FIRE AND FURY

FIRE AND FURY

THE ALLIED BOMBING OF GERMANY, 1942–1945

Randall Hansen

NAL
CALIBER

NAL Caliber
Published by New American Library, a division of
Penguin Group (USA) Inc., 375 Hudson Street,
New York, New York 10014, USA
Penguin Group (Canada), 90 Eglinton Avenue East, Suite 700, Toronto,
Ontario M4P 2Y3, Canada (a division of Pearson Penguin Canada Inc.)
Penguin Books Ltd., 80 Strand, London WC2R 0RL, England
Penguin Ireland, 25 St. Stephen's Green, Dublin 2,
Ireland (a division of Penguin Books Ltd.)
Penguin Group (Australia), 250 Camberwell Road, Camberwell, Victoria 3124,
Australia (a division of Pearson Australia Group Pty. Ltd.)
Penguin Books India Pvt. Ltd., 11 Community Centre, Panchsheel Park,
New Delhi - 110 017, India
Penguin Group (NZ), cnr Airborne and Rosedale Roads, Albany,
Auckland 1310, New Zealand (a division of Pearson New Zealand Ltd.)
Penguin Books (South Africa) (Pty.) Ltd., 24 Sturdee Avenue,
Rosebank, Johannesburg 2196, South Africa

Penguin Books Ltd., Registered Offices:
80 Strand, London WC2R 0RL, England

Published by NAL Caliber, an imprint of New American Library, a division of Penguin Group (USA) Inc.
Previously published in a Doubleday Canada hardcover edition.

Set in Janson
Designed by Ginger Legato

Printed in the United States of America

For Katja

CONTENTS

Preface   *ix*

1. The day Hamburg died   3
2. The Blitz: Bombing civilians and destroying houses   17
3. Bomber Harris takes over   27
4. The Americans   33
5. Building the mighty Eighth   41
6. Burn, Germany, burn   51
7. Killing the Boche   63
8. Cologne   69
9. Göring and Speer   73
10. Churchill, Roosevelt, and the future of bombing   83
11. The Ruhr   91
12. Busting dams   95
13. England, July 27, 1943: "Let us open the window"   105
14. To destroy Hamburg   109

15. Under the bombs   117
16. Speer's nightmare   123
17. The Battle of Berlin   141
18. What the British knew   153
19. Taking out the Luftwaffe   169
20. Germany's Achilles' heel   179
21. Oil and baby killing   189
22. Harris's and Spaatz's orders   207
23. Portal pleads   229
24. Speer despairs, Harris threatens, Portal blinks   241
25. American area bombing   247
26. A crescendo of destruction   259
27. Doubts   269
28. As the last bombs fell   273
29. Conclusion   279

Acknowledgments   299
Notes   301
Selected Bibliography   329
Index   339

PREFACE

On Feb 2, 1945, James ("Jimmy") Doolittle, famous for the retaliatory raids on Tokyo following Pearl Harbor, was awaiting orders. He had been told by his superior, Carl Spaatz, to launch a bombing raid on the heavily populated center of Berlin. For Doolittle, it was a betrayal of the principles to which America had committed itself since the United States' entry into the war: bombing would be precise, would hit industry, and would avoid civilian casualties. "We will," Doolittle had written, "in what may be one of our last and best remembered operations…violate the basic American principle of precision bombing of targets of strictly military significance. . . ." When Doolittle received his reply, it was unequivocal: "hit Berlin—center of [the] city."

Decades later, near the end of his life, Spaatz looked back on the early February 1945 bombing of the German capital with regret. "We never had as our target in Europe anything except a military target—except Berlin."

The debate between Doolittle and Spaatz, and between Spaatz and his own conscience, fit into a larger debate that raged throughout the Second World War: how to bomb Nazi Germany. From the moment the war started, airmen on both sides of the Atlantic were convinced that airpower would play a central role in defeating the enemy. Until 1944, it was the only way in which the Allies brought the war directly to Germany. And until the end of the war, the Allies could not agree on bombing strategy. In this context, the exchange between Doolittle and Spaatz is remarkable. It is remarkable for Doolittle's passion, for his willingness to challenge a superior officer (though also a friend), but also for the result, which was a deviation from American policy. For the majority of the war, the Americans remained publicly committed to the precision bombing of noncivilian targets; their British Allies, by contrast, were committed (from 1942) to the carpet bombing of heavily populated cities.

The American commitment to precision made the American bombing campaign over Europe unique. This important point has been forgotten. In recent years, there has been a great effort, particularly but not only among authors publishing with commercial presses, to downplay if not trivialize the differences between the American and British campaigns. Those holding this view argue that poor weather, German defenses, and often imprecise radar technology meant that while Americans were trying to hit precise targets they were hitting much else, civilians included. This is all true. But it is also true that intention matters: unlike their British Allies, American airmen were, with some important exceptions, committed to the precision bombing of noncivilian targets until the end of the war. At times, they maintained this commitment at very great cost to themselves. As another airman put it, "It is contrary to ideals to wage war against civilians." There is an important and basic difference, often lost to contemporary moralizers discussing Iraq, Afghanistan, or Lebanon, between killing civilians incidentally and killing them deliberately.

The failure to distinguish sufficiently the two bombing campaigns has, this book argues, encouraged a misunderstanding of the role of bombing in ending the war. Authors keen to defend British Bomber Command against the charge that carpet bombing cities was immoral and pointless tend to exaggerate these effects, suggesting that bombing in general and city bombing in particular played a decisive effect in defeating Germany. This view is very hard to credit; on any reading, bombing was just one part of the war, and the role it played has to be considered in the context of contributions made by the Western Armies and Navies in the other theaters of war, and of course by the Soviet Union. That said, it is also a mistake to suggest, as many critics have, that Allied bombing had no effect on the outcome of the war. It did. The question is rather what effect, which type of bombing, and whether the results constituted the wisest use of scarce military resources. On this point, the distinction between the American and British campaigns is relevant. Bearing in mind that determining cause and effect is always very difficult, the evidence, as this book shows, suggests that the bombing that damaged Germany the most—the destruction of industrial targets and the inestimably important obliteration of the German fighter force—was done by the Americans. At three points in the bombing campaign—in 1943 (twice) and in late 1944/early 1945—American precision bombing almost brought the Germans to their knees. Compared with the British, the Americans bombed better, with greater results and lower loss of life, both civilian and military.

Bombing debates were about more than strategy; they were also about morality. This was the case both during the war and after. To the end, the American campaign was affected by a particular concern for the moral implications of bombing. Many writers today deny this, and Spaatz and Doolittle were keen after the war to disassociate themselves from the taint of morality. It is clear why: expressing concerns over women and children was at best unstrategic; at worst, it was unmanly. It is nonetheless impossible to read the exchange above, or other passionate denunciations of area bombing discussed in this book, without seeing a deep and abiding moral concern.

For their part, the RAF led a campaign that was, from 1942, committed, daring, and produced at times spectacular results. In the end, however, the British obsession with the obliteration of German cities (the Commander-in-Chief of Bomber Command, Sir Arthur Harris, promised to take them out one after another, "like pulling teeth") was ultimately counterproductive. It had few direct effects on German production, which rose unchecked until late in 1944. Area bombing's indirect effects (forcing the Germans to transfer resources from other theaters of war to the home front), about which much has been made, could have been achieved at lower cost through precision bombing.

In writing this book, I have relied on a wide range of sources—archives, personal interviews, and memoirs of the key characters involved. None of these is entirely without problems, but they are essential to reconstructing the air war through the eyes of those who arranged it, those who executed it, and those who experienced it. Two types of sources are worth commenting on. The first are interviews with German civilians. Some might be rightly suspicious of accounts given by Germans who lived through the Third Reich, viewing them as an effort in self-justification. Here time was fortunately on my side. Most of those Germans who remember the Third Reich were children at the time. These "children of war" (*Kriegskinder*) were old enough to remember the bombings, but too young to have been involved in the politics that led up to the war. Equally important, whatever one thinks of them, these children were there, and their stories are—subject to all the usual qualifications that apply to oral history—part of the historical record. In many cases, they expressed great appreciation that anyone, above all a foreigner, would be interested in their stories. A daughter of one eyewitness, from Essen, wrote me a touching letter:

We read about your project in our daily newspaper this week. My mother, born 1937, decided to go out on a limb and to give your assistant her phone number. Your assistant called her back and had a long talk with her. This was the best thing that could have happened to my mother.

I grew up with her stories about her experiences during her early childhood, when the war started and everything that seemed to be so reliable fell to pieces. She always told us about [the bombings], but she never had the chance to tell her experiences to strangers. So what became normal to us through endless repetition acquired a disturbing and destructive quality for her. Until this phone call. When the call was over, my mother wept heavily. But after that she told me, she felt relieved. I think it helped her to know someone outside her family recognized that her experiences were traumatic for her and the whole generation. . . . I thank you very much, that my mother had the chance to be heard before dying.

The second source is the memoirs of Albert Speer. Speer was the last man standing; all other senior Nazis killed themselves, were hanged at Nuremberg, or went into hiding. As such, he was able to tell his story without having to worry that those who had been in the room with him would challenge his version of events. His memoirs were, as all memoirs are, an effort in self-justification. They should be treated with caution, but they remain a reliable source. This is partly because they were vetted by the German historian and journalist Joachim Fest. Fest has, however, attracted many critics of his own, and he admitted later that Speer had on some issues led him astray. The controversies surrounding Speer are nonetheless specific: they concern his knowledge of the Holocaust, his use of forced labor, and his claims to sympathy with the German resistance. This book does not use Speer's memoirs on any of these. Where it does use Speer is in his estimation of the bombing war's effects on German war production. It does so because I find Speer more reliable on this topic (he had little to gain in the late 1960s by commenting one way or the other on it) but also because defenders of area bombing quote Speer frequently, one is tempted to say ad nauseam. Given this, I thought it important to provide a fuller picture of Speer's views on area and precision bombing.

There is a time and place for every book. It would be one thing to write a book that covers, as this book inevitably does, German suffering, in the years immediately following the war, before the country faced up to its National Socialist past. It is quite another to write one today, some six decades after the war and some four decades (taking 1968 as a turning point) after the (West) Germans began the long and difficult process of examining and learning from their own history. Although "coming to terms with the past" (*Vergangenheits-bewältigung*) is a process and not an end point, Germany has done more than most nations, probably more than any nation, to discuss, analyze, and remember its own history. As Nicholas Kulish put it in the *New York Times*, whereas "most countries celebrate the best in their past, Germany unrelentingly promotes its worst."

The debate on the bombing war has carried on, with pauses, for decades, and it will continue. All authors would like to believe that their argument will be the last word on their topic of choice, but they know—or should—that it won't be. As that debate rolls on, it is important to bear in mind that an evaluation of the effects and the morality of the British bombing war can cast no aspersions on the bravery or sincerity of the young men who chose to serve in British Bomber Command, still less on the memory of the fifty-five thousand of them who died over Europe. It is to their bravery and that of tens of thousands of others in the Allied armed forces and the navy that we owe our ability to debate these issues free from intellectual and political tyranny. For the Americans, some twenty-six thousand of whom died over Europe, this book is a tribute to that bravery.

New York, January 5, 2009

1889
Hitler is born
Nietzsche goes mad

1918
Hitler weeps in an uncontrollable rage
The Royal Air Force is formed

1943

1

THE DAY HAMBURG DIED

July 27, 1943

A t 4:30 P.M., **a young boy**, Ernst-Günther Haberland, was playing in a bleak courtyard. His mother came to fetch him; they were going to the air-raid shelter early. She collected the family's most important documents, dressed herself and her son in as many clothes as they could wear, and put a rucksack on his back. Her husband was at work and she could not get word to him. They left their flat at Götenstrasse, 55 at 5 P.M. and headed to the Berliner Tor (the Berlin Gate), just a few blocks north.

Their neighborhood was Hammerbrook, a working-class district about two miles southeast of the city center. The architecture was characteristic of turn-of-the-century Germany. Most buildings were blocks of four- or five-story houses. The apartments at the front of these houses were populated by the relatively affluent. The flats at the back were dark and small. They housed the poor. Some eighteen families lived in each house. Between 1928 and 1932, unemployment in the neighborhood had more than quadrupled.

Ernst-Günther and his mother needed to get to the air-raid shelter at the Berliner Tor. The building, called a *Winkel* (tower shelter), had been built in 1939. It was a multi-story bunker with curved outer walls and a peaked, oval roof. Many air-raid shelters were made of solid concrete and looked like massive rectangle blocks, but the one at Berliner Tor was covered in brick. It was almost attractive. There were two large main doors made of steel, with steps leading up to them. From outside, it looked like a windmill without the sails. The outer walls were just over three feet thick at the base (and about half

3

that near the apex); the roof was nine feet thick. Inside, the shelter's services—heating and electricity, toilets, running drinking water, and ventilation—were all contained in a central column-like structure. Between the column and the outer walls were rows of wide, backless benches just a few feet apart. A spiral staircase led down to a deep basement and the floors below. In all, some six hundred people could fit into the bunker, but it was always far too full.

Ernst-Günther and his mother took their places. The majority of people there were women, children, and old men. Each shelter had an air-raid warden, often Wehrmacht soldiers, members of the SS, or Hitler Youth who had sought safety from the bombs. Most of the other young men were away fighting at the front. Soon, all the benches were taken and the aisles were also full of people standing. Sometime after 8 P.M., there were around one thousand people inside and the massive steel door was closed and sealed. Latecomers hoping to enter were left standing on the steps.

Inside, it was horribly uncomfortable. People had barely any room to move. They made stilted conversation. The atmosphere was hot and stale, and everyone was overdressed. They were allowed only one bag in the shelter, so they wore layers of garments. Those who had not drunk enough liquid soon felt desperately thirsty; those who had drunk too much were in need of the toilet. No one dared give up their seat, knowing it would not be there when they returned.

As Ernst-Günther and his mother made their way to the bunker, a thirteen-year-old girl, Elfriede Bock, was at home with her family. Like Ernst-Günther, Elfriede was a native of Hammerbrook. She was raised by a harsh mother and a distant father, who made it clear to her that he had wanted a son. "I had no idea," she said sixty years later, "that women could have any value." The Nazis told her they could, and did: as mothers, they were Germany's future.

Elfriede's father came home at 5 P.M., earlier than expected. He ordered his wife and daughter to pack their things and get ready to go to the shelter. Elfriede's mother looked startled, and in her strong Hamburg accent she said, "Why? It sounds like we will never come back to this apartment again." Elfriede's father barked, "Just do what I say and be quick about it."

Elfriede and her mother left the apartment at 8 P.M., stepped out onto the Süderstrasse, turned right toward the Berliner Tor, and followed the path taken by Ernst-Günther and his mother a few hours earlier. Elfriede was lightly clothed and carried a cardigan. Everything else was in her suitcase in the basement of the house. At Heidenkampsweg, the street showed the scars of stray bombs that had fallen two nights earlier. City workers were clearing the sidewalks and climbing ladders to inspect the roofs for damage. The air was dusty, hot, and stifling.

Outside the shelter, they met Elfriede's friend Kuttl and went in together. Elfriede had hoped they could secure a good spot, but the shelter was already full, and all of the benches were taken. People were pushing past them looking for a place to sit. Elfriede heard a group of women nearby frantically chatting. They spoke of a raid on Hamburg two days earlier, of a thousand planes over the city, fifteen hundred bodies, and tens of thousands fleeing the city. Elfriede viewed such reports as nonsense, though she wondered about the fifteen hundred bodies. She thought, *It must have been horrible to be trapped in a cellar for three hours. But so many airplanes? Almost a thousand? Impossible. The Allies couldn't have so many. No fear!* "Men, hold tight, the Führer will get you out!" (Jungs, haltet aus, der Führer haut euch raus!) *That's the message he sent to the soldiers in Stalingrad. . . . If only these women would shut up.*

They would. At 12:41 A.M., the first alarm rang out over the city, followed by a second at 12:50 A.M. Elfriede heard the bombers fly over, seemingly toward Berlin in the southeast. The airplanes soon turned, though, and the roar grew louder. The wishful belief that the city would be spared lasted only a few seconds. The bombers turned toward southwest Hamburg.

At 8 P.M., as Elfriede was leaving her apartment for the bunker, a boy from an even poorer background, Werner Wendland, was finishing a swim with three friends in the canal. It was close to the river and a favorite spot for working-class boys from the neighborhood. The streets were hot and dusty, and the three of them walked back laughing, shoving each other and thinking about supper. Back on his street, Stresowstrasse, Werner saw people with backpacks heading toward the bunker, pushing bicycles overloaded with belongings. He asked them what they were doing. "There will be a huge air raid tonight," came the response. The boys laughed it off. Until then, every large attack had been followed by a period of calm or nothing more than nuisance raids.

Werner returned home and told his parents the story. They decided to wait and see how the night would unfold. When the first air-raid warning rang out over the city, his father told Werner to go to the shelter, promising to join him afterward. Ten minutes later, Werner, his mother, and his sister joined a neighbor and her daughter. They guessed that the Berliner Tor bunker would be full and went instead to a smaller shelter down the street. An hour later, Werner's father had still not arrived. Following a tip given by his neighbors, Werner went to the nearby air-raid bunker. It was so full that there was no chance of pushing past the crowds to reach his father. Just then, the roar of planes above became louder, and he saw the marker flares gliding down against the night sky. Werner thought, *If this gets worse, my mother and sister will need my help more than my father.* He headed back to the shelter.

He had barely arrived when the first bombs exploded. The floor of the cellar heaved and then fell. The walls cracked. Dust filled the air. Water spurted out of cracked pipes. People moaned and sometimes cried out. Others prayed. Werner thought about his father.

July 28

1 A.M., BERLINER TOR

The bombing began. When the first high explosives landed in Hammerbrook, everyone in the bunker fell silent. Through the thick concrete walls, the distant explosions sounded like dull thuds. But they gradually became louder and closer. For half an hour, a carpet of bombs hammered the city. There were a few minutes of calm, then a massive explosion. The bunker heaved, and then sank. People were thrown from benches and landed on top of each other.

For some time, the light had been flickering in the bunker. Then it went out. The electricity had gone, and with it the pump supplying fresh air. Soldiers forced, at gunpoint, the few men to operate the hand pumps. They got just enough air in to keep everyone alive.

1 A.M., STRESOWSTRASSE

Werner and his family cowered in the cellar. As the fires caused by the incendiary bombs lit up the neighborhood, the temperature in the cellar began to rise. They could either wait there or take their chances in the street. If they stayed, they risked asphyxiation, incineration, or being crushed. If they left, there were the dangers of the open street: bombs (old, unexploded ones and new ones), bomb craters, falling debris, and more fire. One of the men looked through the keyhole in the cellar's steel door to see what was happening. The roof and walls of the passageway were in flames. They had to get out of there.

Werner and some of the men pushed against the door, but it refused to budge. Debris had fallen against it, trapping them. The air grew thinner. Desperate, they searched the walls with a flashlight. They found a breach, constructed to provide a second escape route. Werner took a sledgehammer and smashed through the opening. He saw stairs leading up to an exit that, despite the hammering the house was taking, somehow remained passable. They dashed through a burning stairwell and into the neighboring courtyard.

Holding his sister and mother by the hand, Werner pulled them out into the street. He wanted to get to what he thought would be the relative safety of the banks of the Elbe River, three streets away.

When he had left his street less than an hour before, it had looked like any other in the neighborhood. Now it was an inferno, having been hit by some of the first bombs. The high explosives tore off roofs, and left wood, coal, and plaster exposed. They were followed by wave upon wave of incendiaries, creating multiple pockets of fire that spread across the floors—consuming the furniture, curtains, clothes, and books—climbed the walls, and traveled through the staircases. Air rushed in through the open roofs and smashed windows, and the fires grew more intense, pushing out more windows as the flames shot into the sky and jumped to adjacent buildings. The flames sucked in more oxygen and pushed against Werner, his mother, and his sister with such force that they retreated into the next cellar, one house away:

It was already overflowing with people, tightly packed together. The air was awful and getting worse. It was so bad that some—mostly children—fell from the chairs and benches, and clung to the feet of those standing. People began to scream "we have to get out of here!" A few courageous men forced the reluctant air-raid warden to open the door.

The flames had grown more intense, and a wall of fire stood between Werner and the street. His mother and sister were mad with fear. He took each by the hand, heard someone yell, "To the middle of the street!" and pulled them through the flames. They ran west, past Lindseystrasse, across the hot cobblestones. "It was a terrifying sight," Werner later recalled. "St. Thomas's church in flames, mannequins burning in the window of the C&L Meyer clothing store, trees blown over, and the tram cables snapped and dangling." When they reached the relative safety of the Elbe, Werner left his mother and sister and made one last effort to find his father in the bunker back on the Stresowstrasse.

When he arrived at the bunker, the door was open. The entranceway that had been packed was empty. It was dark and very smoky. Werner could not see anything. He took a few steps into the darkness and heard something: the moans of the dying. Horrified, he ran away.

By 1:20 A.M., the Stresowstrasse and the rest of the neighborhood was an inferno. Fire leaped from windows on both sides of the streets, joining in the center.

The cellars were death traps. Those huddled in the cellars of the neighboring streets—the Wendenstrasse, the Sorbenstrasse, and the Süderstrasse—had a few minutes to make a decision that would save their lives: to leave.

Residents ran for the safety of the canals. Those who tried to cross the main north-south road, the Heidenkampsweg, were stopped by the melting asphalt (asphalt melts at 200 degrees Celsius, twice the boiling point of water). Their feet sank. Their trousers and dresses caught fire, and the flames climbed up them. They screamed loudly at first, then grew quiet, gurgled, and died.

Some followed Heidenkampsweg north or south, past the burning buildings and falling debris. Those who were not crushed by falling buildings made for canals running parallel to the east-west streets. They jumped in and were cooked to death. The water was boiling.

The fires in buildings on either side of the street merged into one and began moving in search of oxygen. The entire neighborhood was in flames. The bombing that night was unusually concentrated. The pathfinders marked the neighborhood with uncommon precision, and there was little "creepback" (which occurred when bombers dropped their bombs before they reached the aiming point). The weather was atypically hot by Hamburg's standards (the city's weather is roughly similar to that of England), and had been so for days. It was 30 degrees Celsius in the early evening and humidity was extremely low. Hamburg had experienced one of largest raids of the war two nights earlier, and the city's Gauleiter (regional head) had ordered the firefighters to concentrate all of their efforts on putting out the fires. The headquarters of the fire brigade was located at the Berliner Tor, but it had dispatched the fire trucks to other parts of the city. As a result, they were on the wrong side of Hamburg when the bombing began and had to fight their way back through bomb craters, abandoned cars, and rubble. When they finally arrived in Hammerbrook, it was too late. They could only combat fires on the neighborhood's periphery, and most of their efforts were directed toward helping the victims. The fire itself raged unchecked.

Somewhere in the middle of Hammerbrook, the flames converged with unimaginable force. As they did so, a chain reaction began: the intense heat led the fires to rise quickly, leaving a gas bubble below. Cold air then rushed in, mixing with the gases and setting the "bubble" alight. As the fires burned, more oxygen was sucked in and the process repeated itself. The inferno became larger and hotter, peaking at more than 1000 degrees Celsius and climbing four miles into the sky. The fire sucked all of the oxygen out of the cellars. Those in them gasped, put their faces to the ground, choked, and died. Then their bodies were incinerated.

On the streets, people were met with a scene of utter chaos. The howling winds were deafening and tore through the streets with a force that ripped stone tiles, doors, and windows from the buildings and carried debris through the air, which then crushed anyone in its path. Mothers struggling against the wind felt their babies torn from their arms. Trees three feet thick were uprooted. Death had a random, godless quality. Some people burst into flames, while those a few feet away from them were spared.

The inferno raged for five hours. At its peak, 133 miles of houses were on fire. The great city of Hamburg was dying. At 2:25 A.M., an hour after the bombing began, the senior officer of Hamburg's air defenses jotted down a novel word in his logbook: *Feuersturm.*[1]

5 A.M., BERLINER TOR

The bunker was still. The minutes ticked slowly by. The bombing had stopped, but Elfriede and Ernst-Günther had no idea of what was going on outside. The air grew worse, and people fell silent. In the early hours of the morning—Elfriede cannot remember when exactly—someone swung the bunker's steel door open, probably hoping to let in fresh air. Instead, people from outside poured in. They were refugees from the firestorm; most were burned and some were naked. There was almost no fat left on their bodies, only burn wounds. Their tongues stuck out and hung down toward their necks. They lay where they fell and died.

Rather than fresh air, the open door brought in billows of smoke. Screams echoed through the bunker, particularly from the children. Elfriede heard confused cries for help, and yet more victims entered the bunker. Someone called out, "Whoever can leave the bunker should do so now!" Elfriede climbed out, stepping over charred bodies. The view outside was extraordinary. She thought, *Is hell like this?* The smoke burning her eyes, she watched walls collapse, the wind and flames twist in a squall. The inferno was unstoppable. It tore through the street and up to the sky. Hydrants were uprooted. Burning debris was carried through the air. Elfriede recognized the old hot dog stand at the Berliner Tor, but it, too, was picked up and swept away. All around her, burning beams, planks, even parts of roofs, windows, and doors were carried through the flames, dust, and ash.

Ernst-Günther and his mother emerged at approximately the same time. "The distant heavens," he later remarked, "were pitch-black, but above us it glowed red. You could hear the awful screams of the injured. More and more came to us with burned and torn clothes; their bodies were covered in phosphorous burns. You could not tell whether clothes or skin were hanging from their bodies." Ernst-Günther recognized a neighbor who, stone-faced, walked toward them with two suitcases—one large, one small—in his hands. He opened them. In the bigger one was a large object that looked like a charred tree trunk; in the other suitcase were two smaller, but otherwise identical objects.

They were the charred remains of the neighbor's wife and children.

Ernst-Günther and his mother sought to escape the heat in the underground railway tunnels beneath the Berliner Tor. From there they were taken by lorry to the Moorweide, a large park in the middle of the city. They joined thousands of others and waited to be transported out of Hamburg.

Elfriede, her mother, and Kuttl pushed their way through the wind and crowds, making their way to the same subway station, where they stopped to rest. They saw screaming women lying on makeshift beds. There was a brownshirt (SA) whose stomach was hugely protruded from smoke poisoning. No doctor came to him, and the efforts of others to help were fruitless. He died and was dragged away.

The three sat near the underground railway tracks for hours. Having no desire to climb up to the streets, they tried to find a way out by following the subway lines. They eventually made their way to the main station, the Hauptbahnhof, where they were reunited with Elfriede's father. He told them what he had seen: "The houses in the Süderstrasse had been flattened, even the cellars were gone. There was nothing left of our house; not even one stone stood atop another. The entire street was a burning mass grave. The flames were shooting out of the cellars! The high explosives knocked the roofs off, and the incendiaries finished the job." He closed his eyes and continued: "On the corner of Süderstrasse and Ausschläger Weg a lorry drove into a deep bomb crater. No one survived. God, there were so many bodies. I saw people running down the street; they suddenly caught fire; they fell to the ground and died there. The air was so hot, it could suffocate you. I jumped into the crater [among the bodies] and stayed there for at least an hour. [The British] dropped phosphorous, liquid phosphorous. People [covered in it] jumped into the canals, but when they came up they were still burning. It was an awful fate, you can't imagine . . . so many charcoaled bodies. They were so small."

Elfriede and her mother joined thousands of other Hamburgers who fled their city. They left that night for the Luneburger Heide, an area of forests and villages south of the city. Her mother spent the next night crying for her lost belongings. And for her lost Hamburg.

The Day After

Hamburg was in ruins. For miles in every direction, all that remained of large apartment complexes were the outer walls. More than forty thousand people were dead. Their bodies would be thrown into mass graves at the city's Ohlsdorf cemetery.

The heat was still unrelenting, and the neighborhood was soon full of the stench of death and the threat of disease. City officials cordoned off the area—they would eventually build a brick wall around it—until the thousands of bodies could be cleared. One determined young woman, Anna Lies Schmidt, managed to get past them. "My uncle and I," she told Martin Middlebrook thirty years later, "went on foot into this terror. No one was allowed into the devastated district but . . . we fought bodily with the sentries on duty and we got in. My uncle was arrested. Four-story-high blocks of flats were like glowing mounds of stone right down to the basement. Everything seemed to have melted. How terribly these people must have died. The smallest children lay like small eels on the pavement. Even in death, they showed signs of how they must have suffered—their hands and arms stretched out as if to protect themselves from the hideous heat."[2]

Among the bodies, she found her parents.

In the City Hall, Karl Kaufmann—the city's Gauleiter and a committed Nazi who had urged Hitler to deport Jews east after the first bombings—had to decide what to do. It was obvious that the Allies would not stop until they had obliterated Hamburg. Kaufmann gave the order to evacuate. Loudspeakers relayed it across the city. Over the next forty-eight hours, 900,000 people— half of the city's 1933 population—left. Hundreds of thousands climbed onto wagons, pushed carts around the hills of bodies and rubble, or boarded ships in the Elbe.

By the evening of July 29, almost all those who could leave Hamburg had done so. The city was empty, and on its knees. And once again, the bombers swept in at 1 A.M. Hamburg's defenses had improved marginally over the raids (German defenders and searchlight operators cooperated more effectively, and ten RAF aircraft would be brought down), but radar was still hugely impaired. The RAF's targets that night were the districts of Rotherbaum, Harvestehude, Hoheluft, and Eppendorf, directly to the north of the city center. They made up a beautiful, affluent residential neighborhood. There was nothing of industrial worth there. That night, the weather came to the neighborhood's aid: heavy winds blew the pathfinders east, over what was left of Billbrook. As the bombers came in from the north, creepback brought bombs to the as-yet-undamaged districts of Eilbek, Uhlenhorst, Winterhude, and Barmbek. The old center of Barmbek was leveled, and 27,945 houses were destroyed. Fires raged, but the districts were—save for the stubborn—empty. One thousand people died. They included two aunts and two uncles of future West German Chancellor Helmut Schmidt.

The next two nights brought only nuisance raids, and on August 3, Bomber Command launched the final raid of Operation Gomorrah. A total of 749 bombers took off from southeast England. When they reached Hamburg, they couldn't see it. For the first time since the attacks began, a thick cloud had descended over Hamburg. The RAF's weather forecasters had got it wrong: not only was the weather over Hamburg not clear, it had become a thunderstorm. The pilots struggled to maintain control as their planes were knocked about the sky. Lightning flashed everywhere. The bombers jettisoned their loads where they could; the bombs fell aimlessly across Hamburg, creating local fires but causing no substantial damage. The firestorm was not repeated. It was, as a local newspaper put it sixty years later, as if the heavens took pity on the razed city and said "enough."

Three weeks after the attack, most of the area around the firestorm was still cordoned off. Rats and large cockroaches swarmed through the ruins. Somehow, Werner managed to get to the bunker at Stresowstrasse, 88. He found his father's hat, and his empty suitcase. He never saw his friends again.

THREE
YEARS
EARLIER

2

THE BLITZ: BOMBING CIVILIANS AND DESTROYING HOUSES

O n September 7, 1940, a Londoner, Colin Perry, was cycling over Chipstead Hill in the south of the capital. He heard the by-now-familiar drone of planes overhead, and looked up to see whether they were British fighters. They were not. "Directly above me were literally hundreds of planes, Germans! The sky was full of them. Bombers hemmed in with fighters, like bees around their queen, like destroyers around the battleship, so came Jerry!"[1]

Over the course of the day and into the evening, German bombers hammered the London docks and the surrounding East End neighborhoods, among the poorest in the city. As an inferno consumed the docks, the destruction spread through the Isle of Dogs, West Ham, Bermondsey, Stepney, Whitechapel, Poplar, Bow, and Shoreditch. In one Bow church, people kneeled on the ground, wept, and prayed. They were spared; some four hundred others were not.

The next night, the Germans were back. More than 170 bombers pasted the East End again, killing another 400. On September 9, still more—200—bombers arrived by day, killing 370. The next night, the Germans set St. Katherine's Dock alight, creating the worst fire in England's history. Flames rose two hundred feet, gutting the factories and destroying the adjacent workers' houses.

As the bombers hammered the city, Londoners first made for the capital's dirty, dank, and in many cases disease-ridden public shelters. Later, they headed to the underground stations. The government initially did not want to open tube stations to the public, but its hand was forced. At Liverpool Street

17

on September 8, workers and soldiers stood off for hours until the latter capitulated. The doors were flung open, and the people scrambled past each other, down the steps, and into the tunnels. Overnight, London's tube lines became the capital's largest air-raid shelter, housing as many as 177,000 people.

They were not always safe there, however. On September 19, as German bombers continued to hammer the capital, bombs landed near the tube station at Balham. The roadway caved in, the mains burst, and the water gushed into the station below. Ballast, sand, and water mixed together and cascaded down the escalators and steps. Slime began filling the station. "All you could hear," remembered one air defense worker, "was the sound of screaming and rushing water." The next morning, sixty-four Londoners lay dead, with a pile of sludge on top of them.[2]

The September attacks were the first serious daylight raids on the capital and part of the Battle of Britain, Hitler's effort to use bombing to prepare for an invasion. It has no clear starting date: air raids occurred sporadically in June and July, and intensified during August. At that time, the German Air Force launched a costly but effective campaign against Britain's industrial production, fighter bases, and shipping. Though the targets were industrial, imprecise bombing (there was little in the way of aiming technology at this point in the war) meant that neighborhoods were also hit. In July, 258 civilians were killed; in August, the figure was three times that: 1075, including 136 children and 392 women.[3]

Despite the imprecision, the bombing of Spitfires and airfields was slowly but surely wearing the RAF down. Then, the Germans switched strategies. Luftwaffe commanders deduced from intelligence reports that Fighter Command was a spent force.[4] The Luftwaffe sought to tame the rest of the country by bombing industrial, military, and transportation targets around large urban centers.[5] German bombers hit Bristol, Liverpool, and Birmingham at night. On September 2, Göring ordered the systematic destruction of targets in London. Three days later, Hitler directed the Luftwaffe to undertake a general campaign against urban targets, including the capital, and against British morale.[6]

For the next nine months, the Luftwaffe launched seemingly indiscriminate raids on London and other British cities. On September 17, 1940, the Germans dropped 350 tons of bombs on London, more than the total tonnage dropped on the entire country during the First World War.[7] By April 1941, they would drop three times that figure—more than a thousand tons—in a single night.[8] In November, the Luftwaffe launched its most infamous raid of the war, obliterating Coventry. Five thousand people were killed. At the same time, a series of raids on industrial targets in heavily populated cities—Liverpool, Manchester, Sheffield, Portsmouth, Plymouth, Swansea, Cardiff, Glasgow, and Belfast—pasted their residential neighborhoods. The attacks seemed wholly indiscriminate to anyone on the ground. In the capital, raids that began on the East End extended westward, hitting Parliament, Buckingham Palace, and West London's more affluent neighborhoods. The rich fled to the countryside, turning some of London's most fashionable streets over to the lower-middle and working classes. By the time the Blitz ended, 40,000 Britons had been killed and 750,000 made homeless. The dead ranged in age from an eleven-hour-old baby to a hundred-year-old pensioner.[9] A million and one-quarter homes had succumbed to the bombs.

The Blitz was not only awful; it was, given the Germans' own aims, counterproductive. Luftwaffe raids on aircraft targets were costly, probably too costly to sustain for long, but they had the effect of wearing down British defenses.[10] Night-bombing city targets, by contrast, was unproductive. It produced little in the way of results and allowed British fighter defense to regroup.[11] British morale famously failed to buckle; rather, it hardened, and Londoners became the heroes of the free world. More than anything else, the bombing of London swung neutral opinion to Britain's side.[12] When Hitler decided, in a typically erratic and ill-advised strategy shift, to turn toward Russia, he left a UK that was physically scarred but morally and psychologically strengthened. And determined to give it back to the Germans.

The question was how. When Britain declared war on Germany, the Royal Air Force (RAF) was made up of three main commands: Bomber, Fighter, Training and Coastal. The offensive component was Bomber Command, which in 1939 had 349 bombers. During the initial year of the war, the first wartime commander-in-chief, Sir Edgar Ludlow-Hewitt, pursued a cautious strategy. He was partly bound by the government: fearing attacks on London, the Cabinet ordered Bomber Command to limit its war to attacks on industrial targets where there was no risk of civilian losses. But Ludlow-Hewitt also took a conservative view of Bomber Command's abilities: if he launched an aggressive war, the Germans would wipe out Britain's bomber force within weeks. During the first seven months of the Bomber War—until May 1940—

Bomber Command limited itself to leaflet campaigns (dropping Allied propaganda over Germany) and largely ineffective raids on naval targets.

Ludlow-Hewitt's caution was probably warranted, but it cost him his job: he was replaced on April 4, 1940, by his protégé, Sir Charles Portal. Portal, a graduate of Winchester and Christ Church, Oxford, was a child of the RAF. He joined the Royal Flying Corps (RFC) at its 1915 creation, and rose quickly to the rank of lieutenant colonel by the end of the war. He was among the first pilots to drop bombs on the Germans. When the RFC became the RAF in 1918, he stayed on, and by 1927 he was running a squadron. After a stint in Aden, where he bombed rebellious tribesmen into submission, he became a lecturer at the Imperial Defence College.[13] Three years later, he was promoted to Air Vice-Marshal and appointed Director of Organization within the Air Ministry. As he took over the post, the RAF was in the midst of a belated and rushed effort to expand in the face of the German air force. Portal was significantly involved in the development of new heavy bombers (Stirlings, Halifaxes, and Manchesters) and the building of airfields; in the organization of personnel, including bringing women into the RAF; and in the creation of Group Pools (later Operational Training Units) for the training of squadron crews. In 1939, Portal was again promoted, joining the Air Council, which was responsible for running the RAF, as Air Member for Personnel, in charge of appointments, promotions, postings, discipline, and awards. From there he was appointed commander-in-chief of Bomber Command.

Shortly after Portal's appointment, the Germans launched their invasion of the Low Countries. On May 14, 1940, the Wehrmacht was outside Rotterdam. The general in command of the 9th Panzer division warned the Dutch defenders that, unless they surrendered, their city would suffer "complete destruction" at the hands of the Luftwaffe. The next day, the surrender hadn't come. German bombers took off for the city, and the Dutch garrison surrendered soon after. Frantic attempts were made to recall the bombers, but it was too late. German bombs laid waste to the city, and the army entered unopposed.

The bombing provided the RAF with the reason—or the excuse—for a shift in strategy. Portal was informed that he could target rail and oil installations east of the Rhine. It did not go well. The main British bomber—the Blenheim—was a slow and fragile airplane that was no match for German fighters. During the June and July raids, many aircraft would turn back. Those that did make it often missed the target. The bombing was in fact so imprecise that the Germans, seeing bombs scattered across hundreds of miles, were genuinely unaware of what the target was. The RAF suffered high casualties in the process. On July 2, twelve aircraft took off for raids on oil targets; ten turned back, and one of the two aircraft that continued was destroyed. The story was the same throughout the rest of the month.[14]

From then, things only got worse. On August 13, as the Battle of Britain was picking up, twelve aircraft were sent to attack a German airfield at Aalborg in northern Denmark, the site of an earlier disastrous raid. Twenty miles from the target, German fighters—Messerschmitt 109s—attacked them. The fighters strafed the formation mercilessly all the way to the target. When the fighters broke away at the last minute, German flak guns opened fire. It was in every sense a massacre. All twelve aircraft were shot down, and only nine of the thirty-three aircrew who left England survived—as prisoners. One was blind in one eye, and another had a broken back.[15]

Aalborg put paid to the belief that the RAF could launch daylight raids on Germany without fighter cover. The RAF switched to night bombing (with some exceptions), but it continued its strategy of precision bombing. Over the summer of 1940, Bomber Command went out night after night. The targets changed frequently, according to no apparent pattern: from oil to shipping, to aircraft, then back to shipping again. Much time and many airplanes were also wasted on pointless schemes (in August 1940, 10 Squadron was ordered to drop phosphorous strips to set German fields alight; the only thing that caught fire was the airplanes themselves). Losses remained low in percentage terms, but combined with the poor results, aircrew morale was slowly being chipped away. At the best of times, an air raid was a brutal experience. On one early 1941 raid, a pilot watched the head of an observer be sheared off by a cannon shell. The gunner climbed to the front of the plane and dragged the body back so that the pilot would not have to be behind a headless corpse all the way home, but it was too late; the pilot never flew again.[16]

On December 12, 1940, ten RAF aircraft set out for Mannheim. They bombed the center of the city successfully and returned home. It was the first area raid of the war, directly ordered by Churchill as retaliation for Coventry.

By then, Portal was no longer commander-in-chief of Bomber Command. He had been promoted to Chief of Air Staff on October 4, 1940. Sir Richard Peirse, an uncompromising advocate of precision bombing, replaced Portal as commander-in-chief. Throughout the autumn of 1940 and the spring of 1941, oil remained the first target when weather allowed, with German barges as the second (Bomber Command would destroy some 12 percent of the German fleet). The RAF made a valiant effort, but poor precision meant that the Germans again hardly realized that oil was the intended target.

As the bombing war progressed without producing results, Portal began to lose faith. He was by instinct a supporter of precision bombing. In 1940, he held the view "that bombers were best employed against target systems and precise objectives."[17] But he was nonetheless moving toward area bombing. In July, he made almost casual mention of the possibilities of attacking German morale. At that time, the aircraft industry was the first target, oil the second. The difficulty with both, Portal (then still commander-in-chief) wrote, was that both targets were "isolated and in sparsely inhabited districts," meaning that "the very high percentage of bombers which inevitably miss the actual target will hit nothing else important and do no damage." Where attacks dispersed over the widest area of Germany, they would increase "the moral effect of our operations by the alarm and disturbance created over the wider area." Here, less than a year into the bombing war, were the seeds of area bombing.[18] Four months later, Portal—now issuing rather than receiving the directives—wrote to Peirse and instructed him to attack electricity and gas plants located in the center of Berlin and other German towns. Bombers on these runs should carry "high explosives, incendiary and delay action bombs"; the first sorties would "cause fires, either on or in the vicinity of the targets so they should carry a high proportion of incendiary bombs."[19] The prime minister was moving in the same direction. "We have seen," he wrote on November 2, 1940, "what inconvenience the attack had on the British civilian, and there is no reason why the enemy should be freed from all such embarrassments."[20]

RAF bombing would remain precision bombing—on oil, aircraft, and, from the spring of 1941, U-boat targets—for the rest of the year, but the policy's days were numbered. It had not produced results: bombs continued to miss their target, and those that hit did little evident damage. A successful precision-bombing campaign required good weather, good visibility, and limited defense. These three conditions were rarely, if ever, met. David Butt, a minor official in the Statistical Department, used reconnaissance photos and Bomber Command's own reports to determine bombing accuracy. He concluded that only two out of every three of the bombers dropped their loads within seventy-five miles of their target.

If it was impossible to bomb precisely, then there were only two choices: bomb imprecisely or don't bomb at all. There was no other way of hitting back, and an end to bombing was unthinkable. British forces had been driven from the Continent, and reestablishing a British military presence was out of the question. The Russians had become an ally in July 1941, but at this point in the war they were wholly engaged in a defensive conflict. Their survival was more in doubt than that of the British. And the Americans were still not in the war. All that was left was area bombing. Few people at this point or any other in the war were prepared to countenance the deliberate killing of German civilians as an end in itself; it had to produce some measurable good for the war. The concept of "morale," which would be worn down through city bombing, seemed to offer hope toward that end.

Portal, who had by late 1941 finally converted to area bombing, put the case for targeting morale to Churchill in a September 1941 memorandum.[21] "It must be realized," he wrote,

> that attack on morale is not a matter of pure killing, although the fear of death is unquestionably an important factor. It is rather the general dislocation of industrial and social life arising from damage to industrial plant, dwelling houses, shops, utility and transportation services, from resultant absenteeism and, in fact, from interference with all that goes to make up the general activity of a community . . .
>
> In highly industrial countries such as Germany and England it is in the thickly populated towns that the morale effect of bombing will be chiefly felt, though the population involved may be a comparatively small proportion of the whole. [By contrast,] in so far as the war effort is concerned, the contribution of the country population is only a fraction of that of the town workers. The conclusion is that the morale of the country as a whole will crack provided a high enough proportion of town dwellers is affected by the general dislocation produced by bombing.

Bombing the Germans into submission required will, but above all it required money. "The strength required to obtain decisive results against German morale," Portal concluded, "may be estimated at 4,000 heavy bombers and that the time taken would be about 6 months."[22] Britain's daily availability of bombs was approximately five hundred at this point.

Churchill wrote back two days later with a letter that—in the light of his earlier support for Bomber Command—was surprisingly blunt and dismissive. "It is very disputable whether bombing by itself will be a decisive factor in the present war. On the contrary, all that we have learnt since the war began shows that its effects, both physical and moral, are greatly exaggerated. . . . The most we can say is that it will be a heavy and I trust seriously increasing annoyance."[23]

Among Portal's merits were a capacity to remain calm in the face of provocation and an ability to deal well with difficult men. He waited five days to reply. When he did, he reminded Churchill of the history of bombing. "Since the fall of France," he wrote,

> it has been a fundamental principle of our strategy that victory over Germany could not be hoped for until German morale and German material strength had been subjected to a bombing offensive of the greatest intensity. This principle was clearly stated [by you] more than a year ago . . . and has been reaffirmed by you in several occasions.
>
> In their recent review of General Strategy, which you approved, the Chiefs of Staff [i.e., senior personnel from the Army, Navy, and Air Force] stated: "It is in bombing on a scale undreamed of in the last war that we find the new weapon on which we must principally depend for the destruction of economic life and morale. . . . After meeting the needs of our own security, therefore, we give the heavy bomber first priority in production, for only the heavy bomber can produce the conditions under which other offensive forces can be deployed."[24]

Portal then threw the matter back into the prime minister's lap:

> I feel bound to restate these facts, because I find them hard to reconcile with your minute of 27 September. The Chiefs of Staff Committee have regarded the bombing offensive on the scale on which we hope to wield it in 1943, as a weapon calculated, if not to break Germany, at least to reduce her strength to the level at which our Armoured forces could hope to intervene successfully on the Continent. If this is a gross over-estimation of the power of the bomber, and if the most we can hope to achieve with our bomber force is a heavy and increasing annoyance, then, as I see it, the strategic concept to which we have been working must dissolve, and we must find a new plan . . .

It is my firm belief that the existing plan is sound and practical. But other plans could be drawn up. We could for example return to the conception of defeating Germany with the Army as the primary weapon. I must point out with the utmost emphasis that in that event we should require an Air Force composed quite differently from that which we are now creating.

Portal ended with a *coup de grâce*. "If, therefore, it is your view that the strategic picture has changed since the issue of your original directive I would urge that revised instructions should be given to the Chiefs of Staff without a moment's delay."

Churchill declined the offer. He was not entirely comfortable with area bombing, but he was still less comfortable with the idea of shifting Britain's strategy from the Royal Air Force to the Army. Britain was in no position to launch an invasion of the Continent in 1941, and even if it were, Churchill recoiled at the prospect of a post-invasion return to the Somme or Passchendaele. Britain had no option but to fight back with the RAF; the RAF could only bomb, and the experience of the last two years of the war had made it clear that the only chance for bombing was area bombing. Churchill was not convinced—and nor was Portal, for that matter—that area bombing would win the war, but hoped it would produce some kind of effect.

Churchill wrote back on October 7 and gave his qualified support to the campaign.

Everything is being done to create the Bombing force desired on the largest possible scale, and there is no intention of changing that policy. I deprecate, however, placing unbounded confidence in this form of attack. . . . It is the most potent method of impairing the enemy's morale at the present time. . . . [However,] even if all the towns in Germany were rendered uninhabitable, it does not follow that the military control would be weakened or even that war industry could not be carried on. It is quite possible that Nazi war-making power in 1943 will be so widely spread throughout Europe as to be to a large extent independent of the buildings in the actual homeland. A different picture would be presented if the enemy's Air Force were so far reduced as to enable heavy accurate daylight bombing of factories to take place. This however cannot be done outside the radius of fighter protection.

This insightful letter was hardly a ringing endorsement of area bombing, but it was enough. "I am now completely reassured," Portal wrote on October 13, "that you accept the primary importance of our bomber operations and of the building up of the bomber force on the largest possible scale." With Churchill's knowledge if not undiluted support, the Royal Air Force had moved toward a policy of destroying Germany's ability to wage war by destroying its cities. There was no better person to implement this policy than the new commander-in-chief of Bomber Command.

3

BOMBER HARRIS TAKES OVER

In **early 1942, a young** police officer pulled over a Bentley speeding on a country road near Uxbridge, west of London. The driver had a stern look and piercing eyes. There was something unnerving and intimidating about the man. The officer told him, "You're liable to kill people at that speed." The driver looked at him coolly and responded, "Young man, I kill thousands every night." He was Air Chief Marshal Sir Arthur Harris, commander-in-chief of Bomber Command.

Harris was born in Cheltenham on April 13, 1892, raised in India (his parents were in the Civil Service), and sent to school in England. After school, he emigrated to Rhodesia, where he drifted between a series of working-class jobs before settling down on the eve of the Great War. When it broke out, Harris, "like all the other damned fools," signed up for the 1st Rhodesian Regiment, but he did not go to the battlefield. After an idle year, he moved to London. He arrived to the *Times* headline of August 21: RISING TIDE OF ENTHUSIASM for forced national service. Tens of thousands of men were volunteering for all branches of the armed services. Harris was keen to be one of them, but he could not find an opening. After being rejected by the Cavalry and Artillery, he remembered an advertisement for the new Flying Corps. Exploiting a connection of his father's in Kitchener's office, he jumped to the front of the line.

Harris was sent to London to defend the capital against German Zeppelin raids. In 1917, Harris saw several months of active service over the Western front, flying dangerous missions over the front line during the bloodiest battles in Flanders. As he flew above the slaughter of Passchendaele, Harris concluded that any price would be worth paying, or for that matter inflicting, to avoid similar carnage in the event of a future war between Britain and Germany.[1] In 1918, British Prime Minister Lloyd George took the decision to combine the Royal Flying Corps and the Royal Naval Air Service (the Navy's air force) into a single Royal Air Force. The RAF came into being on April 1, 1918, with Hugh Trenchard, a man with an almost religious faith in bombing, as its first chief of staff.

After recovering from a potentially deadly bout of the flu, Harris saw out the end of the conflict on training operations in England. By autumn 1918, his squadron was ready and he was given a date to fly: November 11. By then, of course, the war was over.

After the war, Harris was offered a permanent commission in the RAF and was allowed to retain the rank of major. This was unusual. Most people offered permanent commissions were demoted. "The story," Harris said, "was that in the printing of the *Gazette* [which announced the assignments of rank] two sets of names somehow got transposed and having gazetted they couldn't ungazette you. . . . All they could do was hasten the promotion of the poor devils who got into the wrong paragraph!"

After a stint in Mesopotamia (where bombing saw off threats posed by rebellious tribesmen), Harris returned to England to command a squadron (58) until 1927, when he was sent to an army staff college. There he developed his ideas on bombing and became a convinced disciple of the Trenchard school. For Trenchard, future wars would be won by bombers who brought the war directly to the enemy's cities, industries, and people. Harris left the college as a wing commander in 1929 and was posted to Egypt, where he did a tour of duty at Headquarters RAF Middle East in Cairo. While in the city in 1931, he gave an internal RAF lecture on bombing: "What is air bombing today but a reversion to the principle employed by the first intelligent ape, who gave up man handling and fights on the ground because he conceived the more adequate and less risky result to be obtained by pitching a coconut down upon his adversary?"[2] There is no record of the audience's reaction, but the script was sent back to London. It landed on the desk of an official at the Plans Branch of the Air Ministry: Charles Portal.[3]

Harris returned to England in 1932, completed a flying course, and took over command of a base and its resident squadron in west Wales in March 1933. Five months later, on August 11, he was told to report for duty at the Air Ministry. As Hitler became German chancellor, Harris was at the center of power. There, he and two other Directors of Plans—Tom Phillips and Colonel Ronald Adam—drafted a 1937 document entitled "Appreciation of the Situation in the Event of War against Germany in 1939." It is often quoted for its exaggerated prediction of 150,000 casualties in the first week of a German air attack, but it got much else right: France might be unable to cope with an assault by Germany; developing Britain's industrial output and restricting that of Germany might well be decisive; and the intervention of the Soviet Union could decide the war. As Harris's biographer put it, they "succeeded in identifying two of the most crucial factors that were to lead to the defeat of Germany, the others being the protection of sea lanes . . . and the intervention of the USA."[4] The report also argued that demoralizing the Germans by attacking their cities would be impractical and unrealistic.

In September 1939, Harris and his wife were in Norfolk, staying with their friends Jean and Adeline Tresfon. On the night of September 3, two days after Germany invaded Poland, the Harrises and Tresfons were sitting around the fire listening to a crackling radio. Prime Minister Neville Chamberlain, his voice full of melancholy, announced, "This country is"—pause—"at war with Germany." It was, Harris remarked, "uninspired and uninspiring . . . about as stirring as a school-master confirming the fact that mumps had broken out in his prep. school." The four of them sat in silence for a few minutes. Jean turned to Harris and asked, "How long will this one be?" "Five years," replied Harris. And he ran to the phone.

The lines were complete chaos and Harris could not get through to the Air Ministry. He finally demanded that the operator give him "immediate priority." The term lacked meaning or authority, but it worked. He got Portal on the phone and said he wanted a job. Portal replied with words to the effect of "I'll see what I can do."

For the next four days, the minutes ticked by slowly. Finally, the phone rang. Portal would see him in London. There, Portal told Harris that he was to take over as Air Officer Commanding (AOC) of 5 Group, Bomber Command at Grantham. He served there until 1940, when Portal was promoted to commander-in-chief of Bomber Command. Portal contacted Harris and asked him to become his deputy. Harris viewed the thought of returning to desk work with horror but felt he had little choice but to agree.

His fears were soon confirmed. The hours were, in his words, appalling. He arrived at the office at 9 A.M. every morning and rarely returned before midnight. Often he would have to work until three or four in the morning.

Sometimes he didn't go home at all. After three or four weeks without a break, he would be given forty-eight hours to recover. And then the whole thing would start again.

On one of those many late nights, December 29, 1940, Harris was at a desk when he heard a great roar. He left his office and climbed up to the Air Ministry's roof to see what was happening. London was ablaze. The Luftwaffe had launched its massive incendiary attack on the city; St. Paul's Cathedral rose from a vast lake of fire and smoke. At steady intervals, the air would fill with the roar of an arriving bomber stream, followed by a swish as incendiaries fell into the fire below. Harris called Portal to view the scene. They stood in silence for a few minutes. As they were turning away, Harris quietly remarked, "They are sowing the wind."

Harris's earlier work—his speech in Cairo, his 1937 paper, and his pronouncements during the war—had all caught the attention of Portal, who by then had come to share Harris's faith in area bombing. Portal quietly waited for the chance to make Harris his protégé. It came on December 6, 1941. On that day, Sir Richard Peirse resigned as commander-in-chief of Bomber Command. Peirse was blamed, rightly or wrongly, for Bomber Command's poor performance, and by the end of 1941 his days were numbered. On December 10, Sir Archibald Sinclair, a friend of Churchill, former Liberal leader, Secretary of State for Air, and somewhat marginal figure in the war, saw the opportunity to move Peirse sideways. Following the Japanese attack on Pearl Harbor, he needed a new Air commander-in-chief in the Far East.[5] Sinclair saw his chance. He suggested to Portal that Peirse take the job.[6] Harris's experience and his contacts in the United States (he had left the desk for a tour of the U.S.) made him a likely candidate to replace Peirse.

A likely candidate, but not a certain one. Harris's style had already made him enemies. Lord Halifax, in particular, thought he was crude, domineering, and patronizing toward the Americans. During Harris's study trip to the States, his habit of speaking his mind had left his hosts offended. Against this, however, Harris had an inestimable advantage: Churchill's support. Although they differed in background, learning, style, and articulacy, chemistry developed between the two men. They shared a flair for the dramatic and liked to present the struggle against Germany in grand, almost mythical terms. Whether this was enough to explain Churchill's affection for the Rhodesian is not clear, but for whatever reason he remained throughout the war strangely in thrall to Harris. Like another colonial, Beaverbrook, "Harris had a peculiar influence over Churchill which he used to great effect. . . . Although he never got all he asked for, his ability to influence Churchill meant that the Prime Minister essentially allowed Harris to wage a private war."[7] That war began with a mid-December phone call from Portal to Harris, offering him the job. Harris accepted. Portal replied, "Splendid! I'll go and tell Winston at once."[8] On February 10, Harris sailed to England.

As he did, the Air Ministry was drafting a new directive, which it issued on February 14, 1942. For the first three years of the war, Bomber Command had been limited: first, by the need to protect private property; then, by the need to avoid bombing east of the Rhine; and finally, by the need to target industry rather than civilians. In early 1942, before Harris took power, all of this changed. According to the directive, precision bombing was to be abandoned, and from that day forward bombing was to be "focused on the morale of the enemy civilian population and in particular of the industrial workers." To stave off any ambiguity, the Chief of Air Staff, Sir Charles Portal, clarified the directive in a follow-up communication the next day: "Ref the new bombing directive: I suppose it is clear that the aiming points are to be built up areas, not, for instance, the dockyards or factories. . . . This must be made quite clear if it is not already understood."[9] The directive specified "Primary Industrial Areas"—Essen, Duisburg, Düsseldorf, Cologne—and "Alternative Industrial Targets." The directive was meant to be temporary—to apply for no more than six months.

For Harris, the timing could not have been better. The directive gave him exactly what he wanted and he made no bones about it. Although not one to court publicity, he agreed to give an interview a few weeks after taking office. As the newsreel rolled, Harris barely looked at the camera, exuding an air of bored contempt. He outlined his bombing philosophy in cool, clipped tones: "There are a lot of people who say that bombing can never win a war. Well, my answer to that is it has never yet been tried. We shall see."

He nonetheless had to move carefully. Bomber Command was a demoralized animal, and the vultures—in the form of an army and, above all, a navy hungry for more air support—were circling above it. Even more worrying, the politicians' support was beginning to waiver. On February 25, 1942, Sir Stafford Cripps, then Lord Privy Seal, rose in the House of Commons. Cripps was a devout Christian and pacifist. A vegetarian and teetotaller, he hailed from the far left of the Labour Party. In 1936, the party had to repudiate Cripps's argument that it would not "be a bad thing for the British working class if

Germany defeated us."[10] In 1942, Churchill brought him into the Cabinet to shut him up. It didn't work. "A number of honourable Members," Cripps began,

> have questioned whether, in the existing circumstances, the continued devotion of a considerable part of our efforts to the building-up of this bomber force is the best use that we can make of our resources. . . . I would remind the House that this policy was initiated at a time when we were fighting alone against the combined forces of Germany and Italy, and it then seemed that it was the most effective way in which we, acting alone, could take the initiative against the enemy. Since that time we have had an enormous access of support from the Russian Armies . . . and also from the great potential strength of the United States of America. Naturally, in such circumstances, the original policy has come under review. . . . I can ensure the House that the Government are fully aware of the other uses to which our resources could be put, and the moment they arrive at a decision that the circumstances warrant a change, a change in policy will be made.[11]

With the Butt report still fresh in people's minds, another disastrous raid—one producing little damage and losing many planes—might have given Cripps and those of his ilk the excuse they needed to end the bombing war.

Harris was not about to let that happen. Over the next three years, he would fight two parallel battles: a military one with the Germans, and a rhetorical one over bombing with its opponents. He would receive qualified help from individuals whose committment to bombing, albeit bombing of a very different type, made them air purists in Harris's mold: the Americans.

4

THE AMERICANS

In December 1949, Bruce Simmons, a chauffeur, traveled to a modest ranch near Sonoma, California. He was checking in on his employer, a U.S. general. When he entered the semi-darkened bedroom, he saw the general lying in bed. There was no sign of movement. Alarmed, he bent over and put his face very close to the general's, checking for any sign of life. Suddenly, the general's eyes opened and he roared, "What in the hell do you want?" Simmons bolted upright and jumped back. The general let out a loud laugh, and said, "You thought I was gone, didn't you?"

This was Henry Harley ("Hap") Arnold, the commanding general of the U.S. Army Air Forces. At first meeting, one might be tempted to conclude that Arnold was the American alter ego of Harris. He was irascible, gruff, and at times crude. He was ruthlessly driven, and had no tolerance for those who adopted a more leisurely pace. He had even less tolerance for failure. One story about him is legend. On a Sunday in early March 1942, Arnold called a meeting to sort out a bookkeeping issue: he consistently had fewer planes than official tallies stated he should. A lower-level staff officer, Steve Ferson, "slowly and methodically" explained to Arnold that some planes were marked "accepted" (i.e., delivered) even though a part was missing. This was done because the manufacturer needed the money to produce planes for subsequent orders. When Arnold saw that his list of acceptances differed from Ferson's, he laid in to the hapless officer. Standing across the desk from him, Arnold thrust his head forward and screamed. As the harangue continued, Ferson's face turned crimson and his veins bulged. He began to sweat profusely. Ferson opened his mouth, as if to defend himself, but he never uttered a word. He pitched forward and landed face-first on the carpet in front of Arnold's desk. He was dead from a massive heart attack.[1]

Harris's temper—though also legendary—had never killed a man. But Arnold had several advantages over Harris. While Harris would scowl his way through photos, and through life, the natural expression on Arnold's "expressionless" face was a thin smile. It inspired his nickname "Hap" for "happy," and even his enemies found this quality disarming. He could also be charming, smooth, and disciplined. These characteristics served him well.[2]

Henry Arnold was born on June 25, 1886, in Pennsylvania, of a provincial, German-descended doctor, an austere and puritanical man who dominated his household and refused to let his children speak at dinner. Against Henry's will, Dr. Arnold signed him up for the entrance exam at West Point when the doctor's preferred choice, Henry's older brother Tom, refused to sit it. To Dr. Arnold's surprise, and Henry's horror (he was no keener on a military career than Tom was), the boy came second on the exam.

At West Point, Henry resumed his indolent ways. He graduated in 1907 with a mediocre class standing of 60 out of 110 and failed to make it to the cavalry branch he had initially strived for, instead being assigned to the infantry.[3] After two unhappy years in the Philippines and another two in the U.S., he wrote to Washington in 1911 and asked to be detailed for aeronautical work with the Signal Corps. The War Department sent back an official letter asking him if he would be willing to train under Wright in Dayton, Ohio, as a pilot. When he showed the letter to his commanding officer, the man drolly replied, "Young man, I know of no better way for a person to commit suicide."[4]

After two months' instruction under the Wright brothers, completed in June 1911, Arnold was a fully trained pilot. He was one of exactly two in the U.S. Aviation Service, but soon there would be twenty-six more. Of this early cohort, ten died in airplane crashes, twelve quit after a few months, and four died of natural causes. Hap was one of the survivors. After a glittering year in which he achieved a number of aviation "firsts" for high altitude, distance, and speed, a near crash on November 5, 1912, almost ended it all. He swore never to get in an airplane again and was transferred to a desk job in Washington.

In 1914, Arnold returned to Manila, where he and his new bride were forced to share headquarters with one other officer and many cockroaches. The latter were so large that Arnold's wife tried to kill them with a broom and failed.[5] Two years later, Billy Mitchell, the father of modern American air power, asked Arnold to reconsider a career in aviation. Arnold had still not set foot in an airplane since his near crash. He had to decide whether to try again or to bring his aviation career to an end, and with it the anomaly of an Air Force man afraid to fly. On October 18, 1916, he flew as a passenger; a month later he soloed, and in mid-December he was in the air for more than forty minutes, flying upside down and putting the aircraft through stalls, spins, rolls, and loops. "Hap" was back.

After a frustrating attempt to build an air force during the First World War, Arnold was demoted to major and transferred to Rockwell Field in San Diego, where he served as commander. Despite the demotion and more provincial focus of his work, Arnold was ecstatic. He was away from the desk and commanding troops.

The transfer was more fateful than he could have recognized. Arnold had two people to help him in San Diego. The first was Major Carl Spaatz, who was assigned to Arnold as his executive officer. The second was 1st Lt. Ira C. Eaker, who served as their adjutant. The three men would have a defining influence on the development of the U.S. Air Force.

Spaatz's background was similar to Arnold's. His upbringing was rural— he was born in Boyertown, Pennsylvania, on June 28, 1891—and his father was a member of the provincial liberal professions (he owned a family newspaper). Spaatz was of German descent: his grandfather immigrated from Germany and the newspaper, the *Boyerton Democrat*, was originally published in German, the language his grandmother spoke until the end of her life.[6] He attended West Point and ended up with a class standing of 57—three above Arnold. His "conduct" ranking was much worse: 95. He excelled at wit, along with bridge, poker, and the guitar. West Point failed to bequeath him with a love of learning, but it did equip him with things he would carry for the rest of his life: a nickname ("Tooey," because of his resemblance to upperclassman Francis J. Toohey), a love of flying, and a reputation for honesty.

With less fuss than Arnold, Spaatz went from West Point into the infantry, and from there he moved into his chosen branch: Signal Corps Aviation. Spaatz could have chosen the safety of a desk, but he insisted on fighting at the front. In September 1918, he reported for flying duty at the 2nd Pursuit Group, which had entered combat five weeks earlier. One of his first acts was to remove his major's insignia and place it in his pocket. He became one of the regular pilots and immediately won their respect. On September 15, he shot down his first German airplane. Eleven days later, a daring dogfight earned him the Distinguished Service Cross and made the *New York Times*. The headline read, FLYING OFFICER SHOOTS DOWN THREE PLANES—TWO GERMAN AND HIS OWN. When his wife, Ruth, saw the headline, she exclaimed, "That has to be Tooey!" Spaatz's determination to gun down the enemy had led him to neglect his fuel. He ran out of petrol and crashed in no-man's-land. Luckily, the French got to him before the Germans did.

While Spaatz was flying across enemy lines, the third in the air force trio—Ira Eaker—was an infantry officer at Fort Bliss, Texas. In November 1917, Eaker saw an airplane try without success to clear Mt. Franklin after takeoff. When the plane returned, it landed closest to Eaker, who ran to help. He had never seen an airplane engine before, but climbed on and saw a loose spark plug lead.

"Maybe this is your trouble," Eaker remarked.

"Let's find out," the pilot responded.

He showed Eaker how to turn the propeller, and got back into the cockpit. The engine sprang back to life.

"You know so much about engine motors," the pilot replied, "that you ought to come to the aviation section of the Signals Corps."

"How do I do it?" Eaker asked.

The pilot was a recruiter. "Fill out this form and send it in," he replied, "and you'll probably get a call."

In October 1918, after flight training in Austin and San Antonio, Eaker was transferred to Rockwell Field, where Arnold and Spaatz appointed him post adjutant.[7]

Eaker was the son of struggling Texan sharecroppers. He was born in Field Creek, Texas, on April 13, 1896. While Spaatz and Arnold attended West Point, Eaker's only education was at the undistinguished Southeastern Normal School in Durham, North Carolina. What he lacked in education he did not make up for in physical appearance: Arnold was towering and handsome, Eaker short and balding. Eaker was nonetheless able to overcome these disadvantages. Whereas Arnold and Spaatz were the Army equivalent of spoiled Ivy League students yawning over their books, Eaker had a deep and abiding love of learning. Through sheer determination, he became an intellectual, an accomplished writer and speaker. His soft Texan accent and gentle demeanor made him appear the gentleman, Arnold the vulgarian.

In the interwar years, what would become the United States Air Force would develop in tandem with the careers of Arnold, Spaatz, and Eaker. All three were disciples of William "Billy" Mitchell, the American counterpart of Hugh Trenchard and the founding father of American air power.[8] Mitchell had been the first American airman to arrive at the Western Front, the first to fly over enemy lines, and the first to be seduced by the promises of air power. The son of a U.S. senator, Mitchell was—like many bomber heroes after him—dashing, fearless, and flamboyant. He had fought in the Spanish-American War, dressed in sporting fashion, wore high cavalry boots and expensive tailored suits, and spoke flawless French.

Mitchell took inspiration from his experiences on the Western Front—streaking forward over enemy lines in seconds while armies struggled to advance a few inches—and from the writings of Italian theorist, air commander, and fascist General Giulio Douhet. In Douhet's view, the advent of air power meant that the new wars would be offensive, short, "violent to a superlative degree," and targeted at the enemy's homeland. "It is not enough," Douhet wrote, "to shoot down all the birds in flight if you want to wipe out the species; there remain the eggs and the nest." Such war would be total and Cromwellian in its brutality: "Any distinction between belligerents and non-belligerents is no longer admissible . . . because when nations are at war, everyone takes a part in it; the soldier carrying his gun, the women loading shells in a factory, the farmer growing wheat, the scientist in his laboratory."

While Douhet's project was ultimately genocidal—war was a "merciless pounding from the air" aimed at destroying the civilian population—Mitchell's was, or was meant to be, humane (though his views were never entirely consistent).[9] Air wars would be violent, but fewer people would die. Constructing an image that seduced generations of aviators, Mitchell believed that a dazzling bombardment would knock out the pillars of the enemy's war machine, destroy the people's will to fight, and lead to a quick surrender before the Army and Navy had even mobilized. The wars of the future might be nasty and brutish, but they would be—above all, in comparison with the prolonged slaughter of the First World War—short.

Still at relatively young ages, Arnold, Spaatz, and Eaker risked their careers for Mitchell. After accusing the Army and Navy (which blocked his plans for an independent air force) of incompetence and an "almost treasonable administration of the national defense," Mitchell was court-martialed in 1925. Spaatz and Arnold bravely spoke in his defense at the trial. Eaker worked quietly behind the scenes to help shape the defense. Mitchell was convicted of insubordination and given a five-year suspension. Refusing to be silenced, he resigned and pressed the case for air power as a civilian. For their part, Eaker, Spaatz, and Arnold survived the trial, but they drew at least one powerful lesson from it. "There must be something to this public relations business,"[10] they were reported to have said to each other. "I guess we'd better learn it."

Montgomery, Alabama, is most famous for its role in the civil rights movement. It played an equally important role in the history of air power. In 1910, at a muddy site occupied by a few wooden hangars, the Wright brothers opened their flying school. In 1922, the air force designated the site Maxwell Field. In 1928, the Air Corps Tactical School was transferred to it from Langley, Virginia. Over the subsequent decade, some of the most distinguished men in the history of American air power—Eaker, Spaatz, LeMay, and Arnold—would pass through its doors. They—and the less well-known permanent faculty at the school—developed American ideas about air power.

One of the faculty lecturers was Lieutenant Colonel Harold L. George, a veteran bomber pilot who had served in the First World War and the "anonymous warrior"[11] who provided much of the intellectual basis for what would become America's Second World War strategic bombing campaign. During his three-year stint at the school (1933–1936), he worked with Laurence Kuter (who taught bombardment and was known for his sharp mind and brilliant sense of humor), Muir Fairchild (an instructor), Kenneth Walker (an intense, methodological student of strategic bombing), Donald Wilson (an instructor), and Haywood S. Hansell (a southern engineer and fighter pilot with a deeply reflective and analytical mind).[12] Together, they drew on the ideas of Mitchell and Douhet, as well as Liddell Hart and Clausewitz,[13] and added their own, very American twist. Mitchell and especially Douhet had said little about targets (except that, for Douhet, everything was a target) beyond the aircraft industry and the opaque goal of destroying "morale."[14] George and his colleagues thought about nothing but targets: they wanted to identify the critical pillars of a modern industrial economy and how bombing could knock them— and, with them, the enemy's war—out.

Determining this required money, and the Air Corps Tactical School had little of it. They could not hire economists and they were forbidden from studying the economies of Japan or Germany. To get around these constraints, George and his colleagues studied the American industrial system as a (imperfect, as the two economies were different) proxy for the German one. Through this work, they came up with an idea of an "industrial web": modern economies were delicate and interconnected machines that were entirely dependent on the same set of key supports.[15] All industries needed steel, ball bearings, and electricity. All industries needed railroads to transport these materials and to deliver their finished products. What was needed, then, was not Douhet's war of extermination, but rather a precise and relentless bombing campaign against the producers of steel, ball bearings, electricity, and similar targets.[16] If bombing could destroy these "choke points," the wartime economy would collapse, and with it the will to fight on.

Out of these theories emerged daylight precision bombing, America's plan for bringing the war to Germany. The question was how to accomplish it, and it is here that George's ideas showed their American origins: he had an overwhelmingly optimistic faith in the ability of ingenuity and technology to overcome difficulties. In an almost perfect confirmation of cultural stereotypes, early setbacks in the war quickly convinced the British that precision daylight bombing couldn't be done; the Americans, in the face of similar losses, insisted that it could. As a plaque on Arnold's desk read, *The difficult we do today. The impossible takes a little longer.* Added to these beliefs was a moral concern. Commentators have tended to downplay it, insisting that the Americans mainly viewed bombing civilians as pointless. They largely did. As one general put it in 1944, "There was a memorandum on 29 October which said that no German cities would be bombed as secondary targets unless they had military targets adjacent. We said we would never bomb a German city. We will bomb a military target within the bounds of a German city, but not a German city. That is largely because of the fact that the Eighth Air Force does not believe that the morale of Germany is vulnerable to a decisive degree. . . . [Hitler] has made the morale of the German civil population highly invulnerable to either [Allied] propaganda or morale attacks." Otherwise, there would have long been a rebellion against Hitler: "Never before in the history of man has a nation been subject to any pounding like the Germans have."[17]

Strategy explains much of American opposition, but not all of it. The Americans also viewed city bombing as wrong—at least over Europe. "The Tactical School," Hansell later wrote, "opposed the concept which was generally described as an attack on enemy morale. The idea of killing thousands of men, women, and children was basically repugnant to American mores."[18] Daylight precision bombing was a perfect synthesis of American attributes: a belief in the importance of morality in politics, optimism, and a commitment to technological pioneering.[19]

In 1933, the optimism and morality were in place, but the technology wasn't. At least, the lecturers at the Air Corps Tactical School *thought* it wasn't. In fact, in 1931, Carl L. Norden, a Dutch inventor who had emigrated to the United States in 1904, had developed an idea to help naval aircraft bomb with greater precision. Resembling an oversized camera, the bombsight allowed aircrew to input airspeed and altitude on the bombing run. The bombsight would calculate the trajectory of the bomb and the moment when it should be released. The bombsight was originally designed for purely defensive purposes, and the Navy ordered almost a hundred thousand of them to protect the U.S. coastline. The faculty at Maxwell Field didn't hear about this until 1935, but when they did, they knew they had the equipment they needed.

By 1935, what would become the United States Air Force had three of the most talented men in the history of aviation—Arnold, Spaatz, and Eaker; it had the abstract creativity and diligent research of George and his colleagues at Maxwell Field; and it had the technology it believed it needed to translate the theory of precision bombing into a reality. It lacked one thing, however: an airplane.

5

BUILDING THE MIGHTY EIGHTH

On September 12, 1938, President Roosevelt and his adviser and New Deal architect, Harry Hopkins, were in a car in Rochester, Minnesota, where the president's son was undergoing surgery. The radio was on, and they were listening to Hitler's speech at a huge Nazi rally in Nuremberg. The German dictator ranted and threatened Czechoslovakia with invasion if it did not submit to his demands. When it ended, Roosevelt snapped off the radio and turned to Hopkins. He told him to look immediately for new aircraft factory sites on the west coast. Roosevelt "was sure then," Hopkins wrote, "that we were going to get into war, and he believed that air power would win it."[1]

The U.S. Congress did not agree and would not provide the funds. Without them, only two thousand planes were produced in 1939. All of this changed in early 1940, however. In May, as the Germans invaded the Low Countries, Roosevelt issued a public call for an annual output of fifty thousand planes—some twenty-five times the figure produced in 1939! Congress quickly provided the money. After spending years begging for funds to build a handful of bombers, Arnold—now chief of the Army Air Corps—found that "in 45 minutes I was given $1,500,000,000 and told to get an air force."[2]

Arnold had the money; he now needed the power. In 1940, Roosevelt had appointed Harry L. Stimson his Secretary of War. Stimson was a Harvard-educated lawyer, the son of a Union soldier in the Civil War, and a member of upper-class New York. His upbringing emphasized the puritan virtues of work and abstention (though he lived very comfortably) and the not-uncommon early-twentieth-century view of war as a cleansing antidote to the soft mate-

41

rialism associated with American affluence.[3] "Every man," he wrote in 1915, "owes to his country not only to die for her if necessary, but also to spend a little of his life in learning how to die for her effectively."

One of Stimson's first acts was the appointment of a fellow New Yorker, Robert Lovett, to the new position of Assistant Secretary of War for Air. Lovett was a wealthy stockbroker, an experienced pilot (he had flown Navy combat planes in the First World War), and a student of RAF administration. He had a talent for packaging his ideas and for handling difficult people, not least of whom was Arnold. "When I became impatient, intolerant, and would rant around, fully intending to tear the War and Navy Departments to pieces," Arnold wrote, "Bob Lovett would know exactly how to handle me. He would say, with a quiet smile, 'Hap, you're wonderful! I wish I had your pep and vitality. Now . . . let's get down and be practical.' And I would come to earth with a bang."[4]

In 1941, Lovett produced a plan for reorganizing the Air Corps and giving it more autonomy. Roosevelt accepted it. The Army Air Corps was replaced by the Army Air Forces. A new Chief of the Army Forces (who was also Army Deputy Chief of Staff for Air) controlled the entire organization. With the support of General George Marshall (Chief of Staff of the United States Army, the professional head of the U.S. Army), the position went to Arnold. Marshall wrote later: "I tried to give Arnold all the power I could. I tried to make him as nearly as I could Chief of Staff of the Air without any restraint."[5]

The Air Staff was made up of old Maxwell Field lecturers: Kenneth Walker, Haywood Hansell, and Laurence Kuter. They produced a document known as AWPD-1, named after the Air Staff's Air War Plans Division. The plan envisioned four roles for the Air Forces in the coming war: supporting the defensive strategy in the Pacific during the initial phases of war; waging an unlimited strategic offensive against Germany as soon as possible; preparing for an invasion of the European continent; and preparing the invasion of Japan by waging an unlimited strategic air offensive against its homeland. Although a more measured document than the one produced earlier by Britain's Directorate of Plans, it was still beholden to the bombers' dream. "If the air offensive is successful," AWPD-1 read, "a land offensive may not be necessary."[6] Working long hours, Hansell, Walker, and Kuter rehearsed the document with each other until they knew it by heart.[7] The three men then presented it to Marshall, Stimson, and Hopkins. The lecturers, as it were, flew on a wing and a prayer. At a time when the United States had thirteen B-17s, they spoke of thousands. The large figures, Hansell later said, "scared us very badly at the time."[8] But the presentation went over well. It was then leaked to the *Chicago Tribune*, resulting in strong public support.[9] The leak also ensured that the details of the plan were publicized *before* the draft was sent on to the Army, which would have almost certainly reworked it.[10]

Having already won two wars—over money and power—Arnold now needed to win another—over strategy. His opponents were not in the U.S. Air Forces (everyone agreed on daylight precision bombing) but across the Atlantic: the British.

In May 1940, Arnold sent Spaatz to London. Officially, he was there as an "Assistant Military Attaché (Air) to Britain"; unofficially, he was a "high-class spy" studying the air war and the state of Britain in it.[11] Though it was a low point in Britain's war, Spaatz formed prescient views about the limits of German air power and the ability of the British to hold out.[12] A year later, Arnold visited. By this point, America's entry into the war seemed more and more likely. Arnold expected to meet with Portal, then Chief of Air Staff and overseeing an air war that was still formally committed to precision bombing. The RAF was bombing German warships in support of the Royal Navy, a job that the commander-in-chief of Bomber Command, Richard Peirse, resisted. Peirse—supposedly a confident supporter of precision bombing—complained bitterly to Portal that his pilots were wasting hundreds of tons of bombs on a job for which they were neither trained nor prepared.[13]

Beyond Portal, Arnold held out hope for a meeting with Lord Beaverbrook, then Churchill's production coordinator. To his surprise, he was treated as a minor, if not major, celebrity. When he arrived for an overnight stay in neutral Portugal, three members of a UK delegation, led by Air Marshal John C. Slessor (Assistant Chief of Air Staff [Plans], who worked directly under Vice Chief of Air Staff Wilfred Freeman and Portal), were waiting for him. After allowing Arnold a bath and change, they pelted him with questions: What could the Americans do about the U-boat campaign, which threatened the UK with starvation? What could they do about the B-17 (delivered by Roosevelt to England), which was useless in combat? And, above all, did he really believe that precision bombing would work?

Despite his quasi–hero's welcome, the trip nearly went badly. The British found him unprepared. Portal, when he first dined with Arnold, was shocked to learn that Arnold had arrived without an agenda for his visit. Arnold, for his part, found Portal defeatist and demanding. They would "talk about squadrons whereas we would talk about groups." At the same time, they made endless demands for American support. Things looked up, however, when he met Beaverbrook, who was "the one man in London with ideas as large as his own"—perhaps because he, too, was a North American.[14] Beaverbrook agreed immediately to Arnold's request for two each of Spitfires (fighters), Hurricanes, and Wellingtons (bombers) for study, and invited him to view everything the British had. Most revealingly, from Arnold's perspective, Beaverbrook told him that the Germans had reduced British aircraft production by up to one-third as a result of factory bombing.[15] Another of Beaverbrook's comments left a lasting impression on Arnold. At an April 21 dinner, Beaverbrook asked him: "What would you do if Churchill were hung and the rest of us were hiding in Scotland or being run down by the Germans? We are up against the mightiest Army the world has ever known."[16] When Arnold left London, he had the impression that the British were setting their sights far too low and that the gloom that had overtaken the country might lose them the war. He reserved his most scathing views for Sir Richard Peirse. In contrast to the leaders of Fighter Command, who were actually fighting, Peirse was "pathetic."

In August 1941, Roosevelt and Churchill met in Newfoundland. There they outlined the principles that would guide their countries' approach to war. Neither country would seek territorial aggrandizement, and both would foster the freedoms of all people, vanquished and victors. The United States had served notice on Hitler that his enemies had its sympathy. It had also, though this captured less attention at the time, served notice on the British Empire.

Marshall had invited Arnold to attend the conference, and while Roosevelt, Churchill, and their aides drafted the charters, Arnold met with the generals and admirals. He was again taken aback by British shortsightedness and greed. The "British long-range plan," he wrote in his diary, "is to keep giving as little as possible in remote areas where they can meet Germans on even terms, always hoping for a break—a miracle—an internal breakdown of [German] morale."[17] They had no long-term plan that envisaged total victory or even the invasion of the Continent. Yet, they wanted four thousand heavy American bombers at a time when the U.S. was producing five hundred a month.[18]

Arnold returned to Washington in August and spent the next four months building the U.S. Air Force while fighting off British requests for ever more planes. He repeatedly warned Roosevelt that transferring planes to England might leave the U.S. undefended. Roosevelt insisted, and on December 7, 1941, Arnold's fears were realized. The Japanese attack on Pearl Harbor cost the Americans 188 aircraft (with another 159 damaged). The aircraft had been left in tight formations to prevent sabotage, and they formed ideal targets for the incoming airplanes. Four hours later, Japanese bombers destroyed twelve B-17s caught refueling in the Philippines.

The Eighth Air Force would have four commands: Bomber and Fighter Commands, as well as Ground-Air Support Command and Air Service Command (responsible for supply and maintenance). Eighth Bomber Command was organized into combat wings, which were in turn composed of three bomb groups (made up of squadrons), which went together on air raids. Each combat wing was in turn part of a larger structure, first called a bombardment wing (there were two—the 1st and the 2nd—in 1942) and later an air division (eventually made up of three to five combat wings).

With the U.S. now in the war, Arnold needed to rebuild the air forces and to keep them American. The British, led by Portal, wanted U.S. bombers transferred to England and the American air forces under the control of the RAF, to jointly conduct area bombing at night. Arnold was not one to give up on an idea—of an independent air force bombing according to American principles—that he had cultivated and cherished for almost a decade. He formed the Eighth Air Force, and turned to Spaatz for his views on the American bombing offensive. Spaatz told him what he wanted to hear: whatever the British said, daylight bombing was possible and much more likely to win the war than indiscriminately bombing civilians in the middle of the night.[19] Arnold made Spaatz commander of the Eighth.

Arnold's next move was to bring Eaker, who had taken over fighter defenses on the west coast after Pearl Harbor, on board. Arnold met with him in Washington on January 8. "You're going to England. I want you to fly over there and negotiate with the British for headquarters, airdromes, communications, all the stuff we'll need. Understudy the British and work out the plans. Then I'll get you some bombers and crews. You'll be in charge of the Eighth Air Force Bomber Command."

The news surprised no one more than it did Eaker. He had never even been in a bomber.

"Bombers!" he exclaimed. "But I've been a fighter all my life."

"That's why I'm giving you the job," Arnold replied. "I want you to put some fight into the bombers."

Seeing that he had no choice in the matter, Eaker asked, "What do I do for staff?"

"I can spare you two or three good men," Arnold answered. "Beyond that I suggest you find yourself some civilians. You take a smart civilian, you can make a smart officer out of him in six weeks or so. But if you take a dumb officer, you'll never make him a smart officer."[20]

That night, not yet used to the stars on his shoulders, Eaker and his wife, Ruth, accompanied Arnold to a dinner for Portal and Harris. Wine flowed throughout the long meal, and over after dinner drinks Harris subjected Arnold to a harangue on precision bombing.

"I bloody well don't think you can do it," he began in a characteristically truculent mode. "We tried it. We know. We even tried it with your Fortresses."

Arnold, now accustomed to this argument, replied, "Sure. You tried it with one or two B-17s at a time. We don't plan to do it that way. We're going to send them out in mass formations."

Harris was not to be moved. "It doesn't matter a tinker's damn what you send them in," he shot back. "The Boche have too many fighters, too much flak, too much bloody power against that West Wall to make it worth the losses. God knows, I hope you can do it, but I don't think you can."

Turning to Eaker, he said, "Come join us at night. Together we'll lick them."

Eaker, ever the gentleman, sought a compromise and in so doing produced a phrase that would become legend.

"Yes," he said, "we'll bomb them by day. You bomb them by night. We'll hit them right around the clock."[21]

The strategy, which had resulted not from agreement but rather the opposite, would become policy.

On February 4, 1942, Eaker left to take up his assignment in England. He and six staff officers undertook a long trip to England. After a complicated journey, he finally arrived in London on February 21, a day before Harris took over Bomber Command. After three days in London, Eaker and his staff moved on to Bomber Command headquarters in High Wycombe. Harris was there to greet him. Although he and his wife, Jill, had themselves just moved in, he insisted that Eaker stay with him until his headquarters were ready. They lived at Springfield, a two-story, wide brick house. After the war, rumors circulated to the effect that the house was bombproof, but it wasn't.[22] The only bombproof part of the house is a panic room in a bathroom, with a bullet-proof window. The window wasn't installed until the 1980s, when the RAF had the Irish rather than the Germans to fear. In fact, both the house and the town itself—a typical provincial English town filled with rolling hills and streets of terraced, working-class houses—were chosen for their ordinariness. German reconnaissance flights over High Wycombe would see only a clutch of private houses. Harris did not, however, want for comfort. The house has large rooms, a dining hall reminiscent of an Oxford Head-of-House's lodging, and a grand lawn. It is stately but unpretentious and housed both the Harrises and the Eakers comfortably.

The two men could not have been more different: Harris liked a drink; Eaker barely touched the stuff. Harris was hearty, gruff, and deliberately offensive; Eaker was shy and eager to please. Harris was cold and aloof with his staff; Eaker was informal and completely unpretentious. For all that, the two men got along during their stay, and developed a friendship that would outlast the war. Harris had a monster of a personality, but never let his disagreements get in the way of friendship with those for whom he had genuine affection.

After Harris's warm welcome, Eaker received a less enthusiastic one from Major General James E. Chaney (Commanding General, U.S. Army Forces in the British Isles), who had overseen the skeleton staff the Americans had in England. Chaney and Eaker, like most airmen, had known each other for some time, but Chaney was hostile to the American plan for a separate air force under Eaker and Spaatz. He had become anglicized during his time in the UK, and viewed the war with the same set of low expectations as his British hosts. Under Chaney's vision, Eaker and his men would become simply adjuncts to the existing London-based staff of thirty-five officers, only four of whom were airmen.[23] Eaker outflanked him. He pointed out that he was there to understudy the RAF and that he could not do that from London. Fortuitously, he received an invitation from Harris to share space at RAF Bomber Command. Eaker seized upon it immediately and he, his six accompanying staff members, and eventually fifteen additional officers, all moved in.

Until the U.S. Air Force had its own infrastructure in the United Kingdom, Eaker had to play his hand carefully. The British were still pressuring the Americans to join in the area bombing campaign and, when expressed by Harris, that pressure was not subtle. Throughout early 1942, the commander-in-chief pressed Eaker to bomb cities. "It took," Harris told Eaker, "only a year or less to build a tank or a plane but it took 20 years to build skilled workmen, and skilled workmen in short supply would affect war production as much as loss of their factory."[24] Eaker was always careful not to sound skeptical, which some observers have taken as evidence of his and broader American support for Harris. The truth was more complicated: Eaker needed Harris's support and he could not risk that support by telling him that the Americans viewed city bombing as immoral, if not murderous, and pointless. Instead, he steadfastly told Harris and Portal that his orders from Arnold were to bomb by day, that American planes and crews were not trained for night bombing, and that precision daylight bombing could be made to work.[25] It was an agreement to disagree. Portal and Harris did not agree with Eaker, but they helped him. Harris turned over five long-established bases in East Anglia, and the Air Ministry agreed to build another sixty. Eaker could not have been more pleased.

The first job was securing permanent headquarters. General Chaney, clearly accustomed to English privations, suggested tents, but Eaker was able to kill that idea. He also got his way on the location: in High Wycombe, within five miles of RAF Bomber Command. Harris and Eaker drew a five-mile radius around Bomber Command headquarters, and Eaker scouted the area. The only suitable building was the Wycombe Abbey School for girls, a manor house set on a verdant campus, its walkways shaded by linden trees. Harris agreed it would be perfect, but thought that securing it was beyond even his powers of persuasion: "I'm afraid you'll have trouble getting that school. Too many of our Ministers' wives are graduates." Eaker persevered, and applied for the school through the Air Ministry.

An Air Ministry official, also a Lord, came to see Eaker a few days later and told him it was impossible. "Our girls from the colonies, Australia, and Canada are in that school, and we have to keep them there. We can't send them home due to the submarine menace."

Eaker replied in his Texan drawl, "If you're more interested in educating your daughters than in winning this war, I'm glad you've told us."

The official was taken aback and left. The next day, he called: "The school is yours."[26]

Eaker moved in three weeks later. Although formally part of a joint strategy, over the next three years the Americans and British would effectively fight parallel but separate air wars against Germany. While the Americans were preparing for their war, Britain's, under Arthur Harris, would begin in earnest.

6

BURN, GERMANY, BURN

The bombing force that Harris took over in 1942 was small: 407 bomb-ers. Of these, only 136 (29 Lancasters, 62 Halifaxes, and 45 Stirlings, all four-engined aircraft with maximum speeds of some 260 miles per hour) were heavy bombers.[1] A force of that size could be literally wiped out over the course of a few high-loss raids. Harris viewed the situation with his usual clarity. He sought to increase the number of bombers, to expand his crews, and to make sure that both had a better chance of surviving.

All three problems had, as Harris saw it, a single solution: successful raids that inflicted a great deal of damage on Germany at little cost to Bomber Com-mand. A new development in radar, an area in which the British were always ahead of the Americans, Gee (named after the first letter in *grid*), helped. Gee was developed in 1940–1941 and worked like this: three transmitter stations in England (one "master" and two "slave") sent signals that were picked up by equipment carried in the bombers. When the navigator's three signals were plotted, the result was a sort of a grid, and the position of the airplane within it could be estimated to a high degree of accuracy. For the first time in the bombing war, RAF aircrew had a precise measure of where they and their tar-gets were. The only downside was time: the Germans would eventually figure out what the British were up to and jam it. The RAF gave it six months.

Harris made his first move, without Gee, in an unusual precision raid on the Renault works at Billancourt, which produced trucks for the Wehr-macht. On the night of March 3, he sent in three waves of bombers. Tightly concentrated—121 airplanes passed over the target in an hour—the first wave marked the target with flares, while the second and third blasted the target with high explosives (one thousand- and four thousand-pound bombs). The factories suffered severe damage; only one aircraft was lost, though three hundred French people were killed.[2]

Harris then introduced Gee: in a series of raids on industrial targets in Duisburg, Cologne, and Essen, he instructed his crews to mark the targets with flares using Gee alone. When they did, it worked, though crews—unaccustomed to or suspicious of the new technology—often tried to mark visually, with poor results.

By the end of March, the technical pillars of Harris's strategy were being put in place. Gee would guide a first wave of airplanes to mark the target with flares. Subsequent waves of bombers would hit the target with high explosives (blowing off roofs and doing structural damage) and incendiaries would light the target on fire. With radar, markers, and concentrated bombings, Harris was ready to bring his war to Germany.

The question that remained was one of targets. Harris avoided the major industrial cities of Germany: Düsseldorf, Essen, and Stuttgart. They were heavily defended and, in the case of Stuttgart, hard to reach. Harris instead sought a city whose destruction would be so complete that the world would take notice. "I wanted my crews to be well 'blooded,' as they say in foxhunting, to have a taste of success." Such a city would have three attributes: it would be easy to find, not overwhelmingly defended, and likely to burn.[3] The commercial port city of Lübeck fit the bill. Above all, its mass of densely knit, wooden houses meant that it would burn. "It was built," as Harris noted, "more like a fire lighter than a human habitation."[4]

Like Hamburg and Bremen, Lübeck was built around trade rather than industry. The city radiated out from its central markets, around which wealthy trading families had built their famous gabled houses. The city's old center was small and compact—half a mile by one mile—and bounded by canals on all sides. Its two most important public buildings were the Cathedral, for which Henry the Lion, the city's founder, had laid the cornerstone in 1173, and the Church of St. Mary, both famous for their paired steeples. By 1940, the entire city core was under a preservation order. Three years into the war, it was only lightly defended by five heavy and three light flak batteries.

Lübeck, northern Germany

In the early evening of March 28, 1942, the sun was setting. It was the night before Palm Sunday, and across the city churches were preparing confirmations. At around 11:15 P.M., the first air-raid warning rang out.[5] No one paid any attention. For more than two years, air-raid warnings had been followed by nothing, as the bombers flew to Bremen, Hamburg, or Berlin. Lübeckers—believing a story that had many equivalents across Germany—told themselves that the city would not be bombed because Churchill's grandmother lived there.[6] But on that night, the airplanes appeared and Lübeck was bombed in three waves. Pathfinders appeared first and marked the city with their gently descending lights. At 11:29, the first wave of incendiary and 250-pound bombs hit the city, landing near the harbor in the south.[7] "We couldn't believe it," wrote the members of Flak Group 161 later. "Many, probably most of us never thought the enemy would actually attack this city of architectural monuments from distant times . . . but here it was, the attack, far larger than we had expected."[8] Nearly twenty minutes later—at 11:48—a second and far more powerful wave of bombs hit the city. High explosives and incendiaries rained down on the area around the main station and the city's famous two-towered Cathedral. One hit a house on the corner of Ritterstrasse and Gothlandstrasse,[9] outside the main aiming point, killing eleven members of a family who had gathered to celebrate a birthday. Only one son and his grandmother, who were not in the house, survived.

Fires started in the Grosse Burgstrasse, in the southwestern corner of the old city.[10] They quickly spread through the neighborhood, surrounding St. Jacob's Church and the adjacent school.[11] The flames continued to move, and the incendiaries started hundreds of new fires that spread westward, consuming the Königstrasse and the Breite Strasse (which ran north–south, parallel to each other) along with the Kuhberg and the Johannisstrasse (which also stood parallel). They reached the Kohlmarkt and the adjacent Church of St. Mary almost exactly in the middle of the old city. As this was happening, bombs lit fires in and around the Aegidien church, to the southwest. Surrounding the church was the Kaufmannsviertel, the merchant's district, made up of tightly knit narrow streets. The fires tore through them and began leaping over the buildings into neighboring streets. As they did, high explosives shattered houses, giving new oxygen and new pathways to the flames.

At 1 A.M., a final wave of bombers pasted the city. A combination of high explosives and thousands of incendiaries landed across Lübeck: in the east, south, and west. One high explosive landed in the Mühlenstrasse, in the southeast of the old city and only several feet from the Cathedral, and destroyed the city's main waterlines.[12] Firemen's hoses ran dry and were dragged to the city's canals, but the sub-zero temperature meant that the hoses turned to ice. In the Johannisstrasse, flames shot up from the roof of the Karstadt department store, threatening the twin steeples of the nearby Church of St. Mary. At 1:30 A.M., fires appeared in the church's chapel. The church's two bells (one cast in 1390, the other in 1745) fell and broke, crashing through the great organ made by Arp Schnitger. The crown of the choir toppled, burying the wooden high altar and the sedilia, installed in 1310.[13] Firemen tried to put out the flames, but the pipe bringing water from the Trave, the canal in the north of the city, was broken. The fires spread and began leaping out of the domes of St. Mary. At 5 A.M., the helm roof on the southern dome was alight; a few minutes later, the northern dome followed. Nearby, the City Hall (Rathaus) and the St. Petri church also burned. So did the Cathedral. A neighboring museum was hit by the first wave of bombs and, at 1:30 A.M., the fires jumped across to the Cathedral.

Firefighters did not have the blaze under control until 10 A.M. the next day. By that time, two hundred acres of the old town had been demolished. All of the churches were shells. The Kohlmarkt was flattened. More than 320 people were dead, 130 seriously injured, and 15,000 homeless. Bombing destroyed 1063 houses and 21 public buildings.[14] Twenty-five industrial concerns were hit, three significantly: a butcher was destroyed, Drägerwerk (which made breathing equipment for U-boats) lost 30 percent of its power supply, and an armaments factory was seriously damaged.[15] The harbor suffered only light damage. At 10:30 A.M., the Cathedral's northern tower collapsed; four hours later, the southern tower met the same fate. Losses among the RAF were tolerable: twelve bombers did not come back, and only one seemed to have been shot down over Lübeck.

Although Lübeck's historic center had been gutted, the effect of the raid on industrial production was minimal. The city was operating at 80 to 90 percent within days. The Heinkel factory, which suffered during the raid, recovered within weeks.[16] There was no evidence of the widespread panic, fear, and demoralization promised by Portal and Harris. Instead, newspaper reports spoke of the "heroes" that were the flak operators,[17] of "Lübeck's heart" that was "tougher than English bombs,"[18] and of the help that poured in from neighboring cities and beyond.[19] The dead were declared "soldiers" who fell for a Germany that would never forget them.[20] Above all, the city would recover from the "great crime" committed against it by the "British murderers."[21] The rhetoric was no different than that heard in London during the Blitz, as was the effect on morale. "It made us," wrote Lübecker Günther Becker, "harder and more resilient, and we believed even more in Germany's ultimate victory."[22]

For all the official bravado, the Germans feared another attack: not on the city, but on the harbor. A full four months after the attack—on July 24, 1942—the Staatskommissar in the mayor's office in Lübeck wrote to the local Luftwaffe command in Hamburg begging for more air protection from direct attacks on the harbor.

For the moment, this did not matter to the British. The photos of Lübeck's skyline, covered in billows of smoke from the city's shattered Cathedral, made the destruction alone seem like a great achievement. And from a technical point of view, it was. In 1941, a raid involving a hundred bombers over four hours would be considered a great accomplishment. Now, one year later, Harris had managed more than twice the number of bombers in half the time.[23]

These were impressive feats of destruction, and Ira Eaker recognized them as such. Destroying cities was possible, he admitted, but that did not convince him that it was effective. When Harris used Lübeck to press him into the campaign, he reiterated his faith in precision bombing, and repeated his argument that U.S. planes and crews were not prepared for night bombing. He also articulated a more measured vision of what bombing promised. "It would be desirable," Eaker said, "to sit back and put all our efforts into the air and destroy [the enemy's] weapons-making production. But that's daydreaming. . . . In our case the elder service is the Army, and then the Navy has always had great public popularity. There's no possibility . . . that we're going to get the Army and Navy to stay out of it and let the fledgling young Air Force win the war."[24] It would be ideal if bombing could win the war, but if it could not, it would weaken Germany to the point where an invasion was easier. Eaker, along with Arnold and Spaatz, was not yet sure of the best way to achieve this aim, but all three were from the start willing to accept bombing's role as complementary rather than decisive.

Harris was not, and in this he was not alone. One of those impressed by city bombing was Churchill's scientific adviser, Lord Cherwell. Cherwell was courageous, wealthy, and—when he wanted to be—disarmingly charming. He was also vain, arrogant, and unforgiving to the point of being vengeful. He was born Frederick Lindemann in Baden-Baden in 1886 (of a German father who had migrated to England in 1870), studied at Darmstadt, and took a Ph.D. from the University of Berlin. He always viewed his German birth and descent as a handicap, and is said to have overcome it by demonstrating greater enthusiasm than anyone else for killing Germans. True or not, throughout the war he was the most consistent advocate, after Harris, of leveling Germany.

When war broke out in 1914, Cherwell made several unsuccessful attempts to use his scientific background for the war effort before being offered a position at the Royal Aircraft Factory at Farnborough.[25] From there, he was accepted into the Royal Flying Corps, where he developed a mathematical theory of aircraft spin recovery (at that time, it was thought that when an aircraft entered a spin, it was all over). He calculated that if the pilot let go of the controls rather than struggling against them, the plane would automatically come out of the spin. When he presented the findings, his superiors asked him how he could prove it. Cherwell took a plane up, deliberately put it into a spin, and let go of the controls. It worked, and the method is still in use.[26]

In 1919, Cherwell took up a chair in experimental philosophy and became director of the Clarendon library. He saw Nazi Germany for what it was earlier than most people in the UK, and he urged preparation for war. In the 1930s, he was also active in helping distinguished Jewish scientists escape Germany. In the summer of 1933, Cherwell visited Germany to interview scientists and made his recommendations to the UK Academic Assistance Council. With Cherwell's help, more than a dozen scientists found positions in Britain. They included Albert Einstein, who became a fellow at Christ Church—Portal and Cherwell's college. In the college's senior common room (faculty lounge) there is a book of present and former college fellows. In it, not far from Cherwell himself, the casual observer stumbles across the familiar uprush of white hair. In a very Oxonian way, the photograph is neither distinguished nor marked in any particular manner, and does not even have the great scientist's name below it.

Although kind to those closest to him, Cherwell could in no way be described as sociable. His foreign origins and the widespread belief that he was Jewish (*mann* being a common name ending among German Jews) likely created a wall between him and other students (Christ Church's quaint name for fellows) at his college. For his part, Cherwell was rigid and unforgiving. All those who worked with him—first at Christ Church and later in government—had to be careful. Cherwell shared with Harris more than a passion for bombing; both saw little difference between constructive criticism and personal slight. Those who crossed him, whatever their motive, were never forgiven. One evening in the late 1920s, a Christ Church don, Roy Harrod, brought an economics colleague in for dinner. Harrod's colleague ventured a figure on the value of British exports; Cherwell offered another.

> The matter was subsequently looked up, and my colleague wrote to the Prof. to acknowledge the fact that his, the Prof.'s, *guess* had been nearer than his own. The word "guess" was quite fatal; the Prof. never forgave him. I remember that many years later the Prof. had to consider a proposal put forward, and objected to it. "Why did you object, Prof.?" I said. "The proposal seems a very reasonable one." He made some specious criticisms which struck me as quite unconvincing. Then it suddenly flashed across my mind that the proposal was associated with my unfortunate colleague, who had accused the Prof. of "guessing" some twenty years before.[27]

It was at one of Cherwell's rare visits to High Table that he came across an idea that would have an important influence on the bombing war. Cherwell had been Churchill's scientific adviser since 1940. On one evening in August 1942, a young physiologist, Solly Zuckerman, the son of Eastern European Jewish immigrants to South Africa and an Oxford zoologist who conducted early experiments on the effects of bombing, was sitting next to Cherwell.[28] Zuckerman worked at the Ministry of Home Security. The two men found themselves in agreement on Bomber Command: despite the poor results, the case against bombing had not been proved. More importantly, there was no other way of hitting the Germans. Zuckerman suggested to Cherwell that there might be one way of proving the case: survey the damage done by the Germans in their raids on English cities, and generalize the results back to German ones.[29]

Cherwell immediately took to the idea. He threw his support behind the survey and gave Zuckerman three specific questions: How many tons of bombs does it take to break a town? And how should the bombs be delivered—in one sharp attack or over a number of nights? If the latter, in what rations should the total load be distributed and over how many nights?[30] Zuckerman carried out the survey with the help of Desmond Bernal, a Cambridge scientist. They chose Birmingham and Hull as typical manufacturing and port towns. Cherwell sent Zuckerman and Bernal requests for data and had an almost complete tally of the bombs dropped during air raids fed to David Butt in the Statistical

Department.[31] Butt analyzed the results and then presented them to Cherwell. They, but not the Zuckerman–Bernal report itself, formed the basis for a minute he drafted for Churchill. It was ready on March 30.

The following seems a simple method of estimating what we could do by bombing Germany. Careful analysis of the raids on Birmingham, Hull and elsewhere have shown that on average one tonne of bombs dropped on a built-up area demolished 20–40 dwellings and turns 100–200 people out of house and home.

We know from our experience that we can count on nearly 14 operational sorties per bomber produced. The average lift of the bombers we are going to produce over the next 15 months will be 3 tons. It follows that each of these bombers will in its lifetime drop about 40 tons of bombs. If these are dropped on built-up areas they will make 4,000–8,000 people homeless.

In 1938 over 22 million Germans lived in 58 towns of over 100,000 inhabitants, which, with modern equipment, should be easy to find and hit. Our forecast output of heavy bombers (including Wellingtons) between now and the middle of 1943 is about 10,000. Even if half the total load of 10,000 bombers were dropped on the built-up areas of these 58 German towns the great majority of their inhabitants (about one-third of the German population) would be turned out of house and home.

Investigation seems to show that having one's house demolished is most damaging to morale. People seem to mind it more than having their friends or even relatives killed. At Hull signs of strain were evident though only one-tenth of the houses were demolished. On the above figures we should be able to do ten times as much harm to each of the 58 principal German towns. There seems to be little doubt that this would break the spirit of the people.

Our calculation assumes, of course, that we really get one-half of our bombs into the built-up areas. On the other hand, no account is taken of the large promised American production (6,000 heavy bombers in the period in question). Nor has any regard been paid to the inevitable damage to factories, communications, etc., in these towns and the damage by fire, probably accentuated by the breakdown of public services.[32]

The scale of destruction promised captured Churchill's imagination. He forgot the discouraging words he had offered Portal back in September. Instead, he passed Cherwell's minute on to Portal and Sinclair with one sentence added: "What do you think of this?"

Portal and Sinclair wrote back effusively. Lord Cherwell's calculations were "simple, clear, and convincing." Seeing the opportunity, they then argued that the "necessary scale of destruction of Germany" would only be achieved if further conditions were met. They tacked on new demands beyond more bombers: more squadrons, more resources for target finding, and authority to focus on bombing Germany alone.

Cherwell's letter swayed the prime minister, who had only months before come close to writing the campaign off. Throughout the war, Churchill's attitude to the bombers and bombing shifted in a way that frustrated the airmen then and confuses historians now. He would, as in his September 1941 note to Portal, dismiss the airmen's promises as overblown; in the next note, he would blast his airmen for failing to accelerate the campaign. One day he would appear the guardian of European culture; the next he would be prepared to flatten Hamburg or Dresden just to have something in hand at his next meeting with Stalin. Infuriated at the depths to which the Nazis would sink, he at times called for the leveling of everything that stood in Germany. At others, he would read reports of the bombing and doubts would creep in. In the summer of 1943, after viewing film of ravaged Ruhr cities, he wept and asked Jan Smuts (prime minister of South Africa and field marshal in the British Army), "Are we beasts? Are we taking this too far?"

Throughout the war, Churchill was under overwhelming pressure. Every day, he got up around 8 A.M.[33] His staff would bring him a cooked breakfast, which he would eat in bed. His secretary, Miss Hill, followed soon afterward with his boxes. The prime minister did not get out of bed; instead, it became a desk and he got straight to work. Two hours later, his valet would arrive, draw his bath, and lay out his clothes. Miss Hill would leave with the typing.

The rest of the morning was occupied by meetings with chiefs of staff or the War Cabinet. Midday would be broken up by a good lunch with his wife, Clementine, followed by at least an hour's sleep and another bath. If the House was sitting, he would go there to take questions, followed by drinks in the smoking room. He would then head to Downing Street, where there were more meetings and telephone calls, often to Roosevelt. Churchill might then dictate a few more letters to Miss Hill before going for dinner.

Dinner was usually the longest event of the day, accompanied by champagne and a quality claret or burgundy. There were about twelve people around the table, often including Portal and his wife. The women would eventually retire to another room, and the servants would bring brandy and cigars. Churchill would hold forth over a wide range of conversations, falling reluctantly silent only if two or more of his guests entered a debate.

At 11 P.M., the men would rejoin their wives and Churchill would head to his office. His desk there was covered with many sentimental trinkets, gold medals, and toothpicks. Beside it was a table with bottles of whiskey, glasses, soda, and Havana cigars. The night secretary would come in regularly to ensure that a tumbler of whiskey and soda was ready. Churchill would work, drinking regularly, until 3:30 or 4 A.M. He would then get up, say good night as he passed through the door, and collapse into sleep for a few hours.

Added to this crushing schedule was a hatred of detail—above all, mathematical detail. The complex calculations that Portal added to his September 1941 letter bored Churchill, so much so that Portal apologized in advance. Bombing, however, was all about numbers: of bombs, bombers, and bomb loads; of houses, factories, and buildings; of miles flown and acres destroyed. Churchill's time constraints and distaste for detail led him to rely on the judgment of those he trusted. He had no time for Harris's predecessor, Peirse, and only intermittently had patience for Portal. But he listened to Cherwell, right to the end of the war.

And this meant, by definition, that he did not listen to others. One who was shocked by the minute and its logic was Cherwell's Oxford colleague Sir Henry Tizard. Tizard had played a key role in the development of radar, but by the early 1940s his influence was on the wane. He had disagreed with Cherwell more than once (on December 12, 1942, he wrote that an Air Ministry memorandum assumed that night bombing was going to win the war when it would not) and experienced the "Prof.'s" wrath for daring to do so. Tizard finally decided to pack in the dark art of politics for the more genteel world of the Oxford common room. He was likely not cut out for political life anyway. In an interview with an American researcher, he suggested that American and British scientists could work in a vacuum isolated from political considerations. "Between scientists," he said, "there are no barriers except language."[34] This is probably never true, but it was certainly not true in wartime. In 1942, Tizard became president of Magdalen. His last act was to speak out against Cherwell's minute. On April 15, 1942, he wrote directly to Cherwell:

I am afraid that I think that the way you put the facts as they appear to you is extremely misleading and may lead to entirely wrong decisions being reached, with a consequent disastrous effect on the war. I think, too, that you have got your facts wrong. . . .

I conclude therefore (a) that a policy of bombing German towns whole-sale in order to destroy dwellings cannot have a decisive effect by the middle of 1943, even if all heavy bombers and the great majority of Wellingtons produced are used primarily for this purpose.

(b) That such a policy can only have a decisive effect if carried out on a much bigger scale than is envisaged [in your paper].[35]

Cherwell's biographer and those close to the events have pointed out that it is an error to contrast a humane Tizard, who wanted to spare German cities the horrors of bombing, with a sadistic Cherwell. Some of Cherwell's more bloodthirsty comments make the contrast a tempting one, but it is false. As Tizard's point (b) implies, he was willing to carpet bomb the Germans. He simply doubted that it was technically possible to do so and that, even if it were, it would deliver what Cherwell promised. Bomber Command could expect at most seven thousand bombers by mid-1943, not the ten thousand Cherwell promised; bombs would hit, at most, 25 percent of their targets; and the next generation of radar navigation and bomb aids necessary to per-form better would not be available before spring of 1943 at the earliest. Above all, such a large transfer of resources might lose the war elsewhere, notably in the Battle of the Atlantic. Given all of this, bombing on the scale envisaged by Cherwell "would certainly be most damaging, but would not be decisive unless in the intervening period Germany was either defeated in the field by Russia, or at least prevented from any further advance."[36]

Tizard was not alone in his skepticism. When Cherwell's memorandum made its way to Zuckerman, he was taken aback, as it contradicted his and Bernal's report.[37]

In neither town was there any evidence of panic resulting from a series of raids or a single raid. The situation in Hull has been somewhat obscured from this point of view by the occurrence of trekking [people leaving town at night], which was made possible by the availability of road transport which was much publicized as a sign of breaking morale, but which in fact can be fairly regarded as a considered response to the situation. In both towns, actual raids were, of course, associated with a degree of alarm and anxiety which cannot in the circumstances be regarded as abnormal, and in which in no instance was sufficient to provoke mass anti-social behavior. *There was no measurable effect on the health of either town.*[38]

Neither Tizard's nor Zuckerman's views mattered in the end. Only Cherwell had the ear of the prime minister. Cherwell wrote back to Tizard with a dismissive reply. "My Dear Tizard, many thanks for your note. I would be interested to hear what you think wrong with my simple calculation, which seems fairly self-evident. . . . My paper was intended to show that we really can do a lot of damage by bombing built-up areas with the sort of air force which should be available." Whatever gap there might be between the figures and the facts, bombing German cities would be "catastrophic" for the enemy.[39] Whether from exhaustion, distraction, or lack of interest, Churchill accepted Cherwell's standard for judging the bombing war—acres of dense cities flattened—and Portal's call for more money.

7

KILLING THE BOCHE

In April 1942, General Marshall and Harry Hopkins arrived in London. They were there to achieve two goals. The first was to brief General Chaney on the granting to Arnold of direct command over all air forces. What this meant, though they did not have to say it, was that Chaney was being sidelined. The second goal was to convince the British of the need for a 1942 invasion of the Continent. Stalin was demanding the opening of a second front, and the Germans were one hundred miles from Moscow. Although a Soviet counteroffensive had repelled the Germans from the Soviet capital, the German army was far from defeated.

Marshall did not inform Eaker of these developments, but he kept in close contact with him. He praised Eaker's work, lunched with him and Harris, and brought Eaker along to dinner at Chequers, the prime minister's country house. A partnership was established at one of these dinners. It was a good night. The company was glittering: Lend-Lease Ambassador Averell Harriman; the British First Sea Lord, Sir Dudley Pound; and Harris. The conversation, over wine and then whiskey, was about bombing: When would the Americans get their bombers? Could the British borrow them? How could they best take the offensive to Germany, and then to Japan?

In the midst of these exchanges, Marshall offered his views. "I don't believe," he said, "we'll ever successfully invade the Continent and expose that great armada unless we first defeat the Luftwaffe."

Eaker looked at him and replied, "The prime purpose of our operations over here . . . is to make the Luftwaffe come up and fight. If you will support the bomber offensive, I guarantee the Luftwaffe will not prevent the cross-channel invasion."[1]

Harris, unsurprisingly, did not add his agreement, but he may not have even taken part in the exchange. He was in great spirits that night, extolling his city bombing program and boasting about leveling Lübeck.[2]

And boast he could. In the wake of the Lübeck raid, everything was going Harris's way. Portal and Cherwell gave him the intellectual justification he needed, his directive allowed him a free rein to bomb Germany, and more money was flowing to Bomber Command. In late April, Harris was certain he could repeat his success over northern Germany. On April 22, he wrote to Arnold brimming with confidence: "Come on over and let's clean up! 1000 bombers per raid, instead of 2–300 as now, and we've got the Boche by the short hairs . . . Ira [Eaker] will have sent you the Lubeck and other photos by now." He then added a few sentences that generously interpreted the truth: "[Ira] and I see eye to eye in all such matters—and indeed in all matters. He's a great man. I do not thereby infer that I am also! But I find myself in invariable agreement with him—except perhaps that I think he will find it necessary to go easy on the daylight bombing stuff until he has found his way . . . Extraordinary how many people can think of ways of employing air power except the right one! I know you have your problems too. Frightening the codfish over wide open spaces will never win a war. Bombing Germany and Japan will win this one—or else."[3]

Harris's next try came over the northern Baltic city of Rostock. Over four nights, Bomber Command attacked the medieval core of the densely packed city. Despite heavy defenses, the raids were another destructive success: forty thousand were made homeless and two hundred killed.[4]

The raids on both Lübeck and Rostock followed the same pattern. High-explosive bombs landed in the middle of densely packed streets—on houses, churches, museums, and government buildings—and exploded. They created large piles of flammable material as well as air passages through which flames could travel. Incendiary bombs served as matches, creating large fires that would do most of the damage. The Air Ministry had concluded in late 1941 that only the old town centers were suitable targets for large-scale incendiary attacks, and even then the spreading fire would not necessarily develop into a widespread conflagration. To ensure it did required a relentless attack that would overwhelm the fire brigade and interrupt the water supply used to fight the fires; ideally, high-speed winds would carry the flames over fire-breaks.[5] The high explosives also had to do the job right. If they hit buildings but failed to smash out the doors and windows, there would not be enough oxygen to feed the fire. If they leveled the building entirely, what would have been an inferno became a firebreak instead. Rubble, as Harris noted when he explained his tendency to avoid follow-up attacks on a bombed city, does not burn.

These technical questions led to one of many debates between Harris and the Air Ministry. After both raids, reconnaissance flights took photos of the damage, and sent these on to the Air Ministry. In late April, the Vice Chief of Air Staff, Wilfred Freeman, a Rugby graduate, the son of "new" industrial wealth, and an early backer of Harris, was inspecting the photos. To Freeman, it seemed that Rostock—which had been blasted with more high explosives than Lübeck—was in better shape post-bombing than Lübeck (it wasn't, but photos provided only a rough guide). He therefore made a case for using more incendiaries and fewer high explosives in each raid:

My Dear Bert,

The records show that in the attack on Lübeck, you got 45,080 four-lb incendiaries on to the target. As a result, the defences were saturated and the town was set ablaze. In none of the attacks on Rostock was any-thing like so great a number of incendiaries dropped and the photographs suggest that the fires never took hold as they did at Lübeck. The moral seems to be that unless the incendiary attack is on a large scale and con-centrated in time and space, it will not achieve any decisive degree of destruction.[6]

Freeman had drafted the letter carefully. He knew, as the mandarins in the Air Ministry gently put it, that the commander-in-chief "did not welcome independent opinions." He hoped that his gentle, suggestive tone would prevent Harris from overreacting.

It did not. The letter irritated Harris, as it illustrated that, once again, the bureaucrats above him had misunderstood the point of area bombing. It wasn't to destroy houses for the sake of destroying houses. Its purpose was clearer than that. "I am always," he wrote back on April 29, "being pressed to concentrate entirely on incendiaries, but I do not agree with this policy. The morale effect of H.E. [high explosives] is vast. People can escape from fires, and the casualties of a solely fire raising raid would be as nothing. What we want to do in addition to the horrors of fire is to bring the masonry crashing down on top of the Boche, to kill Boche, and to terrify Boche; hence the proportion of H.E."[7]

Harris's reply clarified his views not only on bombing but also on the relationship between Bomber Command and the Air Ministry. He "refused to acknowledge any basis for collaboration between the Air Staff and Command."[8] Bomber Command was *his* baby.

In the days following the Rostock raid, Harris reflected on Bomber Command's success. Under his leadership, the Command had by then destroyed 780 acres of Germany's cities, effectively squaring the UK's account with Germany. But it wasn't enough. The Army and Navy would be quick to point out that neither Lübeck nor Rostock was well defended, and that their destruction could not prove Bomber Command's ability to take out larger targets. Nor had the world paid enough attention. Although the *New York Times* had covered the Lübeck raid, the paper gave it only a few column inches on page four. Harris needed something bigger, something that would make the world stand up and take notice.

This search for the dramatic led him to alight upon "The Thousand Plan." The idea was to put one thousand bombers above a German city in one night and to attack it with the greatest concentration of air power in the history of the world.[9] The plan was bold, and crazy. There was no chance that the Air Ministry would support it; as Harris was conceiving the plan, they were grumbling about the rate at which he was going through bombs. So, he went above their heads. He called Portal and put the idea to him. Portal loved it, and then called Churchill. On Sunday, May 24, Harris visited Churchill at Chequers, and the two spoke about the broad details of the raid over whiskey and soda until 3 A.M. The idea appealed squarely to the prime minister's flair for the dramatic. He agreed to a loss of one hundred bombers, or a 10 percent casualty rate.[10] Harris drove the ten minutes between Chequers and Springfield humming contentedly.

With Portal and Churchill on board, Harris assigned the job of finding a thousand aircraft to his deputy, Robert Saundby. Saundby had just over 800 airplanes at his disposal: 485 in four of Bomber Command's operation Groups (Nos. 1, 3, 4, and 5) and 330 in its two training groups (91 and 92).[11] Coastal Command—then in the middle of the Battle of the Atlantic—first offered 250 aircraft, but then balked at the gimmicky nature of the whole idea.[12] Saundby convinced Flying Training Command to provide another 21 clapped-out airplanes, but that still left him just under 200 short. Harris took the brave and foolhardy decision to use crews who had not been fully trained, and by mid-May Bomber Command had 1046 airplanes ready. As RAF airman Jack Pragnell remarked sixty years later, "They got everything that would move into the sky."

The next question was which city. The obvious choice, Berlin, was too far away and too heavily defended. The next most obvious choice was Hamburg, Germany's second-largest city and Europe's largest port. What was more, the Elbe provided a user-friendly map leading right into the heart of the Hanseatic capital. On May 27, the day originally chosen by Harris for the Hamburg raid, thick clouds covered England and northern Germany. A raid in such conditions risked collisions on a massive scale over the target area and during landing.[13] Such a disaster might have finished Bomber Command. He postponed the operation for twenty-four hours, but Hamburg and eastern England were once again covered in cloud. The operation was postponed until May 29, and then for the same reasons until May 30. The pressure was beginning to mount on Harris. The longer he waited, the stronger his critics would become.

On the morning of May 30, 1942, Harris walked into the operations room at Bomber Command headquarters in rural Buckinghamshire, near the village of Walters Ash. He sat at his desk and tensely waited for the meteorological reports. At 9:10 A.M., the meteorological officer gave him unexpected news: while northern Germany would be covered in cloud, there was a chance that it would break up in the south. Saundby added, "The home base will, on the whole, be clear of cloud."[14] Harris remained stone-faced. He slowly pulled a cigarette pack from his pocket, flicked the bottom with his thumb, and retrieved a protruding Lucky Strike.[15] He set the cigarette precisely within a cigarette holder he retrieved from his right breast pocket and placed the holder firmly between his teeth.[16] Still silent, Harris put a finger on the charts in front of him and moved it slowly from England toward the European continent. It passed Brussels and Loewen in Belgium, and reached the German border. He continued to move it past Aachen and the liberal, Francophile city of Düsseldorf. Then he stopped. He turned to his senior air staff officer, his face still expressionless, and said, "The Thousand Plan. Tonight."[17] His finger rested on Cologne.

8

COLOGNE

Near the bleak north Yorkshire town of Leeming, the crew of 10 Squadron gathered for their briefing. The ritual was the same throughout the war. The men would take their seats, and the briefing officer would tell them whether there was to be a raid. If no, they would slip off to the local pub for a night's entertainment. If yes, they would learn the city, the target, and have an hour to prepare themselves for takeoff.

At 8 P.M. on May 30, the chatter in the room died down as Air Vice-Marshal Sir Roderick Carr stepped up to the front. He began with a formula designed to convey drama and singleness of purpose: "Gentlemen, the target for tonight is . . . COLOGNE." The room erupted in a cheer. The men were not itching to destroy Cologne, but rather relieved that the target was not something further away and more dangerous. Such as Berlin.

Carr held up a hand to silence the men and resumed his speech. "Tonight, gentlemen, the raid is no ordinary one. We shall be bombing with one thousand aircraft!" The airmen could not believe it. Some slammed their desks; others whistled and shouted, "Bloody hell!"[1] Still others stared in silence. "Cologne," Carr continued, "is a highly industrialized centre; it has light and heavy engineering, factories making guns, tanks, vehicles for export to the Russian front. It is also an important transportation junction. Rail lines link it with Hanover, Berlin, Paris, and Vienna; trains ship troops, goods, and war materials. Finally, Cologne has a marshalling yard and factories at Ehrenfeld, Kalk, and Mulheim on the east of the river."

Some of the men wondered which of these would be the target. The engineering works? The train station? The factories across the river from the center of Cologne? The men of "shiny 10," as the squadron was known, were veterans of precision bombing. During the Battle of the Barges, they had attacked the Channel ports of Lorient, Le Havre, Antwerp, Cherbourg, Bologne, and Calais. Against a barrage of flak, they had taken out moving barges of the German invasion fleet.[2] Tonight, however, they would bomb neither ships nor factories.

The Air Vice-Marshal gave the floor to an intelligence officer, a small, pink-faced man who unveiled a large map of the city, raised his cue, and let it rest on a point not far from Cologne's famous Cathedral. "The central point is right here. At the Neumarkt. Look carefully. It's just this western side of the river." It was the heart of residential and cultural Cologne. A few of the men looked at each other, but no one said anything.

The intelligence officer gave the floor back to Carr, who pulled out a piece of paper and read a statement direct from Harris himself. This was unusual, and the men listened carefully. "The Force," it began.

> of which you are about to take part tonight is at least twice the size and more than four times the carrying capacity of the largest Air Force ever before concentrated on one objective. You have the opportunity therefore to strike a blow at the enemy, which will resound, not only throughout Germany, but throughout the world. In your hands be the means of destroying a major part of the resources by which the enemy's war effort is maintained . . . Press home your attack to your precise objectives with the utmost determination and resolution in the full knowledge that, if you individually succeed, the most shattering and devastating blow will have been delivered against the very vitals of the enemy.

Carr paused, and then read the last sentence: "Let him have it. Right on the chin."

That night, more than nine hundred bombers reached Cologne. Wave after wave hammered the city. Forty-five minutes into the raid, one pilot, Micky Martin, could not believe his eyes as he approached the vast red glow ahead of him.[3] He flew in low—at four thousand feet. The fires seemed to lick his wings as he flew past the silhouette of the great Cathedral, rising above the rubble around it. Martin crossed the city three times, wondering whether it was worth it to drop his bombs. At last, he dropped them on the city's battered railway station, just several yards from the Cathedral itself.

As the fires raged, Cologne's fire and air defenses lost control of the city. Searchlights crisscrossed the sky aimlessly, unsure of which of the hundreds of airplanes to trap in their glare. The flak guns began to run out of ammunition, and one by one they fell silent, leaving Cologne almost defenseless.

Almost, but not entirely. Bomber Command lost forty aircraft over Cologne. One of those was piloted by a quiet, shy young man from Manchester named Leslie Manser.[4] Manser's plane and its seven-member crew were "coned" (trapped in searchlights) over Cologne. As Manser tried to shake the lights, flak guns sprayed the underbelly of his plane, wounding the rear gunner. Manser dived from seven thousand to one thousand feet. He could have then ordered a bailout, but he feared the consequences for his crew of going down over Germany. Instead, he brought the airplane up to two thousand feet. The port engine burst into flames. The airplane was losing speed and altitude fast. Smoke began to billow into the cockpit. Manser ordered the bailout. The plane was bucking against him, but he held the controls tightly, keeping it stable enough for a safe jump. The other six members bailed out successfully. As they were slowly carried to earth by their billowing white parachutes, they watched their plane explode in a ball of flames.

Down below, the citizens of Cologne had the first taste of what awaited many other German cities in the course of the war. Under the city's streets, tens of thousands of citizens cowered in cellars. In earlier raids on Cologne, the all-clear signal rang after a few minutes. That night, it didn't come. Instead, civilians heard the drone of bombers flying over their city, punctuated by the great crash of landing bombs. Gertrud Türk was eighteen years old at the time and worked as a bookkeeper. She was with relatives in the Auguststrasse, in the north of the city, that night and they went to the cellar together. The detonations shook the house, and dust and dirt fell from the cellar walls and ceilings. Every so often, the drone would stop and she would think, *It's finally over.* But then another wave would come in and the whole thing started again. "It just wouldn't stop . . . when every second, every minute is an eternity, the fear, it becomes so unbearable."[5]

Across the city, twelve thousand individual fires merged into seventeen hundred infernos. They tore through the Hohestrasse, which had followed the course of the Roman main street, disfiguring it forever, and they consumed the western gallery of the eleventh-century church St. Mary in the Capitol.[6] Those who had taken shelter in cellars cowered in fear of the bombs. They struggled to breathe through the clouds of dust from the flying debris and the stifling heat as their city burned around them. Gertrud was among them, and they were the lucky ones. The unlucky died in their living rooms or bedrooms, or out in the street. They were buried alive by collapsing roofs, crushed by flying debris, or shredded by high explosives. In the morning, rescue workers had to collect hundreds of charred and crumpled bodies. The only consolation was that it could have been far worse. The city's water mains had held under the strain of intense bombing. A call went out to Düsseldorf, Duisburg, and Bonn, and before the bombing was over, 150 fire departments sent equipment racing for Cologne. The casualties numbered 480, the highest figure yet but only 30 percent higher than Lübeck, a smaller city attacked by many fewer planes. The city itself was badly damaged, but not leveled.

On the evening of May 30, as fleets of squadrons were taking off for Germany, Arnold, Eaker, Portal, Harriman, U.S. Ambassador John Gilbert Winant, and Dwight D. Eisenhower, who had just replaced a sacked Chaney as overall commander of the European theater of operations, were dining at Chequers. Arnold had arrived in the UK a week earlier to convince the British to allow aircraft shipments previously promised them by the Americans to be given to Eaker instead. The Americans at this point hoped for an early invasion of the Continent. At midnight, Churchill stood up and announced, "Gentlemen, at exactly this moment one thousand of our bombers are attacking Cologne!" He made a less dramatic, but equally important remark to Eaker that same night: "Perhaps your program is too ambitious."[7] The prime minister was serving subtle notice of his opposition to the American plan for invading France early, putting forward instead his preferred option: an invasion through North Africa.

At this point in the war, as Harris was hitting Cologne, the United States had only 1871 men in England—mostly ground staff—and not a single airplane.[8] The next day, Winant sent an urgent message to President Roosevelt: "England is the place to win the war. Get planes and troops over here as soon as possible."[9] Roosevelt would, but for the moment it was the British who brought the war to Germany.

9

GÖRING AND SPEER

Hermann Göring was the most colorful figure among the senior Nazi hierarchy. As a young man, he was rakishly handsome, with haunting pale eyes. Throughout the 1930s and into the war, his hunger for food, luxury, and fame had been insatiable. He became fatter and fatter. Heavy perfumes, large rings, mountains of clothes, and even lipstick were standard features of his wardrobe. Göring would never take a trip to Paris or Vienna without trolling through the shopping districts for fine clothing, art, and jewelry. This decadence horrified the somber and snobbish soldiers and bureaucrats who met him.[1] When Göring attended the first launch of Germany's ill-fated wonder weapon, the unmanned V-2 (*Vergeltungswaffe 2*, or revenge weapon 2) rocket, the general in charge—Dornberger—looked at him with disgust.[2] "Soft Morocco leather riding-boots of glaring red with silver spurs," Dornberger later wrote, "a very voluminous greatcoat of Australian opossum fur with the hide turned outside. Platinum rings with big rubies." In an odd sort of way, Göring's flamboyance endeared him to Hitler. The Austrian was himself always keenly aware of his status as an outsider, and he indulged Göring's vulgarity and ostentation precisely because they made him so different from the austere German upper and middle classes.[3]

Göring's odd personality also earned him a few sympathetic remarks from his British adversaries. The British have always been much more celebratory of eccentricities than the Germans, and the English upper class found Göring's dress and manners amusing rather than offensive.[4] As one of his critics, Sir Eric Phipps, British ambassador to Berlin, 1933–1937, put it, "Lunching with the Warden of New College [Oxford], General Göring might pass as almost civilized."[5] Lord Halifax was even more positive. After meeting Göring, Halifax had to admit that he had found the Nazi "immensely" entertaining. "Göring met me on the way, dressed in brown breeches and boots all in one, with a green leather jerkin and full-collared short coat on top. . . . Altogether a very picturesque and arresting figure, completed by green hat and large chamois tuft!"[6]

Göring's oddities and his charm—which would briefly serve him well at the Nuremberg trials—might encourage the view that he was less sinister than the other senior Nazi colleagues, even harmless. He was anything but. When the Reichstag fire broke out, Göring launched an indiscriminate wave of repression, instructing the Prussian police to shoot anyone who demonstrated and giving the SA (Ernst Röhm's brownshirts) a free hand to terrorize left-wing opponents.[7] The Prussian police largely ignored the order, but the SA went on a rampage. A little over a year later, Göring played a decisive role in The Night of Long Knives. On June 30, 1934, partly in response to Göring's prodding, Hitler moved against his erstwhile friend and ally Röhm. On that infamous day, Göring presided over the liquidation of his enemies.[8] Later, Göring oversaw the expropriation of Jewish property and the Aryanization of the German economy, and he ensured that both policies were carried out ruthlessly. During the war, he worked closely with the SS on the "recruitment" of slave labor.[9]

Göring was born on January 12, 1893. Like so many Germans of his generation, he was defined by the First World War. A fighter pilot awarded the prestigious *Pour le Mérite* by the Kaiser in June 1918, he was an uncritical subscriber to the "stab-in-the-back" theory.[10] He met Hitler in 1922, and was immediately convinced that Hitler had the keys to Germany's greatness. By 1939, Göring was in charge of a rambling empire that controlled the police, the air ministry, and industrial policy across an increasingly centralized Germany. As more territories fell into German hands, Göring established an economic empire, based on pure exploitation and extending eastward.

To add to his own glory, Göring made a point of surrounding himself with mediocrity and incompetence. His appointee in 1936 to head German aircraft production, Colonel General Ernst Udet, told a friend, "I don't understand anything about production. I understand even less about airplanes."[11] Udet's chief merit was that he had been part of the same Richthofen squadron as Göring, and Göring instinctively trusted him.[12] The downside for Udet was that Göring held him fully responsible for any failures. After five years of ill health, bullying and manipulation from everyone around him, and constant harangues from Göring over his failure to increase airplane production, Udet killed himself. Before he died, he scrawled a suicide note on the wall, blaming Göring for his death. He was succeeded by Field Marshal Erhard Milch, a commander in the Norwegian campaign with close contacts to the armaments industry. At Göring's request, Hitler Aryanized Milch when rumors of his Jewish father circulated. "I decide who's a Jew," Göring is reported to have said.

On the morning of May 31, 1942, Göring leaned over a report from the mayor of Cologne. His assistant and another high-ranking Nazi official were also in the room. "Impossible," he said to his assistant. "You can't drop that many bombs on a city in one night." Göring got Cologne's mayor on the phone and told him: "Your police report is nothing but lies. I'm telling you as Reichsmarschall that the figures you gave are too high! How can we give the Führer such figures? I'm telling you, they're too high!" Göring allowed the mayor a short response, and then continued: "Are you telling me I'm lying? I'm giving the Führer the correct figures, and that's it!"

Göring had good reason to deny the report. Since being appointed leader of the Luftwaffe, his career and influence within the Nazi party had been in decline. The Blitz, which he oversaw, had failed to bring Britain to its knees, and he had rashly staked what was left of his reputation on one claim: "If a single bomb falls on the Ruhr [valley], you can call me Meyer [a twit]." Cologne was in the Rhineland, but Essen, in the heart of the Ruhr valley, was next. Harris hit it the day after Cologne, and three more times in June 1942 alone. He also repeatedly bombed Bremen, Emden, Duisburg, Düsseldorf, Osnabrück, Hamburg, the great medieval city of Frankfurt, the small Hanseatic city of Wismar, Aachen, Stuttgart, the northern city of Kiel, and the southern city of Munich.

The bombings made Göring and his Luftwaffe look incompetent. More importantly, they strengthened the hand of the other official in the room with him as he screamed down the telephone: Albert Speer. Speer was born in the then-prosperous bourgeois town of Mainz in 1905. His father, an architect by training, had grown rich through buying, redesigning, and selling property, and it was he who convinced Albert to study architecture rather than his true love, mathematics.[13] Beyond that fateful moment, there was little personal or social contact between the two men. Albert Sr. liked his boys robust and he instinctively preferred his two other sons over the bookish and fragile Albert Jr. As Albert grew older, the differences became political. His father was by inclination liberal, and he clung to that embattled creed throughout the 1920s and 1930s. As Europe marched to war, he aligned himself with the visionary pan-European ideals of Count Coudenhove-Kalergi, one of the earliest intellectual influences on European integration. Until the 1930s, Albert Jr. was deeply apolitical. He thought, as all Germans did without thinking, that Versailles was a travesty, but he barely noticed the postwar world around him. The revolution, the Kapp putsch, the assassination of Rathenau, and the Munich putsch all occurred under Speer's radar. Thanks to his father's decision to divest himself of Reichsmarks in favor of dollars, Speer even escaped the inflation, receiving a princely sum as an allowance.[14] Weimar Germany was fun if you had a lot of U.S. dollars and little social conscience.

Speer Sr., again very much unlike his son, also had a deep sense of morality. In the mid-1930s, he attended a Berlin theater with Albert, and Hitler unexpectedly invited him to his box at the interval.[15] When Speer's father met the dictator, he began to tremble and turn pale, reacting viscerally to what Speer Jr. later called Hitler's "otherness." By contrast, Speer Jr. only developed a moral sense—if he ever did—while in the docks of Nuremberg.

Speer studied first in Karlsruhe and then in Munich before finally settling at the Technical University of Berlin, where he studied with Heinrich Tessenow, an apostle of simple, unadorned architecture that was the antithesis of Speer's later bombast. On December 4, 1930, he heard a speech by Hitler in working-class southeast Berlin. Drawing on mostly inaccurate historical examples, Hitler told a story of his struggle, of the battle of good against evil, of the manifest threats to Germany—communism, unemployment, economic stagnation, and political impotence—and of his determination to see them all off. When he ended, the room exploded in rapturous applause. Speer felt energy and excitement shoot through him. Four months later, he joined the National Socialist German Workers Party and was given membership number 474,481.[16]

Speer spent the next eighteen months in demoralized boredom, living with his parents in Heidelberg. Neither the July 1932 elections nor the hundreds of people it left dead stirred his interest. On July 28, three days before the election, he was preparing for a three-week journey to the isolated East Prussian lakes. A few hours before he was to leave, he got word that the organizational head of the Berlin region (Gau), Karl Hanke, urgently needed to speak to him. Hanke invited Speer to Berlin to renovate the Gau's new head-quarters on the Vosstrasse, a few minutes from Potsdamer Platz. Speer immediately canceled his trip and headed to the capital. Three hours later, he would have been unreachable.[17]

Speer finished the Vosstrasse project in record time and found himself back in Heidelberg, where he slipped back into depression. He barely took notice of January 30, 1933, when Hitler became Chancellor. But three weeks later, Hanke called again. Speer was to come back to Berlin. Hitler's propaganda minister, Goebbels, wanted him.

Goebbels set Speer to work on the renovation of Schinkel's Leopold palace on the Wilhelmplatz. When Speer was finished, Goebbels loved it. So did Hitler. Speer's career took off. Commissions poured in daily, including one for a May 1 mass rally at the Tempelhof football field, now Tempelhof airport. Hitler stood on a wooden platform; behind him were three massive flags—swastikas at each end and the black, red, and white Reich flag in the center. He was surrounded by dozens of soldiers, and the field was packed with thousands of spectators. It was the world's first taste of the haunting Nazi aesthetic, and Speer was its author.[18]

Goebbels then had Speer renovate his official residence. Then Hitler commissioned him to work on the Chancellor's residence. During the renovations, Hitler lived on the first floor, in a temporary apartment. He made frequent and unannounced visits to the worksite. On one of these, he suddenly asked Speer to lunch. Speer had entered the inner circle.[19]

The commissions continued to come in, and more and more they were official. Speer became chief designer of the Nuremberg rallies. There, on massive platforms, were huge perfectly symmetrical rows of men in black and brown T-shirts; 150 projectors 36 feet apart shot columns of light 6 miles into the sky; and 30,000 banners streamed into the arena. The effect was intoxicating, not least on Speer himself, who was both seducer and seduced.[20] In Nuremberg's aftermath, Speer was given the commission for the German embassy in London and the Olympic Stadium in Berlin. The young architect caught Göring's attention. The Reichsmarschall took him to his apartment behind Leipziger Platz, and told him to renovate it. "It must turn out like the Führer's."[21]

After his Nuremberg triumph, Speer set his sights on a glittering prize: the transformation of the Third Reich's capital. Hitler viewed the city with a mix of hatred and hope. He loathed its liberality and permissiveness; its Jewish theaters, homosexual bars, and Negro bands; its left-wing politics and skeptical citizens. But he believed it would, following Germany's victory, be the capital of the world. He wanted to tear out its center and transform it into an architectural wonder that would outclass Paris, Vienna, and Rome. In late 1936, Hitler summoned Speer without warning and charged him with rebuilding Berlin.

Speer saw himself as a modern Hausmann. As the latter had transformed Paris's tiny, irregular streets into grand, uniform avenues, Speer would sweep away Berlin's neighborhoods in favor of bombastic public buildings, expansive boulevards, and clean, crisp lines. Speer's first task was Hitler's new Reich chancellery. Hitler gave him the order to start on it in January 1938, and insisted it be finished within a year. It was a seemingly impossible task, but Speer worked feverishly throughout 1938 and into 1939. On one Thursday morning, near the project's completion, Speer took the Fasanenstrasse, in Charlottenburg, to work. He passed the smoldering ruins of a public building at number 70–80. The date was November 10, 1938; the building was the Berlin Central Synagogue. Goebbels had sent his SA dogs on a rampage across the country, destroying 270 synagogues, wrecking 7500 businesses, and killing 190 Jews. Hundreds more killed themselves. Goebbels had singled out the Fasanenstrasse synagogue for destruction. As Speer passed the collapsed facade, perhaps even stepping over one or more of the charred beams scattered on the street, his thoughts were elsewhere. Three months after Kristallnacht, the Reich chancellery was opened on schedule. Speer showed his teacher, Tessenow, the plans and noted that he had managed to finish the building in only nine months. Tessenow dryly replied, "I would have preferred you to have taken nine years."[22]

The chancellery was the beginning and the end of Speer's Berlin. The city's mayor, Julius Lippert, was a Berliner first and a Nazi second, and he threw up every bureaucratic obstacle he could think of to prevent the destruction of his city's core. Speer's redesign of Berlin amounted to the moving of the victory column from the Reichstag to the Tiergarten, the widening of the east–west axis leading to the column, and the installation of new lampposts around it. That was it. In September 1939, war began. Hitler wanted him to continue, but Speer knew better. He went to the office of one of his collaborators, his face pale. Pointing to plans scattered around the room, he said, "It's all over."[23]

After the war started, Speer made a transition from architecture to armaments. He spent the first two years of the war overseeing demolition work in the run-up to his never-realized building projects. Most of the demolished buildings were residential, and a Central Department for Resettlement was created as part of Speer's empire. Many of the demolished apartment blocks had Jewish occupants. Still more Jews were evicted as these buildings' non-Jewish occupants were quickly rehoused. The legal basis for this was found in an April 1939 "law on rental contracts with Jews," which allowed the eviction of Jewish tenants if "alternative accommodation" could be found. In Berlin, Speer's Central Department for Resettlement was charged with overseeing the evictions and finding new accommodation for the evicted.[24]

Speer's resettlement department was not his first contact with the Jews. Thousands of Jews had been arrested during Kristallnacht, and afterward many others fled. Across the city, hundreds of apartments previously occupied by Jews were vacant. As Speer's redevelopment plans would require a great deal of excess housing, he was very keen to get hold of the vacated apartments, and to ensure that he had access to those forcibly vacated by Jews in the future.[25]

At this time, the notorious anti-Semite Goebbels and his subordinate Adolf Eichmann began cleansing Berlin of Jews. On October 13, 1939, hundreds of Jews received expulsion orders. The next day, SS units burst into their flats and ordered them to pack a few belongings immediately. The SS transported them to a collecting camp run by Jews in a synagogue on Levetzowstrasse. On October 17, the Jews were slowly marched in pouring rain through the leafy streets of Grunewald to the suburb's railway station. A day later, the first trains left for Lodz; others left for Riga, Minsk, and other points east. Across Germany, suicides became more and more common, to the point where the SS Sturmbannführer Alois Brunner (who had organized the expulsion of Jews from Vienna) wrote to Jewish leaders and demanded that they "prevent this flight into suicide."[26] In early 1940, some nine months into the operation, a Gestapo official gleefully announced to the Jewish community office on Oranienburgerstrasse that the Jews of Berlin were no more.

Speer was keen to see that all of the expulsions happened quickly. He had his close friend Rudolf Wolters keep a log of the bureau's chief activities. Several entries refer to the eviction, resettlement, and, later, deportation of Jewish tenants. On November 27, 1940, Speer wrote to an assistant to ask him: "How is the clearance of those thousand Jewish flats going?"

_____

By some quirk of fate, Speer's fortunes changed forever in exactly the same month that Harris's and Eaker's did: February 1942. If Harris's predecessor suffered from a lack of self-assurance and an unwillingness to speak truth to power, Speer's had the opposite problem. Fritz Todt was born in 1891 to a wealthy upper-middle-class family similar to Speer's. He joined the Nazis in 1922 and remained a committed national socialist throughout his life.[27] Almost immediately after the Nazi seizure of power, he was tasked with overseeing the construction of the autobahns. He then organized the building of the West Wall (the Siegfried line). In 1941, Hitler appointed him Reich Minister for Armaments and Ammunition and Inspector-General for Water and Energy. His bureaucratic empire was exceeded only by that of Göring, and Todt's was far better run. Todt's power flowed partially from his competence, but above all from the admiration, bordering on reverence, with which Hitler viewed him.[28]

In late 1941, Todt visited the Russian front. He saw firsthand how winter had stopped the German soldiers in their tracks and revealed how hopelessly overextended they were. Back in Berlin, he arranged a meeting with Hitler on November 29. He told him that opening a second front was a strategic blunder. The war could not be won and it was time to seek a political solution. Hitler replied that there "was hardly any way of reaching a political solution."[29] Todt did not back down. Now was the time to act, when Germany was still in a position of strength and could trade withdrawal from occupied Europe for major Allied concessions. Hitler simply ended the discussion. Two weeks later, as if in deliberate rebuke of Todt, he declared war on the United States.

By January 1942, the tide was beginning to turn. It looked as if Germany could lose the war. On January 20, the Nazis formalized the "final solution" to the Jewish question in Europe at Wannsee in southwest Berlin. It was a bureaucratic tidying-up rather than a policy change. Within weeks of invading Poland in September 1939, the SS had murdered hundreds of Jews in the streets, savagely beaten thousands more, and destroyed synagogues.[30] Jews, gays, communists, and other enemies of the new social order were crowded into concentration camps. A November 1940 report on Auschwitz described how, as a reprisal for the killing of two guards, a group of prisoners was taken into a field, ordered to run around, and machine-gunned; their bodies were thrown into a local crematorium.[31] Seven months later, as German armies

invaded the Soviet Union, Nazi murder squads (*Einsatzgruppen*) moved eastward behind the armies, rounding up and shooting hundreds of thousands of
Jews on the spot.[32] On December 8, 1941, several hundred Jews from three
Polish towns were taken to a forest outside the village of Chelmno, where they
were gassed.[33] Within months of Wannsee, the Treblinka extermination camp
was established in occupied Poland. All the while, reports of German massa-
cres of civilians were turning up in the Soviet Union and the West. On January
30, 1942, ten days after the conference, Hitler gave a speech, reported in both
Washington and London, at the Berlin Sports Palace: "The war will not end
as the Jews imagine it will, namely with the uprooting of the Aryans; rather,
the result of this war will be the complete annihilation of the Jews." Trainloads
of Jews began traveling to death camps at Chelmno, Belzec, Sobibor, and
Treblinka.

In February 1942, Todt made one last attempt to change Hitler's mind
about negotiating. On February 7, he flew to see Hitler at Rastenburg. Those
outside the room heard shouts. In the middle of the meeting, Speer arrived
unexpectedly and tried to see Hitler. When an aide announced Speer's arrival,
Hitler refused to see him. Speer made his way to the officer's mess for dinner.
Just before midnight, Todt came in looking exhausted and despairing. He said
nothing about his argument with Hitler and instead offered Speer a seat on
his airplane leaving for Berlin the next morning. Speer, concluding that he
would not see Hitler, agreed.

After Todt left, Speer lingered. At almost 1 A.M., an aide arrived and told
him that the Führer wanted to see him. When Speer entered the room, Hitler
looked as depressed as Todt had. As was often the case with Hitler, conversation was painful. But when it strayed to architecture, Hitler perked up. Discussion of what Nuremberg and Berlin would become allowed him to escape
from the gloomy news from the front. They spoke for two hours before Hitler
dismissed Speer at 3 A.M. Speer, utterly exhausted, rang to cancel his flight
with Todt and went to bed.

The next morning, well before he had planned to get up, the phone rang.
It was Karl Brandt, Hitler's personal physician and head of the Nazi euthana-
sia program. Brandt gave Speer the news: Todt was dead.

That morning, witnesses saw Todt's Heinkel HE-III taxi onto the runway
and lift off. The plane began to gain altitude and then, very suddenly, it
turned and headed back toward the runway. With the aircraft only sixty feet
from the ground, a vertical jet of flame shot out of the fuselage. The machine

plummeted. With a great crash, it broke apart on landing, setting off further explosions.

The circumstances behind Todt's death were never clarified. Was Speer tipped off the night before, leading him to cancel his flight? Did Hitler himself order Todt's execution? Were Himmler and the SS, without Hitler's knowledge, behind it? Todt himself seemed to have suspected something. Shortly before his death, he deposited a large sum of money in a safety-deposit box and left instructions that it was to go to his secretary if anything happened to him.[34]

Whatever the cause of Todt's sudden death, when the news was passed on to Hitler, he paused briefly and then declared that Speer would be Todt's successor. Speer was summoned into Hitler's rooms, where he was surprised to see the dictator standing up to receive him. Hitler solemnly declared, "Herr Speer, I appoint you successor to Dr. Todt in all his posts." Before waiting for a reply, he extended a hand to dismiss Speer. Speer stammered a reply, saying he would do his best but suggested that his work should be limited to taking over Todt's construction tasks. Hitler cut him off, telling Speer that he had his unbounded confidence. Speer then had, as he later put it, "one of the best and certainly most useful ideas of my life." He asked Hitler for a "Führer Order" giving him "nothing less than an unconditional promise of support." From that moment forward, Speer's orders would be Hitler's orders. Hitler hesitated briefly, then agreed.

By February 1942, the die was cast. With Göring sidelined, Albert Speer had total, if not uncontested, control over German war production. Ira Eaker and, after him, Carl Spaatz had total, if not uncontested, control over the Eighth Air Force. Arthur Harris had total, if not uncontested, control over Bomber Command. For the next three years, there would be a silent but furious struggle between the men who wanted to destroy Germany's effort to wage war and the man who wished to sustain it.

10

CHURCHILL, ROOSEVELT, AND THE FUTURE OF BOMBING

On January 13, 1943, Eaker was just settling into his new house at Kingston Hill and was entertaining guests. He had been commander of the U.S. Eighth Air Force since December 1, 1942, when he replaced Spaatz, who had been transferred to North Africa. Midway through the soup course, a message from Eisenhower arrived: "Proceed at earliest practicable time to Casablanca for conference, reporting there to General Patton. Conference involves method of air operations from United Kingdom."[1]

The night before, Churchill had boarded a small plane with Charles Portal. They were bound for Casablanca, where they were to meet with Roosevelt. The meeting was originally planned as a "big-three" summit between Roosevelt, Churchill, and Stalin, but the Soviet leader's refusal to leave Moscow turned it into an Anglo-American summit. The meeting had been called to reach agreement on Allied tactics in the run-up to D-Day.

The flight to Morocco was not an auspicious start. The airplane was a "Commando," a converted bomber. It had no central heating unit, so the RAF had installed a petrol heater in the bomb alley and linked it to heating points throughout the airplane. One of these was below the toes of the sleeping prime minister. At 2 A.M., the point had become red hot, and Churchill's burning toes woke him. He climbed down from his bunk and woke Portal. Together, they found two other equally hot points, and traced them back to the bomb alley, where two men were industriously keeping the flames going. Fumes were filling the alley and drifting up toward the red-hot points. "I decided," Churchill wrote later, "that it was better to freeze than burn, and I ordered all heating to be turned off, and we went back to rest shivering in the ice-cold winter air, about eight thousand feet up."[2]

At Medouina airport, not far from Casablanca, security men were on the tarmac waiting for the prime minister's plane on the morning of January 13. The Commando duly appeared over the horizon and landed safely, but security was in for a surprise. The meeting was meant to be top secret, and the plan was to whisk the British prime minister discreetly to safety. Instead, Churchill emerged in a bright blue RAF uniform that would catch the eye of anyone within sight. Matters got worse still. After he descended to the tarmac, Churchill asked about a second plane coming to land. When told it was the chiefs of staff, Churchill insisted on waiting for them. For minutes that must have seemed like hours to security, Churchill stood on the empty tarmac in full view, puffing on a large cigar and waiting for the plane to land.[3]

The Allies had cleared Casablanca of German soldiers, but the city was swarming with German agents and retained the air of intrigue made famous in Michael Curtiz's film. Berlin radio delighted in reporting unpublicized events in Morocco an hour after they happened.[4] The Luftwaffe occasionally launched nuisance raids over the city.

Since nowhere in Casablanca was safe, the security agents decided that the visitors might as well be comfortable, and they commandeered the modern Anfa Hotel and a clutch of elegant private villas.[5] The villas were reserved for Churchill, Roosevelt, and French general Charles de Gaulle. President Roosevelt occupied a spacious villa known as Dar es Saada. Churchill's Villa Mirador was about fifty yards away.[6] When Churchill arrived, it wasn't clear whether de Gaulle would show, as he had refused to work with Henri Giraud, who had the Americans' backing.[7] Giraud, though thoroughly anti-German (he became a national celebrity through a daring escape from a Nazi prison), incurred de Gaulle's wrath by supporting Pétain.

Both Churchill and Roosevelt were in good spirits, and they set the tone of the conference. De Gaulle wasn't due to arrive until January 16, and the first two days of the summit were conducted in a relaxed atmosphere. As Churchill put it, "I had some nice walks with Pound and other Chiefs of Staff on the rocks and the beach. Wonderful waves rolling in, enormous clouds of foam."[8] Roosevelt was, if anything, even more at ease. The president repeatedly let everyone know how delighted he was to escape Washington's 24-7 pressure-cooker politics, and his "mood was that of a schoolboy on vacation."[9]

Roosevelt's only complaint was of the "Winston hours"—post-dinner drinks that lasted until 2 A.M.[10]

Frivolity did not mean agreement, however. The most important differences concerned invasion tactics. The British wanted to concentrate on North Africa and delay the invasion of the European continent; the Americans wished to hold on North Africa and speed the invasion.[11] General Marshall viewed Allied activities in the Mediterranean as a diversion from the real show: a head-on invasion of the Continent.

There were also disagreements over bombing. Except for Harris, all participants agreed that bombing alone would not win the war. Even Portal, an advocate of area bombing, conceded that it would be necessary to "exert maximum pressure on Germany by land operations; air bombardment alone was not sufficient."[12] The 1942 bombings of Bremen, Emden, Duisburg, Düsseldorf, Lübeck, Osnabrück, Hamburg, Frankfurt, Rostock, and other cities had not brought Germany to its knees, and both Portal and Churchill were starting to view Harris's promises with skepticism. There was also agreement on the overwhelming necessity of beating the U-boats at sea,[13] with the predictable exception of Harris. In June 1942, he said of Coastal Command: "It achieves nothing essential. . . . It abates little. . . . It aids by preventing a few shipping losses. A very few."[14]

Eaker arrived in Casablanca on January 15 and took his rooms. He tried to reach Arnold right away, without success. Arnold wasn't able to escape meetings until that evening, when he joined Eaker and Harriman for dinner. He told Eaker that "the President is under pressure from the Prime Minister to abandon day bombing and put all our bomber force in England into night operations along with (and preferably under the control of) the RAF."

Eaker exploded. "General, that is absurd. The cross-Channel operation will then fail. Our planes are not equipped for night bombing; our crews are not trained for it. We'll lose more planes landing on that fog-shrouded island in darkness than we lose now over German targets. If our leaders are that stupid, count me out. I don't want any part of such nonsense!"

Arnold, himself given to flying off the handle, was amused to see the usually controlled Eaker do so. He chuckled and replied, "I know all that as well as you do . . . [in] fact, I hoped you would respond that way. The only chance we have to go get that disastrous decision reversed is to convince Churchill of its error. I have heard him speak favorably of you. I'm going to try to get an appointment for you to see him. Stand by and be ready."[15]

Eaker returned to his villa with his assistant, James Parton, took a pencil, and began outlining his argument, sending Parton off to check the occasional fact. They sat at one end of a long dining table. At the other end, Robert E. Murphy of the U.S. State Department huddled with Harold Macmillan, trying to broker a compromise between Giraud and de Gaulle.[16] Eaker's work was interrupted frequently by visitors. At one point, General Patton—who was guarding the Anfa and the surrounding villas—strolled in wearing his pistols. Harry Hopkins, whose recent marriage had given him a new spring in his step, also visited. Breaking only for these brief chats, Eaker wrote all afternoon and the next day.[17] With an eye to Churchill's distaste for verbosity, he limited his reasons in favor of daylight bombing to seven, keeping another sixteen in his pocket as backup.

Eaker handed the document to Parton for typing and flew to Algiers to confer with Spaatz. The two returned to Casablanca on January 19 after Arnold arranged a meeting with Churchill.

Churchill, dressed again in his blue Air Commodore's uniform (which Eaker found "resplendent"), came down the stairs. He said to Eaker, "I understand you are very unhappy about my suggestion to your President that your Eighth Air Force join the RAF in night bombing." Without waiting for Eaker's reply, he continued: "Young man, I am half American; my mother was a U.S. citizen. The tragic losses of so many of our gallant crews tears my heart. Marshal Harris tells me that his losses average two percent while yours are at least double this and sometimes higher."

Churchill had this backwards—American losses had been 2.54 percent; British 4.7 percent—but Eaker resisted the temptation to correct the prime minister. He presented Churchill with a short memorandum, less than a page long, making his case. "I hope," he said to the prime minister, "you will read it."

Churchill had Eaker sit on the sofa beside him. Reading half-aloud, he absorbed Eaker's arguments. Toward the end, Churchill began to speak louder, rolling the words and adding emphasis to his rounded English tones:[18]

Day bombing is the bold, the aggressive, the offensive thing to do. It is the method and the practice which will put the greatest pressure on Germany, work the greatest havoc to his war-time industry and the greatest reduction in his air force. The operations of the next 90 days will demonstrate in convincing manner the truth of these conclusions. We have built up slowly and painfully and learned our job in a new theater against a tough enemy. Then we were torn down and shipped away to Africa. Now we have just built back up again and are ready for the job we all cherish—daylight bombing of Germany. Be patient, give us our chance and your reward will be ample—a successful day bombing offensive to combine and conspire with the admirable night bombing of the RAF to wreck German industry, transportation and morale—soften the Hun for land invasion and the kill.[19]

The memo still in his hand, Churchill chatted with Eaker as if the two were old friends. After Eaker argued his case further, Churchill handed the memo back to him. He said, "Young man, you have not convinced me that you are right, but you have persuaded me that you should have further opportunity to prove your contention. How fortuitous it would be if we could, as you say, bomb the devils around the clock. When I see your President at lunch today, I shall tell him that I withdraw my suggestion that U.S. bombers join the RAF in night bombing and that I now recommend that our joint effort, day and night bombing, be continued for a time."[20]

Arnold was delighted. "We had won a major victory," he later wrote, "for we would now bomb in accordance with American principles, using the methods for which our planes were designed."[21] The Americans were now ready to enter the bombing war on their own terms.

Churchill might have been agreeable because he had won the other two arguments: over de Gaulle's threatened boycott and, more importantly, over the date of the Continental invasion. He did so by playing good cop and bad cop. To de Gaulle, he was bad cop: he threatened to cut off British financial aid. To the Americans, he was good cop: anticipating Marshall's "diversion" argument, the British prepared what they called a compromise. After the North African campaign, Allied troops would make their way step-by-step through Sicily and into northern Italy. The Channel crossing would be delayed from 1943 to 1944. To concentrate American minds, the British brought to Casablanca a six-thousand-ton ship, converted into a reference library. It was crammed with all of the essential files from the War Office and had a complete staff of file clerks prepared to make the case for the "compromise."[22] In the face of such supposedly overwhelming evidence, and needing a way out of the deadlock, the Americans caved. Rather than simply a quick fight in Africa as a prelude to a Continental invasion, Eisenhower found himself agreeing to a protracted campaign in the Mediterranean, a traditional British sphere of influence. His troops would be making their way to Germany, but only gradually.[23]

Having reached agreement on who would bomb *how*, the Allies now needed to decide on *what*. In the run-up to the conference, the Americans had put a great deal of thought into how best to defeat the German menace at sea. They agreed on the need to destroy the factories producing U-boats, the Luftwaffe planes protecting them, and the raw materials that made them. Closely following this logic, they specified five essential targets: submarine yards and bases; the German air force, its factories and depots; ball bearings factories; oil installations; and facilities producing synthetic rubber and tires. There was not a word about cities.

The conference ended on January 23. Roosevelt was getting ready to return to the States when Churchill came to see him. "You cannot come all this way to North Africa without seeing [the Oasis of] Marrakesh. Let us spend two days there. I must be with you when you see the sunset of the snows of the Atlas Mountains."[24] Glad to have another reason to delay his return to Washington, the president joined Churchill on a five-hour drive across the desert and saw out the day with dinner and a view of the sunset.

Even before Churchill and Roosevelt went off on their journey, officials at the Air Ministry began drafting a new directive (christened "POINTBLANK") for Harris. It was ready on January 21, 1943, and came across his desk on February 4.[25] The directive began with these words: "Your primary objective will be the progressive destruction of the German military, industrial and economic system and the undermining of the morale of the German people to the point where their capacity for armed resistance is fatally weakened." If Eaker and the Americans had their way, there would have been a full stop after the "economic system." The armed forces were not prepared to admit that the invasion of Germany was dependent on bombing, and the Americans viewed the destruction of morale through bombing as a lost cause.[26] However, they agreed to insert the sentence on morale to satisfy the British. The directive continued:

Within that general concept, your primary objectives, subject to the exigencies of weather and of tactical feasibility, will for the present be in the following order:

(a) German submarine construction yards
(b) The German aircraft industry
(c) Transportation
(d) Oil plants
(e) Other targets in enemy war industry

It went on to specify other worthwhile targets: submarine operating bases of the Biscay coast, Berlin (inserted at Churchill's insistence), and northern Italy in support of the navies. The directive ended by summing up the two air forces' role:

> You should take every opportunity to attack Germany by day, to destroy objectives that are unsuitable for night attack, to sustain continuous pressure on German morale, to Impose heavy losses on the German day fighter force and to contain German fighter strength away from the Russian and Mediterranean theatres of war.
>
> Whenever Allied armies re-enter the Continent, you will afford all possible support in the manner most effective.
>
> In attacking objectives in occupied territories, you will conform to such instructions as may be issued from time to time for political reasons by His Majesty's government through the British Chiefs of Staff.

The commander-in-chief was unimpressed. The directive, like so many others that issued from the Air Ministry, was based on a flawed idea: that bombing one or more precision targets would be a panacea. Harris was convinced it wouldn't be. The whole point of bombing, for Harris, was to take out German cities and everything within them. All German cities, not simply Berlin. The question was how he would continue to do so while respecting the directive. As one author puts it in the doublespeak common to Harris's defenders, "he felt [the directive] was open to a certain amount of interpretation."[27] The official history put it slightly differently: Bomber Command interpreted the directive as allowing "general attacks necessary to render the German industrial population homeless, spiritless and, insofar as possible, dead."[28] The word *morale*, sprinkled uncomfortably throughout the document, certainly helped, but it could not hide the fact that the order called for the overwhelming weight of British and American bombs to fall on industry. Harris waited several weeks to reply, and when he did he offered a "commentary" on the directive. It suggested a slight rewording, stating that "the primary objective of Bomber Command will be the progressive destruction and dislocation of the German military, industrial and economic system aimed at undermining the morale of the German people to the point where their capacity for armed resistance is fatally weakened." Read this way, it implied that the main point of bombing was the undermining of morale rather than the destruction of industry. Harris was convinced it gave him exactly what he wanted. The Casablanca directive, he wrote after the war, "allowed me to attack pretty well any German industrial city with 100,000 inhabitants or above."

Although the directive was meant to wind down city bombing, not to launch a new wave of it, Harris exploited the directive's ambiguity to continue his city-busting campaign. There were only two men who could stop him: Churchill and Portal. The prime minister, following a year of bombing with few results, no longer believed the airmen's exaggerated promises, but he could never resist the appeal of bombing Berlin. On January 27, he sent a note to Sinclair urging him to "keep on at the big city." Portal, for his part, knew that his subordinate was not implementing the directive, but he—for reasons that are not entirely clear—chose to turn a blind eye.[29] Harris continued his effort to wreck Germany from end to end.

11

THE RUHR

The Ruhr valley stretches over some seventy miles. In the west it begins in Wesel near the Rhine, and in the east it ends at Hamm. Slightly wider than it is long, the area begins in the north at the Lippe River and ends in the south at the Ruhr River. It contains a series of midsized cities—Bochum, Essen, Dortmund, and Duisburg—that are actually parts of Germany's largest conurbation of five million people. Before Germany's late industrialization, the area was made up of small market towns: Essen, Bochum, and Dortmund. The only exception was the old trading port of Düsseldorf. The region's industrialization, like so much else in German history, was rapid and jarring. Property prices exploded—in Hamborn, they rose hundredfold in twenty years as workers poured into the area.[1] The housing shortage was intense, but the demand was almost entirely working class. With the exception of those in Düsseldorf, there was no middle class to pay for the elegant, decorative turn-of-the-century apartments found in Berlin, Pforzheim, Würzburg, or Hamburg. The result was hastily built rental apartment blocks with small, crowded back courtyards. The materials were cheap, the buildings often badly built, and little attention was given to such matters as plumbing and safe drinking water. It was not unusual for a recently built house to collapse.[2] The region's occupants were thoroughly proletarian: simple, poor people who—to the horror of the bourgeois residents of Düsseldorf—enjoyed fairs, drink, and illegal bars.[3]

The area was Germany's industrial heartland and home to some of Europe's most important producers of oil, steel, and chemicals. In the spring of 1943, the Ruhr became the focus of Harris's war. "At long last," he said, "we are ready and equipped. Bomber Command's main offensive and task is to destroy the main cities of the Ruhr."

The night of March 5, 1943, was moonless, and the industrial skyscape of Essen was barely illuminated.[4] The old city center was a dense pocket of small streets with shops and houses, of grand turn-of-the-century hotels, and of elegant churches.[5] A dark industrial haze hung over the otherwise clear and cloudless city. At 8 P.M., eight plywood airplanes were streaking toward Essen. They were de Havilland Mosquitoes, made almost entirely of wood and capable of speeds greater than 400 miles an hour. They made up the pathfinder force and were carrying Oboe tracking equipment, which allowed them to pinpoint with great accuracy the marking point, and red flares. Once over the city, they began circling and dropping the flares. Minutes later, hundreds of bombers, including seventy-eight from 6 Group,[6] swept in. For the first time in RAF history, the bombers would drop their loads on the flares rather than on anything the pilots could see on the ground.

At 8:37 P.M., the air-raid warning rang out across the city. Eighteen-year-old Paul Werner was on the night watch at his local school, the Burggymnasium. During air raids, it was his duty as a volunteer in the local air defense to stand ready. He would cycle through the city reporting fires, damaged buildings, craters, and broken pipes. The one place he wasn't allowed to visit was an air-raid shelter.

The signal brought eleven-year-old Horst Rübenkamp to the window. He lived in the west of the city, not far from the Krupp steelworks. He had viewed all previous raids as a game, and he found the lights, flak, and occasional explosions exciting. Tonight would be different. The sound of hundreds of bombers and hundreds of flak guns was deafening. Horst ran to his mother and they made for the house's cellar. The noise penetrated the walls. After ten minutes, everything fell silent. The next bomb was theirs. A massive explosion shook the cellar. The lights went out. Water pipes broke, and plaster came raining down. Horst's mother grabbed his hand as she tried to climb the stairs to safety. They were gone. The explosion and ensuing fire had left only ashes. Horst's mother lifted him up, and then scrambled over the wall after him.

When they came out into the street, houses were ablaze and bombs were falling. Dodging incendiaries and explosions, they struggled fifteen hundred feet to the nearest concrete, aboveground air-raid shelter. Horst picked up a stone and hammered on the door. A Nazi party member opened it and ushered them inside. He told them to say nothing about what was going on outside, as it might create a panic. Covered in chalk from the cellar ceiling, they took their places and waited.

Not far away, Paul left the school. One high explosive had hit its steps, smashing them and leaving a crater in its wake. Next to the school, another high explosive had destroyed a house, killing seventeen people. Across from the school, the Cathedral was burning. The minister tried to put out the fire, but the flames licked at his clothes, caught fire, and burned him to death. Paul climbed up to the church attic, where the fire extinguishers were kept on the assumption that the roof would burn first. He ran down to the cellar and ordered it cleared. Twenty-four children came out into the street. Paul led them through the burning streets and to the subway near the main station. His arms and hands were covered in burns.

At 4 A.M., the door of the shelter housing Horst and his mother was opened. "I," he said sixty-five years later, "could not believe my eyes. . . . There were smoking piles of rubble everywhere. Our house was gone, and so was our neighborhood. Eighty percent of it had been destroyed." Western Essen was hardly unique. When the flames subsided, 479 people were dead and another 30,000 were homeless. Horst and Paul stayed in the city, and a week later—on March 12—they watched the rest of it go under in a second devastating RAF raid.

Essen was the opening salvo in the Battle of the Ruhr. Over the next five months, Harris launched more than forty raids. Bomber Command poured fifty-eight thousand tons of bombs on Germany, more than the Germans dropped during the Blitz and more than Bomber Command had dropped during the whole of 1942. One by one, the cities of the Ruhr were turned into ash and rubble. The effects of these raids on production were minimal. Although two hundred thousand tons of bombs would fall on Germany in 1943—five times the figure for 1942—its wartime production increased dramatically. It would only begin to fall in the last six months of the war. During the Battle of the Ruhr, the country faced nothing approaching a labor shortage. There were 1.4 million workers still employed in household service (at a time when two-thirds of British servants had joined the war effort), and Hitler insisted on importing five hundred thousand Ukrainian women to join them. By the end of 1943, the Reich still had six million Germans employed in consumer industries. The result was the overproduction of consumer goods. From October 1942 to October 1943, Germany produced 120,000 typewriters, 200,000 domestic radios, 150,000 electric blankets, 3600 refrigerators, 300,000 electricity meters, 512,000 pairs of riding boots and 360,000 spur straps. According to the official British historians Sir Charles Webster and Noble Franklin, the Battle of the Ruhr—during which fifty-eight thousand tons of bombs had been poured on Germany—cost the area between one and one and a half months' loss of output. The price for Bomber Command in men and matériel was enormous: 872 aircraft (4.7 percent of the 18,506 sorties flown). On some nights, 30 percent of all aircraft would come back damaged or not at all.[7]

From Harris's point of view, the raids were an extraordinary success. In mid-May, Churchill was caught up in the drama again, and he wrote to Harris asking for a list of the one hundred most important towns in the German war effort. Harris gladly complied. On May 15, his confidence reaching a new high, Harris told Portal that "staggering destruction [has] been inflicted throughout the Ruhr to an extent that no nation can stick it for long. If we can keep this up it cannot fail to be lethal within a period of time which in my view will be surprisingly short."[8]

12

BUSTING DAMS

I n the early hours of May 17, 1943, Speer was still working. An assistant
handed him a report. The largest of the Ruhr dams—the Möhne—had
been shattered. It was one of four dams supplying the Ruhr with water
and electricity. When it collapsed, the floods covered fifty square miles. They
extinguished gas furnaces, flooded coal mines, and swamped more than one
hundred factories and many homes. More than one thousand people were
drowned. Speer drafted a report on the damage and delivered it personally to
Hitler at his headquarters. It made a "deep impression" on him.[1]

The "dambuster" raids—formerly known as Operation Chastise—are the
stuff of legend, perhaps the most famous of the RAF raids.[2] The idea behind
them—that a bomb could bounce into its target rather than being dropped on
it—was conceived by the eccentric scientist and aircraft designer Barnes
Wallis.

Wallis was obsessed with bombs: how big they should be and how
much they could destroy. The Möhne dam was 112 feet thick at the base, 25
feet thick at the top, and 130 feet high. Wallis originally suggested that a ten
thousand–pound bomb would wreck it, depriving armaments makers of electricity and people of water. In 1943, however, Bomber Command had no
airplane capable of carrying such a weight. Wallis was sent back to the drawing
board. He then thought about the position of the bomb rather than simply its
size: a small bomb exploding right next to the dam wall might do more damage than a larger one going off several feet away. After countless experiments and calculations, he concluded that a 6000-pound bomb, if placed right
up against the dam wall, would destroy it. The question was how to manage

the placement. Further experiments led Wallis to the now-famous idea of a bouncing bomb. A round bomb that looked like a cement roller—technically, a mine—when dropped low would skip across the water and hit the side of the dam at the right speed and spot: 240 miles an hour and sixty feet above water level. The spinning motion of the bomb would cause it to roll down the side of the dam, exploding underwater like a depth charge. If the bomb created a hole, even a tiny one, in the dam, the force of the water would do the rest.

When Harris first heard of the idea, he was scathing: "With some slight practical knowledge and many previous bitter experiences on similar lines I am prepared to bet that this is just about the maddest proposition as a weapon that we have yet come across." The bouncing bomb was a precision bombing proposal created by an inventor. In other words, it combined the two things that Harris hated most. Harris refused to meet with Wallis and was only talked into it by Air Chief Marshal Sir Ralph Cochrane (AOC 5 Bomber Group). When he was brought in to see Wallis in March, his first words to the scientist were: "My boys' lives are too precious to be wasted on your crazy notions."[3] Despite this inauspicious beginning, chemistry formed between the two men. They had more in common than either realized. As Harris's biographer put it, they both "mistrusted politicians, disliked senior civil servants and despised obstructionists; possessed determination and originality far beyond most of their contemporaries; and between them . . . had as much diplomacy as a circus prize fighter." Rather than follow his initial insult with a swift exit, Harris listened patiently to Wallis, watched the scientist's film, and admitted that he had not been aware of all of the details. On March 15, Harris told Cochrane that he should form a special squadron and suggested Guy Gibson to command it. Gibson, a dashing young man with a lovely smile, was already known as a crack pilot who had flown a hundred missions over three bombing tours— one tour more than was usual.

Harris rarely admitted he was wrong, but on those rare occasions when he did, he did not hesitate to change his behavior. From then on, the dambuster raid had his full support, and by May, 617 Squadron was ready to attack the Ruhr dams. On the night of May 16, nineteen aircraft—specially designed Lancasters—took off for the Ruhr. Nine were to attack the Möhne, five the Sorpe, and five were in reserve. En route, the Sorpe force was savaged. Guns raked one of the planes, while another grazed the water while taking evasive action; both had to return.[4] Between Harderwijk and Apeldoom, ground fire sliced into the lead planes; they crashed to the ground, taking all fourteen crew members to their death.

Gibson's Möhne force fared better, but one plane was lost on the way. Flak tore a Lancaster from the sky; another three Canadians died in the crash.[5] When Gibson's plane reached the Möhne, there were eight airborne and ready to attack. Under intense flak fire in the full glare of the searchlights, Gibson's aircraft swept in low across the water. He dropped his bomb and pulled up hard. The bomb skipped across the water, hit the side of the dam, and exploded underwater. A perfect hit. When Gibson looked back, however, the dam was still standing. A second plane, piloted by John ("Hoppy") Hopgood, came in next. Hopgood's plane had already been raked by ground fire on the way over, wounding his rear gunner. He was bleeding from the head and Hopgood could have easily returned to base with honor. Instead, he had chosen to press on. As he came in over the water, he did not enjoy Gibson's element of surprise. Flak strafed his airplane, setting his starboard wing on fire. His bomb-aimer, John Fraser, released the bomb. It bounced over the dam and destroyed the pumping station. The burning aircraft crossed the dam. Hopgood held it steady and ordered his crew out. Fraser "kneeled facing forward over the escape hatch and . . . saw that the trees looked awful damn close. I thought there was only one thing to do and that was to pull the rip cord and let the pilot chute go out first and then let it pull the chute out and me after it and that's what I did. I rolled out and the tail wheel whizzed by my ear. I swung to the vertical and within 2 or 3 seconds I touched the ground."[6]

In the plane itself, Hopgood shouted to his rear gunner, Tony Burcher. "Get out, you damn fool!" He struggled to hold the plane as his men escaped. Burcher, who had been wounded in the first strafing, managed to throw himself through the bomb chute. He bounced off the tail plane and broke his back, but he lived. Hopgood stayed at the controls as the plane went down, crashing some two thousand feet from where Fraser had jumped. Above, over the squadron radio, someone said, "Poor old Hoppy."

As Hopgood sacrificed himself to save his crew, a third plane attacked the dam. Micky Martin, an Australian, followed the same path blazed by Gibson and Hopgood. To draw off German fire, Gibson joined him. In what must have been an awing and fearful sight to anyone watching from the dam, Martin and Gibson came in together, all guns blazing. Martin's bomb skipped and scored another direct hit. But the dam still held. Next on the attack was Dinghy Young. Young was raised in California, educated at Cambridge, and joined the Royal Canadian Air Force. Young's airplane came in with Gibson and Martin on each wing tip, using their guns to draw enemy fire. Once again, the dam withstood an accurate hit. Young pulled his plane up, while Gibson and Martin swung around to join David Maltby on a fourth run. The three planes came in at sixty feet above water. Maltby scored a third accurate hit, and the three planes pulled up just as the bomb exploded. The planes circled the valley, preparing for a four-plane attack with David Shannon carrying a bomb. Then, suddenly, the dam cracked and collapsed. "A wall of water twenty-feet high surged over the masonry and swept off into the night."[7] As the water rushed into the valley, Gibson led those planes that had not dropped their bombs toward the Eder valley dam. After three runs, during one of which Henry Maudslay's plane was caught in the explosion, the second dam collapsed. The raid had cost Bomber Command fifty-six aircrew, only three of whom survived in POW camps. Of the twenty-eight Canadian aircrew on the raid, almost half died.[8] The surviving aircraft headed home.

A hero's welcome was waiting for the airmen. On their arrival, they learned that the Sorpe raid had failed to breach the much stronger earthen dam, but it hardly mattered. Canadians Ken Brown and Steven Oancia were awarded medals (a Conspicuous Gallantry Medal and a Distinguished Flying Medal, respectively) for their efforts. The bouncing bomb had been a stunning success, and the two raids showed that Bomber Command was capable of precision that no one would have imagined possible a few months earlier. The casualty rate had been extremely high—some 24 percent—but the absolute losses—eight aircraft—were no higher than on the average raid, and small compared to the vast degree of destruction meted out against the dams. Gibson became a national hero, though he did not enjoy his status for long. He was above all a bomber, and could not forgo the thrill of the air. After writing his bestselling book, *Enemy Coast Ahead*, and going on a lecture tour of the U.S. (paid for by the British government in the vain hope of keeping its hero on the ground), Gibson continued to badger Bomber Command for a return to operations. He volunteered for still more bombing runs and, in 1944, his plane went down on its way to a raid over Rheydt, a suburb of Monchengladbach. The man who had dodged dozens of Luftwaffe fighters and tons of flak had run out of luck. And fuel. His plane crashed near Steenburgen in the Netherlands. He was twenty-six years old.

Since Harris had taken over Bomber Command, the organization had gone from strength to strength. In the early years of the bombing war, Bomber Command—under the leadership of the hapless Peirse—had difficulty getting a hundred planes into the air. Once there, some of them would become hopelessly lost, failing to find Germany much less any particular city in it. Those planes that did reach their target would circle pathetically above it, trying to identify without radar the precision target they had been assigned. They were easy prey for the Luftwaffe, and Bomber Command suffered terrible casualties. As the Butt report had made clear, the bombs that did fall barely hit anything. Those crew members that did not crash and were not shot out of the sky could not but despair.

In contrast with those years, the first six months of 1943 must have seemed like a miracle. Over the space of four months, Harris had taken out major German cities and brought Bomber Command to industrial Germany's beating heart. And, finally, as a definitive answer to the sniping of the Butt report, the dambuster raid had hit a target with a precision measured in inches.

The effects among the Allies were energizing. The Lübeck and, above all, the Cologne raids had made the world stand to attention. In the United Kingdom, the Blitz was over, but only the most empathetic could fail to take pleasure at the Germans finally receiving something of what they had dished out against Rotterdam, Warsaw, Coventry, and London. The aircrew had gone from being the whipping boys of the war effort—chronically short of funds, demoralized, and viewed as pointless by large sections of the Army, Navy, and political elite—to the public and very glamorous face of the war itself. The *Times* headline of May 18, 1943, shouted their triumph.

RUHR DAMS BREACHED *** DARING LOW-LEVEL ATTACK *** WALLS BLASTED OUT BY 1,500 LB MINES *** VAST DAMAGE BY FLOODS

Peppered with exciting reports from the pilots themselves, the story told of a secret operation that was months in the planning, of a handpicked crew, and of the bravery and thrill of the raid itself. Quoting Air Minister Sinclair, full due was given to Harris himself: "Our praise is due to that resourceful and determined Commander-in-Chief, Air Chief Marshal Harris, who planned the details of the operation, and those superbly daring and skillful crews who smote the Germans so heavily last night. It is a trenchant blow for the victories of the Allies." The article ended with Harris's own words: "Please convey to all concerned my congratulations on the brilliantly successful execution of last night's operation. To air crews I would say that their keenness and thoroughness in training and their skill and determination in pressing home their attack will forever be an inspiration to the Royal Air Force. In this memorable operation they have won a major victory in the Battle of the Ruhr, the effect of which will last until the Boche is swept away in the flood of final disaster." He might as well have been looking Stafford Cripps right in the eye.

While the United Kingdom was celebrating, Speer was making his way from Berlin to the Ruhr. As he inspected the Sorpe Valley reservoir, his fears were confirmed. The center of the dam had taken a direct hit. The hole was just above water level. Had it been a few inches lower, the pressure of the water would have swept the dam away. With the two successful hits, the RAF "with just a few bombers [nineteen] . . . came close to a success which would have been greater than anything they had achieved hitherto with a commitment of thousands of bombers."[9] The RAF had made one mistake: the Eder Valley dam had nothing to do with the water supply to the Ruhr. Still, Speer's relief that three dams were still standing was marred by a gnawing fear: when would the British be back?

They wouldn't. Speer ordered seven thousand men from the West Wall to the Ruhr, where they feverishly repaired the dams. They erected vast wooden scaffolding across the breach in the Möhne dam and began cementing it in from the bottom up. Every night, they listened for the bombers. "A few bombs," Speer observed, "would have produced cave-ins in the exposed building sites, and a few fire bombs would have set the wooden scaffolding blazing." But they never came. On September 23, 1943, just before the rains that would have flooded the valley again, the workers managed to close the breach. "The British air force," Speer sighed with relief, had "missed its second chance."[11]

Harris did not have the benefit of Speer's views, and he in any case thought the advantage of the dambuster raids lay in their effect on Bomber Command morale and popularity. Cities remained the key to Germany's war effort. In the months after the dambuster raids, Harris returned to them. On May 28, 826 bombers lit Dortmund's medieval center on fire, knocking out the Hoesch steelworks with it. The following night, almost five hundred bombers attacked Wuppertal. Fires tore through the city center's narrow streets, destroying half of the city and leaving thirty-four hundred dead and a hundred thousand homeless. The bombers had developed a new technique. The first wave of planes dropped the high explosives that tore off the roofs of the houses and public buildings. The second wave followed with incendiaries, which lit the houses' contents and interior walls on fire. Fires spread from one building to another, and soon the neighborhood was a conflagration. With any luck, the high explosives would also break underground waterlines, making it impossible to fight the fires. The ratio varied, but Portal viewed the ideal as one-third high explosives to two-thirds incendiaries.[11]

This technique was again employed to devastating effect on the Rhine city of Düsseldorf on June 11–12. The high explosives–incendiaries sequence started 8000 fires, destroyed 25 miles of the city center, and left 1400 people dead and another 140,000 homeless. On June 21–22, the fires did their work on Krefeld, destroying half of the city, killing five hundred people, and making another seventy thousand homeless. The next night, 550 aircraft destroyed 60 percent of Mülheim an der Ruhr. The night after that, Bomber Command destroyed the other half of Wuppertal and left four thousand dead. By July, Bomber Command had carried out twenty-two major raids. The raids had killed fifteen thousand civilians, and seven thousand aircrew.

The Battle of the Ruhr ended with the destruction of the medieval city of Remscheid; a July 30–31 raid flattened the city center. After twenty minutes, "the town," as one Group captain put it, "had ceased to exist."[12] The RAF lost fifteen aircraft. One—a Halifax—landed near Hermann Josef-Baum's Flak Batterie.[13] Hermann was an eighteen-year-old flak operator from Oberkassel, a Düsseldorf suburb. He had been called up to serve in air defense as a schoolboy, on February 15, 1943.[14] A German fighter raked the Halifax with bullets, and it made an emergency landing. When Hermann's crew reached it, only one aircrew was alive. Badly wounded, he was transported by Hermann's Batterie to a POW camp hospital. Hermann removed and kept the plate bearing the Halifax's serial number: E.E.P. 108770.

Speer viewed coal (of which one-third of Germany's supply was in the Ruhr), but also steel and chemicals, as key spokes in the German war economy. He feared that sustained attack on them—meaning an initial raid that destroyed the factories and subsequent raids that frustrated efforts to repair them—would cripple Germany's capacity to wage war. In the early years of the war, such precision would have been impossible; by 1943, as the dambuster raids had so clearly proven, it was possible. "The principle followed [in the dambuster raids] was to paralyze a cross section, as it were—just as a motor can be made useless by the removal of the ignition."[15] As Speer surveyed the damage, he concluded that the results for Germany could well be disastrous. "I had early recognized," Speer wrote, "[that] the war could largely have been decided in 1943 if instead of vast but pointless area bombing, the planes had concentrated on centres of armaments production."[16]

For his part, Harris obviously recognized the importance of oil, steel, ball bearings, chemicals, and much else to the war effort, but he thought it pointless to single out any one of these as the magic bullet. Strangely, for a man who seemed so hostile to ideas, he took a much more subtle, abstract, and almost theoretical view of the German war machine. It was a complex and integrated machine in which the component parts depended on the operation of the whole. Industries depended on people, people depended on food and infrastructure, infrastructure depended on resources, resources depended on transportation, and transportation depended on industry. To target any one industry would be to overlook this interlocking structure. Attacking a factory here or there was like a pinprick. It hurt a bit, but healed quickly (factories were easy to rebuild). Bombing an entire city would take out everything in it and wreck the very complex, integrated machine on which Germany's ability to wage war depended. Added to this was the particular role of workers: without them, there could be no industry. As Harris put it, replacing a building takes a few months; replacing a worker takes twenty years. He saw little distinction between attacking the soldiers who occupied the battlefield and attacking the workers who armed them.[17] If it was morally acceptable to starve the Germans in the hundreds of thousands (as the Allies did with their First World War blockade), how could it be immoral to attack them in their cities?

Area bombing, Harris also argued, was a modern, almost civilized, way to fight, and one that particularly suited Britain's circumstances. "Involvement in land campaigns," he wrote to Churchill in June 1942, "especially Continental campaigns, serves but to reduce us to the level of the Horde. We are not a Horde. We are a highly industrialized, under-populated, physically . . . small island. Our lead is in science, not spawn; in brains, not brawn."[18] It was also the best way. "Victory," he wrote in the same letter, "speedy and complete awaits the side which first employs air power as it should be employed. . . . [City bombing will] knock Germany out of the War in a matter of months."

Harris's theory had been tested, but not proven, in the Ruhr. The cities had suffered extensive damage. Only one major urban center—Hagen—was standing by the end of the battle, and it would be finished off on a single night in October.[19] Harris had every reason to believe that industry had suffered as well—reconnaissance photos showed direct hits on the Krupp works in Essen, for instance. He was right. The problem, however, was that the industrial damage that did occur was repaired by the end of September. For all its accomplishments, Bomber Command had yet to achieve the sort of decisive blow that would knock out a city on a single raid. Even Essen, which suffered more than any other city, had to be bombed twice during the Battle of the Ruhr, and it would be hit hundreds of times before it was wiped off the map. The death toll had reached new highs, but remained in the thousands.

Part of the problem was the cities themselves. The Ruhr is Germany's most populated region, but it is made up of a series of medium-sized cities. While Harris was happy to see them go under, they were not his main target. Germany's largest and most famous cities—Berlin, Munich, Hamburg, and Frankfurt—were all outside the Ruhr. Up to this point in his command, Harris had been salvaging the credibility that Bomber Command had lost during the first three aimless years of the bombing war. He was able to turn to his main targets once credibility had been unquestionably restored. At the top of the list was Berlin, the capital of the Reich, the world's third-largest city in 1943 and Germany's largest by far. For the moment, however, it was too far away and too well defended for Harris to be at all confident of a successful raid. Berlin's time would come, and soon, but Harris looked elsewhere. He alighted on a city that was second only to Berlin in its importance, that was on a readily identifiable river, and that was easy to reach from England: Hamburg.

13

ENGLAND, JULY 27, 1943: "LET US OPEN THE WINDOW"

They did not look like much: small paper strips, about a foot long and an inch wide, silver on one side and black on another. They were tied together in a tight bundle and ready to be loaded into Jack Pragnell's airplane, a Halifax with 102 Squadron. Jack had joined the RAF in 1940 with his twin brother, and the two had trained together in South Africa before being assigned to different Bomber Command squadrons. He had no particular hatred for the Germans. Even the loss of his brother did not change his views. On the contrary, like many members of Bomber Command, he developed a deep respect and near affection for his opposite numbers in the Luftwaffe. They alone understood, in a way that no armchair critic could, what bombing meant for the bomber. "It was only a shame," he later remarked, "that they weren't on our side." Jack's motivations were simple, and powerful. There was a war that England had to win, and he had to contribute somehow. He had considered joining the Army or the Navy, but couldn't bear the thought of dying in the foul depths of a submarine or crawling through mud and barbed wire. The RAF, by contrast, offered glamour. "I had always wanted to fly," he said sixty years later.

The strips were code-named Window. They were a further advance in a silent radar war conducted between the British and the Germans throughout the conflict. The idea of radar itself was a fantastic notion from the pages of sci-fi writers: deadly rays could penetrate enemy aircraft and kill the pilots.[1] The man tasked with the job of transforming this idea into reality was the onetime friend of Cherwell, Henry Tizard.

Tizard's civil service work had put him back in contact with Cherwell.

While the two men's careers followed an at-times eerily similar trajectory, they were very different characters. When Tizard was in Berlin, he lived in a cold rented flat and looked with envy at the warm coats of wealthy Berliners strolling down the Unter den Linden, Berlin's grandest boulevard. Cherwell lived on the Unter den Linden, at the city's most prestigious address, the Adlon Hotel, overlooking the Brandenburg Gate. Back in England, their lifestyles continued to differ. Cherwell was a gentleman and lived the life of one. He would rise late, have a leisurely morning, and send his manservant to pick up his car—a grand Mercedes—around 11 A.M. He would be driven to the lab to put in a few hours' work before returning to his rooms at Christ Church—a very grand set overlooking Christ Church meadow and the chapel.[2]

Tizard's was an altogether different character: unpretentious and suspicious of unjustified privilege. When he learned during the war that an official car was kept continuously at his disposal, he gave it up in favor of that most proletarian means of transportation, the bus.[3] Tizard also possessed a work ethic more like that of an American entrepreneur than an English gentlemen. From 1929, Tizard had been rector at Imperial College, London, and he combined that position with his civil service work. He would put in a full day at Whitehall and return to Imperial as late as midnight. He would then rouse the college secretary, G. C. Lowry, and work until 3 or 4 A.M. Then the whole thing would start again.[4] In both committee and college, Tizard had the gift of making everyone—professors, students, bureaucrats, and office messengers—feel that their views were of enormous interest to him.

On January 28, 1935, a committee, soon called the Tizard committee, met for the first time. Harry Egerton Wimperis, a scientist who had been researching bombing since the 1930s and on whose suggestion the Tizard committee was initiated, made a startling announcement. A short time before, he had asked Robert Wattson-Watt, superintendent of the Radio Division of the National Physical Laboratory, to look into the possibility that a projected beam of electromagnetic radiation might destroy an aircraft. The hypothesis was a version of comic book fantasy—that laser beams shot at an airplane might penetrate it, killing the pilot and crew.[5] Wattson-Watt dismissed the idea in a note a few days later, but he suggested another: that enough energy might be reflected from an aircraft, with radio field strengths that could be readily created, to create an echo that could be detected by a radio receiver on the ground.[6] An excited Wimperis presented the idea to the committee, and it requested a full memorandum from Wattson-Watt. It arrived on February 12, and practical tests were hastily arranged. From these tests, the committee concluded that if the time it took for a beam to return from an airplane was multiplied by the speed of the signal and divided by two, it was possible to find and then follow the airplane.[7]

Wattson-Watt's early work also showed how radar might be rendered useless. When he conducted early tests on RAF planes, he noticed that anything close to the planes—a bird, for instance—would interfere with their radar equipment. If the British could drop objects from their planes continuously, they might disrupt German radar and protect their aircraft. Out of this simple idea emerged Window: metal strips, dropped in the thousands, would render German radar useless.

Window was on course for early adoption in 1942, but then Cherwell—who "rarely found it possible to believe in an idea unless he was at least a midwife at its delivery"[8]—intervened. He pointed out the obvious—if the strategy worked against German radar, it would also work against the British. And then he posed a question that still shook a bombing-weary country: What if the Germans launched a new and more devastating blitz against Britain?[9] The idea horrified those responsible for defending London: Fighter Command, Anti-Aircraft Command, and Minister of Home Security Herbert Morrison. Tizard threw his weight behind Bomber Command, which was firmly in favor of Window, but it was not enough. Its introduction was delayed.

Harris was disgusted, and he did not hesitate to let the Air Ministry know. Directly addressing Cherwell's "tit-for-tat" argument, "it is generally wise," he wrote in late May 1942, "when you think of a weapon first to use it. Otherwise you lose all chance of profit before the enemy, as he will think of it and get it into service. This weapon is adjudged to be of benefit to the bomber. The bomber crews have more to face than anyone else in our war. They should be given all reasonable preference. But because we are defensively minded—and that never yet won a war—everyone else always gets preference over the Bomber!"[10] He did not, however, follow up his missive with his usual insistence. He let the matter rest and only raised it again when radar-directed night fighters began imposing higher losses on Bomber Command in the summer of 1943.[11] At that time, he went directly to Churchill. The issue was finally settled at a June 22, 1943, meeting. R. V. Jones, the young Assistant Director of Intelligence [science], Wattson-Watt, and the obstinate and hot-tempered commander-in-chief of Fighter Command, Sir Trafford Leigh-Mallory, were there. All sides repeated their arguments while Churchill listened.

Finally, after an hour and a half, Sir Trafford switched sides. "I have heard both sides of the argument," he said, "and I still believe that launching this weapon will wreck our defences. I am, however, prepared to take the risk."

"Very well," Churchill said. "Let us open the window."

It was a smart move. The heart of the anti-Window case was that using it would remove all moral constraints. Seeing their defenses overwhelmed and their cities wrecked, the Germans would retaliate. British defenses would be equally overwhelmed and London would be open to a second, much more devastating blitz. The result would be an early form of what was called mutual assured destruction (MAD) during the Cold War. As it happened, the opponents had underestimated German reticence. In one of the war's ironies, British angels were prepared to go where German devils feared to tread. At the same time as Window was being tested over East Anglia, the Luftwaffe was testing the German equivalent, Düppel, over the Baltic. Reports about Düppel's destructive effect on radar were sent back to Göring. He read them and was horrified by the possibility that the British would discover and employ the technique. He had all of the documents destroyed and ordered an end to the research.[12] The Germans would eventually learn to counter Window; in some ways, they actually benefited from it. Window forced the Germans to trade their ineffective static defenses for aggressive counterattacks. Before any of this occurred, however, a heavy price would be exacted at Hamburg.

14

TO DESTROY HAMBURG

July 24, 1943, 10 A.M.

A t air bases all over eastern England, airmen were relaxing in the sunshine.[1] The last two night raids had been canceled because of poor weather over Germany, and they wondered whether the same would be true on this day. The most curious went to the base's station office to hear the orders rung through from High Wycombe. The rest headed to the messes, where the operations were pinned to a board. There were sighs across the country: the "ops" were on, though they wouldn't learn the target until that evening's briefing.

The pace quickened across hundreds of bases. The men headed to their airplanes to get them "bombed up" and to help the ground crew check that the planes were ready for battle. As they approached, they saw brown paper parcels, endless numbers of them, piled up on the tarmac next to each plane. Some of the men could not contain their curiosity and opened the bags to find the strips. "We couldn't make head or tail of it," an airman of 47 Squadron later said. "One chap peed on it to see if it reacted."[2]

Once the planes were ready, the men had to live through the dead time between bombing-up and the 5 P.M. briefing.[3] At that hour (or thereabouts), they took their places in the briefing room. Someone closed the door behind them, and the officer in charge—a flight commander or the commanding officer—pulled down the flight map. On it was a red line of ribbon leading to the target. As the men strained forward to identify the city, the officer uttered the standard phrase: "Your target for tonight, gentlemen, is . . . Hamburg."

The briefing followed. The officer told them about the route. The weatherman explained the conditions they would face on the way to and over the target. The armament officer discussed their bomb loads. And the signal-man covered radar.

The intelligence officer then took the floor. He explained that Hamburg was Germany's second-largest city, a manufacturing hub, and a center of submarine production. Taking it out would be of great benefit to the Battle of the Atlantic. Finally, he told them about their aiming point: a few miles north of the submarine yards, in the center of the city, and almost exactly above the St. Nicholas (St. Nikolai) Church.

He then briefed them on Window:

> It has been worked out as carefully as possible to give you maximum protection, but there are two points which I want to emphasize strongly. First, the benefit of Window is a communal one: the Window protects you and is not so much that which you drop yourself as that which is already in the air, dropped by an aircraft ahead. To obtain full advantage, it is therefore necessary to fly in a concentrated stream along the ordered route. [It is equally important] that the correct quantities of Window are discharged at the correct time intervals ... When good communication is achieved, Window can so devastate a [radar] defence system that we ourselves have withheld using it until we could effect improvements in our defences, and until we could be sure of hitting the enemy harder than he could hit us.

"The time has now come," he concluded, "when, by the aid of Window in conserving your unmatched strength, we shall hit him even harder."[4]

The officer took the floor again and asked if there were any questions. There were not. He said words to the effect of, "It is now time to synchronize your watches. Good luck."[5] Then he turned and left the room.

The men regrouped around 7 P.M. in the mess, where they had the usual bacon and eggs. Everyone knew that it would be the last meal for some of them. After eating, they donned their gear and waited to be transported to the planes.

At 9 P.M. or so, they were at their planes, and half an hour later they were in them, ready for takeoff. At 9:45 P.M., a New Zealand squadron, piloted by Sergeant P. Moseley, was the first to take off. Minutes later, hundreds of airplanes were screaming down runways across England. Once in the air, Moseley's Stirling was overtaken by the Lancasters in the pathfinder force.

At around 10 P.M., Jack Pragnell's Halifax took off and slowly began to gain altitude. His first job was to get the heavy plane as high in the air as possible. Down below, in Wellingborough, his fiancée, Brenda, could often hear the planes and wondered which one he was in. When he approached the English coast, his squadron joined the others high above the seaside towns below. They fell into three large bomber streams approaching the coast. By 11 P.M., Jack's was one of 791 airplanes in the skies heading out to sea. At almost exactly this moment, Freya radar beams (which showed a plane, but said nothing about altitude) sent from the Germans' Ostend radar station, some seventy-five miles away, silently made contact with the planes and instantly relayed the message. The Luftwaffe had been warned.

About eighty miles from the German coast, three bomber streams converged into one. With the pathfinders in the lead and the bombers stretching two hundred miles behind them, a vast flotilla of airplanes was droning toward Hamburg.

Northern Germany

Stade is a small Hanseatic town with half-timbered houses following the curve of the city's harbor situated between Hamburg and Bremen. In 1943, its airfield housed a massive, bombproof bunker. Inside was a raised balcony overlooking a huge, frosted glass screen, some fifty feet across. From the balcony, General Lieutenant Schwabedissen, cigarette in hand, looked down on the screen and the fighter-control officers, who manned the radios, below. On the screen itself, projected spots of lights represented every plane in the air—white spots for enemy planes, green spots for German planes—with details of each plane's position and flight direction.[6] From his vantage, Schwabedissen oversaw air defense for whole of northeastern Germany.

12:30 A.M., THE German coast

Hundreds of German fighter planes hovered, circling in tightly organized boxes, over the coast. They made up the Kammhuber Line, brainchild of General Joseph Kammhuber. He was the son of a Bavarian farmer, had lived through Verdun, and had managed to stay in Germany's small post-Versailles army. He was sent secretly to the Soviet Union for flight training at the end of the 1920s, and when he returned he was instrumental to Germany's efforts to set up a strategic bombing force. When the war started, he was one of three chiefs of staff in the Luftwaffe—Hans Jeschonnek and Hans-Jürgen Stumpf being the others. Early on, he had the first of many disagreements with Göring. Hitler, with an eye to Britain's rapidly expanding bombing force, ordered Göring to devote sixty billion Reichsmarks to the building up of Germany's bombing force. Kammhuber and the rest of Luftwaffe High Command knew that such overnight expansion was impossible. German industry could not produce the materials fast enough. They told Göring so, presenting Kammhuber's alternate plan for twenty billion Reichsmarks at one-third of the production levels. Göring looked at them and said, "The Führer's program has to be carried out as planned. You will somehow meet the quotas." It was an invitation to lie.

Kammhuber had had enough of Göring and he requested active duty. He was sent to France, quickly shot down and captured. After France fell, he was released and sent back to Germany for Luftwaffe service. Erhard Milch, always a backer, put him in charge of coordinating Germany's air defense.

The result of Kammhuber's efforts was the XII Fliegerkorp—a dedicated night-fighter force—and the Kammhuber Line, which linked the three spokes of air defense—flak, fighters, and searchlights—in a single integrated defense system. The first spoke was made up of the fighter forces, which were organized into "boxes" (*Himmelbetten*, or sky beds, in German) stretching along the German coast.[7] Each had a radius of about twenty-two miles and was linked with a Würzburg mirror, which covered the twenty-two-mile range and could follow a bomber in every direction. From the ground, vast searchlights illuminated the darkened sky. When a bomber entered a box, the night control officer would use the radio to direct the fighters to exactly the point where the bomber crossed over the searchlight. From that moment, the bomber had three minutes to identify and engage his target. The whole thing would be over in ten minutes. The bomber would be spinning toward the ground or he would be through the box. Fighters did not pursue bombers that made it through.

The next obstacle was a chain of searchlights further east, about eighteen miles deep, stretching from the Skagerrak Strait (between Norway and Denmark) and ending in northeastern France. The searchlights were themselves divided into quadrants made up of three sections of nine sixty-inch searchlights. In the center was a main searchlight. The center light and those around it rotated 360 degrees in unison. Behind the wall of light, the squadrons of fighters (*Helle Nachtjagd*) were waiting. It was a massive, unprecedented, co-ordinated death trap, waiting for word from Schwabedissen.

12:30 A.M., RAF BOMBER STREAM OVER THE NORTH SEA

At about 12:30 A.M., Jack's flight engineer climbed to the back of his plane. He took out a stopwatch, which would allow him to throw down the bundles every sixty seconds exactly. Around him, seven hundred other flight engineers were doing the same. They would continue to do so for the next two hours, as the planes flew to Hamburg and back, stopping only on the outward flight once they were sixty minutes away from the city.

At half past midnight, the pathfinders had the German coast—and thus the Kammhuber Line—in their sights. They approached it, waiting for the flak and the fighters. Their breath quickened, and their hands gripped the controls more tightly. From the back, the rear gunner's eyes strained against the darkness, trying to pick up enemy fighters. The coast was closer. Three . . . two . . . one . . . and . . . Nothing.

The pathfinders streaked through the Kammhuber Line unimpeded. Hundreds of bombers followed them. Whereas dozens upon dozens of Luftwaffe fighters might normally attack the bomber stream, only a handful—drawn by the pathfinders' first flares—were there tonight. They only managed one "kill," an unfortunate Lancaster.

12:30 A.M., STADE

Schwabedissen and his officers watched the screen intensely.[8] Scores of white dots—bombers they had known about since 11 P.M.—were making their way across the screen. Radio operators relayed their positions to Luftwaffe fighters, who had already engaged. Then, suddenly, something incredible happened. The tail of the bomber stream began to expand while the front continued to surge forward. The bombers seemed to be reproducing themselves. Schwabedissen screamed at the staff: "What in the hell is going on here?" But they had no better idea than he did. Down below, radio operators patched through calls to radar stations throughout the northwest; they were all told the same story: there were not hundreds of bombers, but thousands, and seemingly more by the minute. Some radar screens showed general "fuzz" rather than distinct blips, as if a solid wall of bombers, several miles wide, was moving across Germany.[9]

In the air, the confusion was total. German fighters followed instructions, only to find themselves not in the middle of the bomber stream but rather in empty sky without an airplane in sight. Others were ordered to turn to port, then starboard, then port again with dizzying speed. Others still were sent around in endless circles. As one Luftwaffe pilot said, "The radio reports kept contradicting themselves. Now the enemy was over Amsterdam and then suddenly west of Brussels, and a moment later they were reported far out to sea. . . . [In a typical exchange, a comrade suddenly shouted] 'Tommy flying at us at great speed. Distance decreasing . . . 2000 yards . . . 1500 . . . 1000 . . . 500 . . . gone."[10] They were fighting phantoms.

At a few minutes before midnight, the pathfinders were leading the bombers up the Elbe and toward the outlines of the city. As the planes approached, the crews grew nervous. Despite the promising words about Window, veterans of even a few raids were all too familiar with the violent ritual. The regular, steady drone of the engines would be interrupted by gunfire, searchlights, and the sound of a nearby bomber going down. Planes not hit by flak would be "coned" and had at most a few seconds to go into a deep dive before the flak guns took aim. The dive itself was no guarantee of salvation. The searchlights sometimes followed the plane down. Other times, pilots shook the searchlights only to be trapped in the dive. Unable to pull up, they crashed into the ground. Some crashed into another bomber, handing the Germans two kills rather than one.

Thanks to Window, that night was different. For the first time in the bombing war, bomb aimers could do their job without mortal fear of the flak that was spraying wildly but aimlessly around them.

At exactly 12:57 A.M.—right on schedule—two Lancasters of 83 and 97 squadrons and one Halifax of 405 Squadron opened their shoots. Pilot Officer A. C. Shipway of 405 called out, "It is about time that someone started this party." All three planes dropped the first line of high explosives, and the Halifax marked the city with yellow target indicators, which guided other aircraft to the aiming point. The next wave of pathfinders dropped more yellow markers and white flares.[11] The yellow target indicators guided the other pathfinders into the city, and the white told them whether to drop their red indicators.[12] Within a few minutes, thirty-nine yellow and red target indicators were cascading down over Hamburg, forming a rough rectangle over the city center.[13] These markers served as maps for the incoming bombers.

Minutes later, some seven hundred bombers swept in over the northeast of the city,[14] over Elmsbüttel and into the city center, toward Altona (southwest of the center) and Wandsbek (northeast of the center).

They were aiming for the middle of the city, near the Rathaus and Alster, at a point exactly above a church—St. Nicholas, the city's highest peak. The goal on July 25, 1943, was to drop the bombs within 3 square miles of the twelfth-century church, destroying a pear-shaped area covering 3 miles by 1.5.[15] It was the center of administrative, cultural, and residential Hamburg.

The first high explosives landed southwest of the city center just before 1 A.M. They were designed, in the words of one Bomber command veteran, to "open up" the houses. The bombs hit the roofs of the residential areas below within a few seconds. The high explosives sliced into the houses. Shingles, dust, brick, sometimes cabinets, beds, tables, children's toys, and whatever else was in the flat followed the bomb down with a deafening crash. Seconds after drawing the house into itself, the process was reversed: the bomb detonated. Within the blink of an eye, shingles became dust; wood, brick, stone, and—if the house was occupied—body parts exploded outward in vast arcs in all directions. The house either collapsed or stood gutted. The shattered roofs, blown-out windows, and debris were manna for the incendiary bombs. Fires spread along the floors and walls, and out the windows. Very quickly, entire neighborhoods were ablaze. It was, an RCAF aircrew later noted, "a volcano belching fire and smoke."[16]

As the pathfinders were coming in over the city, Hamburg's defenses sprung into action. Searchlights came on, and the great flak guns began to fire. Hamburg had among the most extensive air-raid defenses in the Reich: fifty-four heavy flak batteries, twenty-six light ones, and twenty-two searchlights.[17] But they were to no avail. Window was reaching the peak of its effectiveness. Radar controllers could provide no information on the incoming planes; searchlight operators flashed their lights randomly across the sky or pointed them directly upward, and the guns sprayed barrages of flak indiscriminately, in all directions and in none. Experienced pilots reaching the city could not believe it: they were not caught in searchlight cones, which all but promised death, and suffered no targeted bursts of flak.

The bombing of Hamburg occurred in six waves. The first five waves lasted eight minutes, during which more than a hundred planes dropped a line of bombs on Hamburg.[18] Each high explosive was followed by a quick, violent flash and the delayed echo of the explosion. The 4000-pound bombs created a still larger, though slower, explosion. Between these flashes were thousands of twinkles, as incendiary bombs set the houses, clothes, cars, and, in some cases, people on fire. In the last wave, sixteen planes finished the raid at 1:50 A.M. Five minutes later, a straggler, a main force Halifax that would no doubt have been brought down had German defenses been operating, passed over the city and dropped its load. Then, an intact bombing formation turned from the city, banked north, and flew home. It was over.

The raid had been one of the easiest in the RAF's history. Of the 791 bombers that left for Hamburg, a handful failed to return. Mechanical problems led forty-five to turn back before reaching the German coast, another two jettisoned their load just inside Germany (dropping a bomb load anywhere on German soil constituted an operational flight), and five crashed. Two Halifaxes—from 51 and 158 squadrons—strayed badly off course and were brought down by German fighters well north of Hamburg. The men were on their first and second operations, respectively. Their fate was all too typical of young, inexperienced aircrews; many would fly over Germany only once. The final three were brought down over Hamburg. German fighters shot down a Halifax in the second wave and a Stirling in the third—the Luftwaffe's only successes over Germany's second most heavily guarded city. Only one member of each crew survived. The third plane came down when a Stirling dove to escape a searchlight and crashed into another plane head-on. The second aircraft went into a deep dive and crashed into the ground, but the pilot of the Stirling, Flying Officer Geoff Turner, brought his plane safely back to England, despite having lost a four-foot section of the plane's starboard wing. After he touched ground in England, he had less than two months to live: Turner and his entire crew were shot down on a September 23, 1943, raid on Mannheim.

15

UNDER THE BOMBS

In the early evening of July 24, 1943, Gerhard Lange, a soldier on leave, was at his parents' spacious flat in Wandsbek, a suburb northeast of the city center. He was not a Hamburger by birth, and was one of few Germans who could view Hamburgers as southerners. Gerhard was born in Flensburg, now Germany's northernmost city, close to Denmark, but moved to Hamburg in 1933. The transition from Flensburg to Hamburg coincided with Gerhard's own transition from childhood to boyhood. Although his youth would be lived out against the backdrop of the Nazi period, Gerhard was not by inclination political and he took little notice of events around him. Nazi flags flew from public buildings and some private homes, and there were SS marches, but these did not mean much to Gerhard. He would later march too, when he belatedly and under teachers' pressure joined the Hitler Youth, but it had hardly more significance to him than school exercise. He gave almost no thought to the "Jewish question," and though a Jewish boy lived on his street, Gerhard neither knew him well nor noticed his disappearance. He was nine years old when the Nazis came to power, and the next few years were occupied by typical boyhood concerns: school lessons, friends, and, later, girls. When war broke out, his parents were only grateful that he was too young to be called up. However, his time came soon enough, when, in 1943, he was sent to France. His parents did their best to remain hopeful and optimistic, but Gerhard was haunted by a peculiar dream. In it, the war was over; Germany had lost, and he was in captivity in England.

———

Shortly before 1 A.M. that night, Gerhard was in the cellar of the apartment block in which he and two other families lived. At 1:02 A.M., the raid officially began. The bombers opened their hatches, and the first line of high explosives was dropped. The bombs hit the roofs of the residential areas below within a few seconds, tearing them open.

After a few minutes, the sound of the bombs became more intense, and it was possible to identify them by the piercing howl and the change in air pressure. As Gerhard and his family sat in the cellar, it was clear that the bombs were coming closer. The house shook with each one. As he huddled with the others, Gerhard thought of the difference between a soldier and a civilian: the soldier meets his death head-on, in the open; a civilian hides from it in his own coffin. Then, a pattern in the bombing emerged. One whistle and then an explosion; another, this one closer; a third, and then a fourth. Each whistle was louder, and each explosion was closer. A line of bombs had been dropped as the plane passed over the neighborhood. Then, suddenly, there was silence. People in the cellar began to scream. Intuitively, collectively, they knew that the next bomb was theirs. Women hugged their children; wives grasped their husbands' hands. The high explosive hit the house with a deafening explosion. It cut through brick and mortar; the walls caved in and the ceiling came down. Everything was dark.

Gerhard felt something on his legs. He tried to move them, but they were pinned. He opened his eyes and made out the blurry outlines of a beam above his head. He had crouched under a door frame. It had held as it fell with the house and landed at an angle that created a gap beneath it. Without that, the beam would have almost certainly crushed Gerhard's head. He heard no one. The only sound was of wood creaking and dust settling. He called out to his parents: "Mama? Papa?" There was no reply. He called again, but still nothing.

Gerhard turned his head and could make out the outlines of the garden. The door frame created a gap in the rubble. Carefully, he pulled his legs out from under the debris, squeezed through the gap, and stepped onto the grass. It was covered with dust, glass, smashed stone, and dozens of paper strips. Dazed, he stumbled toward the street and ran. He continued for five or ten minutes. Then he felt nothing.

He was in the air for a second, and then landed on raw soil. He had fallen into a bomb crater. He climbed out on his hands and knees, pulled himself up, and continued running. There was fire everywhere, and he no longer had his bearings. Finally, a mile or so from his house, he came across a police station. Screaming, he burst through the door. Hysterical, he spoke of the bombing, his house, his parents. The guard on duty had already heard enough horror stories that evening and was unimpressed. Without listening to more, he sent Gerhard downstairs to see a doctor. After a quick look, the doctor advised him to lie down. Gerhard protested as he did so but then passed out.

Sometime later, he woke up. Dizzy, he got up and spoke to the doctor, who allowed him to go home. As he stepped out of the station, he could hardly believe his eyes. The city was covered in black clouds. The streets were filled with rubble, bombed-out streetcars, and people moving aimlessly. He walked toward his house, averting his eyes from the cityscape. The house was gone. In its place was a smoldering heap of rubble. He saw a neighbor standing in the street and asked him what had happened. The man told him: "They're all dead. Nobody got out." All eight had died there. They were crushed, or asphyxiated. They died quickly, or slowly. They knew nothing of their fate, or they spent hours trying to move under slabs of brick and mortar before allowing death to take them. Nobody knows the details.

Throughout the night, in street after street, small scenes of horror played themselves out. Karl-Heinz Alfcis lived a few streets away from Gerhard in the Schlosstrasse, but he and Gerhard did not know each other.[1] All Hitler Youth had the job of heading for the street as soon as the bombing stopped. The work was often gruesome. One such boy, fourteen-year-old Hans Pauels, was clearing rubble in Aachen after a 1944 bombing raid. Suddenly, the stones felt lighter. He looked down and realized he was holding his school friend's head. His friend's entire family—seven people—had died in the bombing.[2]

Back in Hamburg, Karl-Heinz left his house, walked west along the Schlosstrasse toward Wandsbeker Allee. He then turned north, following it to the Wandsbek Markt. When he reached the Markt, he saw the lovely Christuskirche (now a nondescript 1950s construction) in flames. On the street across from it, he saw small, black packages. They were people: the charred and shrunken bodies of those who had run into the street to escape the flames. They had sunk into the asphalt, burned to death, and cooked.

Another boy, Otto Mahncke, made his way through bombed Hamburg in search of his parents.[3] On the corner of Elbstrasse and Marienstrasse, he saw a woman screaming and pointing at her burning house: "My baby, my baby!" The child had burned to death. When he reached the Schaarmarkt, near the

Michaeliskirche, he saw sailors pulling people out of a burning house, passing them down to safety from balcony to balcony. As Otto watched, the house collapsed and the sailors fell into the rubble. They and those left in the house were crushed.[4]

A few blocks further, at the Michaelis shelter, Otto saw hundreds of people seeking refuge; many were wounded and dying. When he could not find his parents there, he made his way back to the Grossneumarkt. He looked up at one of the many burning buildings. An old woman was calling for help at the third-floor window of a half-wooden house. Her room was on fire. Otto and others ran for a ladder that would reach the third floor. Several men tried to climb it, but the heat kept them from making it beyond the second floor. The woman looked down at them with wild, desperate eyes. The fire climbed up her body and she fell back into the room.

Another Hamburger was returning to his city as a soldier: Herbert Heinicke was making his way back by train from East Prussia. He disembarked at unscathed Bergedorf and caught a slow-moving lorry into Hamburg. Along the way, they stopped a boy of about twelve, carrying a rucksack, to see if he needed help. Herbert then recognized what was sticking out of the rucksack: a head. The boy said it belonged to his brother.

Although the raid was at best a modest success, Hamburg would burn for days. Fifteen minutes after the first bombs hit, the telephone link between the area's fire station and the central station was knocked out, and the bulk of Hamburg's firemen responded to calls from the southeast of the city, which was suffering only relatively mild effects of scattered bombing.[5] Wandsbek's beleaguered firemen had no backup, and their call for help only reached those working in the east hours later. At their peak, the fires created a wall between the Reeperbahn and Altona station, a distance of more than one mile.[6] Before they died down, the fires had a circumference of sixteen miles, and fifty-four miles of streets in western Hamburg were in flames.[7] In the city center, the Rathaus had been hit, and St. Nicholas Church was burning. The house in which Johannes Brahms was born, in the Speickstrasse, was rubble. Twenty high explosives had hit the Hagenbeck zoo, and there were more than one hundred dead and dying animals. Fifteen hundred people were dead. And the bombing had only begun.

The next major raid was the firestorm, and the end of Hamburg.

AFTER HAMBURG

16

SPEER'S NIGHTMARE

By mid-1943, as the air war went worse and worse for Germany, Speer assumed more and more of his rival's power. In February 1942, he had also taken over all of Todt's responsibilities. In the days after Todt's death, Speer saw off attempts by Ley, Funk, and Bormann to limit his power. On February 18, Speer persuaded Milch (who coordinated aircraft production), Funk (Minister for Economic Affairs), and representatives of the country's leading industries to countersign a document granting him "a mandate for full authority" to direct armaments production.[1] That left only Göring. When Speer went to see him, Göring was seething with anger over the signatures, which he claimed wrested responsibility from him and undermined his position and his prestige.[2] Speer was conciliatory and soothing. With feigned sincerity, he assured Göring that he had no intention of reducing the Reichsmarschall's competencies, and ended the meeting by offering what he hoped would seem like a major concession: he, Speer, would perform his duties "within [Göring's] four-year plan." This was, in fact, meaningless; Göring's role as Commissioner of the Four-Year Plan was at most ceremonial without the powers that Todt and, above all, Speer had assumed. But the promise left Göring "deeply satisfied" and he signed the document.[3] In doing so, he signed himself out of industrial and armaments policy, and tied his star to an air war that was already going badly.

That was spring 1942. In summer 1943, Speer was in front of the Central Planning committee (*die Zentrale Planung*), an overarching body presided over by Speer and Milch that coordinated raw-material supplies across the German economy.[4] That morning, Speer had been briefed on what had happened in

Hamburg: smashed water pipes, hurricane winds, cyclone-like firestorms, blazing asphalt, and incinerated civilians. As he reported to the committee, the words he spoke seemed to be a vindication of Harris and his whole bombing strategy. "If the air-raids," intoned Speer, "continue at the present scale, within three months we shall be relieved of a number of questions we are at present discussing. We shall simply be coasting downhill, smoothly and relatively swiftly. . . . We might as well hold the final meeting of [the] Central Planning [committee] in that case."[5]

Over the next few days, apocalyptic reports continued to come in. Repeated telegrams were sent by Kaufmann, begging Hitler to visit the devastated city. He simply refused. Kaufmann then asked Hitler to receive some of the city's more heroic rescue crews; Hitler refused again.[6] Three days after the bombing, Speer went to see Hitler himself. "I told him," Speer wrote after the war, "that armaments production was collapsing and threw in the further warning that a series of attacks of this sort, extended to six more cities, would bring Germany's production to a total halt."[7]

Hitler remained unimpressed. Calmly, he replied to Speer: "You'll sort it out." Speer did. Within days, public transportation in Hamburg was running again and people were getting to work. Far from being demoralized, Hamburg's workers turned up for their shifts in the days and weeks after the bombings, and they worked with an enthusiasm and determination that left Speer speechless.[8] This is not surprising. Like James Joyce's snow, Harris's bombs rained down on both the living and the dead, the innocent and the guilty, the collaborator and the resister. When one survivor took the hand reaching out from the rubble of a bombed house, he did not ask if it belonged to a Nazi. Even those with the most reason to hate the Germans were not immune: in some cases, hidden Jews went through the streets helping bomb victims. The bombing made Hamburgers, always a proud people, love their wounded city more than ever. Within five months, the most important factories had reached 80 percent of pre-bombing production levels.

Speer nonetheless had reason to worry. Since becoming armaments minister in 1942, he had made relentless efforts to increase Germany's industrial production. He created the Central Planning committee for overseeing German industrial production, rationalized steel and coal production, and linked the production of arms with the production of their component parts.[9] The achievement was near-miraculous, but it came at a price: bottlenecks, particularly in ball bearings production. A sustained attack on ball bearings factories would slow and, in the worst case, halt the growth of industrial production. Surveying the Axis Powers' industrial landscape, Speer sketched out the scenario that would lead to Germany's defeat. It had three steps.

1. In a coordinated U.S.–British bombing, the Allies would attack all ball bearings factories—Schweinfurt, Steyr, Erkner, Cannstatt, as well as targets in France and Italy—simultaneously.
2. The Allies would press their advantage by repeating these attacks every two weeks for another six to eight weeks.
3. From October 1943, as the Germans attempted to rebuild, the Allies would launch two large and successive attacks every eight weeks.

If this happened, he thought, industrial production would plummet in two months, and be brought to a standstill within four. Speer and his ministry were gripped with the fear that the Allies had developed a new strategy of repeatedly bombing five or six essential precision targets.

Two weeks after the Hamburg raid, Speer's nightmare came true.

On August 16, 1943,[10] the men of the U.S. 351st Bomb Group were having beers at the RAF base at Polebrook, in Northamptonshire. They had only two each, since they might need clear heads in a few hours' time. As the beer was "bitter"—a flat, warm, and accurately named drink most Americans could not abide—few were tempted to drink more. They were in bed by 10 P.M.

A few hours later, they were awoken. The orderlies screamed at them, and the exhausted men got out of bed and made their way to the mess, where they met good and bad news. The good news was that they were being served fresh rather than powdered eggs, and an unusually large number of cooks were there to prepare them to the men's liking. The bad news was that this could only mean one thing: they were being sent out over Germany.

At 2 A.M., in bomb groups across England, the men went to their briefings. It followed the same ritual everywhere, and used the British format. Each briefing took place in a classroom-like venue, with a large, covered map of Europe at the front. Once the men had taken their seats, the briefing officer removed the cover. Some men groaned and put their heads in their hands; others cursed, and a few even stood up and shouted abuse. The marker showed a route from England deep into Germany, deeper than anyone had flown before, and then on to Africa. One formation was to execute a precision raid over aircraft factories at Regensburg; another was to bomb Schweinfurt. And they were to have no fighter cover. The bombings were undertaken under a June 3, 1943, joint directive, which updated POINTBLANK: in the light of the threat posed by the Luftwaffe to plans for invading the Continent, Bomber Command and the Eighth were to concentrate on targets associated with the aircraft and ball bearings industries.[11] The briefing ended, the crews hurried to their planes, and they and ground support began bombing up. By around 5 A.M., the force was ready to take off.

The word was to be given by Eighth Bomber Command headquarters, fifty miles from the nearest bomber base. There, its head, Fred Anderson, was studying the weather reports. Born in Kingston, New York, Anderson had attended flying school at Kelly Field in Texas in the late 1920s. He was widely known as a fiercely aggressive commander who looked with an admiring eye to Harris's techniques. Commenting on the Eighth's engagement with the Luftwaffe, he once said that "if it comes up here where we get one of those damn cities that we can see and have our force on . . . there won't be a damn house left."[12] Frustrated with the slow pace of the U.S. bombing war,[13] the ever-impatient Arnold had forced Eaker to take on Anderson as the new commander of the Eighth's Bomber Force in Europe. He had arrived in July, and Schweinfurt was his first test. Anderson was in phone contact with the two commanders in charge of the missions: Brigadier General Williams (of 1st Bombardment Wing, responsible for Schweinfurt) and Colonel Curtis LeMay (of 4th Bombardment Wing, responsible for Regensburg). Of the two men, LeMay would become by far the most infamous, viewed as a ruthless airman who rained fire down on Japan. But he also possessed a basic humanity. In the spring of 1938, he had heard about a military plane that crashed into a crowd at a Colombian air show, killing sixty people and mutilating many others. That night, he dreamt of the time his brother had fallen from a barn roof onto a pile of broken bottles. Blood spurted everywhere; people began screaming. A few days later, LeMay, on the start of a South American tour, attended the funeral of the Colombian victims. Viewing the weeping relatives, he remembered airmen who had died in training missions. LeMay thought "how very much alike we are after all."[14] Similarly, speaking of Germany, he said that "if you're cursed with any imagination at all, you have at least one quick horrid glimpse of a child lying in bed with a whole ton of masonry tumbling down on top of him; or a three-year-old girl wailing for *Mutter . . . Mutter . . .* because she has been burned. Then you have to turn away if you intend to retain your sanity."[15]

On August 17, 1943, as LeMay awaited the order, the skies above Anderson at headquarters were clear, but clouds covered all of the bomber bases. Almost four hundred planes were to take off in rapid succession, and doing so through clouds would inevitably lead to collisions. Anderson told LeMay and Williams to wait an hour. An hour later, things hardly looked better. Anderson rang LeMay and Williams and asked them if he could wait another hour. LeMay told him that he could not: the Regensburg force had to fly on from Germany to North Africa and needed to land before daylight. The most he could offer, LeMay told Anderson, was thirty minutes.

At 6:40 A.M., the weather had cleared somewhat, but not much. Anderson had to decide whether to call off the whole thing, send up LeMay's force alone, or take the risk and send up both forces together. None of the options was appealing. Sending them together would lead to crashes. Delaying the mission might be career suicide, as Arnold was demanding results. And sending only one of the forces would mean that Regensburg's chief advantage—as a diversionary raid to draw off Luftwaffe fighters, thereby allowing the other planes to bomb Schweinfurt more effectively—would be lost. Under enormous pressure, Anderson made his call: he ordered LeMay to prepare for immediate takeoff, and had Williams delay. LeMay put down the phone and ran to the car standing outside his headquarters. The car sped along the fourteen miles between Eighth Bomber Command's headquarters and Snetterton Heath, the base of the 96th Bomb Group. When he arrived, LeMay got out of the car in his flying clothes and his driver carried his parachute and kit to the plane. Archie Olds, who had intended to fly the lead aircraft, asked LeMay, "What in the hell are you doing here?" LeMay was there to lead the mission.

Under heavy fighter attack between Antwerp (when the escort fighters left the bombers) and the Alps, LeMay pushed on. Emergency hatches, exit doors, prematurely opened parachutes, airplane parts, and bodies shot past them in the slipstream.[16] LeMay soldiered on. The target was hit successfully and Regensburg itself was untouched. LeMay's force suffered high losses—twenty-four aircraft, or 16 percent of the planes that went out—but he remained undaunted. "We have never turned back from a target and never will be turned back from the target," he said a few weeks after the raid.[17]

A full four hours after LeMay's bombers had taken off for Regensburg, some two thousand men of the 1st Bombardment Wing were still grounded. They had been awake for eleven hours and waiting in and around their planes for five. A mission had never before been delayed so long. "Perhaps the thing that still remains most vivid of the memory of that long and arduous day," one veteran later wrote, "was the awful wait as take-off was postponed again and again. If there be a limit to human endurance of that sort of thing, we must have approached it that day."[18]

Two hours later, LeMay's bombers were crossing the English coast and flying over the North Sea. At 12:30 P.M., German radar picked them up. At the Dutch coast, they were met by eight squadrons of Spitfires that would accompany them to Antwerp, fifteen minutes away. The Americans loved the Spitfires. They were often flown by Poles, who—motivated by an intense hatred for the Germans—were particularly aggressive. Regulations at the time told the Americans to treat *any* plane that turned toward their formation as an enemy. But if the Poles saw a Luftwaffe fighter in or on the other side of an American formation, they would come straight at it. Wiggling their wings, they would blast right through the formation to hunt the Germans down.[19]

At Antwerp, American P-47s met them and flew with them until Eupen. At 2:10 P.M., the head of the bomber force passed Eupen. One had already been shot down, and several more had to turn back. But the bulk of the force was on its way to Schweinfurt, fifty minutes away. They had, however, reached the limits of their escort range, and from Eupen they had to continue alone.

Wilbur Klint of the 303rd Bomb Group was the co-pilot in one of the B-17s. He had flown his first mission the day before, as part of an American raid on the le Bourget airport at Paris. As the bombing formation came toward the target, a small number of fighters turned on them. As they opened machine-gun fire, the wings lit up, and looked like long neon tubes. The formation blasted past the fighters with no difficulty. "We were young and confident," Wilbur observed six decades later, "and I thought, *This is a piece of cake.*"

Schweinfurt would be anything but. At Eupen, Wilbur watched the P-47 escort fighters turn away. They were on their own. Almost immediately, pilots in the leading aircraft made out black dots coming toward them, seemingly straight on. They were German Luftwaffe fighters, dozens of them, bearing down on the B-17s. Within seconds, the Germans were all over them. They flew straight at the Americans, all guns blazing. Out for blood, the fighters attacked mercilessly. They fired upside down. They fired as they did mid-air rolls, bearing down on the B-17s. American pilots saw dozens of aircraft sailing right at them and then, at the last second, diving and shooting past. "I witnessed," a waist gunner in the 384th Bomb Group later reported, "something that mankind will never see again . . . a parachute invasion of Germany. There were planes in flat spins, planes in wide spins. Planes were going down so often that it became useless to report them."[20] The attacks would come in waves, every ten minutes or so. A group of fighters would finish their attack, land to refuel, and come back up again. "They kept coming and coming and coming," reported one navigator, "and we still had miles to go before the target."[21]

The bombers pressed on. Ineffectively trying to dodge the incoming fighters, they absorbed round after round of bullets from the front and flak from below. Flaming bombers fell away on all sides. By the time they reached the city's three ball bearings factories, thirty-two bombers had been lost. The remaining 298 began bombing at 4 P.M. local time, unloading 265 tons of high explosives and 115 tons of incendiaries on the factories and, in some cases, the surrounding neighborhoods.

It was a beautiful, clear day when Wilbur's B-17 reached Schweinfurt. Still under fighter attack, the crew approached the target area. As they turned at the initial point where all of the bombers began their bomb runs, the flak guns opened. Shells began exploding all around and shrapnel began ripping holes in the fuselage. As it did, the bomb bays opened. The lead bomber dropped his bombs, and the B-17s behind him followed.

The moment the group was out of flak range, the German fighters were back. Under heavy Luftwaffe attack, the Americans flew north out of Schweinfurt, banked west, and continued on to Eupen and the waiting Spitfires. By the time they reached England, they had lost thirty-six heavy bombers, a staggering casualty rate of 20 percent. The Schweinfurt raid shook American confidence.

They had paid a high price, but had exacted a heavier toll. The Americans were only able to drop thousand-pound bombs (the British had 4000-pound bombs by this point) and one-third of the bombs missed their targets and landed on houses. Nonetheless, the destruction caused Germany's ball bearings production to fall by 38 percent. Hitler was furious, and he placed the blame squarely on Hans Jeschonnek, the Luftwaffe's Chief of Staff. The next day, Jeschonnek shot himself, leaving a note stating that Göring should not attend the funeral; the Reichsmarschall did anyway. The day after the raid, on August 18, Schweinfurt was at its most vulnerable. The Luftwaffe had lost forty-seven fighters in the previous battle and would be less able to defend the city. The American bombing had blown off factory roofs, collapsed the upper floors, and punched great gaping holes. The ball bearings machines on the ground floor were exposed.[22] That night, Speer waited for news of the follow-up RAF raid. It never came.

The British Air Staff had been pressuring Harris to bomb Schweinfurt throughout late 1943, and continued to do so for months after the raid.[23] "It is essential," Norman Bottomley, Deputy Chief of Air Staff, wrote to Harris on December 23, 1943, "that the attempt to achieve within the time available the maximum destruction of the major built-up areas in Germany should not be allowed to prejudice the implementation of the Joint Anglo-American policy of employing the night bomber force whenever possible for the destruction of vital centres associated with . . . vital industries, e.g. ball-bearing and fighter assembly plants; these industries have been accorded the highest priority in the combined bomber offensive plan. . . . Your night bomber forces would make the greatest contribution by completely destroying those vital centres which could be reached by day only at a heavy cost; examples are Schweinfurt, Leipzig and centres of twin-engined fighter industry." Drawing on an intelligence report, Bottomley continued, "whereas the German people feared the night attacks, Hitler and the German High Command feared the daylight precision attacks on individual factories. Hitler openly boasted that he could, by means of his party organisations, control the morale of the population from some considerable time. . . . The Air Staff," Bottomley added, "must take a somewhat less confident view than [you do] of the possibility of causing the enemy to capitulate by reason of area attacks alone . . ."[24] Bottomley was third in the chain of command after Portal and the Vice Chief of Air Staff, and the man from whom, in Harris's words, "on policy and strategy I take my instructions."[25] You would not have known it. In his reply, Harris wrote: "Hitler's record as a prophet is not such as to inspire confidence. . . . It is surely impossible to believe that an increase by more than one half of existing devastation [through city bombing] within four months could be sustained by Germany without total collapse."[26]

In the days after the American raid, Harris responded with delaying tactics, finding one excuse after another not to bomb Schweinfurt.[27] On August

18, it was the weather. Harris sent his bombers to destroy the V-2 factories at Peenemünde instead. In a tightly executed attack, three waves of bombers hit the plants. Sixty-one planes from 6 Group (formed from RCAF crew in January) made up one-half of the third wave, and the lion's share of the losses. A full 20 percent of the crews dispatched would not return—a figure four times the maximum acceptable loss rate.[28]

The concentration/labor camp, Dora, next to the facility was also hit by stray bombs, killing some five hundred forced laborers. Germany's V-2 production was knocked back by six months. It was an important hit, but the V-2s were—and always would be—less important than ball bearings. They would prove an ineffective terror weapon when they were finally produced and, more importantly, without ball bearings there would have been no V-2s, because there would have been no war. Once again, luck was on Speer's side. LeMay's Regensburg raid, a tactically more successful attack with a lower casualty rate, had diverted airplanes that may have added to the destruction at Schweinfurt. And the RAF did not follow up, not on August 18, August 19, or on any other night in 1943. "We barely escaped," Speer wrote, "a further catastrophic blow."

Speer immediately got to work on recovering from Schweinfurt. He gave brief thought to relocating the factories, but moving them would have held up production for three to four months.[29] He ordered his men instead to patch up Schweinfurt as best they could, and began to draw on Germany's reserves. Within eight weeks, those reserves were gone. The few ball bearings produced were carried—often in rucksacks—from what was left of the Schweinfurt factories to the assembly line each night.[30] Each day, Speer listened for the bombers and worried about Berlin-Erkner, Cannstatt, and Steyr. "In those days we anxiously asked ourselves how soon the enemy would realize that he could paralyze the production of thousands of armaments plants merely by destroying five or six relatively small targets."[31] Instead, the British "continued [their] indiscriminate attacks upon [German] cities."[32]

No good deed goes unpunished. Back in America, Arnold's whole precision bombing project was coming under renewed attack. On August 14, he was at the QUADRANT Conference, a meeting in Quebec of Roosevelt, Churchill, and William Lyon Mackenzie King, along with the Combined Chiefs of Staff, the supreme Anglo-American military authority from early 1942. The main argument was over when the British would commit themselves to invading the

Continent. Arnold had written in a memorandum of record back in May that "it is becoming more and more apparent that the British have no intention of invading France or Continental Europe."[33] Arnold had the impression that Churchill was using an attack on precision bombing to divert attention from the subject of a Continental invasion.[34] This might have been paranoia; some of his evidence came from a conversation between Marshall and Simmons that was overheard by his chauffeur.[35] Arnold was in any case determined to put up a staunch defense of American daylight bombing. He found an unexpected backer in Charles Portal.

On the opening day of the conference, August 14, Field Marshal Sir Alan Brooke, Chief of the Imperial General Staff, summarized the "present situation in the European theatre," and gave the floor to Portal.[36] Exaggerating somewhat, Portal opened with the claim that "the German Air Force was now completely on the defensive . . . [while] the United Nations Air Forces . . . were everywhere on the strategic offensive." Less than a year after pleading with Eaker to join the night offensive, Portal gave the RAF campaign short shrift. "The night offensive," he continued, "is steadily increasing. Radio aids to navigation have proven immensely effective. Certain steps are now being taken to baffle the defences which have resulted in a decrease in casualties from five-to-six percent to only three percent."[37] This out of the way, Portal turned to the Americans: "The daylight bombing—the most important phase of all—is being extraordinarily effective. The first object of POINTBLANK was to knock out the fighter factories and to destroy fighter planes in the air to achieve complete mastery in the air over Germany. The forces available to the Eighth Air Force have done remarkable work but the program is behind schedule for reasons, however, which are quite understandable. The targets are being hit, the enemy aircraft are being shot down and a high percentage of the aircraft are returning safely, but it is a great battle which hangs in the balance."

Arnold saw his opening and jumped in. "It is difficult," he added, "to confine a discussion on the air war to Europe since available resources must be spread between all theaters. Early estimates, based on British experience, of the replacements of men and machines have proved too low in the case of the operations of the Eighth Air Force. . . . There is [also] the problem of war-weary crews. General Eaker has at present some 800 aircraft, but only 400 crews."

Whatever the differences between Arnold and Portal, they were less important than emphasizing the importance of air power in the face of Army, Navy or political opposition. Those differences, in any event, were decreasing by the summer of 1943 as Portal began to lose faith in Harris's area bombing, for precisely the same reason he had earlier lost faith in precision bombing—its failure to deliver results. Picking up from Arnold's points, Portal continued: "The battle against the German fighter force is a vital battle. . . . If the German strength is not checked in the next three months, the battle might be lost. . . . It is impossible," Portal concluded, "to judge the strength which the German fighter forces might obtain by next spring if our attack is not pressed home."

Again and again, Portal came back to the decisive importance of the American daylight campaign. "On the one hand, German fighter strength is stretched almost to breaking point, and in spite of their precarious situation on the Russian and Mediterranean fronts, they have found it necessary to reinforce their fighter forces on the Western Front from these sources. On the other hand, the expansion of German fighter strength is continuing and has increased 13 percent this year. It was hoped that this expansion would by now have been stopped. The Eighth Air Force, who were achieving a great task with their existing resources, believe they can achieve even greater successes if their strength is increased." It was imperative, Portal argued, to ensure a victory in the battle for air supremacy by autumn 1943. Without it, the Germans, "by conservation of their strength and by the development of new methods of defence, might be in an unassailable position by the spring." The key to winning this battle was to put an end to the constant drain on the Eighth's forces: "To achieve our object diversions from the Eighth Air Force should be stopped, loans of aircraft from the Eighth Air Force to other theatres must be returned and the bomber command of the Eighth Air Force must be built up and reinforced to the maximum possible."

Portal drew heavily on a recent report from the British Intelligence Appreciation:

Germany is now faced with imminent disaster if only the presence of POINTBLANK can be maintained and increased *before* the increase in the GAF [German Air Force] has gone too far . . . The *daylight* "Battle of Germany" is evidently regarded by the Germans as of critical importance

and we have already made them throw into it most, if not all, of their available reserves.[38] If we do not now strain every nerve to bring enough force
to bear to win this battle during the next two or three months but are
content to see the Eighth Bomber Command hampered by a lack of
reinforcements just as success is within its grasp, we may well miss the
opportunity to win a decisive victory against the German Air Force which
will have incalculable effects on all future operations and the length of the
war. And the opportunity, once lost, may not recur.

Quoting directly from the British Intelligence Appreciation he circulated,
Portal ended with a ringing endorsement of the American strategy: "The dou-
bling of the German S.E. [single engine] fighter force on the Western front
and the allocation of this increase to Belgium, Holland and Northwest Germany are attributable solely to the development of Allied day bombing of
Germany. The defence of Germany against these attacks has in fact become
the prime concern of the GAF ... There can be no doubt that Germany
regards the defence of the Reich against daylight air attack as of such supreme
importance that adequate support for military operations in Russia and the
Mediterranean has been rendered impossible."

If Arnold arrived at the meeting feeling beleaguered, he left victorious.[39]
Portal's views were accepted without substantial debate. Eisenhower returned
the Eighth's three Bomb Groups of B-24s. Arnold himself set about increasing the number of service personnel in the Allied Air Forces. By December,
forty-five thousand enlisted men and officers would arrive in the United
Kingdom.

After the conference, Arnold traveled to England. He arrived in good
spirits, and took the losses at Schweinfurt in stride. Employing a calculation
that might have served Bomber Command well, he pointed out that a 15 percent loss in one raid was no worse than 5 percent over three.[40] Arnold gathered
two impressions while he was in England.[41] The first was that his B-17s were
taking a beating; in addition to the losses, those that returned had been ravaged by bullets and flak. The second was that the losses were worth it. He
pored over British and American aerial photographs showing extensive damage to German industry. He was particularly impressed with the Schweinfurt
photos. Although the raid was costly, it had inflicted a great deal of damage on
German industry.

A great deal, but not enough. Speer's frantic efforts to secure alternate supplies had not gone unnoticed. By the end of August, Swedish and Swiss sources were sending reports to England. Photo-reconnaissance revealed frenetic repairs at Schweinfurt itself. And ULTRA (intelligence secured using Enigma to decrypt German codes) revealed how worried the Germans were about a follow-up attack and how urgently they were building up their forces.[42] Arnold told Eaker, "I know you'll get to it as soon as the weather permits."[43] Curtis LeMay, for one, was ready to go.

As Arnold and Eaker conferred in High Wycombe, Speer and Milch were at Rechlin am Müritzsee, home of the Air Force Experimental Center. Milch was presenting charts on American and German aircraft production. "What alarmed us most," wrote Speer, "were the figures on the future increase in four-motored daylight bombers. If these figures were accurate, [the U.S. bombing] we were undergoing could be regarded only as a prelude."[44] When asked how much Hitler and Göring knew about the figures, Milch was incensed. He told Speer that he had been trying for months to get Göring to accept an Air Ministry expert report on enemy armaments. Göring refused to look at it. "It was all," Göring said, "enemy propaganda." The Führer had told him so. Speer tried to raise the matter with Hitler after the meeting, but he fared no better. "Don't let them fool you," Hitler replied. "Those are all planted stories. Naturally those defeatists in the Air Ministry fall for them."[45] It was, Speer thought, the same attitude Hitler had taken to 1942 warnings about upcoming RAF raids on German cities, cities that were now rubble.

Göring's (and Hitler's) delusions were again on display in an exchange between General Adolf Galland, head of Germany's fighter command, and the Reichsmarschall.[46] Galland had reported to Hitler that several American fighter planes had been shot down over Aachen. The Americans, in other words, were sending escort fighters deeper into German territory, a development that could spell disaster for the efforts to protect German industry. Hitler relayed the news to Göring, who next saw Galland on the Reichsmarschall's special train, which was to depart for Rominten Heath. Surrounded by his usual store of clothes, jewelry, perfumes, and most likely pilfered art objects, Göring snapped, "What's the idea of telling the Führer that American fighters have penetrated into the territory of the Reich?"

Galland stayed calm. "Herr Reichsmarschall," he replied, "they will soon be flying even deeper."

Göring screamed at him, "That's nonsense! What gives you such fantasies? That's pure and utter bluff!"

Galland looked at him, a long cigar clamped between his teeth, his hat askew, affecting a casual air. "Those," he said, "are the facts, Herr Reichsmarschall. American fighters have been shot down over Aachen. There can be no doubt about it."

Göring wasn't listening. "That is simply not true, Galland. It's impossible."

Galland remained calm. "You might go and check the situation out yourself, sir. The downed planes are at Aachen."

Göring then tried substituting jocularity for truculence. "Come now, Galland," he said, "let me tell you something. I'm an experienced fighter pilot myself. I know what is possible. But I know what isn't, too. Admit you made a mistake."

Galland only shook his head, until Göring, now clearly grasping, said, "What must have happened is that they were shot down much further to the west. I mean, if they were very high in the air when they were shot down they could have glided quite a distance further before crashing."

Galland was deathly still; without moving a muscle, he replied, "*Glided* to the east, sir? If my plane were shot down . . ."

But Göring didn't let him finish. Fuming, he said, "I officially assert that the American fighter planes did not reach Aachen."

Galland tried one last time. "But, sir, they were there!"

Göring finally exploded. In an unintentionally comic replay of his reaction to news of the thousand-bomber raid on Cologne, he screamed, "I hereby give you an official order that they weren't there! Do you understand? The American fighters were not there! Got it?! I intend to report that to the Führer."

Göring stomped off, leaving Galland standing there. Before he was out of earshot, however, he turned and called back menacingly, "You have my official order!"

A thin smile—"unforgettable," according to Speer—crossed Galland's lips, and he replied, "Orders are orders, sir!"

A month later, Speer would learn how vulnerable the German position had become. He was at the East Prussian headquarters going over armaments production with Hitler. Hitler's adjutant, Julius Schaub, interrupted them. "The Reichsmarschall urgently wishes to speak with you. This time he has pleasant news."[47] Hitler left to speak with an almost boyishly giddy Göring. A few minutes later, Hitler came back in good spirits. "Another daylight raid on Schweinfurt ended with a great victory for our defenses." He spoke of downed American bombers littering the German countryside.

On October 14, Wilbur Klint of the 303rd Bomb Group was part of the second wave of bombers that attacked Schweinfurt. His group took off from Molesworth, joined the bombing formation, and flew on to Germany. Just beyond the border, the escort fighters reached the end of their range and pulled off. Then, as Eaker put it, "the Hun sprang his trap."[48] Immediately, a row of single-engine fighters flew at the bombers, firing 20mm cannons and machine guns just before they dived. Then, large formations of twin-engine fighters attacked in waves, firing rockets from underneath their wings. In the meantime, the single-engine fighters had re-formed, and they attacked, this time from all sides. No sooner were they done than the twin-engine fighters re-formed, launching rockets from the front and the back and blasting a single formation until their rockets were expended. "I had no idea the Germans had so many airplanes and so many different types," Klint later said.

American bombers were falling out of the sky left, right, and center. Once a B-17 got into trouble, the pilot—if he had any control at all—would pull off from the formation to avoid a mid-air crash. The bomber was then finished. The fighters would sweep in for the kill. From his cockpit, Klint saw two B-17s hit by rocket fire; they disintegrated. In front and below him was a sea of parachutes. The German attacks, Eaker wrote, "were perfectly timed and coordinated and skillfully executed. . . . One of our combat wings was practically wiped out."[49]

As ever, the surviving bombers pressed on. As Klint approached the target, the fighters were replaced by a barrage of flak. He saw the flash from the first group. After hearing "Bombs away!" he flew on, into the waiting fighters, which continued their attack all the way to the border.

Despite all of the downed bombers on German soil, Speer could not share in Hitler's joy. He asked for a short recess in the conference and left the room to telephone Schweinfurt. He couldn't get through. Communications with all factories were down. Finally, by going through the police, he managed to get on the line one factory foreman who sketched a picture for Speer: a direct hit had shattered machinery, lit the oil baths, and sent fires racing through the buildings. His factory was hardly unique. Armaments production was down 67 percent, almost twice that of the earlier raid.[50] In the darkest hours after the raid, as the Americans were reeling from the loss of sixty bombers, Eaker had bravely told Arnold that "we are convinced that when the totals are struck yesterday's losses will be far outweighed by the value of the enemy materiel destroyed."[51] He was right.

Speer adapted to the crisis quickly. He appointed one of his closest associates, Phillip Kessler (a general manager from industry), as special commissioner for ball bearings production. They managed to import small quantities of ball bearings from Sweden and Switzerland. Factories were ordered to substitute slide bearings for ball bearings. Speer was able to keep production going, though at a sharply reduced level, until the Schweinfurt factories were repaired. His actions were not, however, decisive. "What really saved us," said Speer, "was the fact that from this time on the enemy to our astonishment once again ceased his attacks on the ball-bearing industry."[52]

All of Speer's efforts had in fact been picked up by Air Staff in the UK, who urged Harris to attack Schweinfurt again.[53] Harris of course had no intention of hitting Schweinfurt, but the Americans—mindful of their losses—also paused to regroup. The losses they sustained on the first Schweinfurt raid ruled out a quick follow-up. Instead, the Americans looked to easier targets, and to easier bombing in the run-up to the second Schweinfurt raid. The targets were limited to cities in the western reaches of Germany: Emden (October 2), Bremen (October 8), and Münster (October 10). In the first two raids, the Americans experimented with a new radar technique, H2X. Through a signal under the airplane, H2X produced a rough outline of the earth's surface, distinguishing water, forests, and cities. It allowed the Eighth to bomb through the dense cloud covering Germany in winter. The problem was that the radar could not make out factories. The Americans continued to aim at precision targets, but they were effectively bombing blind.

Then, on the morning of Sunday, October 10, members of the 95th Bomb Group were told that "unlike all previous military and industrial targets attacked . . . today you will hit the center of [Münster], the homes of the working population of those marshalling yards. You will disrupt their lives so completely that their morale will be seriously affected."[54] A young Group Navigator, Captain Ellis Scripture, was "shocked to learn that we were to bomb civilians as our primary target for the first time in the war." Scripture approached the Group commander, Colonel John Gerhart, and said he couldn't fly the mission. Gerhart replied: "Look, Captain, this is war . . . spelled W-A-R. We're in an all-out fight. The Germans have been killing innocent people all over Europe for years. We're here to beat the hell out of them . . . and we're going to do it. . . . You have no option! If you don't fly, I'll have to court-martial you. . . . Any questions?" There weren't. The bombers pasted the center of Münster, leaving seven hundred people dead.

17

THE BATTLE OF BERLIN

On August 19, 1943, Churchill wrote a letter to the Air Ministry. He stated his satisfaction with the Regensburg and Hamburg raids (curiously, as the purpose of the two raids was very different) and urged attacks on Berlin. It was one of several such requests made in 1942 and 1943 by Churchill, who believed that such raids would help—and impress—the Soviets. Portal passed the prime minister's letter to the Vice Chief of Air Staff, Sir Douglas Evill, who conveyed the news to Harris.[1]

Churchill was pushing at an open door. Harris had long viewed Berlin as important, if not key, to the air war against Germany. He had specifically declined follow-up raids on Schweinfurt so that he could preserve his forces for the German capital. He wrote back to Churchill immediately. He wanted to attack Berlin "as soon as the mood wanes." The battle, however, would have to be "prolonged" and would require "40,000 tons of bombs." The load was five times that dropped on Hamburg.

The only problem was that Berlin was not covered by the joint Allied directives, which ordered attacks on aircraft and ball bearings production. These aims had just been reaffirmed at the QUADRANT Conference. Portal wanted to see Harris implement the directive, but he was reluctant to interfere with Harris's role in interpreting the directive as he saw fit. And, in any case, Churchill—whom Harris continued to visit regularly at Chequers—could override any directive.[2]

The Air Ministry was frustrated, above all by Harris but also by what they saw as Portal's indulgence of him. As Sydney Bufton, Deputy Director of

Bombing Operations at the Air Ministry, told Martin Middlebrook after the war:

> Portal showed extraordinary patience, hoping that Harris would con-
> form. There was much correspondence over a long period. Harris
> replied with his tactical reasons why he would not conform with the
> directives, and all the time doing his own thing. We suspected that we
> were being put off but we had nothing cast-iron and, as background,
> Harris had this access to Chequers where he was at least once a week.
> In a way, it was subversive, going behind Portal's back, and in my
> opinion he was thoroughly disloyal to Portal in pursuing his own idea
> of how to win the war.[3]

Yet, even the Air Ministry could not resist the image of German cities consumed by flames. As Bufton admitted, "Hamburg had come like a bolt from the blue. We didn't mind if Harris was able to mount a successful repetition on any industrial area, Berlin or anywhere else, as long as he intended to start toward the specific targets eventually."[4] Among even his critics, Harris had won himself some freedom.

On the evening of August 23, Harris launched the opening raid in the Battle of Berlin. By 10 P.M., more than six hundred bombers were streaking toward Berlin, their bays packed with the bundles of Window that had proved their salvation over Hamburg. When they reached the Kammhuber Line, it seemed to work again. The bomber stream sailed past the boxes and lost only two aircraft, at least one of which fell because of mechanical problems.

At around 12:35 A.M., a Lancaster of 7 Squadron, piloted by Charles Loft-house, was over Berlin. He was one of the pathfinders, whose job it was to mark the city with flares. Then, very suddenly, the dark plane turned bright white. It had been coned. Lofthouse dived, hoping to shake the cone. It didn't work. He jettisoned his flares and tried again to shake the searchlight. Again, no luck. Then a "great bright 'whoosh' of tracer" streamed past the cockpit. He was under fire: "I don't suppose anyone saw the attacking plane; the gunners must have been blinded by the searchlights. This colored tracer just raced by us and the damage was on the port side. The wings and engines were badly hit."

While the engineer frantically tried to put out the engine fire, the naviga-tor, Denis Cayford, bravely asked if he could try crawling out onto the wing to put out the fire there. As this would have been a certain death, Lofthouse said no. He ordered his crew to dump the bomb load and shouted, "Abandon!"

> The flames were very fierce by now, stretching back from each engine, and there was a large hole in the wing between the two nacelles, with flames coming out of it, being beaten back by the airflow. The crew started [jumping through the bomb chute]. The flight engineer put my parachute ready beside me. The wireless op came forward and gave me a thumbs-up to indicate that the boys at the back had gone. Cayford came back at that stage, went back to his "office" [the navigator's bay], and then went forward and out. He told me later that he had come back for a gold signet ring from his girlfriend, which he always took off when flying because it got so cold. That horrified me because I was fighting the controls hard by then, but I managed to get out.[5]

Lofthouse broke his arm as he jumped, and his parachute came down in a tree. He was hanging outside the window of a wooden barrack building, easily visible to anyone inside. The building was used by concentration camp laborers sent to work in the fields and watched over by camp guards. Lofthouse was a POW within seconds. But he was alive, as was—he would learn later—the rest of his crew.

Many others were not so lucky. Flight Lieutenant Kevin Hornibrook's plane, a Halifax in 158 Squadron, was coned as it flew toward the aiming point. Kevin tried for a minute or two to shake it, when the rear gunner shouted, " 'Fighter approaching!' Almost at the same moment, there was a burst of machine-gun fire which we heard striking in the mid-upper area and then we started to burn there."

As Kevin took evasive action, the bomb aimer, Pilot Officer Alan Bryett, went to the mid-upper section of the plane to see if he could put out the fire. As he arrived, he saw the gunner getting out of his turret. He had been shot in the face. Unable to see, covered in blood and bone fragments, he staggered around the back of the plane. The other gunner had also been shot and wasn't moving. Then:

> We were attacked again. I went back to [Kevin]. We had our intercom and he shouted "Don't bail out." But the intercom was very bad and

cracking and I think that some of them only caught the last two words. The wireless operator, the navigator and the flight engineer all went out. . . . One gunner was probably dead, the other probably dying and three men had bailed out, leaving just Kevin and myself.

Kevin struggled with the controls, but the fire had burned through the control cables. The plane went into a sudden dive, "with a terrible screaming sound." The g-force threw Kevin and Alan back against the seats, a few feet from the escape hatch in the nose of the aircraft. Alan later said, "We were going to go down in this bloody plane."

As the plane dived toward the ground at incredible speed, Kevin, struggling against the g-force, grabbed the escape hatch's latch and wrenched it open. Still hanging on, he reached back and got hold of Alan. He pulled him toward the hatch, let himself fall behind him, and pushed him out with his feet. As he did, he said, "I'll follow you."

Alan came out of the plane and almost immediately crashed into a dense forest; Kevin never got out. Alan saw the fires burst up as the plane exploded three or four hundred yards away.

Kevin was a twenty-one-year old Australian with a brother, Keith, a year younger than him and also in Bomber Command. They were the only sons of a Brisbane couple. A year after Kevin died, Keith's plane went missing in operations.

ONE AND A HALF HOURS EARLIER

There were only a few Luftwaffe fighters placed across the Kammhuber Line as the RAF bombing stream approached. They knew, as did Stade, that Window made their radar useless, so they simply waited. A few pilots tried to attack the bombing stream without radar, hoping to identify the bombers visually. One may have managed to take down a Halifax. The others simply waited as the bomber stream flew past. As was their order, they hung back and made no effort to pursue. They knew that something was waiting for the bombers in Berlin.

Over the German capital, hundreds of fighters, including all of the crack crews that had previously been assigned to boxes along the Kammhuber Line, were circling. They had no radar and no contact with ground control. Their only help from below was an agreement from the local flak command to restrict the height of the flak to about twelve thousand feet, so the fighters could circle safely above it, and the support of two hundred searchlights lighting up the Berlin sky.

The searchlights were operated by *Luftwaffenhelfer* (antiaircraft auxiliaries). The young boys, usually fifteen and rarely older than seventeen, were drafted from schools and lived in barracks together. There, they waited for the alarms that called them—before the rest of the city was warned—to the flak guns or searchlights. Werner Schenk, who was a Luftwaffe helper from January 1944 to February 1945, recalled the cadet's typically cheeky Berlin humor. *"Heil Hitler!"* one boy would say; *"Heil du ihn doch!"* (you heal him—playing on the double meaning of *Heil*) another would reply.[6] During one raid on Berlin, antiaircraft fire brought down an Allied bomber. The Luftwaffe helpers saw the parachute coming down and made for it en masse. The airman, who had no doubt heard the stories of airmen being shot by the SS or lynched by furious citizens, could not but have feared for his life. But this time he was descended upon by a horde of grinning boys who could not contain their joy at having arrested an enemy combatant. They were finally real soldiers.[7]

At 12:40 A.M., as planes came in over Berlin, Hans-Werner Mihan was manning a machine gun, but the height of the planes meant that he was a spectator rather than a participant in the battle. He watched the searchlights twist in every direction, trying to cone one of the incoming bombers. Wave after wave of them crossed the city. All around him was the constant sound of blazing flak guns. The ground shook as bombs exploded. Fires and exploding airplanes made the sky shine bloodred. Deadly flak splinters hit the ground around him; he was more afraid of them than of the bombs. "It was," he wrote after the war, "a symphony of hell."

German fighters swept in on the bombers. They were above, below, and around the British, trying to identify individual planes. One was Peter Spoden, flying a Messerschmitt 110:

I had never seen so many aircraft at one time before. There must have been thirty or forty of them. Some were night fighters, but the majority were four-engine bombers. Most of the planes seemed to be flying from south to north, but the tracer was going in every direction. There were searchlights—hundreds of them—and they caused me to lose my bearings. I saw one Lancaster in a steep dive, trying to get out of the searchlights, and another which dived steeply and then reared up and actually looped right over—I swear it. [The battle] was terrible for a kid like me, and I think it must have been just as bad for the British boys. It was the most intensive night battle of the war I ever saw, a terrible inferno, still following me in nightmares in the next decade.

Peter felt paralyzed. His heart was pounding. Then a bomber came directly in view in front of him, caught in the searchlight. From about two hundred yards away, Peter opened fire, aiming at the fuel tanks between the two engines. He scored a direct hit. For two minutes, nothing seemed to happen, then the plane went down. Peter didn't see any parachutes.

Peter's next sighting was a Stirling. Peter fired, but the pilot corkscrewed abruptly and unpredictably, which saved his life. The plane disappeared into the darkness. Peter flew on, and then spotted another Stirling well ahead of him. As he flew toward it, something unexpected happened. The Stirling turned and flew back toward him. Peter fired right into it, scoring a hit. Then, the Stirling dived underneath him. As it did, the tail gunner sprayed bullets into the underside of Peter's Messerschmitt.

I heard them hit my fuselage and a small fire started behind me. I checked with the crew but received no answer; the intercom was not working. When the heat of the fire became unbearable, I shouted, "GET OUT!" four or five times as loud as I could. Then I jettisoned the cockpit canopy and went out myself. It was not easy; I found out later that my left thigh had been hit by a bullet and the bone was broken.

As Peter flew through the air, the crashing machine's tail plane caught him. His stomach was flat against it, his head over its top, and his feet underneath. The angle of the plane meant that he was pinned between the tail plane and the force of the air. For a few minutes, he was trapped there, hurtling toward the ground. He thought he was finished. His plane was coned, and he expected to be strafed by a round of what we now call friendly fire. In fact, the searchlight commander below had recognized Peter's plane as a Messerschmitt and hoped the searchlight would help him. Somehow, Peter managed to free himself from the tailplane, pulled his chute, and passed out.

He landed unconscious in the garden of Grunewalddamm, 69. As he woke up, he felt dull pain all over his body. He looked up to see a crowd of civilians and an SS man. They had mistaken him for an RAF airman and were beating him. He shouted at them in German and they stopped.[8]

The defense technique employed by Peter and the other fighters was called *"Wilde Sau"* (Wild Boar), and it was the brainchild of Hajo Herrmann. Incredibly, Herrmann had never been in a fighter plane; he was a bomber pilot with a long string of operations over the United Kingdom.[9] By early 1943, he had a staff appointment with the Luftwaffe, and he worked on strategies to counter the mounting effectiveness of Harris's bombing campaign. Even before Hamburg, it was clear that the Kammhuber Line was not working; fighter pilots would pick off a few bombers as the bombing stream flew past, but the majority of planes always made it past. When Herrmann was surveying German defense capabilities, two things stood out.[10] The first was that, with the Blitz over, the Luftwaffe had a surplus of trained bombers who were skilled in flying blind. The second was that single-engine day fighters could be produced more quickly and in larger numbers than twin-engine night fighters. From this, Herrmann developed the idea that single-engine fighters should be placed above German cities. Rather than having one shot at the British bombers crossing the Kammhuber Line, they would have many. Over the city, the fires, searchlights, and flares would illuminate the incoming bombers, making them easy targets for multiple attacks by the German fighters. His unit was named Jagdgeschwader Herrmann, but later renamed Jagdgeschwader 300 (JG 300). Herrmann probably did not take to the omen implied by the first title: most Luftwaffe units had been named after dead heroes.[11] The Luftwaffe allowed Herrmann to try out Wild Boar over Cologne. The results were inconclusive, but he was allowed to create a group of thirty fighters and try again.[12]

Three weeks later, after the catastrophe of Hamburg, Herrmann's quirky idea—until then indulged like a German equivalent of Wallis's bouncing bomb—was thrust front and center in Luftwaffe strategy. A few days after the firestorm, a conference of twin-engine commanders was held in Holland. Herrmann presented his idea. Whatever doubts they might have had, the commanders had little choice. Until a new technique was found for responding to Window, both single- and twin-engine fighters would be used in Wild Boar tactics. The Luftwaffe gave the fighters one full Wild Boar practice run, during the August 17, 1943, Peenemünde raid. Despite a clever RAF diversion force of a few Mosquitos that held most of the fighters back, the run was a success for the Luftwaffe and a slaughter for the bombers: forty were shot down that night.[13] The fighters did not save Peenemünde, however. The RAF's costly but successful precision raid destroyed the factory trying to produce Hitler's "wonder weapons," delaying by six months the V-1 (*Vergeltungswaffe-1*, "revenge weapon 1") and V-2 ("revenge weapon 2") rockets that would terrorize London. Regardless, less than a month after Hamburg, the Germans had rendered Window ineffective. The Wild Boar fighters were sent to Berlin. On the first night of the raid, August 23, they killed 298 RAF aircrew, including Kevin Hornibrook.

The next two nights of the Battle of Berlin would go equally badly for Bomber Command. On August 31 and September 1, it lost 333 men—225 died and another 108 were taken prisoner. By contrast, eighty-seven Berliners lost their lives. Only ten out of almost four hundred aircraft managed to bomb Berlin that night; the rest dropped their load on the Brandenburg countryside, south of the capital.

On the night of September 3–4, 130 aircrew died and 10 were taken prisoner. After two more costly raids—on Mannheim, where Bomber Command lost thirty-four bombers, and on Munich, where it lost sixteen—the weather over Berlin worsened. Bomber Command had lost one-third of its four-engined strength and one-quarter of its aircrew in nineteen days. It could not continue; Harris decided to delay the Battle of Berlin until Bomber Command could respond to Wild Boar.

That took almost six weeks. With more heavy bombers, the Lancasters, better radar, and better weather, Harris was again ready to attack the German capital. On November 3, 1943, Harris wrote a letter to the prime minister in which he took stock of the bombing war.[14] Bombing had "virtually destroyed" nineteen cities, including Cologne, Hamburg, Hanover, the Ruhr cities of Düsseldorf, Remscheid, Bochum, Deutz, Krefeld, and Mülheim. The Hanseatic city of Rostock, Charlemagne's Aachen, and the medieval city of Kassel had also gone under.

On October 22, at 8:45 P.M., more than 550 bombers had attacked Kassel. It was a hot, still, and clear night much like the one on which Hamburg was destroyed. The aiming point was the Martinsplatz, right in the center of the city, and the bombers scored a near-perfect hit. Almost two thousand tons of bombs rained down on the city. The bombing was so intense that, on average, two incendiary bombs landed on every square yard. The fires rose further and a firestorm raged. Temperatures reached 1500 degrees Celsius, the winds 100 miles per hour. People struggled against the winds and were pulled into the flames. The oxygen was sucked from the cellars and their inhabitants suffocated and burned. By morning, ten thousand people, 5 percent of Kassel's population, were dead.[15] The Fieseler fighter factory remained untouched.

Along with Berlin, Harris believed that there were some sixty cities (including Leipzig, Dresden, Erfurt, Weimar, Frankfurt, and Munich) left to destroy. When that was done, Bomber Command would only have to "mop up the few small coal and steel towns" in the Saar and "when the occasion serves . . . tidy up all around" by taking out Solingen, Witten, and Leverkusen. But it would not come to that. Harris concluded: "I feel certain that Germany must collapse before this programme which is more than half completed already, has proceeded much further." The key was getting the Americans to cooperate.

> We have not got far to go. If they will only get going according to plan and avoid such disastrous diversions as Ploesti [Germany's main oil supplier] . . . we can get through it very quickly. We can wreck Berlin from end to end if the U.S.A.A.F. will come in on it. It will cost us 400–500 aircraft.
>
> It will cost Germany the war.

Over the next seven months, from August 1943 to March 1944, Bomber Command attacked the capital nineteen times; 10,813 bombers dropped 17,000 tons of high explosives and 16,000 tons of incendiaries, killing 9390 civilians. Two thousand seven hundred aircrew died. As always, the bombs did much damage: the opera house in Charlottenburg, much of Potsdamer Platz, the villas of Potsdamer Strasse, many museums, all were destroyed. But Berlin was not "wrecked." It continued to function as an administrative and commercial capital and the seat of a few industries. Although a few of the latter were "caught" by bombing, most bombs hit targets of no importance to the war effort; in some cases, bombing helped it: when retail shops, hotels, and other businesses unrelated to the military were destroyed, their workers were immediately transferred to more productive tasks.[16] Hitler, famously, stayed in the city until the end. Berlin's solid, modern architecture, wide streets and open spaces (thousands of bombs landed pointlessly in the Tiergarten), and sheer size (nineteen times larger than Paris) meant that it could withstand bombing far more readily than Germany's older, more compact cities. Harris promised that an average monthly bomb tonnage of 13,500 would lead to the Reich's collapse; however, throughout the Battle of Berlin, he dropped a monthly average of 14,915 tons on German cities without bringing the country remotely close to collapse.[17] As Alec Coryton, Assistant Chief of Air Staff (Operations) (and former AOC of 5 Group), noted in November, even if Berlin had been destroyed, it is doubtful that it would have meant the end of the war.[18] The city simply never enjoyed the same singularly important industrial and financial role played by the British capital. The elusive search for a leveled Berlin was motivated by symbolism rather than sound strategy.

April 1, 1944, came and went without the promised German capitulation. The failure of the Berlin campaign did not discourage Harris. Rather, he looked to a whole new set of cities. While the Berlin campaign was still under way, 596 aircraft destroyed the ancient city of Augsburg on February 25–26 under the fire of only token flak defense.[19] On March 1–2, Stuttgart was hit, destroying the Neues Schloss and killing 125 people.[20] On March 18–19 and again on March 22–23, Frankfurt was hit, flattening the old center and ending "the existence of the Frankfurt which had been built up since the Middle Ages."[21]

Throughout this period, the British death toll climbed: in January 1944, Harris lost 6.1 percent of aircraft sent to Berlin, and 7.2 percent of those that went to Stettin; in a February raid on Leipzig and a March raid on Berlin, the casualty rate was greater than 9 percent.[22] Six days after the end of the Berlin campaign, on March 30–31, Harris dispatched 795 aircraft on an attack on Nuremberg. Although the city—like all German cities—had some industries, none of these, with the exception of a small aircraft repair plant on the outskirts, was specified under the Casablanca and POINTBLANK directives.[23] Like Berlin, Nuremberg was appealing more for its symbolism than its industrial importance: Harris wanted to flatten the city of the Nazi party rally. The raid was a disaster: ninety-six planes, or 11.8 percent of those that took off, did not return. The casualty rate was a staggering 20.6 percent. Nuremberg itself got off relatively easy: 265 buildings of little or no industrial importance were destroyed, 75 people (including 15 foreign workers) were killed, and 11,000 were made homeless. Ironically, many pilots mistook Schweinfurt for Nuremberg and successfully dropped ten blockbusters (4000-pound bombs with light casings), three hundred other explosives, and thousands of incendiaries on a city that Harris claimed they could not attack.[24]

After two years, the failure of the bomber dream and its costs were obvious to everyone but Harris himself.[25] For the moment, however, he had to deal with what he called a "diversion."[26] Operation OVERLORD—the invasion of the European continent.

18

WHAT THE BRITISH KNEW

The *Times* **was the most** venerable institution on Fleet Street. Founded in 1788, it was Britain's newspaper of record for almost two centuries. Throughout the war, it recorded Bomber Command's successes (but almost never its failures). From the beginning, but particularly as Harris ramped up the bomber war, it was the most important voice of Bomber Command.

And it was generally loud and proud. Following a March 9, 1942, raid on Essen, the paper reported:

> During the heavy air attack on Essen and objectives elsewhere in the Ruhr on the night of March 9, a small number of aircraft bombed the August Thyssen Steelworks, which lie between the town of Hamborn and the Rhine. Photographs taken during the bombing fully confirm the pilots' reports that there were large fires in the area of the works, and that high-explosive bombs were accurately aimed at the fires. There can be little doubt that substantial damage was done.[1]

The reports rarely described the destruction of cities, and never the killing of civilians. Only two reports, over the last three years of the war, could be construed as anything close to an accurate picture of area bombing. In August 1942, Sinclair, the British Secretary of State for War, gave a speech at Swansea, the Welsh port city that had suffered so much during the Blitz. In a speech rallying the beleaguered citizens, he informed them that:

we intended to press home our attacks on Germany ruthlessly. . . . The destruction which Bomber Command has wrought in Germany and in German-occupied territory in recent months has been terrible. . . . Bomber Command has destroyed between a quarter and a third of the whole of Cologne. . . . The effect of Bomber Command's mighty raids are well exemplified in this extract from the diary of a German soldier killed far from home on one of Hitler's many battlefronts. "The last mail made an overwhelming impression. On everybody's lips are the words Cologne and Essen. Relatives wrote terrible things. Max was informed that life had come off the rails and people simply could not recover after this dreadful disaster."[2]

In a similar vein, the *Times'* aeronautical correspondent provided a report on the extent of bomb damage in Germany on the first day of 1943. He had been briefed or given information by Harris or someone close to Harris, as he measured bomb damage with a technique favored by the commander-in-chief: acres destroyed. "The damage caused by the Luftwaffe in Britain during 1940 and 1941," the correspondent wrote,

and that caused by the R.A.F. in Germany during 1942 make an interesting comparison. The City of London contained less than 120 acres of devastation. In Bomber Command's big raid on Cologne more than 600 acres were devastated. In Luebeck more than 40 per cent of the property, totalling more than 200 acres, had been destroyed or damaged beyond repair. The damage in Rostock was greater, in proportion to the total area, than in any other city, being about 70 per cent. No city in the world had a greater acreage of damage than Cologne. Other damage caused by the R.A.F. included: Duesseldorf, more than 380 acres; Mainz, 130 acres; Karlsruhe, 360 acres; Emden, 60 per cent destroyed; Bremen, nearly 20 per cent; Aachen, 30 per cent (nearly 160 acres); Muenster, 260 acres devastated; and Nuremberg, 106 acres.[3]

The only discussion of people as distinct from buildings came on June 21, 1943. Most likely relying on Swedish reports on German morale, the *Times'* diplomatic correspondent wrote:

The signs are that German propaganda is now going to play up the R.A.F. attacks as vigorously as it had hitherto played them down. Goebbel's speech at Wuppertal on Friday, in which he described the sufferings of the victims of bombing, is now said to have broken the spell—meaning, presumably, that facts which have been suppressed are to be disclosed in the future.

Hans Fritsche, the wireless commentator, said on Saturday of Goebbel's speech: "The spell was broken that had thus far lain over the sufferings of that part of our people which is exposed to these terror attacks." . . . Now all Germany was to be told of the sufferings and sacrifices of the bombed districts. . . . Large-scale evacuation from the Ruhr is taking place, and the housing of the refugees in what are regarded as safe areas is not proving easy. Some of the bombed-out people have not been sympathetically received, and in the German Press there have been complaints of this lack of considerateness.[4]

With some imagination, Sinclair's vengeful rhetoric and Fritsche's stories of evacuations could have conveyed the idea that not everyone could be successfully evacuated. With a little more imagination, the rather dry figures on acres destroyed might have provided the reader with a view of what German cities were starting to look like in early 1943. Likewise, some reflection might have led a reader to conclude that, if large numbers of civilians were being driven out of their homes, some of them, perhaps many of them, must be dying in the process. Throughout the war, Vera Brittan, a pacifist and activist, published pamphlets denouncing RAF bombing as murder. In a March 1944 issue of *Fellowship*, an American religious publication, one of her ritual attacks on Allied bombing was accompanied by the signatures of twenty-eight noted clergymen and anti-war activists.[5] "Christian people," the text went, "should be moved to examine themselves concerning this participation in this carnival of death." The result was a flurry of controversy in the American media.[6]

Such relatively honest reports were not the only ones consuming column inches. Equally typical was a *Daily Sketch* report on the bombing of Lübeck: "Lübeck, important German U-boat building yard on the Baltic and thirty-five miles north-east of Hamburg was still on fire late yesterday. RAF long-distance bombers pounded this vital port on Saturday night. . . . Surface vessels, as well as submarines are built in the Lübeck yards. The port is also used for sending military supplies to Norway, Finland and the Northern Russian front . . . [Twenty minutes] after the start of the attack at about 10:30 P.M. . . . the fires had spread right across the port."[7] But the port hadn't been the center of the bombing at all; the old city was.

In a similar vein, the *Times* report on Hamburg in the summer of 1943 states that:

Air bombing reached a new intensity on Tuesday night, when the R.A.F. made their fourth successive night attack on Hamburg, which experienced its sixth raid in 72 hours. In 45 minutes—five minutes shorter than on Saturday in the first of the present series of raids—a total exceeding the previous record weight of 2,300 tons of bombs was rained on the still blazing docks and industrial quarter, causing damage which it is expected will far exceed that caused in any previous attack.[8]

The date was July 27, 1943; the target area was residential working-class Hamburg, and the firestorm left forty thousand people dead.

A few weeks before Hamburg, the Archbishop of Canterbury wrote to Sinclair for clarification. "I am bombarded," he wrote, "by statements that we have evidently changed our policy in bombing and are now deliberately destroying cities irrespective of military objectives. I have continued to say that I see no evidence of this . . . but I should be grateful if you could let me have a line to assure me that this is correct."[9] Sinclair was glad to: "It is no part of our policy wantonly to destroy cities—regardless of military objectives—as the German Air Force attempted to do . . . [though] we cannot attack factories without damaging the surrounding buildings."[10]

Two weeks later, British readers were informed that the small city of Bonn was an "important railway centre on a trunk line serving the Ruhr and southern Germany, and [was] the site of a precision instrument factory."[11]

Throughout the war, the government was sensitive to public opinion on bombing, and watched it closely. The evidence was inconclusive. According to polls conducted by Mass Observation, during the worst of the Blitz, the public was evenly divided—45 percent in favor, 45 percent against—over revenge attacks.[12] In answer to the more specific question, posed by the British Institute of Public Opinion, of whether the German civilian population should be a target for attacks, the answers varied for reasons that are not entirely clear. In 1940, support for such attacks stood at 45 percent; in 1941, it rose to 55 percent; in 1943, it peaked at 83 percent.[13] In 1944 and 1945, it fell off again. In themselves, however, these figures say very little; as any political scientist knows, answers to public opinion questions depend greatly on when and how they are asked. It is one thing for people to say they support attacks on the "civilian population"; it is another to say so after seeing the pictures of burned and maimed children. Someone who called for revenge attacks after seeing their hometown bombed might (or might not) have changed his views with the passage of time.

In the end, the attitude of the British to civilian bombing is necessarily ambiguous. Enough information—including pictures and occasional apocalyptic imagery conjured up by politicians ("a crescendo of destruction")—leaked out during the war to give the curious a clear picture of what was going on. Still, the press reports were vague enough, and the claims of industrial targets and precision capabilities sincere enough, to allow everyone to believe what they wanted to. For those who wanted to smash the Huns where they lived and breathed, they had Cherwell's intervention. For those who believed that Britain was mainly bombing industries, there was no end of official statements to confirm it. Activists such as Brittan were rare, and they were viewed as extreme if not treasonous. No country had ever been bombed on the scale that Germany was being bombed, and it would have been difficult to imagine exactly what it was like for civilians on the ground. After the war, many pilots and other aircrew would admit that, in the air and under a barrage of flak, they thought little about the civilians in the cities as they bombed them. If the tens of thousands of feet between aircrew and civilians created moral distance, how could the six hundred miles between London and Berlin not?

The Air Ministry sat in a large, sandstone corner building at Whitehall. It was a slightly bombastic, largely interwar structure. The Air Ministry issued bombing directives and oversaw the bombing war. It was also responsible for RAF publicity, issued press releases, and provided instructions on what could and could not be said to the press. On October 21, 1943, Air Commodore Howard Williams had been authorized by the Ministry to write a story for the *Daily Telegraph* on the bombing campaigns from the previous July. "Bomber Command's nightly average on Germany," Williams wrote, "was equal to the

Luftwaffe's effort for the whole 100 days on Britain [during the Blitz]. . . . the
total load on 35 of our larger-scale raids was 50 tons more than the Luftwaffe's
greatest effort against Britain"—450 tons on Coventry in 1940. "The campaign," he continued, was providing "direct help to Russia":

> When Gen. Smuts stated this week that some 2,000,000 people were
> engaged in Germany in meeting our air offensive in some form or
> other, he more than confirmed Sir Archibald Sinclair's estimate that
> some 750,000 were employed in active defences and another 750,000
> on the passive side. In addition hundreds of thousands of workers are
> in the repair and ancillary industries. Many of these would otherwise
> be fighting the Russians.

The article later added that "the effect of the night and day bomb offensive on
events on the Russian front is known to be very appreciable."

Williams went on to explain the difference between area bombing and
precision bombing. "Comparing our 'area bombing' by night [with precision
bombing by day]," he wrote, "an RAF commentator pointed out that the enemy's cities were now great labour camps, employed almost solely on the war
effort."

The purpose of the night attack, he added, was to destroy Germany's capacity to wage war by "striking out of her hands the weapons she seeks to use
against us."

> While it is not practicable at night to bomb precise targets, as by day,
> a very high measure of precision occurs over the target area. The ef-
> fect is to smash not only arms factories and their satellites, but [also]
> the virtual barracks of those who work in them, driving sometimes
> literally millions to their shelters below ground.
>
> It has to be remembered that every man who works in these in-
> dustrial "divisions" is only doing so because he is of more use to the
> enemy's war capacity than he would be as a soldier.

At this point in the war, Williams concluded, Germany's aircraft factories were
one of its "high spots," central to the war in general and the Russian campaign
in particular: "We have long known that the German fighter force has been
steadily increasing since last January. It is now disclosed that there are about a

third more fighters now operating against Air Chief Marshal Sir Arthur Harris by night and Gen. [Ira] Eaker by day."

The result was that massive numbers of fighters had been drawn off the Eastern Front. Of the 2750 fighters available to Germany, the RAF estimated that 1900 were on the Western Front, 300 on the Mediterranean Front, and 550 on the Eastern Front. The consequences for Germany were disastrous:

> When it is realized that some 550 fighters, of which probably only 60% are serviceable, have to cover the entire Russian battle front of 600 miles, the extent of the enemy's shortage can be gauged. . . .
>
> The one thing on which the Germans are relying to stave off defeat is their fighter force, which, by night and day, is being whittled down by every conceivable means in our power.[14]

Harris was not briefed on the letter; he read it in the *Telegraph* itself. It made him furious. The article suggested that the targets of Britain's bombing campaign were industrial, that the most important of these targets was fighter production, and that the point in drawing off and destroying fighters was to help the Russians. He sat down and penned a response to the Air Ministry. In an October 25 letter, Harris urged the Ministry's policy on press releases be urgently modified. He wrote that the Ministry had failed to convey the fact that "the position of Germany as a result of 8 months' intensive bombing and the advance of the Russian armies across the Dnieper is such that the possibility of her collapse at a very early date must be seriously envisaged."

If Germany collapsed, the Air Ministry would have wholly failed to make clear Bomber Command's decisive role in it:

> The manner in which the aim and achievement of the combined U.S.–British Bomber Offensive have been presented both in the Press and public pronouncements by authoritative speakers in both Britain and the United States has encouraged the view that it is in the nature of an experiment or a side-show which is important but is not the major part of the United Nations' war effort in the European Theatre. . . . No one could possibly gather from casual reading of the British Press that the enemy openly admits the results of our bombing to be his most serious problem, ie, of greater importance than the advance of the Red Army.

This "writing down" of Bomber Command was, Harris concluded,

> the outcome of deliberate policy. So also, it must be assumed, is the fact
> that the quite considerable space which is nevertheless devoted to the
> part of Combined Bomber Offensive entrusted to Bomber Command mis-
> represents both the aim and achievement of that part. This misrepresenta-
> tion consists in the continued suggestion that Bomber Command is
> concerned, not with the obliteration of German cities and their inhabitants
> as such, but with the bombing of specific factory premises. What all official
> talks and handouts emphasise is not that Cassel contained over 200,000
> Germans, many of whom are now dead and most of the remainder home-
> less and destitute, but that the Henschel Locomotive works and various
> other important factory premises were in or near the city.

The problem with this presentation was that it gave the impression that
the Americans and the British were trying to do the same thing, but that the
Americans were simply better at it. This, Harris continued, had three consequences. The first was that it made Bomber Command's exploits seem "dull
and unconvincing" compared to those of the Russians, the Allied armies in
Italy, or the U.S. Eighth Air Force. The truth was exactly the opposite:

> The aim of our Bomber Force which went to Cassel on October 22/23 was
> to wreck the city. . . . In the course of the proceedings, the Henschel Works
> and a number of other factories probably got damaged, and this makes
> the loss to the enemy all the greater. But the fundamental purpose was to
> knock another great German city out of the war and add it to the growing
> list of those which are now liabilities and not assets to the enemy from the
> point of view of morale and production. By obscuring this purpose, we
> simply rob the whole operation of its point.[15]

The second consequence was that it gave the crews the impression that
"the authorities are ashamed of area bombing." This could not stand. Men
could not to go on "risking their lives to effect a purpose which their own
Government appears to consider at least as too disreputable to be mentioned
in public." The third was that it gave "unlimited scope for pushing their view"
to "those elements in this country who hope to accumulate political capital by

Churchill's role in the bombing campaign was controversial. He was an erratic supporter of area bombing, but distanced himself from it later in the war.

Sir Arthur Harris, Commander-in-Chief of Bomber Command (standing at left) listens to a report on the dambuster raids with Ralph Cochrane (on Harris's left), who formed the squadrons.

The crew of the "Question Mark." At left are Carl Spaatz and Ira Eaker.

Curtis LeMay, viewed as one of the most brutal American airmen, confessed a deep concern for the fate of civilians killed by bombing.

Sir Charles Portal, Chief of Air Staff for most of the war.

A symbol of London's resistance: St. Paul's Cathedral rises from the smoke at the height of the Blitz. As Arthur Harris viewed the scene, he remarked, "They are sowing the wind."

German bombers hit a school in January 1943, killing thirty-eight children and six teachers.

Recalled too late: German bombers lay waste to Rotterdam on May 14, 1940.

Hamburg before the firestorm:
A typical house on Ernst-Günther
Haberland's street.

After the firestorm, Haberland's
street was sealed off.

Private Collection

Top: Working-class Hamburg: Hammerbrook after the firestorm. Most of the forty-thousand-plus people who died during the raids lived in or near this part of the city.

Left: Old Hamburg: Across Germany, ancient, narrow streets were ideal fire starters.

Denkmalschutzamt Hamburg

Right: A cellar in Hamburg: The majority of those who lost their lives during the firestorm died in their own basements.

Archives of Michel Foedrowitz

An old woman stands before
the piled-up bodies of children
in Brunswick.

Bundesarchiv Koblenz

Bildarchiv Preussischer Kulturbesitz

Angry German civilians threaten a downed American airman: Wehrmacht soldiers would
generally protect Allied aircrew, but they had to get to them before the SS or angry mobs.

Area bombing tested: Rostock after the April 1942 raids, some of the earliest in Harris's city-busting campaign. Note that the shells of the buildings are largely intact.

Area bombing perfected: Darmstadt after a single September 1944 raid. By then, a routine raid by Bomber Command could flatten a city.

The interior of Cologne's famous Cathedral a year after the thousand-bomber raid. By 1945, the Cathedral would still rise above the shattered city.

Bildarchiv Preussicher Kulturbesitz

Members of Hitler Youth try to put out fires during a bombing raid.

Bundesarchiv Koblenz

Firefighters attempt to put out the fires in Hamburg following an early 1943 raid.

Private Collection

Kiel: Following the collapse of a building under the weight of high explosives, two men rush in to help those trapped in the rubble.

Precision bombing: In the Americans' August 17, 1943, raid on Schweinfurt, they suffered a 20 percent casualty rate, but German ball-bearings production fell by 38 percent. That night, Albert Speer waited for news of a follow-up RAF raid.

Blind bombing: Although the Americans were aiming at industrial targets, heavy cloud cover often meant that precision bombing was only a hope and a prayer.

Oil raids: From 1944, the Americans began bombing oil targets whenever they could. The effect on the Nazi war effort was devastating.

Photos on both pages: National Museum of the United States Air Force/U.S. National Archives

American casualties: Throughout the war, Allied airmen faced the prospect of a terrible death. Here, the wing of a U.S. bomber is sheared off by flak.

Jack Pragnell (right) with his brother, Tom. Jack, RAF navigator in Operation Gomorrah, would survive the war. His brother would not.

Bomber Command casualties: Over the course of the bombing war, eighty-thousand Allied airmen, most of them still boys, lost their lives.

Hitler with Albert Speer (at far right): From 1942 to 1945 there was a silent but furious struggle between Speer, on the one hand, and Arthur Harris, Ira Eaker, and Carl Spaatz, on the other.

Senior National Socialist officials in Würzburg, 1934.

Heinrich Giesecke (right) and his brother in old Würzburg.

Würzburg after its 1945 destruction.

Bremen: Inmates clear out Senator Bernhard's house following a raid. Forced laborers were denied entry to air-raid shelters and were ordered to provide relief during and clear rubble after the bombings.

A dead city: An American soldier surveys the remains of Nuremberg. Allied soldiers entering Germany were first awed, then dismayed by the endless devastation.

Inferno: Nothing can save this Berlin publishing house.

minimising our contribution to the defeat of Germany as contrasted with that of the USSR."

Unless the British people were told the truth of the bombing campaign, they would never understand its importance in bringing about Germany's defeat:

> The fact that bombing has won the war and forced the German armies to give in to the Russians will never be accepted in quarters where it is important that it should. Nobody will believe ex post facto that for 8 months Bomber Command was winning resounding and indeed decisive victories and that they were nevertheless deliberately represented as of less importance than very minor encounters with the enemy at sea and on land.

To avoid such a "deplorable result," the Air Ministry needed a new publicity strategy. Above all, the aim of the U.S. and, especially, the UK claims should be "unambiguously stated":

> *That aim is the destruction of German cities; the killing of German workers; and the disruption of civilized life throughout Germany. It should be emphasized that the destruction of houses, public utilities, transport, and lives; the creation of a refugee problem on an unprecedented scale; and the breakdown of morale both at home and at the battle fronts by fear of extended and intensified bombing, are accepted and intended aims of our bombing policy.* They are not by-products of attempts to hit factories.[16]

The success or failure of Bomber Command, Harris concluded, should be "publicly assessed in terms of the extent to which they realize this policy."[17]

Alarm bells began ringing in the Air Ministry, and officials penned frantic minutes to each other rejecting Harris's claims. On October 28, Sir Arthur Street, Under Secretary of State in the Air Ministry, wrote to Portal about the matter. "In my public statements," Street stated, "I always emphasize that our objectives are the centres of war power and that the damage to built-up areas, though inevitable and huge, is incidental. If we were to abandon this line and to adopt as the principal measure of our success the number of men, women and children killed and the number of houses burnt out rather than the numbers of factories destroyed, we should provoke the leaders of religious and humanitarian opinion to protest."[18] "There must," he concluded, "be no departure from our present line without consultation with me."

Air Marshal Sir Richard Peck, Assistant Chief of Air Staff, was given the job of drafting a response to Harris. Before he did so, he wrote to Bottomley and asked him directly about the Allies' policy on bombing civilians. In his reply, Bottomley stated that "there is no indication [in the directive] of any deliberate attack upon the civilian population as such. It would be quite wrong to say that destruction of civilian lives is an accepted and intended aim of our bombing policy; nor is the aim of the destruction of German cities as such unless those cities have an important part of the military, industrial or economic system of the enemy."[19]

Over the next three weeks, the Air Ministry produced multiple drafts of a response to Harris. On December 15, it went out under Street's signature. The letter made several attempts to minimize the differences between the Ministry and Harris. On the question of the armies', navies', and Soviets' contributions, the minister argued that it was

> obliged to exercise great discretion in drawing comparisons between the importance of land and air operations. Whatever high hopes [the Council] may entertain for the results of the combined bomber offensive, the fact is that the British and United States Governments have made plans for major land operations on the Continent at a comparatively early date. In framing their publicity policy, the Council cannot ignore this basic concept of Allied strategy. Nor can they ignore the vast significance of the Russian land offensive which jointly with the bomber offensive is placing Germany under a strain that may at any time prove fatal. Subject only to these considerations, the Council will continue to stress in their publicity the critical importance of the bomber offensive and the outstanding achievement of air power in creating the conditions of victory.

But, in the end, the response had to address directly Harris's claim that the bomber offensive was aimed at "the destruction of German cities, the killing of German workers. . . ." "The Council," Street wrote,

> recognise, of course, that night attacks directed against the German war economy involve the virtual destruction of those German cities which are essential to the enemy's war effort and that such destruction entails heavy

casualties to the civil population and disruption of the organized life of the
community . . . but your directive neither requires nor enjoins direct attack
on German civilians as such.

Street denied that the Ministry was concealing "from the public the immense devastation that is being wrought to German industrial cities . . . Every
one knows that, in attacking the sources of Germany's war potential, Bomber
Command is bound to destroy large areas of German cities." This "widespread
devastation" was, however, "not an end in itself but the inevitable accompaniment
of an all-out attack on the enemy's capacity to end war." To say any more than
this, Street concluded, would be politically unwise. "It is," he wrote,

desirable to present the bomber offensive in such a light as to provoke the
minimum of public controversy and so far as possible to avoid conflict with
religious and humanitarian opinion. Any public protest, whether reasonable or unreasonable, against the bomber offensive could not but hamper
the Government in the execution of their policy and might affect the morale of the aircrews themselves.

The Council are therefore unwilling to change the emphasis of their
publicity. They do not, however, wish to imply that the objects of your
Command should be represented as confined to the bombing of specific
factory premises.[20]

A devious character would have interpreted this wink-and-nod as an open
invitation to carry on, which it probably was. But Harris was not devious. As
he wrote a week later, the Ministry's answers to his questions were, "in spite
of [my] most careful examination . . . ambiguous." With regard to the Soviets
and the Western ground forces, Harris did not want to imply that their successes or their significance should be ignored. Rather, he

asked simply that adequate emphasis as distinct from occasional and casual references should be made to the fact that these successes have been
made possible largely by the Bomber Offensive, and also to the truth, of
which the enemy is well aware, that the reduction to ruins of Berlin, Hamburg, Cologne and many other cities is of incomparably greater significance to the German people than the recovery by the Soviets of the ruins
of Kharkov, Kiev and Gomel.

The point of these bombings, Harris continued, was not to kill the old, invalid, and very young. Indeed, doing so would be irrational. Children, the handicapped, and the aged consume more than they produce and are thus a drain on the German war effort. The logical corollary of this, however, was that it was rational to kill civilians who were productive. The Ministry was therefore wrong in implying

> that *no* German citizens are proper objects for bombing. The German economic system, which I am instructed by my directive to destroy, *includes* workers, houses and public utilities, and it is therefore meaningless to claim that the wiping out of German cities is "not an end in itself but the inevitable accompaniment of an all out attack on the enemy's means and capacity to wage war." I repeat that the cities of Germany including their working population, houses and public utilities are literally the heart of Germany's "war potential." That is why they are being deliberately attacked.[21]

Harris blasted the Ministry for the contradictions in its letter. The Ministry had in the same two pages claimed that cities were legitimate targets ("the objects of Bomber Command are not confined to ... specific factory premises"); that they were not legitimate targets ("widespread devastation is not an end in itself "); and that the real objective could not be specified for fear of alienating "religious and humanitarian opinion." As a result, Harris was "completely unable to discover from the Air Ministry letter whether or not [he was] in agreement with the views of the Air Council."[22]

Not without reason. The occasional rhetoric of Churchill and Sinclair ("laying waste"), and a few dry statistics (percentages of cities bombed, acres destroyed), had hinted at what Bomber Command was doing. But the Air Ministry and the government shied away from a full statement of what Bomber Command was up to. When Sir Richard Rapier Stokes, Labour MP, asked the government whether "on any occasion instructions have been given to British airmen to engage in area bombing rather than limit their attention to purely military targets," the reply was: "The targets of the Bomber Command are always military, but night bombing of military objectives necessarily involves bombing of the area in which they are situated."

As Harris well knew, this was false, or at least highly misleading. He was by nature an honest man, and he was confident in his policy and that the British people would support it. He also suspected that, if he allowed the Air Ministry to continue its dissimulation, it and the UK government would be allowed to escape responsibility for a policy that, Harris believed, they had supported from the beginning. "I submit," he wrote, "that this is far too serious a matter to be left in this position of obscurity. If the authorities are in doubt that cities, including everything and everybody in them which is a help to the German war effort, are the objectives which Bomber Command in accordance with its directive is aiming to destroy, they should at once be disabused of this illusion, which is not merely unfair to our crews now but will inevitably lead to deplorable controversies when the facts are fully and generally known."

The question was more than one of publicity. It went to the very cause for which thousands of young men were dying:

It concerns the whole aim and scope of the activities of Bomber Command, since, unless my interpretation of the situation . . . is accepted without ambiguity or evasion of the issue, it is clear that our crews are being sacrificed in a deliberate attempt to do something which the Air Council do not regard as necessary or even legitimate, *namely eliminate entire German cities*. . . . It is not enough to admit that devastation is caused by our attacks, or to suggest that it is an incidental and rather regrettable concomitant of night bombing. It is in fact produced deliberately and our whole [pathfinder force] and navigational technique is primarily designed to promote it. This is the truth which cannot be denied without implying that Bomber Command is attempting to do the same thing as the Americans do occasionally and doing it comparatively ineffectively. Failure to assert it openly will, as I stated in my previous letter, inevitably affect adversely the morale of our crews and I would urge that this rather than the appeasement of the sentimental and humanitarian scruples of a negligible minority should be our primary consideration.[23]

Harris's letter, as ever a model of clear thought and frankness, left the Ministry with little choice. It could no longer pretend that there was no difference of principle between it and Harris. Instead, it had to tell Harris directly whether his own view of the bombing war accorded with official policy as dictated by the POINTBLANK directive and interpreted by the Ministry. In its reply, the Ministry noted that there could be no question that the "indirect and inevitable consequences" of attacks on "factories, industrial premises, public utilities and means of communication" would be "heavy casualties to the population of the city and destruction of buildings and monuments which are not themselves universally recognised as legitimate objects of attack." But this, the Ministry argued, was as far as it went:

> What is in dispute is whether, in order to maintain the morale of Bomber Command air crews and avoid unfair comparison with the methods adopted by the U.S.A.A.F. in their daylight attacks, it is necessary to include in the definition of avowed targets for direct attack civilian workers and the whole of a city including dwelling places and cultural and religious monuments.
>
> The Council cannot agree that it is.

The issue for the Council, though it did not use the word, was a moral one. There was a difference between trying to minimize civilian casualties but causing them anyway and deliberately trying to maximize those casualties:

> The effect may be the same but the emphasis placed on the motive is profoundly important.
>
> War itself is regrettable. So too are almost all the consequences of war and the conscience of all humanitarian people, and not merely of a negligible minority, would be shocked if such a misdescription were applied to the objects of our attacks as to lend colour to the German description of them as "terror" raids.

The Council had no moral objections to area bombing as such: "[We] have no compunction whatever in publicly justifying the adoption of area bombing as a stern necessity of war involving though it must as an indirect but inevitable consequence heavy casualties to the civil population whoever they may be." The point of area bombing, however, had to be to destroy industry, not to kill civilians: "[We] are unable to agree that it is necessary to this justification to imply that a deliberate attempt is made to take the lives of German civilian workers."[24]

The distinction might seem like hairsplitting, but it was not. Under the Ministry's understanding, area bombing was justified so long as it was the only or the best way to destroy industry, as well as much else. Under Harris, area bombing was justified whether it damaged industry or not: it was more effective to destroy cities and the people in them, regardless of any concomitant damage to industry. This fundamental difference of interpretation would grow more important as the war continued, and it set the stage for a final battle between Harris and his direct superior, Charles Portal.

19

TAKING OUT THE LUFTWAFFE

Ⓘ **n early 1944, General Arnold** sent a memo to Carl Spaatz. It instructed him to "seek out and destroy the German Air Force in the air and on the ground. The defensive concept of our fighter command and air defense units must be changed to the offensive."[1] Arnold was preaching to the converted. "Destruction of the Luftwaffe," Anderson noted after the war, "was priority number one. [The entire] war was hinged—even strategically—to a successful defeat of the German Air Force, the German fighter forces."[2] It was the clearest lesson of the second Schweinfurt raid. On the morning of October 15, as sixty American B-17s lay on German soil, Eaker penned a passionate letter to Arnold:

> This does not represent disaster; it does not indicate that the air battle has reached its climax. Our answer to this challenge [will be]:
>
> 1. More fighter cover at longer range;
> 2. Multiple attacks by 7 or 8 combat wings of 54 bombers;
> 3. Greater emphasis on counter Air Force operations, striking all fields with medium and pressing destruction of aircraft factors and repair establishments with heavies;
> 4. Bomb through clouds when his fighters will often be fogbound.[3]

Urging Arnold to rush replacement aircraft, crews, and fighters, and to supply droppable tanks for fighters (allowing greater range), Eaker ended his letter on a defiant note: "We must show the enemy we can replace our losses; he

169

knows he cannot replace his. We must continue the battle with unrelenting fury. This we shall do."

Spaatz had arrived back in the UK in December 1943. He had commanded the United States Eighth Air Force, but he took over the Americans' North African campaign in November 1942, before they began bombing Germany. He returned to England to assume full command over U.S. air forces in Europe and to prepare for the invasion of the Continent. Spaatz worked with Sir Arthur Tedder, General Eisenhower's chief deputy at Supreme Headquarters Allied Expeditionary Force (SHAEF). Spaatz was given overall command of a new organization, the United States Strategic Air Forces in Europe (USSTAF), which coordinated both the Eighth Air Force and the Fifteenth Air Force (U.S. heavy bombers based in Italy). The USSTAF was effectively the Eighth in new clothes, and Eighth Air Force Bomber Command was officially disbanded. Eaker, very much against his will, was pushed out and "promoted" to command Allied air operations in the Mediterranean. Major General James ("Jimmy") Doolittle (a hard rock miner, amateur boxer, daredevil stuntman, MIT Ph.D. in aeronautics, and hero of the first April 1942 bombing raids on Tokyo) was brought in to replace him, and Major General Frederick Anderson became Doolittle's Chief of Operations. In a final move, Major General Nathan F. Twining was transferred from the South Pacific to assume command of the Fifteenth Air Force.

For Doolittle and Spaatz, there was no question that defeating the Luftwaffe was USSTAF's overriding goal. When Doolittle entered the office of General William Kepner, the Eighth's fighter chief, he saw a sign that said THE FIRST DUTY OF THE EIGHTH AIR FORCE FIGHTERS IS TO BRING THE BOMBERS BACK ALIVE.[4] "Take that damn thing down," Doolittle ordered, "and put up another one saying 'the First duty of the Eighth Air Force is to destroy German Fighters.' "

"You mean," Kepner replied, "you're authorizing me to take the offense?"

Doolittle replied, "I'm directing you to."

Of all the reasons behind American air force losses—bad weather, faulty equipment, flak, and fighter defenses—the Luftwaffe was the most important. It always had been, but the German air force—largely because of Galland's efforts—was becoming an increasingly vicious force. Escort fighters were able to offer a great deal of protection to American bombers, but the Luftwaffe quickly developed a technique for dealing with them. When incoming U.S. bombers were picked up on radar, the German fighters would go up but hover just beyond the limits of the escort fighters' range. Once the escorts turned back and the bombers continued on alone, the Luftwaffe swept in for the kill. It was often, by no means only over Schweinfurt, a massacre. Ridding the skies of the Luftwaffe had to be done, for the U.S. air forces and for POINT-BLANK. Only if the Luftwaffe was knocked out could Allied bombers attack Germany's submarine, tank, and oil targets. Recognizing this, the Eighth Air Force and Air Ministry drew up plans in early 1943 for altering POINT-BLANK priorities: destroying the German fighter force, previously priority two, became priority number one.[5] Eaker and Portal agreed, and they presented it to the Combined Chiefs of Staff at the May 1943 Trident conference.[6] These discussions became the basis of the June 1, 1943, directive. The force they set out to destroy was an ever-growing one: German fighter production had increased throughout the summer and into the autumn of 1943.[7]

The outlines of the plan for destroying the Luftwaffe had been sketched out by Eaker at least since the April 1942 dinner at Chequers. The idea was to deliver a massive blow against the German aircraft industry. Eaker formalized the plan of attack in Operation Argument, which envisaged continuous, coordinated strikes by the Eighth Air Force, the Fifteenth Air Force, and Harris's Bomber Command.

Spaatz's idea for destroying the Luftwaffe was contained in the words "seek out and destroy"; he may have in fact suggested them to Arnold. Until 1944, the fighters played an important but essentially defensive role. They would accompany the bombers on their flight to Germany and defend them against any Luftwaffe fighters they met. Otherwise, the striking force—a very large one by early 1944—would be on the ground or in training flights, waiting for the next precision bombing run. Spaatz transformed this defensive role into an offensive one. On bombing missions, the fighters would not simply accompany the bombers into Germany. Instead, they would surge ahead and seek out the Luftwaffe, attacking them and knocking enough of them out of the air to allow the bombers to get through.

Bombing escort was, however, only one part of the fighters' role, and possibly not the most important part. Spaatz decided that, whenever he could, he would send out his dogs. The goal was "nothing less than the annihilation of the Luftwaffe. The strategy [was] to bait them and kill them. Send in the bombers—the bait—to destroy the aircraft factories and then massacre the planes and pilots that came up to defend them."[8]

The idea was a daring one, but it faced a powerful opponent: time. Spaatz knew that his forces, both bombers and fighters, would be called away to support Operation OVERLORD, the invasion of the Continent. He had until April 1—only ninety days—to ruin a large, powerful, and modern air force.[9]

The first forty-five of them were lost to poor weather, and to arguments within the Allied air forces about the proper command structure. For an all-out war on the Luftwaffe, Spaatz needed the support and involvement of all Allied air forces over Europe: the Eighth Air Force, British Bomber Command, and the Ninth Air Force, which was built to support the Allied invasion of the Continent. In this he ran up against Sir Trafford Leigh-Mallory, head of Fighter Command and, from August 1943, the Allied Expeditionary Air Force (a complex and rambling organization that was to coordinate Allied air forces in the run-up to D-Day). Spaatz viewed Leigh-Mallory, not without some justification, as pompous, haughty, and naive. Leigh-Mallory could be highly inarticulate, which made his pomposity even more annoying, and his inability to be shaken from an idea once he adopted it as his own made Arthur Harris look like a model of flexibility. His view of a fighter's role was thoroughly defensive: his four years of experience successfully defending the United Kingdom had convinced him that there was no point in trying to get the Luftwaffe to fight if it did not want to.[10] The head of the Ninth Air Force, General Lewis Brereton, wanted to keep it independent of both Spaatz *and* Leigh-Mallory. As Brereton saw it, the Ninth would spend the time in the months leading up to D-Day on training exercises, with a few raids being launched on V-1 production sites. Added to all of this was general confusion about how the Allied command structure would operate once Eisenhower assumed control of the integrated British–American forces.

The whole matter came to a head in mid-February. Spaatz undercut Leigh-Mallory, who played his last hand by writing directly to Portal, who acted as the agent for the Combined Chiefs of Staff in matters relating to the air war. Portal, increasingly an ally of the Americans, sided with Spaatz. "I have had the various directives looked up," Portal wrote to Spaatz on February 15, "and it seems quite clear that A.C.M. Leigh-Mallory is bound . . . [to] lend maximum support to the strategic air offensive," and to do so on both cloudy and clear days.[11] On that night, Harris dropped 2642 tons of bombs on Berlin, killing 320 people.[12]

Having sidelined Leigh-Mallory, Spaatz then took care of Brereton. At a February 19 meeting, Brereton, facing a united front of Doolittle, Spaatz, and Anderson, agreed that the Eighth would issue primary orders to the Ninth, either through Brereton or directly.[13] Spaatz then put the matter in writing after the meeting. Brereton received an official letter: "The Commanding General, USSTAF, will exercise control of all administrative and training matters pertaining to the Ninth Air Force and will assume direct responsibility to higher headquarters for the proper performance of those functions."[14] If Brereton thought of objecting, he didn't for long; Spaatz's administrative control of the Eighth and Ninth gave him power over promotion.

Spaatz was gaining full control of American air forces, but not of the capricious north European weather. To help him understand it, he enlisted the help of yet another eccentric professor, Irving P. Kirk of The California Institute of Technology. Kirk researched fifty years of European weather patterns, leading right up to February 1944, and theorized that weather patterns repeated themselves.[15] On February 18, he rang Spaatz with his findings: on February 20, a high-pressure system would settle over central and southern Germany and it would last for several days. Spaatz leapt on the news and gave Anderson permission to schedule a maximum strike on the morning of February 20. He still faced opposition outside the air forces—Churchill refused to transmit a cable to Eaker requesting help from the Fifteenth and doubts were raised about the P-38s—but Spaatz, with Anderson urging him on, refused to be knocked off course.[16]

Spaatz and Anderson were staking the entire American armed forces on the musings of an obscure and probably nutty professor. The price of this folly seemed to become clear on the evening of February 19. Heavy clouds hung over England and reconnaissance flights to Germany could find no break in them. The next morning promised icing conditions. Doolittle recommended postponing, and William Kepner, the leader of Eighth Fighter Command, agreed. Anderson, ever the risk-taker, argued the opposite, urging Spaatz on and assuring him that the operation was worth two hundred bombers. Spaatz stayed up all night listening to the conflicting advice of his opponents. As dawn broke, he had gotten no sleep. But he'd made up his mind. He put a three-word message through to his base commanders: "Let 'em go."[17]

On February 20, more than one thousand bombers and nine hundred fighters took off for Germany.[18] Six combat wings flew unescorted to targets near Posen and Tutow. The other ten and the entire fighter force headed off to the massive assembly and component plants in the Brunswick-Leipzig area. When the ten combat wings entered German airspace, the professor was proved right: the sky cleared quickly and completely. Incredibly, for February, there was snow in Los Angeles and bright sun in Leipzig.[19] The leading bombs were accompanied by nine hundred fighters (P-47s, P-38s, and P-51s). They had new 150-gallon tanks that allowed them to fly all the way to Hanover, some 400 miles from their base. Just as they were ready to break off their escort on the left side of the bombing formation, they saw a stream of Messerschmitt fighters. The Germans were planning—following a tried and tested technique—to attack the fighters from below, blasting them as they remained glued to the bombers. This time, however, it was different: the Americans attacked them. The Thunderbolts swooped down onto the Luftwaffe fighters, chewing into them. Only one Messerschmitt escaped undamaged.[20] The Americans did not lose a single plane.

While the Thunderbolts were engaging the Luftwaffe, the six other combat wings flew to northern Germany and the Ninth Air Force sent 135 medium bombers to attack airfields in western Germany. The largest force ever dispatched by the Eighth Air Force was hitting the Luftwaffe front, middle, and center.

That night, some twelve hours after his men left, Spaatz was waiting nervously for news at Park House. He was determined to see POINTBLANK through to completion, and he was willing to lose hundreds of bombers to do it. Anderson, who was even more gung ho than Spaatz, was prepared to see seven thousand American pilots and aircrew die—two-thirds of his entire crews and one-third of the number of Marines that would die taking the Pacific—to see the Luftwaffe destroyed.[21] But a large number of losses at this early point in Spaatz's war on the Luftwaffe, even if (as at Schweinfurt) they inflicted heavy losses on the Germans, would have been severely damaging. It would have given fodder to Churchill and other enemies of precision bombing and strengthened the hand of those, such as Brereton, who opposed the concentration of power and authority in Spaatz's hands. As the evening wore on, group after group reported, and the story was always the same: they had losses of only one or two, many times none at all.[22]

The attacks had damaged four plants producing Luftwaffe night fighters/bombers (Junkers Ju88s), and two others producing day fighter aircraft

(Messerschmitt Bf 109s). More importantly, only twenty-one American heavy bombers and four fighters had been lost, half the figure lost on a January 11 raid on the same targets and one-third of the losses of Schweinfurt/Regensburg. Of the 11,000 men who went out, all but 214 came back. On the other side, the Germans had lost 150 fighters. Spaatz was ecstatic, "on the crest of the highest wave he had ever ridden."[23]

Over the next five days, until the weather turned, the Eighth and Fifteenth air forces fought their way to and from targets deep inside Germany. The Americans attacked shipyards in Rostock, railway and power stations in Berlin, aircraft industry in Brunswick, Daimler-Benz in Stuttgart, Messerschmitt factories in Regensburg and Augsburg, and more.[24] The Luftwaffe fought back viciously, and the American fighters responded with aggressive attacks. The "Big Week" cost the Americans 266 bombers, 2600 aircrew (killed or captured), and 28 fighters.[25] Fully one-half of these losses occurred on the last two days of the battle, when the Germans exploited mistakes that left bombers unescorted or without sufficient escorts.[26]

The British joined in on the Big Week, but with different targets. From February 20 to 25, the RAF bombed the centers and/or residential sections of Leipzig, Berlin, Aachen, Stuttgart, Munich, Keil, Augsburg, Saarbrücken, Mannheim, and Schweinfurt. Augsburg—an ancient city—was entirely obliterated.[27]

Speer was in bed at the Red Cross's Hohenlychen Hospital when he got the news of the American attacks. He had fallen ill in January and, at his worst, was delusional and unable to get out of bed. Himmler had assigned Dr. Karl Gebhardt, his personal physician, to look after Speer. Gebhardt had been a doctor at the Ravensbrück and Sachsenhausen concentration camps, where he deliberately infected women with gas gangrene to test the effectiveness of new drugs.[28] Gebhardt misdiagnosed Speer with muscular rheumatism, for which he prescribed sulfonamide and bee poison. "I think," Speer said after one of Gebhardt's rounds, "he's trying to kill me."[29] He might have been: in February 1944, Speer's secretary, while hiding behind a door, heard Himmler say to Gebhardt, in apparent reference to Speer, "Well, then, he'll just be dead." When Gebhardt protested, Himmler replied, "Enough! The less said the better."[30]

On February 23, a few weeks before Speer was able to transfer out of the hospital and away from Gebhardt's clutches, Milch came to see him. The

Americans, he told Speer, were concentrating their bombing on German air-craft industry, "with the result that our aircraft production would be reduced to a third of what it had been, for at least a month."[31] Speer decided he had to "leave nothing untried to help the hard-pressed Luftwaffe."[32]

Alexander Witzigmann was a seventeen-year-old antiaircraft auxiliary who manned one of Germany's great flak guns. He was one of 750 defending the heavily protected capital. Across the city, there were hundreds of searchlights, heavy gun batteries, flak towers, and rocket launchers (single guns). Operating together, they were capable of creating a ceiling of death over Berlin.

On March 6, which came to be called Bloody Monday, Alexander watched a fifteen-mile-long parade of American bombers thunder across the capital. Wave after wave of fighters flew head-on into them. Flashlights coned them and flak blasted them. And yet they kept coming. "I was so frightened," Alexander later said, "by the display of strength by the enemy [that] I began to shake."[33]

Determined to defend the capital, Luftwaffe fighters lined up fifty abreast and flew head-on into the bombers. When they were within five hundred yards of them, they would fire a single half-second burst before pulling up violently. These daredevil, almost proto-kamikaze techniques cost the Americans dearly. By the time they were over Berlin, they had lost twenty bombers. The 100th Bomb Group had suffered particularly badly, losing one-half of its force. But it cost the Germans even more: American fighters, Mustangs, shot down between 70 and 170 out of 400 fighters. And though the ball bearings factory itself was hardly touched—many of the bombs hit the city, killing and maiming seven hundred people—the raid was unquestionably a success. In New York, reporter James B. Reston wrote, "The time of what was once called air-raids has passed. The Allied Army of the air has started a campaign of attrition against the Luftwaffe which must be recognized as one of the decisive military campaigns of the war. . . . From now on the Allied leaders of this campaign will send their aerial artillery anywhere in Germany where the German fighters are made and to any point where German fighters will give battle."[34]

Harris had always counseled against hitting the same targets successively, as it gave the Germans a clear warning of what to expect. But, two nights later, the 100th Squadron was back, blazing exactly the same trail across Germany. At Drummer Lake, in northern Germany and the scene of the majority of the 100th's losses, the first wave of escort fighters, Thunderbolts, turned away. They should have been replaced immediately by Mustangs, but they weren't: the second wave of escorts was late. The Luftwaffe saw their chance and attacked: German fighters flew en masse into the bomber formation. The leader of the bombing formation, the head of the 45th, became confused and lost, and missed the turn to Berlin. Major John M. Bennett, head of the battle-scarred 100th, moved his wing in front of the 45th and led the Eighth Air Force into Berlin.[35]

Galland was waiting for them there. He had deliberately saved up the bulk of his fighter forces for the Eighth's bombing run. As Bennett's and the other bombers came over Berlin, they responded to Galland's tactics by bearing straight ahead, and the B-17s blasted through the fighters. As the bullets pelted them from the front, flak hit them from below. The airplanes, and men, shook. Hot shrapnel cut through the bottoms of the planes, killing some men and castrating others.[36] By the time it returned to England, the Eighth Air Force had lost thirty-seven bombers and eighteen fighters. But they had again exacted so heavy a toll on the Germans that, three nights later, the Luftwaffe stayed on the ground during a precision raid on Berlin.

Over the course of the March 1944 raids, the Americans suffered terrible losses—153 bombers in just three raids—but they imposed equally terrible losses: 40 to 50 German fighters per raid. By the time the Americans paused, they had destroyed almost all of Germany's existing night fighters, seven hundred night fighters that were in production, and three-quarters of all manufacturing facilities. It was, as Speer's biographer put it, "very nearly the end of the Luftwaffe."[37]

20

GERMANY'S ACHILLES' HEEL

Oil had been on target lists from the earliest days of the war, but the major refineries were out of the range of early RAF bomb runs and the few raids on closer targets produced little. In February 1944, Spaatz became a convinced advocate of new attacks on oil. As air attacks on the Luftwaffe produced early results, Spaatz ordered the formation of a USSTAF planning committee to consider future targets. With Spaatz urging them on, the committee produced a report on March 5. It called for combined RAF–American attacks on oil targets across Germany and into central Europe. If fourteen synthetic oil plants (which extracted oil from coal) and thirteen refineries could be destroyed, 80 percent of German production and 60 percent of readily usable refining capacity would be destroyed.

Spaatz's urgency was driven by the British as much as the Germans. Solly Zuckerman, who had been fully behind Spaatz's attacks on the Luftwaffe, had been studying attacks on communications in the Mediterranean theater. He became convinced that the best way to weaken Germany in the run-up to D-Day was through destroying the country's transportation system, and above all its large railway centers and rolling stock.[1] Sounding rather like Harris on cities, Zuckerman argued that a country's railways were its nervous system: if you damaged one part of it, you could cripple the whole.[2] Specifically, destroying these transportation nodes would paralyze the Germans as they tried to ship men and materiel to Normandy. Zuckerman calculated that about 40 percent—45,000 tons out of a total preinvasion program of 108,000—of all Allied bombs should hit communication targets. The work would be roughly divided between the RAF and the Eighth and Ninth air forces. Zuckerman presented his conclusions, which were not radically different from those of a 1943 report by the Ministry of War Transport, in early 1944.[3]

The plan went before a newly formed Allied Air Forces Bombing Committee on January 10, passed through several other committees, and finally reached Eisenhower and Tedder on February 1. The plan proposed attacks on rail targets. They liked it. The report convinced Tedder of the merits of attacking transportation. Eisenhower was similarly won over, but one of the plan's merits had nothing to do with bombing at all: the integration of all available air forces nicely complemented Eisenhower's assumption of overall command. As the plan circulated, the battle lines quickly became clear. Eisenhower, Tedder, Leigh-Mallory, and Zuckerman supported the plan; the prime minister, the bulk of the War Cabinet, the War Office, the Air Ministry, Bomber Command, and the USSTAF opposed it.[4]

Added to this mix was an institutional debate. Tedder was given the job of reconciling differences between Eisenhower, who wanted total control, and Portal, who wanted autonomy for RAF Coastal, Fighter, and Bomber Command. Tedder—who saw air power as complementary to the Army and Navy—was able by April to get all parties to agree to a compromise.[5] Eisenhower would have overall direction of the strategic air forces for a limited period, only until September 1944.

Throughout February and March, the debate over transportation versus oil raged. Tedder's support for transportation was matched by his suspicion of oil, as he had been "led up the garden path before." He doubted that refineries could be knocked out and believed that any damage that was inflicted would be answered by aggressive German conservation. Spaatz countered that attacks on northern France would not bring the Luftwaffe up into the air, and that the inevitable civilian casualties would destroy French goodwill.

As the argument rolled on, Eisenhower grew increasingly irritated. In late March, he threatened resignation: "I am going to take drastic action and inform the Combined Chiefs of Staff that unless the matter is settled at once I will request relief from this command."[6] At a March 25 meeting, Spaatz, Tedder, Eisenhower, Harris, and Leigh-Mallory, along with representatives from the War Office, Air Ministry, and Joint Intelligence Committee, met to have it out. Spaatz and Eaker had already spent the morning lobbying Eisenhower, but the general would not show his hand.[7]

When the meeting started, Tedder was in the chair—a crucial advantage. He secured general agreement that the Luftwaffe, including ball bearings production, remained the highest priority, and that the air forces would only target oil or communications *after* they targeted the German Air Force. Tedder then put the case for the transportation plan, and Eisenhower swung in behind it. "Everything," he said, "I have read convinces me that, apart from the attack on the German Air Force, the Transportation Plan was the only one which offered a reasonable chance of the air forces making a real contribution to the land battle during the first vital weeks of OVERLORD."[8] He continued: "In fact, there is no real alternative."

The argument was not going Spaatz's way, and he did himself no favors. When he presented the oil plan, he highlighted the transportation plan's problems *without* emphasizing strongly enough how the oil plan would aid OVERLORD. Worse still, he spoke in a wooden and unpersuasive manner. Among the English, wit and rhetorical persuasion matter. Immensely.

After Spaatz's speech, Anderson came in with the honest admission that the oil plan would not guarantee a decisive influence during the initial stages of OVERLORD. What it would do, however, was have a devastating effect on the enemy within six months. The transportation plan, by contrast, might affect neither OVERLORD nor the overall war effort. At this point, a British oil expert from the Ministry of Economic Warfare offered his "help"; attacks on oil would drive down German supplies by 25 percent in three months, and would significantly affect German production (they would "feel the pinch") within four to five months.

Portal leapt on this. The official's comments "showed conclusively that the oil plan would not help OVERLORD in the first few critical weeks."[9] Eisenhower agreed, and it was all over. Transportation, not oil, would be the primary target in the run-up to the invasion of the Continent.

Arthur Harris had been unusually quiet during the discussion. He naturally detested the transportation plan, as it was precision bombing *par excellence*. With his usual wit, he wrote to U.S. Assistant Secretary of War for Air Lovett that "our worst headache has been a panacea plan devised by a civilian professor whose peacetime forte is the study of the sexual aberrations of the higher apes. Starting from this sound military basis he devised a scheme to employ almost the entire British and US bomber forces for three months or more in the destruction of targets mainly in France and Belgium."[10] Bombing transportation, Harris told Spaatz, would "never work."[11]

A few weeks before the March 25 meeting, Harris had pleaded with Portal in favor of all-out area bombing. "Any serious reduction of our rate at striking at German production," he wrote, "will inevitably make possible industrial recovery which would, within quite a short period, nullify the results achieved by tremendous efforts during the past 12 months."[12]

Portal decided to call his bluff. On March 4, he ordered Harris to undertake precision raids on marshaling yards in France. The results were outstanding. On March 6–7, Bomber Command blasted railway tracks, rolling stock, and railway installations, doing "enormous damage."[13] The next night, the RAF dropped 300 bombs on railway yards at Le Mans; they destroyed 250 wagons, hit 6 locomotives, sliced through many railway lines, and burned out a store of railway sleepers.[14] Only thirty bombs fell outside the target, killing thirty-one French people. Not a single aircraft was lost on either raid, and it was made crystal clear that Bomber Command was capable of a high degree of precision. Less obviously, the raids also showed that the cantankerous commander-in-chief would, when push came to shove, obey a direct and unequivocal order. When the March 25 meeting occurred, Harris's success left him unable to make a tactical case against transportation targets. His views on all "panaceas" were well known, and restating them would have gained him nothing. Instead, he reserved his invective for Leigh-Mallory, who let it be known that he was "reluctant to go down to posterity as the man who killed thousands of Frenchmen." Harris shot back: "What makes you think you're going to go down to posterity at all?"[15]

Spaatz left the March 25 meeting disappointed, but not dejected. Although transportation won out over oil, he was still left with much that he liked. For his part, Harris had been assigned twenty-six rail targets in France, so he could not go on bombing cities while Spaatz was diverted from his own preferred targets. More importantly, the overall agreement on the importance of destroying the Luftwaffe gave Spaatz a wedge into oil attacks. If bombing oil targets brought a fierce Luftwaffe response, then oil targets would fall squarely within his primary order to destroy the Luftwaffe.[16] At the same time, poor weather limited the number of direct raids of transportation, freeing up surplus bombers for oil.[17] After a long fight over transportation and oil, it was proving possible to hit both.

Within a week of his March 25 loss, Spaatz regrouped and made his case to Portal and Eisenhower. In a March 31 memo, he defended his oil plan with a clarity that had escaped him six days earlier. "The effect from the Oil attack," he wrote, while offering a less definite input in time, is certain to be more far-reaching. It will lead directly to sure disaster for Germany. The Rail attack can lead to harassment only. In weighting these two, it appears that too great a price may be paid merely for a certainty of very little.[18]

As oil depended, like everything else, on transport, the two targets might be viewed as complementary. Knocking out both oil production and the trains that brought the men and equipment to repair the damage would be disastrous for Germany's war effort.

Spaatz sketched out the target priorities for the two air forces. The Eighth would attack:

- The Luftwaffe and ball bearings.
- The nineteen rail targets in occupied countries already selected through the Transportation Plan.
- The thirteen major synthetic plants.

At the same time, the Fifteenth would target:

- The Luftwaffe and ball bearings.
- Rail transport in Romania and selected targets in southern France.
- Synthetic oil targets in southern Germany.
- Political targets in the Balkans.[19]

Spaatz envisioned a two-part attack: first, a concentrated raid on Germany's main supply of crude and refined petroleum, which would cut production and force the Germans to use synthetic oil; and, second, concentrated air attacks on synthetic oil production that would, over several months, cripple German industrial production. By March 1944, Germany's main source of crude and refined petroleum was to be found in Romania, at the sprawling refineries of Ploesti. In 1943, they had supplied two million tons of oil.[20]

Changing the mind of either man was not easy. The Supreme Commander remained convinced that the transportation plan would provide the greatest support for the invasion. Portal maintained that oil fell outside POINTBLANK, and in late March he sent out an official minute ruling Ploesti out as a target.[21]

Spaatz went ahead anyway. On April 5, the Fifteenth Air Force launched a raid on Ploesti. As required by the transportation plan, the target was the town's marshaling yards.[22] The bombers, however, "missed" the yards and hit the adjacent refineries. A few days later, they "missed" again, and scored another direct hit on Ploesti. Spaatz was convinced that the raids had been successful, but he could not launch a full-blown oil campaign without Eisenhower's support.

On April 10, the British War Cabinet and British Chiefs of Staff invoked an escape clause in the air agreement, declaring V-1 rockets a threat to the security of the British Isles. Tedder phoned Fred Anderson to give him a new bombing directive: Operation Crossbow, the destruction of German long-range missiles and missile sites, had priority over POINTBLANK. In early 1944, the War Cabinet had asked for a military report on gassing German launching sites.[23] Portal had to point out that the Vice-Chiefs of Staff had already considered such a proposal in late 1943, along with the related idea of gassing German civilians. The Vice-Chiefs thought gas attacks on civilians would cost Britain the moral high ground and invite retaliation, and that gas attacks on projector sites did less damage than high explosives.[24]

Spaatz was livid, and on the night of April 19 he went to let Eisenhower know. The timing turned out to be bad. Minutes before Spaatz arrived, Eisenhower had learned that the commanding general of the Ninth's Air Force Service Command, Maj. Gen. Henry J. F. Miller, had gotten obnoxiously drunk in a London hotel and proceeded loudly to take bets that the invasion would come before June 15.[25] It was not an auspicious start, but Spaatz made good by having Miller arrested and confined to his quarters. Spaatz then vented his anger over Tedder's decision to grant V-1 rocket sites priority. If they worried the British so much, the RAF should be sent to destroy them. The case was clear and Eisenhower agreed.

Spaatz then used the chance to reopen the oil debate. He argued that two recent raids on transportation targets at Berlin and Kassel had cost the USSTAF only fifteen bombers between them. While a great relief, it meant that the transportation attacks were not bringing out the Luftwaffe. Oil attacks, Spaatz argued, would. Eisenhower would not be swayed. He repeated his arguments against moving from transportation to oil. But then he relented. No one knows exactly what Spaatz said to change Eisenhower's mind—the two men made a point of leaving no official record—but he probably threatened resignation. Spaatz was permitted any two days before the invasion to hit oil. Then it was back to transportation.

Spaatz was ready to go, but the weather was not. It was not until May 12 that the clouds had cleared, and then only over England and Germany (Ploesti remained covered in clouds). Synthetic oil plants in eastern Germany would have to be the target. That day, 15 combat wings—886 bombers and 735 escorting fighters—took off from English bases and streaked across Germany. Their targets were synthetic oil plants at Zwickau, Merseburg-Leuna, Brux, Lützendorf, Bohlen, and Zeitz. They flew across the English Channel toward Frankfurt am Main, where the bulk of the force banked northeast toward Zwickau.

German radar picked up the bombing formation as it approached the Dutch coast. Galland, who had deliberately preserved his fighters as Speer tried frantically to rebuild, quickly guessed where the bombers were headed. He sent up four hundred fighters to attack.[26] At Frankfurt, a mass of German fighters attacked the leading division, which was low on escorts because one of its fighting groups had mistakenly rendezvoused with a trailing division.[27] The remaining escort fighters were overwhelmed. Within forty minutes, the Germans downed thirty-two bombers—some two-thirds of the total forty-six bombers lost on the mission. Two others were lost to fighters, twelve to flak.

After these early kills, the Luftwaffe ran out of luck. Subsequent bombers were better protected, and the fighters engaged the Germans in ferocious dogfights. They destroyed sixty Luftwaffe fighters, protected the majority of the bombers and allowed them to fly on to oil targets. They blasted synthetic oil plants with 1718 tons of bombs.

On the day of the attack, Albert Speer had been back in Berlin for four days. May 12 was a date he would never forget. "On that day," he wrote, "the technological war was decided. . . . Until then," he continued, "we had managed to produce approximately as many weapons as the armed forces needed, in spite of their considerable losses. But with the attack of [the American daylight bombers] upon several fuel plants in central and eastern Germany, a new era in the air war began. *It meant the end of German war production.*"[28]

On May 13, Speer accompanied some technicians on a visit to the Leuna works. Stepping across broken and twisted pipes, he received a report on the damage. The chemical plants had proven "extremely sensitive to bombing."

By the most optimistic forecasts, production could not be resumed for weeks. Daily output dropped by 1000 metric tons: from 5850 to 4820. It was a huge drop, but not a disastrous one. Germany's reserves could see the country through for another nineteen months.[29]

On May 13, the day after Spaatz's oil raid, ULTRA intercepted an order from Luftwaffe Operations Staff in Berlin. It called for the stripping of heavy and light antiaircraft guns from the Eastern Front and from plants manufacturing fighters in Oschersleben, Leipzig-Erla, and Wiener Neustadt. They were to be sent to Zeitz, in eastern Germany, and Politz, near Stettin. Spaatz was ecstatic: the Germans obviously dreaded attacks on oil, even more so than on fighter production, and they were gathering their air force around oil targets. He had successfully predicted both. A week later, ULTRA intercepted a second order, this time to convert an even higher percentage of motor transport to power supplied by inefficient wood fuel generators.[30] Oil attacks were working. Even Tedder came around: "I guess we'll give the customer what he wants."[31]

As the second intercept arrived in London, Speer left Leuna after a week of fact-finding. On May 19, he flew to Obersalzberg, where he met Keitel and Hitler.[32] Looking straight into Hitler's eyes, Speer said, "The enemy has struck us at our weakest points. If they persist at it this time, we will soon no longer have any fuel production worth mentioning." In a reference probably to Göring, he added, "Our one hope is that the other side has an air force of general staff as scatterbrained as ours!" Keitel, always the sycophant, tried to brush this aside. He argued that the reserves would see Germany through, and he added a typical National Socialist appeal to past glories. "How many difficult situations we have already survived!" Turning to Hitler, he said, "We shall survive this one, *mein Führer.*"

This time Hitler did not allow himself to be taken in by cheap optimism and flattery. He arranged a meeting with Göring, Keitel, Milch, four industrialists, and Hans Kehrl, chief of the Planning and Raw Materials Department. Göring tried to keep the representatives of the fuel industry out—arguing that the matter was best dealt with in private—but Hitler brushed him aside.

Before the meeting, Speer urged the industrialists to tell the whole truth. Göring, however, got to them a few minutes before it started and, fearing the blame would fall on him, urged them to retain their optimism in Hitler's presence. They gathered outside Hitler's office and watched several hurried and harried senior military officers rush past. Then they were called in. Hitler tersely shook each man's hand and bid them to sit down. "I have called this meeting," he said, "to be informed about the consequences of the last air-raids."[33] He then asked the industrialists directly for their views. One by one, they testified in sober and dispassionate terms, furnishing their arguments with statistics, that the situation would be hopeless if a systematic campaign against oil were launched. Hitler at first reverted to platitudes: "We've been through worse before," and "You'll manage it somehow." Göring and Keitel took their cues, and gushed in confident terms. Keitel in particular harped on about the oil reserves. In a manner that commanded Speer's respect, the industrialists would not be swayed. They reiterated their conclusions and supported them with hard data.

After the meeting, the guests returned to the anteroom, where Göring scolded them for having "burdened Hitler with such anxieties and pessimistic nonsense."[34] The cars then picked up the guests and took them to the Berghof, where they had coffee and cake before the fireplace. The talk became trivial, and Hitler retreated into one of his friendlier worlds. He said nothing ever again to Speer about American bombing.

Speer left the meeting and oversaw two weeks of feverish repairs. Production was just about at its former level. It was May 28, 1944. That day, Spaatz sent out more than four hundred bombers to attack synthetic oil plants at Ruhland, Magdeburg, Merseburg-Leuna, and Lützendorf. The results were devastating. At Merseburg-Leuna, Italian forced laborers added to the chaos by pouring fuel on the flames.[35]

The results of the May 28 raid were more devastating than on May 12. The two blows halved German oil production. As Speer wrote, "Our pessimistic statements at Obersalzberg had thus been fully confirmed only five days later, and Göring's bluster had been refuted."[36] Looking back at the campaign after the war, Galland noted that "it is difficult to understand why the Allies started this undertaking so late, after they had suffered such heavy losses in other operations. Right from the start fuel had been the most awkward bottleneck for [Germany's] conduct of the war."[37] The oil campaign was "the most successful operation of the entire Allied strategical air war" and the "fatal blow for the Luftwaffe."[38]

A further Ploesti raid occurred almost exactly a week before a vast armada of troops landed at Normandy, with more than six thousand planes—from Bomber, Fighter, and Coastal Command, the Second (tactical) Air Force of the RAF, and the Eighth and Ninth American air forces—flying overhead.

They were prepared for bitter resistance from the Luftwaffe, but none came. Only 320 aircraft—making odds of 1 to 20—were there to meet them.[39]

The air forces' support for ground troops was impressive, but their greatest contribution to Normandy occurred well before June 6, 1944. Over five months, they had destroyed the factories producing fighters, used decoys and attacks to draw out the German fighters, and shot them out of the sky in the hundreds. The transportation plan, despite Spaatz's skepticism, had also produced results. Bombing had almost entirely dismembered the rail network of northern Belgium and France, choking off the supply channels feeding the German army.[40] Trucks that tried to move toward the front found gullies where bridges had been. German fighters that had hoped to land at little- or never-used bases in northern France found them ravaged by bombs. Any trucks or trains that managed to find a route to the front were blasted by Allied fighters. "The Allies have," the commander of the 2nd Panzer Division reported, "total air supremacy. They bomb and shoot at anything that moves, even single vehicles and persons. . . . The feeling of being powerless against the enemy's aircraft . . . has a paralyzing effect."[41] The morale that mattered in a totalitarian state—the morale of its military and political leaders, rather than its citizens—was being undermined.[42] And it was being undermined by precision bombing.

21

OIL AND BABY KILLING

On June 7, 1944, Portal was sent a message from Luftwaffe Operations Staff that ULTRA had intercepted. It read:

As a result of renewed encroachment into the production of a/c [aircraft fuel] by enemy action, the most essential requirements for training and carrying out production plans can scarcely be covered with the quantities of a/c fuel available. *In order to ensure the defence of the Reich and to prevent the readiness for defence of the GAF [German Air Force] from gradually collapsing,* it has been necessary to break into the strategical reserve.[1]

Portal was above all a pragmatist. He had once believed that area bombing would win the war. When the evidence suggested otherwise, he changed his views. In early 1944, he had been very skeptical about the effectiveness of oil targets; when the evidence showed how effective those targets were, he changed his mind again.[2]

Portal sent a copy of the decryption to the prime minister and added a note: "I regard this as one of the most important pieces of information we have yet received." He recommended to Churchill an all-out attack on synthetic oil plants by all Allied strategic bombers as soon as they were free. Piecemeal and sporadic attacks by small forces would only give the Germans time to increase flak and smoke defenses. Churchill replied with one word: "Agreed."[3]

On June 3, Bottomley had asked Harris for his views on bombing oil targets as soon as OVERLORD allowed him to.[4] Harris had waited ten days to reply and then stated that the targets could be destroyed with thirty-two thousand tons of bombs, perhaps less, but that it would be a waste of bombs to do so. Harris also reminded Bottomley that any plans would have to go through the deputy supreme commander. Tedder had already signed on. Thus, through an informal arrangement between Eisenhower and Spaatz and between Tedder and Harris, oil became an unofficial RAF target.[5]

Later in the month, Eisenhower made the clandestine oil plan public, and the attacks continued. Throughout the month, the Eighth Air Force launched three all-out raids on oil. On June 18 and 20, the Eighth attacked oil facilities near Munich, losing fifty bombers. Nine days later, the Fifteenth Air Force once again hammered Ploesti.

In Berlin, Speer felt as if his world was imploding. His remarks of May 12 had proved all too accurate. On that day, Germany had 715,000 tons of petroleum at its disposal. By June, it had 472,000 tons. In April, the Luftwaffe had 180,000 tons of aviation spirit; by June, only 10,000.[6] On June 30, Speer wrote to Hitler. "My Führer,"[7] he began,

> in the course of June the enemy's attacks on the synthetic oil plants and refineries were carried out with increased strength . . . *The enemy succeeded, on June 22nd, in bringing the loss of aviation petrol up to 90%.* Only through the most rapid repair of the damaged [facilities], whose return to production was in every case far in advance of the originally laid down date, will it be possible to restore a part of the catastrophic loss of June 22nd. *Nevertheless, the output of aviation spirit is wholly insufficient at present.*
>
> After the first attack of May 12, you were told on the Obersalzberg that the output for the month of June would be 126,000 tons of aviation petrol . . . Owing to the continuing attacks of the month of June production fell considerably short of this stated total. . . . *The production of the second half of June has again fallen considerably and is only at the rate of 42,000 tons a month, which leads to the certain conclusion, even today, that there will be an extraordinary fall in the July production if the attacks continue.*

Unless synthetic plants and refineries could be protected, Speer concluded, "it will be absolutely impossible to cover the most urgent of the necessary supplies for the Wehrmacht by September, in other words, from that time onwards there will be an unbridgeable gap which must lead to tragic results . . .

I beg you to take the strictest measures to provide additional protection for these plants."

On July 9, ten days after Speer's letter to Hitler, ULTRA picked up another intercept, this time from Göring. It read: "The deep inroads made into the supply of aircraft fuel demand the most stringent reduction in flying. Drastic economy is absolutely essential." Three weeks later, the Americans launched a raid on Germany's largest single synthetic oil plant, at Merseburg. The intercept read: "Heaviest attacks so far; heavy damage—works provisionally 100 percent out of action."[8] The impact of oil attacks was decisive and unquestionable. Up to this point, during the whole of 1944, Bomber Command had not launched a single attack on oil targets.[9]

On July 7, both the Eighth and the Fifteenth air forces launched oil raids on Germany. The Eighth hit targets in central Germany; the Fifteenth bombed synthetic oil plants at Blechhammer, in Upper Silesia, forty miles from Auschwitz.

The Allies had definitely known about Auschwitz since April 1944.[10] On April 4, an American reconnaissance plane had flown toward the I.G. Farben synthetic oil and rubber plant at Monowitz. Four miles before reaching the plant, he turned on his camera. The film rolled as he passed over the plant, and then for another four miles. On his return, he had twenty-three exposures, including three of Auschwitz.[11]

On April 7, Rudolf Vrba and Alfred Wetzler, both Slovak Jews, had escaped the camp and hid themselves in a woodpile just outside it. For three days, the SS and their dogs searched the camp and its surroundings. Then, after SS procedure dictated that the search be called off, Vrba and Wetzler escaped.

Two weeks later, they arrived in Slovakia. On April 25, 1944, the Vrba-Wetzler Report (also known as the Auschwitz Protocols) told the world of the camp and its locations, of crowded trains arriving at precise times, of the separation of prisoners, and of ovens:

> At present there are four crematoria in operation at Birkenau, two large ones, I and II, and two smaller ones III and IV. Those of type I and II consist of 3 parties, i.e.: (A) the furnace room; (B) the large halls; and (C) the gas chamber. A huge chimney rises from the furnace room around which are grouped nine furnaces, each having four openings. Each opening can take

three normal corpses at once and after an hour and a half the bodies are completely burned. This corresponds to a daily capacity of about 2,000 bodies. . . . The gassing takes place as follows: the victims are brought into hall (B), where they are told to undress. To complete the fiction that they are going to bathe, each person receives a towel and a small piece of soap issued by two men in white coats. Then they are crowded into the gas chamber (C) in such numbers that there is, of course, only standing room. To compress this crowd into the narrow space, shots are often fired to [force those at the front] to huddle still closer together. Then, there is a short pause, presumably to allow the room temperature to rise to a certain level, after which the SS men with gas masks climb on the roof, open the traps, and shake down a preparation in powder form out of tin cans. [It is marked] "CYKLON. FOR USE AGAINST VERMIN."

The report was sent to Rudolf Kastner, leader of the Jewish Agency Rescue Committee in Hungary. Rather than disseminating the information to that country's Jews, Kastner showed the report to Adolf Eichmann, head of the Jewish section of the SS. Eichmann feigned an interest in negotiating to keep the report secret.

Kastner, however, didn't have the only copy. Another copy, together with a further eyewitness report on deportations from Hungary (the "Mordowicz-Rosin" report), was forwarded by Slovak Jewish leaders to Dr. Jaromir Kopecky, the Geneva representative of the Czechoslovakian government-in-exile.[12] Kopecky sent both reports to Gerhart Riegner of the World Jewish Congress in Switzerland. Riegner had a summary of the report forwarded to Elizabeth Wiskemann, an expert on Czechoslovakia at the British legation in the Swiss capital, Bern, urging that the BBC broadcast the details.[13] Wiskemann then sent the summary immediately to Allen Dulles, head of U.S. Intelligence in Switzerland. On June 16, Dulles forwarded it to Roswell McClelland, the War Refugee Board's representative in Switzerland. The Board had been established by Roosevelt in January to "rescue the victims of enemy oppression." Dulles attached a note: "Seems more in your line."[14] McClelland cabled John Pehle, the head of the Board, in Washington: "There is little doubt that many of these Hungarian Jews are being sent to the extermination camps of Auschwitz and Birkenau in western Upper Silesia where, according to recent reports, at least 1,500,000 Jews have been killed . . . It is urged by all sources of this information in

Slovakia and Hungary that vital sections of these [railway] lines and especially bridges . . . be bombed as the only possible means of slowing down or
stopping future deportations."[15] Two days later, another cable arrived, this
time from the Orthodox community in Bratislava, urging the bombing of
railways and of towns that served as major railway junctions.[16] On June 24,
Pehle went to see John McCloy, Assistant Secretary of War and another
Stimson protégé. Without endorsing the proposal or even formally asking
McCloy to act on it, he suggested that the assistant secretary "explore it."[17]

The report was definitive proof of Auschwitz (the concentration camp)
and Birkenau (or Auschwitz II, the gas chambers and crematorium), and what
was happening there. Much information on the Nazi murder of Jews had
leaked out and been reported, and by 1942 the Allies knew the name and location of four of the death camps: Chelmno, Treblinka, Sobibor, and Belzec.[18]
Auschwitz-Birkenau, the principal site of mass murder, nonetheless remained
shrouded in secrecy. Specific information about the camp—through ULTRA
intercepts, for instance—had come to the Allies sometime before, and by mid-
1943 a number of officials had enough details to determine the site and purpose of the installation. It is, however, a matter of debate whether they had
analyzed the disparate pieces of information in a systematic enough way to
know with certainty at that point. By June 1944, they had. By the time the
Allies had the knowledge, they also had the capability: bombing Birkenau
required in practice heavy bombing missions from northern Italy. By April
1944 at the latest, the Fifteenth Air Force was capable of destroying Auschwitz
in four precision raids, spread over several weeks and involving some
seventy-five bombers each.[19] It would have diverted 7 percent of the Fifteenth's
bombers from the oil offensive. Only a raid on the camp itself would have
worked: bombed rail lines were easily repaired, and the more ambitious project
of taking out the rail nexus leading to Auschwitz-Birkenau would have
required a massive diversion of air power.[20]

In June, the Eighth Air Force began flying missions in support of the
Soviet summer offensive from bases near Kiev ("Operation Frantic"). An attack on Auschwitz from Soviet bases would have required Stalin's approval,
however, and they were much more vulnerable to Luftwaffe attack.[21] It is
possible that low-level raids by RAF Mosquitoes, flying from bases near the
Adriatic Sea, might also have destroyed Birkenau in June 1944, but it is doubtful that they could have covered the distance undetected, or had enough impact to destroy Birkenau if they did.[22] The Fifteenth, by contrast, could have

done the job. By this point, 250,000 Jews had already been deported from Hungary to Auschwitz.

On July 2, a few days after the report reached McCloy, Spaatz launched a series of heavy raids on military targets around Budapest. They had nothing to do with the deportations or with diplomatic efforts to stop the deportations by Sweden, Roosevelt (who appealed to the Hungarian people to help Jews to escape and to "record the evidence"), and the Vatican.[23] The puppet government in Budapest interpreted the bombing as reprisals, panicked, and told Eichmann on July 7 that they were halting the deportations. Three hundred thousand Jewish lives were temporarily saved.

The day before, Chaim Weizmann and Moshe Shertok, two of the most senior representatives of the Jewish Agency for Palestine in London, went to see the Foreign Secretary Anthony Eden.[24] Much of their conversation concerned the tragically hopeless proposals by Joel Brand of the Zionist Rescue Committee to negotiate with the Gestapo over trading Allied goods for Hungarian Jews. But they also raised the issue of bombing. The same day, Eden sent an account to Churchill. He reported Weizmann's appeal that "we should do something to mitigate the appalling slaughter of Jews in Hungary," and suggested himself bombing the railway lines and the camps, "so as to destroy the plant used for gassing and cremation."

Churchill replied on July 7, the following day. Negotiation was a nonstarter: "On no account have the slightest negotiations, direct or indirect, with the Huns." Bombing, however, had the prime minister's support: "Get anything out of the Air Force that you can, and invoke me if necessary."[25] The same day, Eden wrote to Sinclair: "*Both the Prime Minister and I are in agreement with [Weizmann's] suggestion* that something might be done to stop the operation of the death camps by (1) bombing the railway lines leading to Birkenau (and to other similar camps . . .); and (2) bombing the camps themselves. . . . Could you let me know," Eden continued, "how the Air Ministry view the feasibility of these proposals. I very much hope that it will be possible to do something. I have the authority of the Prime Minister to say that he agrees."[26] There were more than 300,000 Jews in Hungary.

On July 11, the Jewish Agency intervened again, sending a note to Roosevelt urging the bombing of Auschwitz itself. Doing so would "give the lie to the oft-repeated assertions of Nazi spokesmen that the Allies are not really so displeased [with] ridding Europe of Jews" and would "convince the German circles still hopeful of Allied mercy of the genuineness of Allied condemnation of the murder of the Jews."[27]

Eight days later, Sinclair replied with a cursory report stating that "bombing is out of the possibility for Bomber Command, because the distance [from the UK to Upper Silesia] is too great for the attack to be carried out at night." Sinclair made no mention of the possibility of using the Fifteenth's bases in Italy. Even if they could, however, Sinclair suggested there wasn't much point: "Even if the plant was destroyed, I am not clear that it would really help the victims." (Eden scribbled next to this: "He wasn't asked his opinion of this; he was asked to act.") Sinclair ended the note by suggesting an alternative: "I am proposing to have the proposition put to the Americans, with all the facts, to see if they are prepared to try."[28]

They weren't. McCloy had already blocked the proposal on July 4. "The War Department," he wrote to Pehle, "is of the opinion that the suggested air operation is impracticable. It could be executed only by the diversion of considerable air support essential to the success of our forces now engaged in decisive operations and would in any case be of such very doubtful efficacy that it would not amount to a practical project."[29] McCloy maintained for decades that the decision was his own, but in 1986, he attributed it to Roosevelt. "I remember talking one time with [the president] about it and he was irate: 'Why the idea! They'll say we bombed these people, and they'll only move down the road a little . . . We'll be accused of participating in this horrible business.' "[30] There is no written record of the conversation.

In August, the Poles launched the Warsaw uprising in the futile hope of liberating themselves from the Germans before the Soviets reached the city. Two full RAF squadrons, relying on volunteers, flew missions supplying the Poles for six consecutive days. Flying from Italy, they passed over Auschwitz on their way to the Polish capital.

During the same month, the debate over bombing Auschwitz continued. On July 26, unaware of the Americans' rejection of the idea, the Air Ministry planned to raise the issue with Spaatz. A week later, Bottomley reported that he had been "most sympathetic," but wanted more information about the "precise location, extent and nature of the camps and installations at Birkenau." The Ministry passed a request for photographic intelligence to the Foreign Ministry, but never got a reply.[31] Meanwhile Allied bombers continued to fly over Auschwitz and reconnaissance flights seeking evidence of industry and bomb damage to it brought back photographs of the camps. One of these photos, near the end of the month, showed Jews walking from a train toward a gas chamber.[32] On August 7, American bombers hit oil refineries at Trzebina, thirteen miles from Auschwitz.[33] One week later, another appeal, from the World Jewish Congress, to bomb the gas chambers and crematorium at Auschwitz was rejected by John McCloy as a costly diversion unlikely to succeed.[34] On August 27, 350 U.S. bombers again hit Blechhammer, and two days later they bombed Trzebina again.[35]

Three months after McCloy's July 4 cable, Pehle forwarded another recommmendation that Auschwitz be bombed, this time from the Polish government-in-exile. It was sent along to Spaatz on October 3. It was the first and last time that the War Department sent a proposal for bombing Auschwitz to an air force official in the European theater.[36] General Frederick Anderson urged him "to give no encouragement to the project. . . . There is the possibility of some of the bombs landing on the prisoners. . . . In that event the Germans would be provided with a fine alibi for any wholesale massacre that they might perpetuate."[37] The matter went no further.

Months before Anderson's dismissive communication to Spaatz, Shalom Lindenbaum arrived at Auschwitz with her father in a sealed goods wagon. A week later, she and other Jews who had arrived with her were summoned for a roll call near the camp gate. They were:

> . . . afraid that it was our turn, because normally before dusk there were no transports to other camps. On the nearby road, which led to the sauna (bath house) and gas chambers a new transport, which had arrived from ghetto Lodz, passed by. There was no doubt where they were taken. . . . I ran ahead to my father in order to be together in what seemed to be our last hour.
>
> [Then,] Allied bombers appeared in the sky. It will be difficult to describe our joy. We prayed and hoped to be bombed by them, and so to escape the helpless death in the gas chambers. To be bombed meant a chance that also the Germans will be killed . . . We were deeply disappointed and sad when they passed over . . .
>
> Fortunately we were taken back to the barracks, after a search of our bodies. But we didn't speak about our unexpected return, only about the Allies' reluctance to bomb the gas chambers.[38]

The chance flyover of Allied bombers probably saved Shalom's life. As the Allies never tried, we will never know how many others the bombers might have saved.

While the final chapter in the Jewish tragedy was coming to a close, Spaatz's overwhelming concern was oil. While he was bombing oil targets, the seductive if elusive target of morale was brought back onto the agenda. On June 21, Harris—having forgotten his June 1942 prediction that "once we get a footing on the continent our last bomb will have been dropped on Germany"[39]—asked Portal to schedule a joint U.S.-Bomber Command daylight raid on residential Berlin. The backdrop was the failure of Bomber Command raids to stem the assault on London. Silent, unmanned missiles launched from the Continent sailed over the British capital, then stopped and crashed down on the city. The military effect was negligible, but it was pure terror bombing and thousands of Londoners were dying.[40] Pressure for retaliation was growing and Churchill wanted something done.

Under Harris's plan, two thousand bombers—double that of the famous thousand-bomber raid two years earlier—would drop sixty-five hundred tons of bombs on Berlin. Portal supported the idea, as did Eisenhower. In a note to Churchill, Portal argued that, at the least, such a raid would "be a pretty good answer to the results achieved in the last few days by the 'flying bomb [the rockets].' "[41] At 1 A.M., Harris—with an eye to poor weather and Doolittle's reluctance to share his fighter escorts—canceled the mission. Instead, the Eighth Air Force sent one thousand bombers over Berlin. One-third of them bombed industrial targets in the outskirts; the others bombed the city center.

On Saturday, July 1, Churchill was in a meeting with the Chiefs of Staff. Out of the blue, he came up with a new idea for seeing off the V-1s: Britain should "announce [its] intention of flattening out in turn the lesser German cities if the 'CROSSBOW' attack is continued."[42] Such cities would be "small towns of 20,000 inhabitants or fewer, well known for historical or other associations, and not particularly connected to the war effort."[43] The idea was not entirely new—Anthony Eden, the Foreign Secretary, had suggested it back in 1943—but Churchill's intervention revived it.[44] There were suddenly two plans on the table: one for flattening Berlin, the other for ignoring Berlin and flattening dozens of provincial cities. Churchill's Chief of Staff, General Hastings Ismay, threw his enthusiastic support behind the second idea. Sir

Douglass Evill (who succeeded Freeman as Vice-Chief of Air Staff) countered that the policy would be immensely costly: the obliteration of a single city would require up to seven hundred sorties, whereas Churchill and Ismay's plan assumed that only one hundred or so would be required. Seeing that Churchill was committed to the idea, he appealed for time: the Chiefs of Staff should be given the chance to think it over. Churchill agreed.

The next day, Evill worked to kill the idea. He spoke with Tedder, who rejected the attacks as "wickedly uneconomical." He also had Coryton from Operations Planning prepare a short report on the proposal. Coryton's report drew up a list of fourteen towns that could be destroyed by joint U.S.–British bombing:[45] Wiesbaden, Mainz, Solingen, Saarbrücken, Bielefeld, Freiburg, Bonn, Osnabrück, Koblenz, Kaiserslautern, Oldenburg, Worms, Pirmasens, and Speyer.

The report concluded that attacking the towns would "have little effect upon the German war affect, is unlikely to impinge upon the confidence of the German High Command, and would impinge upon the morale of only some 1.9% of the population of Germany."[46] It might actually have given the Germans the idea that the V-1 attacks were working (if not, why retaliate?). Most importantly, it would distract from the oil campaign: "the opportunities available for the prosecution of our strategic attacks against enemy oil production, which Intelligence suggests may well have a decisive influence upon Germany's military capabilities, are few. . . . If the proposed policy of retaliatory attacks is adopted in full it will mean the abandonment of many, if not all those opportunities over the next one or two months."

Evill added pencil edits to the list—Mainz had already been destroyed, and Osnabrück and Saarbrücken had been "well-hit"—and attached it to his note. He concluded by saying, "I expect that you will wish to take steps to scotch this idea in the C.O.S. [Chiefs of Staff] on Monday."[47]

On July 4, Portal arrived at the meeting prepared. He argued that Churchill's threat would be the equivalent of an invitation to negotiate; that the Germans would not alter their behavior to save militarily irrelevant towns; and that bombing them would divert Allied air forces from attacks on oil, communications, and the battle in France.[48] The committee agreed to "further careful consideration and discussion at a future date"—an old bureaucratic trick for shelving an issue.

Churchill, however, was in a vengeful mood and was not prepared to let the matter rest.[49] At a War Cabinet meeting that evening, he ordered his

Chiefs to take up the issue the next day.[50] Portal argued still more forcefully against it: "No threat is likely to deter Hitler in his present fix. Indeed, it may well encourage him to order more F.B.s [Flying Bombs] and make still further efforts to increase the scale of the attack."[51] The only effect would be to distract bombers from military targets, including V-1 launch sites. The Chiefs of Staff agreed to a report on all aspects of retaliatory bombing, including poisonous gas. The report was turned around within hours. Heavily steered by Portal, it repeated the Chief of Air Staff's arguments about costs, diversions, negotiating, and retaliation.[52] It also argued that such wanton destruction was inconsistent with liberal democracy and Britain's moral stance. The Germans did not face the constraint of "moral scruples or public opinion" and would win in a tit-for-tat game of destruction. Britain would surrender the moral high ground by adopting a policy of reprisals.

> We have hitherto always maintained consistently in all public statements regarding our bombing policy that it is directed against military objectives and that any damage to civilians is incidental to our attack on the German war machine. This is a moral and legal point of great importance, both now and in the maintenance of our position after the war, and it would be greatly weakened should we now for the first time declare that we intended deliberate attacks on the civilian population as such.[53]

On July 5, the Chiefs of Staff approved the report, but —partly unable to shake the lingering belief that still more bombing might bring results—left the door open for future destruction of small cities. "The time might well come," the Chiefs agreed, "when an all-out attack by every means at our disposal on German civilian morale might be decisive."[54] In the end, the Chiefs recommended to Churchill that the methods of such an attack should be examined and all possible preparations made. Despite Portal's objections, the train had left the station.

In the United States, a similar argument was being played out. In June 1944, an intelligence officer in Washington, Colonel Lowell P. Weicker, drew up several plans for destroying German morale by blasting small German towns. Throughout June and July, an official under General Charles P. Cabell, the USSTAF Director of Plans, worked to scuttle the idea. The official's name was Colonel Richard D. Hughes. He had worked in the Air War Plans Division and came to London to serve on the Enemy Objectives Unit, which selected the target systems most vital to the Nazi war effort.[55] Hughes was no sentimentalist; he believed the Germans should suffer for what they had done. It was just that there were plenty of ways to make them suffer without killing them, and killing them would do nothing to serve the interests of the Allies during the war or after it. Hughes attacked Weicker's plans as yet another stab at the "will of the wisp of 'morale.' " Nazi repression made German resistance impossible, so terror bombing would only serve as confirmation of German propaganda. It would lead to a reaction among the American people against "indiscriminate area bombing," and would—not least—violate the principles to which the country had committed itself. Although the United States may have at times been hypocritical on moral issues, the country nonetheless "represented in world thought an urge toward decency and better treatment of man by man."[56] The Japanese might shoot American POWs; the Americans would never do the same to the Japanese. "Hot blood is one thing," Hughes added. "Reason and the long view is another." Cabell, who was a principled opponent of indiscriminate area bombing, agreed, and he asked that Spaatz reject the plan. Eisenhower, however, had the last word, and while he did not order the bombing of small towns, he told Spaatz to be ready to bomb the center of Berlin at a moment's notice.[57] Notice was not given, at least not in 1944.

While all of this was going on, the case for attacking oil was growing. On July 9, the day of the ULTRA intercept confirming how deeply affected German oil supplies had been, the British Air Ministry announced the formation of a joint Anglo-American oil targets committee, which was to keep the Axis oil position under review, to assess the damage inflicted, and to determine the priority of further attacks.[58]

During the month of July, then, two different committees were established: a joint Anglo-American committee to look at oil, and a working committee (made up of Air Staff, Foreign Office, MEW, and USSTAF representatives) to look at morale. At the end of the month, they both reported. The joint committee concluded that "Germany will be unable to continue the struggle beyond December given intensive fighting on three fronts and the continued success of Allied air attacks." Thanks to bombing, the report noted, Germany was consuming 300,000 more tons of oil each month than it produced. This was fact. At the same time, the working committee offered its recommendations. On July 22, the committee argued that the point of a morale attack was "to influence the minds of the German authorities in such a way that they prefer organized surrender to continued resistance." The target for a morale-busting campaign would be Berlin. A few months after Harris's five-month-long effort to "wreck the city from end to end," the committee promised that twenty thousand bombs delivered in a four-day and three-night round-the-clock bombing raid would disrupt government services, destroy communications, and lead to an overall breakdown of morale. This was fiction.

Two nights later, Harris launched just such a campaign on a different city. Over four nights—from July 25 to 29—Stuttgart was flattened. From the twelfth century, the city had grown up in a series of narrow valleys. Its old city core centered around the castle, the city hall, and the market square. Elegant, densely packed businesses, set alongside houses with sloping roofs, radiated out from the core. At 1:38 A.M. on July 26, 474 bombers razed the city.[59] The first wave of high explosives destroyed the city hall, and knocked out the water lines under the market square. The houses burned and collapsed, burying the remaining water hoses. By morning, the palace was an empty shell, 885 people were killed, and 87 percent of the city was gone. Stuttgart joined an ever-growing list of dead cities.

The following week, on August 3, the working committee presented its final draft to the British Chiefs of Staff. By then, Portal had successfully deflected the conversation away from destroying German towns.[60] That left Berlin: Harris's plan for pasting the city's residential neighborhoods was still on the table, and the Chiefs of Staff had left open the possibility of a massive area raid in their August 1 memorandum. The Directorate of Bombing Operations did some calculations on the bombing needed for a raid—code-named THUNDERCLAP[61]—that would devastate Berlin. It suggested that two thousand Eighth Air Force bombers drop five thousand tons on two and a half square miles of central Berlin. The attack would be by day, when the area had a population of 375,000 people. If the Eighth achieved a bomb density of 2000 tons per square mile, they would kill 110,000 and maim or otherwise seriously injure another 110,000.[62] In order to bomb "for purely moral effect," wrote the Director of Bombing Operations, Bufton, on August 1, "that attack must be delivered in such density that it imposes as nearly as possible a 100% risk of death to the individual in the area to which it is applied."[63] If the Eighth didn't do the job on the first day, the Fifteenth could pelt the area with incendiaries on the next. Such death and destruction, the Air Staff subsequently argued, would be a "spectacular and final object lesson to the German people on the consequences of universal aggression."[64]

Despite the failure of area bombing to deliver results, and the clear evidence that precision bombing of oil was working, few people in the British military command were entirely willing to give up on the idea of area bombing. Tedder showed great interest in the idea of attacking morale, and even Portal seemed for a while to favor it.[65] In the end, the plan foundered—at least temporarily—on the rocks of American opposition. Cabell dismissed THUNDERCLAP as another "baby killing scheme."[66] Spaatz led the opposition against the proposal. "It was one thing to kill non-combatants in raids on military installations inside urban centers, a 'revolting necessity,' in the opinion of most American air commanders. It was quite another to aim bombs at residential neighborhoods."[67] As Major General Laurence Kuter, by then Spaatz's Assistant Chief of Staff for Plans and Combat Operations, argued, "It is contrary to [American] ideals to wage war against civilians."[68] The policy was not only morally untenable; it would not work. Drawing the obvious conclusion from the previous two and a half years of the RAF's bombing campaign, Kuter noted that the "area bombing of Cologne, Berlin and [other] cities has apparently not created large scale absenteeism in industry. Apathy and discouragement mark the German population; these are doubtful qualities from which . . . to generate revolt." Kuter also raised questions about British motives: "Since any such attack will feature U.S.A.A.F. [U.S. Army Air Force] units in the limelight, we should consider whether the recent buzz bomb attacks have not instilled in the British Government a desire for retaliation in which American air units will be called upon to share with the R.A.F. Bomber Command the onus for the more critical features of area bombing."[69] He was not alone in this view. Speaking before the debate over THUNDERCLAP, Cabell observed that "the British were building up this terrific resentment on the part of [bombed] peoples, whereas we were being looked at as being a little 'pure' in our motives . . . I feel that the British are now anxious to have some of that odium shared by other nationals—in other words, by the United States."[70] On the Air Ministry proposal itself, Cabell was even more to the point. "I have just read the great opus: 'Operation Thunderclap,' " he wrote to Hughes. "To my mind . . . this would be a blot on the history of the Air Forces and of the US. We should strongly resist being sucked into any such venture. It gives full reign to the baser elements of our people." The cause of civilization and world peace, he concluded, would not be advanced an iota "by killing more women and children."[71] On August 27, Spaatz wrote to Arnold: "I have been subject to some pressure on the part of the Air Ministry to join hands with them in morale bombing. I . . . have maintained a firm position that our bombing will continue to be precision bombing against military objective[s]. So far my stand has been supported by Eisenhower."[72] Although pressure in favor of bombing Berlin seemed to be emerging from the "highest levels" (most likely a reference to Churchill), "I personally believe that any deviation from our present policy, even for an exceptional case, will be unfortunate." Picking up Kuter's point, he ended with a prescient remark: "There is no doubt in my mind that the RAF very much want to have the U.S. Air Forces targeted with the morale bombing aftermath, which we feel will be terrific."

Arnold was not willing to let the proposal die, for he was always more aggressive and bloodthirsty than his generals (when German booby traps were found in Italy, he wasted weeks trying to convince U.S. government officials to make booby-trapped pens, pocket watches, and pocket books for the U.S. Air Forces to drop on German soil).[73] On September 8, he called for a joint British-American plan for "an all-out, widespread attack, of perhaps six or seven days duration, against Germany."[74] By then, however, the vision had subtly changed. Rather than flattening Germany's small cities, the goal would be to get enough planes above them and do just enough damage to impress on the Germans how pointless continued struggle was -a "stinging rather than a numbing blow" as Cabell, who opposed the idea, put it.[75] Both bombs and leaflets would be dropped. When the plan demanded by Arnold was duly produced ten days later, it suggested the targets should be military rather than industrial and should allow for the easy rebuilding of the towns after the war.[76] It failed to conclude whether hitting Germany's small towns would work (though it noted that, if it did not work, the war would "be drawn out over a long period that would be highly costly for the Allies"). The proposal was shelved.

By this point, Churchill had moved on to the idea of conciliating rather than killing German civilians. On August 23, he suggested that the Allies publish a list of fifty to one hundred German war criminals "who will be executed if they fall into the hands of the Allies."[77] "At the present moment," he continued, "none of the German leaders has any interest but fighting to the last man, hoping he will be that last man. It is very important to show the German people that they are not on the same footing as Hitler, Göring, Himmler and the other monsters who will infallibly be destroyed." Nothing came of the idea.

While the "baby-killing" plan was grinding to a halt, the oil plan was gaining traction. On August 18, an intercepted telegram from the Japanese ambassador in Berlin quoted Speer saying in confidence that "the attack on oil installations was the problem to which they attached the greatest importance at the moment. . . . The only sound method of combating [such] air attacks . . . was to regain air superiority."[78] Three days later, Bufton and Air Vice-Marshal D. Colyer, Assistant Chief of the Air Staff for policy, wrote that "serious consideration should be given to according overriding priority to the attack of oil targets by the Allied Strategical Bomber Forces."[79] This was English mandarin speak for "bomb oil immediately!" Doing so would cripple German production and, because planes need fuel to fly, the Luftwaffe.

The Americans were doing just that. During July, Spaatz took every opportunity to bomb oil targets. The cost over 12 raids was 247 bombers—212 lost and another 35 written off—or 70 percent of the Eighth's total losses for the month. The Fifteenth launched 13 missions (out of a total of 15) against oil, at the cost of 196 bombers. In July alone, the Fifteenth hit Ploesti five times.

Oil was not the Eighth's only target. Spaatz also backed up the Armed Forces' advance, and he launched a series of city raids. Munich was bombed on July 11, 12, 13, and 16; what was left of Stuttgart was hit on July 16. The Munich raids targeted BMW and were meant to be precision raids. Weather and H2X's imprecision meant that the city was also hit. As Anderson said on July 21, "We will conduct bombing attacks through the overcast where it is impossible to get precision targets. Such attacks will include German marshaling yards whether or not they are located in German cities."[80] The intention remained the same, however: they hit industry when they could. As the same letter put it, "We have in the past, and will continue to do so in the future, directed our efforts toward precision targets . . . We will not, at any time, direct our efforts toward area bombing." On July 19, clear weather allowed a successful Eighth–Fifteenth precision raid on BMW. When precision bombing became blind bombing, the Americans asked—as they had asked since 1943—that history judge them on their intentions rather than on their results.[81]

On August 7, the British Joint Intelligence reported that the Germans had launched a vast program for repairing oil plants. Speer was trying to work his magic. Spaatz responded by redoubling his efforts. From late August to early September, Spaatz launched ten more attacks, seven of which were directed at oil. The Fifteenth flew thirteen missions against Balkan and German oil targets.

One of the Fifteenth's missions was conducted on August 10, 1944. Walter Gilbert of the 450th Bomb Group, a bombardier, was just above the target.[82] Flak sliced into engines #1 and #2, sheared off half of the rudder, damaged the nose and bomb bay, and mangled the left wing. It ripped through the floor, grazing the crew and injuring the co-pilot badly. To protect the other planes, the B-17 left the formation. As the fighters swept in for the kill, First Lieutenant Vernon E. Mikkelson ordered his crew to bail out. Gilbert was immediately captured by Romanian and German troops, and taken to a military outpost where he rejoined the co-pilot and nose gunner. All, according to Gilbert, were well treated. For the rest of the month, Gilbert and the rest of the crew witnessed the American bombings from captivity.

Two weeks later, in one particularly spectacular raid, the Eighth and the Fifteenth joined forces on August 24 for combined raids on synthetic oil plants. All oil production ceased, and the plant was occupied by the Soviets a few days later.[83]

As the Americans hammered oil targets, Speer urged a massive transfer of resources to protect these targets. Aviation fuel and airplanes had to be conserved. Fighter protection had to be increased. More flak defense was needed, "even at the expense of the protection of German towns." Speer got Hitler to agree to the training of two thousand pilots.[84] He and Galland had calculated that one fighter would be needed to bring down one bomber, but that the cost of replacing bombers and their pilots was much higher. As in the Blitz, the defending fighters would have the advantage: they could return to duty once they parachuted to German soil, whereas Allied pilots would become POWs. This advantage, thought Speer, might just be enough to do it.

On August 10, all of this was thrown into question. Galland, clearly upset, called and asked Speer to fly with him to headquarters. Without warning, Hitler had suddenly ordered the transfer of fighters from hydrogen plants to the Western Front. Together, Galland and Speer visited Hitler. Speer spoke first. "I," he later wrote, "began by . . . explaining the catastrophic situation in armaments production. I cited figures and sketched the consequences that would follow from continued bombings." Every available fighter in Germany, Speer argued at length, would be needed to combat the bombers.

Hitler became nervous and angry. His hands fluttered. He chewed his fingernails. His face flushed a deep red when Speer stopped. And then he exploded. Screaming at the top of his lungs, he turned on Speer. "Operative measures are my concern! Kindly concern yourself with your armaments! This is none of your business." Then, without letting either man reply, he threw them out. "I have no time for you."

The next day, Hitler summoned them back. His rage, if anything, was more out of control. He spoke quickly, his anger forcing him to stumble over his words. "I want no more planes produced at all. The fighter arm is to be dissolved. Stop aircraft production. Stop it at once, understand? . . . Let all the workers produce antiaircraft guns. Use all the material for that too! Now that's an order. Send Saur to headquarters immediately. . . . A program for flak production must be set up. . . . A program five times what we have now. . . . We'll shift hundreds of thousands of workers into flak production. Every day I read in the foreign press reports how dangerous flak is. They still have some respect for that, but none for our fighters."[85] Galland tried to speak, but Hitler had them thrown out once again.

The two were escorted from the room. They and Karl-Otto Saur (head of the Armament Ministry's technical bureau, an intemperate bully known to assault his workers, and a close confidant of Speer) decided to ignore Hitler.[86] The next day, Speer spoke with the Armaments staff: "We must maintain the production of fighter planes at a maximum." Three days later, Speer arranged, with Galland present, a meeting of air industry representatives and urged them on to higher productivity. "By sending the production of fighter aircraft soaring we can meet the greatest danger we face: the crushing of our armaments manufacture on the home front."

It was a fight to the finish. Speer was in a last, desperate race to produce enough fighter planes to defend the Reich's oil supply well enough to keep Germany's war machine going. He would once again have help from the most unlikely of allies.

22

HARRIS'S AND SPAATZ'S ORDERS

On September 11 and 12, 1944, Spaatz sent the Eighth Air Force on two daytime raids against oil plants. To their surprise, large numbers of Luftwaffe fighters appeared. It was the first time since the May raids on Ploesti that the Eighth had encountered such fierce fighter resistance. The Americans lost seventy-five bombers.[1]

That month, a war that had seemed to go so well after Normandy began to go badly and the Allies suffered a series of setbacks. On the afternoon of September 17, the first of three divisions of Allied paratroopers landed at Oosterbeek, near Arnhem. Two more divisions were preparing to land. The plan was to take the bridges along the Rhine and allow the Allies' armies to sweep into Germany. Operation Market Garden failed miserably. Nine days later, twelve hundred men from the British 1st Airborne Division were killed and another six thousand captured.[2]

On September 27, during a raid on industrial and transport targets, the 445th Bomb Group strayed from the protection of fighter escorts. The Luftwaffe savaged them. In the three minutes between the bombers' call for help and the arrival of American fighters, the Germans shot down twenty-six bombers. Another two crashed. Only the American fighters' quick arrival spared the remainder of the Bomb Group.[3]

On October 1, 1944, General Courtney Hodges and his First Army were forty miles west of Aachen and the Rhine. For four days, the Americans had subjected German positions north of the city to bombardments that recalled the ferocity of the First World War. The Germans didn't budge. It took three more days to pierce the West Wall, and nine more days to advance on Aachen.

On October 16, the Americans offered the German garrison at Aachen the opportunity to surrender. It was refused. For five days, air and ground troops hammered the city until, on October 21, resistance ended. Although the Americans might have progressed much faster if they had ignored Aachen and pressed on eastward, Aachen made clear that German resistance was fierce.[4]

These surprising setbacks shook Allied confidence. Occupying Germany was not going to be as easy as OVERLORD had led them to believe. The question was how to respond to what seemed to be a revival of German strength and fortunes. The Western Allied armies, mindful of casualties in a way that the Germans and Russians were not, opted for a more conservative strategy, one that inadvertently allowed the Germans to regroup along the Western Front. In the air forces, people divided on predictable lines. Harris remained committed to cities; Spaatz to oil and German fighter production; and Tedder to communications.

In practice, the division between Tedder and Spaatz didn't matter much. On the ground, both the oil and the communications campaigns were doing their work. The bombing of rail lines, bridges, tanks, and anything that moved had severely hampered the Germans' ability to get troops to Normandy. Now that the Allies were on the Continent, Allied bombing of communications continued to be the Germans' worst headache on the Western Front. Whereas German troops could go for days without seeing Allied armies, the bombers hammered them constantly. As Max Hastings writes, "Every German was dismayed by the ubiquity and impact of air power. Any German vehicle movement in daylight was likely to be rewarded by fighter-bomber attack, of an effectiveness unknown on the Eastern Front."[5] By contrast, thanks to American attacks on the Luftwaffe, the Allies themselves moved freely behind the front by day or night.[6]

Overall command of the strategic bombing war had been returned from Eisenhower to Spaatz and Harris on September 14. On that day, Portal and Arnold issued a new directive, which Bottomley passed on to the commander-in-chief on September 25. Compared with past directives, it was a model of clarity. It instructed the Allied Air Forces to make attacks on oil their first priority, with transportation targets and tank and motor production as the second priority. After that, it listed German air force targets and support of land and naval action. Like all directives, it left open room for area attacks when these targets could not be hit: "the bombing of important industrial areas when weather made other targets impractical." Who judged the weather and a raid's practicality? Harris and Spaatz.

The directive effectively told the Americans to do what they had been doing, with the added benefit of satisfying Spaatz's long-held wish to rank oil above transportation—though Spaatz had by this point come to view the two as complementary. Both oil and transportation were precision targets, both required successive bombing raids to be decisively destroyed, and the destruction of both materially affected Germany's capacity to wage war. But there was a basic difference between the two. Oil refineries and synthetic oil plants were located outside the cities, in the countryside of Central and Eastern Europe. They were usually ideal precision targets; bombing destroyed them or it destroyed nothing. The situation for marshaling yards and railway stations was entirely different. Big rail yards were located in central urban districts, next to workers' housing. The train stations, or at least the main ones, were right in the center of the cities. Destroying these targets inevitably meant destroying houses and killing workers.

These risks to civilians were compounded by strategy and, that great wild card, worsening weather. The Eighth had adopted Curtis LeMay's policy of "bombing on the leader." Only lead aircraft were given Norden bombsights, and the others were instructed to drop their bombs as soon as they saw bombs fall from the lead plane. The technique increased accuracy enormously, but it ensured that when things went wrong, they went horribly wrong. If the lead pilot bombed the wrong target, they all did. And if the bombing formation stretched back too far in poor weather, the bombers behind the leader blasted whatever was just before the target. Sometimes, in the case of rail centers in small cities, it was the whole town itself. "My squadron was on the tail end of a bombing strike against a railroad yard in a small industrial town," Eighth Air Force pilot Craig Harris told Donald L. Miller in 2003. "There were about 400 bombers in front of us as we approached the target. Our shadow, if we had one, would have covered almost the entire town. The clouds were so thick that we couldn't see a thing on the ground. The lead plane carried the radar equipment. When it passed over the target it dropped its bombs, along with a smoke maker, the signal for the rest of the formation to drop. The planes at the head of the formation wasted the marshaling yard, but the rest of us wasted the town."[7] When a target was cloud-covered, H2X would identify the city but not the targets. In these situations—such as at Kassel (October 2, 1944),

Nuremberg (October 3), and Mannheim (October 19)—the Eighth threw its bombs at the city. They wanted to avoid hitting towns if they could, but hit towns if they could do nothing else.

Wasting towns—deliberately, not incidentally—was of course exactly what Harris wanted to do. On September 6, a week before the September directive, Harris sent his bombers to attack Emden. The daylight raid, free from the recovering Luftwaffe, destroyed the city at the cost of one Lancaster. Four days later, Bomber Command "tore out the heart" of Mönchengladbach without losing a single plane.[8] Two days after that, it was Darmstadt's turn. In the early morning of September 12, the city in which Cherwell had studied, loved by English tourists for its richly detailed residential architecture, was set alight. At five minutes before midnight, 221 Lancasters and 14 Mosquitoes dropped 1000 tons of bombs on the city.[9] A Hamburgesque firestorm tore through the city, leveling its center and the city's castle. Temperatures reached 1000 degrees Celsius, and the flames could be seen 180 miles away. By morning, ten thousand people were dead. For the RAF it was, as one captain reported, "A quiet trip all around with everything going to plan."[10] All of the city's industry was located in the suburbs, and the incidental damage it suffered was repaired within a month.[11]

Two days before destroying Darmstadt, the RAF attacked oil refineries at Dortmund, Beur, and Wanne-Eickel. The Dortmund refinery was badly damaged, but smoke pots and flak protected the other two.[12] Seven aircraft were lost. The day after, on September 12–13, RAF area raids smashed what was left of Münster (killing 144 people), Frankfurt (killing 469), and Stuttgart (killing 1171). Three nights later, Bomber Command devastated the center of Kiel. Then, a week after the mid-September directive on oil and transportation, on September 23–24, Bomber Command dropped three thousand tons of bombs on the town of Neuss in a single night.

Shortly after the Neuss raid, Churchill invited Harris to Chequers to dine and discuss an ULTRA report confirming that Germany faced a crippling oil shortage. ULTRA intelligence had made this clear more than two months earlier—on July 9—and Harris had been specifically ordered to hit oil by the September 14 directive. Churchill either sensed that Harris was not doing his job and used ULTRA to raise the matter, or wanted to be reassured that the city bombing campaign still had worth. In either case, Harris, citing a cold, declined the invitation and instead set out his views on paper.[13] He began by dismissing the source. "Of [sic] our past experience the Jap diplomats are usually stuffed with Boche propaganda, and incline to swallow it, hook, line and sinker." Before altering bombing strategy, he continued, "we should, I feel, take a more sober view of what has so far occurred on the western front. The German Army . . . collapsed in the face of attack by superior and better equipped forces. But it collapsed mainly because it was beleaguered by air power." This happy result was achieved despite giving Germany "considerable breathers" through "necessary and avoidable diversions" during the previous six months. Now that they were out of the way, "we should now get on and finally knock Germany flat."

Churchill responded right away: "I agree with your very good letter," wrote Churchill, "except that I do not think you did it all or can do it all. I recognize however that this is a becoming view for you to take. I am all for cracking everything in now on to Germany that can be spared from the battlefields." It was exactly what Harris wanted to hear.

If September was a bad month for German cities, October was worse still. Harris launched his heaviest attack ever. In October, 80 percent of RAF bombs fell on cities. Harris launched twenty raids, nine of them by daylight. Two of these attacks—on Kleve and Emmerich on October 5 and 7—were requested by the Allied ground forces to aid advancing troops, but they were pushing on an open door. On October 14, Duisburg was smashed twice in twenty-four hours: 5029 tons hit the center by day, 5093 by night. "The record," writes historian Richard G. Davis, "of more than 10,100 tons of conventional explosives dropped on a single target in a day probably still stands."[14] On the same night, the RAF destroyed—on its fourth try—Brunswick. Fire engulfed the old city center, and only the firefighters' determination kept the death toll to a relatively low 561. Over four hours, they fought their way through the ring of fire until they managed to reach eight public shelters housing twenty-three thousand people.[15] They got all but two hundred out. Without their efforts, Brunswick might have been another Hamburg. Three nights later, in Bonn, the university, many cultural and public buildings, and large residential areas were smashed. The firefighters managed to save Beethoven's house; they weren't able to do the same for 313 people. What was left of the Ruhr cities of Essen, Dortmund, and Duisburg was also bombed, as were untouched residential parts of Cologne.

Throughout September and October, the RAF's loss rate was a low 1.8 percent.

In September, U.S. Air Forces continued their assault on the Luftwaffe, dropping five thousand tons of bombs on aircraft targets.[16] They dropped an equal amount on tanks, and somewhat more—fifty-six hundred tons—on oil. Another twelve thousand fell on marshaling yards, which had positive knock-on effects for the oil offensive: they destroyed rail lines, trains, and trucks and interfered with Speer's race to repair the oil damage.

The cumulative effects of the oil and transportation campaigns were spectacular. The production of aviation fuel temporarily halted. German oil production had halved over the summer, and the campaign had important secondary effects. The production of synthetic nitrogen (used for explosives) fell 63 percent; synthetic methanol (used for more advanced explosives) fell 40 percent; and synthetic rubber fell 65 percent.

Harris, too, hit oil targets. In September, fourteen RAF raids were city raids, but eight targeted oil. When he did hit oil—for instance, at Dortmund on September 12 or at Kaiserslautern on September 27–28—the results were impressive. The larger size of British bombs meant that a single British raid was worth more than an American raid. Bomber Command played a role in the oil campaign; it simply could have done more, perhaps much more. During October, only one-twelfth of RAF bombs hit oil targets, and there was only one significant transportation raid—on October 5, on marshaling yards at Saarbrücken. None of this is remarkable: Harris made no secret of his contempt for oil and his support for bombing cities.

And this left Portal in a dilemma. Harris was immensely popular with the British public, and the Air Ministry had spent the last two years making "Bomber Harris" the public face of the RAF. But his obsession with bombing cities was standing in the way of the thorough execution of his orders. Not one for confrontation, Portal began by trying to reason with Harris. On October 28, Portal and Spaatz agreed to Strategic Directive No. 2, which placed transportation again at the top, followed by oil, making those the only two target systems (except when specific requests were made by the other forces). The directive left in the "important industrial areas" exception, but Bottomley modified the language to emphasize that these areas must be clearly linked with oil and transportation. Portal then wrote a gentle letter to Harris, encouraging him to implement the oil directive. He enclosed a document called "Notes on Air Policy to be adopted with a view to rapid defeat of Germany," which presented the American case in favor of the precision bombing of oil targets.

The letter and notes hit Harris at a particularly bad moment. On Bottomley's note, he scribbled the words "here we go around the Mulberry bush."[17] These notes would have angered him at the best of times, but on Tuesday, October 31, another Air Ministry official had questioned his judgment. "Why," he asked Harris, "did you bomb Cologne last night?" The implication was clear: why did you *not* bomb oil plants? The combination of the two sets of criticism infuriated Harris, and he wrote back immediately. He began with an unapologetic defense of the bombing campaign:

> The war has already been vastly shortened by concentrating the bomber effort in the past three years against war potential industrial targets inside Germany. . . . A major reason for the success of the Russian offensives has been the destruction of the German war potential, and the chaos and confusion created in Germany by the heavy bombing campaign. . . . There is also no doubt that the walk-over which the armies experienced in the invasion of France, while mainly due to the destruction of communications in France, was also largely due to the general shortage of equipment and man power in the German forces, to which the general chaos in Germany, the past strategical bombing of Germany very heavily contributed.[18]

Whether he recognized it or not, Harris's argument had shifted importantly over the last two years. He had once claimed that bombing cities would avoid the need for the invasion. Now that it had occurred, he claimed to be responsible for its success.

Harris then went on to argue that he was implementing the September 14 directive:

> In his paragraph 9, the Deputy Supreme Commander makes certain recommendations as to the best targets to be attacked. Apart from diversions forced upon us for tactical bombing, bombing coast guns, invested ports, the Tirpitz, submarine bases etc. the recommendations in that paragraph are precisely what we have been doing and are doing. . . . The main concentration [of our bombing] has been against the Ruhr whenever conditions made this economical. The targets selected have been oil targets, rail centres, canal systems and the major centres of population. . . . Area bombing must enter into any scheme, because in bad weather we have to use sky markers, we must have a large target within Oboe or G.H. range and we necessarily in those conditions paint with a large brush.

When he was not implementing the directive, or appeared not to be, it was for reasons beyond his control:

> There is . . . an aspect of bombing which it is always difficult to impress or to keep impressed upon those outside the immediate Command, and that is the decisive effect of weather and tactical factors on what can be done at any given moment. Taking into account the low ceiling of our bombers and the high ceilings of many cloud formations, particularly those associated with high icing indices it is frequently impossible to go where one wants to go and it is as frequently necessary to do something of value even though it is not always something near the head of the priority list.

And when he could implement it but chose not to, there might be tactical reasons for doing so:

> It is not tactically feasible to go on slamming at the same type of target day after day and night after night, without making the proposition of the defences unnecessarily simple. It is often necessary from time to time to hit the enemy where he least expects he is going to be hit, in order to make him spread his defences out and keep them spread.

Given these constraints, the only certainty in bombing, Harris concluded, is that something is to be bombed. "The final type of target which is liable to questioning after the event," Harris wrote, "is the target which is attacked merely because it is the only thing open to attack in prevailing conditions. In Bomber Command we have always worked on the principle that bombing anything in Germany is better than bombing nothing."

Harris was not one to let a charge go unchallenged, and he used the letter to respond to the question about Cologne, although Portal had not asked it.

> (a) Cologne was the best point at which the weather front gave reasonable possibility of our low ceiling bombers getting sufficiently above the elsewhere high cloud ceiling.
> (b) It was the nearest we could get to the Ruhr.
> (c) It was the furthest I proposed to send the force in . . . full moonlight.
> (d) As a most important communication centre and industrial area it was of direct value to the Army and generally in line with the Directive.

(e) It was big enough to be dealt with using sky mark technique [i.e., drop-
    ping flares to mark the target]. Sky marking requires a big, compact,
    and preferably isolated target.
(f) It was already burning from previous attacks and two important satel-
    lite areas remained to be burned. There is something in continuity of
    attack, within limits, from the morale point of view.
(g) It was as far as we could go and get back before the bases gave trou-
    ble.
(h) Anything worth while further south would have been outside Oboe
    range and would have meant flying low inside American [range] and
    would [have] resulted in [the Americans] shooting at lethal height.

In the letter's last passages, Harris moved from the specific—Cologne—to
the general—the nature of his bombing crusade itself. "In the past 18 months,
Bomber Command has virtually destroyed 45 of the leading 60 German cities.
In spite of invasion diversions [i.e., the invasion of Normandy], we have so far
managed to keep up and exceed our average of 2.5 cities devastated a month.
In addition others have been 'started on' to the extent where they are already
damaged beyond anything experienced in this country. There are not many
industrial centres of population left intact."

Harris ended the letter with a call for a total bombing war. "Are we," he
wrote, "now to abandon this vast task, which the Germans themselves
have long admitted to be their worse headache, just as it nears completion?
[The destruction of] Magdeburg, Halle, Leipzig, Dresden, Chemnitz, Breslau,
Nuremberg, Munich, Coblenz, Karlsruhe, and the completion of Berlin and
Hanover are required to finish this plan. . . . Its completion will do more toward accelerating the defeat of Germany than the armies have yet done—or
will do."

Harris was not in an easy position. He genuinely did not believe that
bombing oil would work. It had not worked in 1940–1941, and in the ensuing
years the Ministry of Economic Warfare (MEW) had come up with many
"panaceas." The clamor continued into late 1944. As he wrote in the same
November 1 letter, "during the last few weeks every panacea monger and
'me too' expert to many of whom we had already (we hoped) given the quietus
in the past, has raised his head again. The Tirpitz has gone within range and
the Admiralty has resuscitated a U-boat threat. The ball-bearing experts have
again become vocal . . ." Everything being said about oil had been said

before, in 1940–1941. And where had that led? To high British casualties, plummeting pilot morale, and no obvious effect on Germany.

The weather also did present a serious problem; any bombing, but above all precision bombing, required cooperative weather conditions. If the target was obscured by cloud, or if there was a storm over it, bombing was difficult, dangerous, or both. Most importantly, Harris continued to believe in area bombing. His entire mission since 1942, if not earlier, was founded on this policy; he had publicly and repeatedly staked his reputation on it; and he had sent tens of thousands of young men to their death in executing it. It was hardly that surprising that he was unwilling, just as Germany finally seemed to be collapsing, to give up on it.

The difficulty for Portal was that, while he recognized all of this, Harris was playing a double game. He was arguing at once that (a) he was bombing oil targets when he could, (b) he mostly couldn't bomb oil targets, and (c) it wasn't worth bombing oil targets. If (a) and (b) were true, there was no need to add (c).[19] There was also something patronizing in Harris's letter. It was as if he were writing to someone who knew nothing about bombing, rather than to his superior and a man who had worked his way through the RAF hierarchy, much as Harris had, from its earliest days.

Harris's last paragraph, on abandoning his task, was equally ambiguous. He seemed to be sliding from a purely instrumental argument—that bombing Germany would end the war—to an absolutist one: that destroying all German cities was an end in itself.

On November 2, the day after Harris wrote about his "vast task" of destroying Germany's remaining cities, the Eighth Air Force launched a routine raid on Germany. The Luftwaffe again surprised the Americans: a supposedly beaten force got five hundred fighters in the air. The escorts were there to protect the bombers—they shot down 102 German fighters—but the show of force took Spaatz aback. Combined with the broader Allied setbacks, it showed that the Germans were not yet conquered. "It has been increasingly evident," Spaatz wrote to Arnold, "that the GAF was being processed to become a major threat to our deep penetrations, in daylight, into Germany." The American victory over the Luftwaffe was "decisive," but only because of "almost perfect fighter cover" and "a fortunate chain of circumstances."[20] Arnold agreed: the USSTAF had to get the German fighters off the Continent, once and for all.

Spaatz's fears were confirmed on two further U.S. raids—on November

21 and 26, against Bremen—when the Luftwaffe responded with some five hundred fighters. The three November interceptions were the largest of the entire war.[21] Under Speer's guidance, the Germans were clearly recouping after their devastating spring and summer losses.[22]

As Spaatz saw it, he had two options for responding to the Luftwaffe's seemingly renewed strength: *reducing* the number of bombers—to the point where adequate fighter cover could be provided—or *increasing* the number of bombers—sending out the maximum number of bombers on each mission.[23] A larger mission might ensure that, even if large numbers of bombers were lost, enough would get past the fighters to do substantial damage. Increasing the number of bombers was the riskier of the two strategies: if a bombing formation were underescorted or if substantial parts of it blew off course, the Luftwaffe would chew even a large force to pieces. Reducing the number of bombers was safe, but it came at a price: the lousy autumn weather reduced the number of raids to a handful, and a small bomber stream would lead to limited damage. Spaatz decided to risk it all. On November 27, he picked a fight with the Luftwaffe. One thousand American bombers left England in two groups. The first was made up of 515 heavy bombers, escorted by 241 fighters. It raided marshaling yards in southern Germany. The second, composed of 460 planes, headed for oil centers in northern and central Germany. The idea was to trick the Germans into thinking that the fighter force was in fact bombers.

It worked. The Luftwaffe attacked the fighter formation, leaving the bombers relatively unimpeded. The American fighters countered viciously. They shot down ninety-eight enemy fighters—double the average of the spring raids—at the cost of twelve of their own. As the reports of the November operation reached Spaatz, he wrote to Lovett with confidence. "In spite of the buildup of strength, the [Germans'] overall effectiveness has not increased. . . . [Recently], we have destroyed as much as 25% of [their] forces." All that was needed was a break in the weather, and the USSTAF could finally destroy the German fighter force.

Three weeks before Spaatz rolled the dice, Portal was mulling over a reply to Harris. As he did so, the commander-in-chief bombed Homburg (twice), Oberhausen, and Düsseldorf. The Düsseldorf raid finished the northern half of the city, destroying five thousand houses and killing some seven hundred people.[24]

On November 4, Portal wrote to Harris. He began with an apology.

Referring to my inquiry of 1st November about the bombing of Cologne in preference to oil or the Ruhr . . . I do hope that you will not resent my asking for such information as I consider it necessary to enable me to explain, and if necessary defend, your decisions; and that you will not think that when I do so I am ipso facto exhibiting a lack of confidence in your direction of Bomber Command's operations. My own belief is that true mutual confidence can only exist on a basis of thorough mutual understanding and that the question of amour propre or "face" should be completely excluded.

If you concede this, I would go on to say, at the risk of your dubbing me "another panacea merchant," that I believe the air offensive against oil gives us by far the best hope of victory in the next few months. It will be a terrific battle between destruction and repair and we cannot afford to give a single point away over and above the many that we shall be compelled to give away in direct support of the land offensive and in deference to the Admiralty's uneasiness about the coming U-Boat offensive. . . .

[In this vein] I was very much worried about the German recovery in oil production in October.

Portal then went on to reject each of the arguments offered by Harris to justify his decision to bomb Cologne rather than oil. On bad weather: there was no difference between Cologne and the Ruhr. On cloud cover: this was true, but there were oil targets near Cologne that were ignored in favor of the city itself. On Cologne as a rail center: true, but oil was more important than transport (here Portal was himself going against Strategic Directive No. 2, which placed transportation first and oil second). On sky-marking: it had been successfully done in the Ruhr. On repeatedly bombing the same targets, or continuity: true, but it was more important to bomb oil targets continually. On distance: the Ruhr is no further from England than Cologne. Finally, on the difficulty of reaching the south of Germany: the Ruhr is not in southern Germany. In short, all eight reasons offered by Harris failed to stand up to scrutiny.

Portal knew his commander-in-chief well; there was little point in directly provoking him. Instead, he offered Harris an out, another reason to favor area bombing over precision bombing. Perhaps, he said, the commander-in-chief had been thinking of the greater publicity benefits that came from destroyed cities. Despite this, he continued, the issues at stake were too important. "In view of the vital importance of getting the German war finished as soon as possible and of the disastrous delay that would result from any substantial recovery of the German oil position, I make no apology for inflicting this letter upon you, and I trust that you will accept it as a sincere attempt to discharge a not altogether pleasant duty."

Portal paused. He had not enjoyed writing the letter, and looked with still less enthusiasm on the prospect of sending it on to Harris. He decided to leave it for a day.

That night, the skies were clear over central Germany, over the damaged but functioning factories in the Ruhr valley and over the benzol plants at Gelsenkirchen. As ever, the air-raid sirens went off and the flak guns began shooting. Gelsenkirchen was not, however, the target. Seven hundred and fifty RAF aircraft flew just south of it and bombed the center of Bochum. More than 4000 buildings were destroyed or seriously damaged; 980 Germans and 14 foreigners were also killed.[25] The same night, Harris sent 176 aircraft to the Dortmund-Ems Canal. The banks of the canal were breached, barges were stopped, and smelting coke en route to steelworks at Brunswick and Osnabrück was stranded.

Reading the reports on Bochum, Portal could not believe it. There could not have been a better opportunity to hit Germany's oil supply. He returned to his desk and continued his letter to Harris. In the face of another affront, he raised his tone slightly. But only slightly:

This morning I see you made an attack in clear weather which I imagine is the weather you expected since you also attacked the Dortmund-Ems canal. The destruction of Bochum as part of the Ruhr is of course very desirable and thoroughly covered by your directive but unfortunately so far as I know it contained no oil targets. To the outsider who knows the vital importance of oil it would have seemed more valuable if you could have attacked, say, Gelsenkirchen, which has two high priority oil targets and a largish, relatively undamaged built-up area into the bargain. Having risked your wrath already and in pursuance of my strong desire that we should understand each other may I ask you to let me know if you think I am wrong on this particular point. . . . My excuse for all of this is that in the light of all available intelligence I feel that the whole war situation is poised on "oil" as on a knife edge, and that by a real concentration of effort at this time we might push it over on the right side. On the other hand if we give away anything in this battle the Germans may get into quite a strong position in the air and hold it long enough to prolong the war by several months at least. Feeling like this I am bound to put you to a certain amount of trouble but I assure that I am perfectly ready to be convinced by reasonable arguments.[26]

After ending the letter in the same apologetic style in which it began, Portal signed it and passed it on for delivery to Harris.

That night the RAF pasted Solingen. Almost exactly a year earlier, Harris had promised to destroy Solingen in order to "tidy up all around." Over two nights—on November 4 and 5—Harris shredded the old city, leaving seventeen hundred people dead.[27]

By the time Harris read the letter, his anger over the "why did you bomb Cologne?" question had passed. He had seen nothing that would change his views on oil, and his natural stubbornness inclined him, when pushed, to push back. However, as Portal had all but begged him to explain Bochum away, Harris saw no need to be truculent. He decided to draft what was for him an unusually soothing letter. "I agree," he began, "with what you say about the urgency and effectiveness of the oil plan. But in any case as the running of the Bomber offensive is now out of my hands, it is not for me to argue over the main Directive."

The second sentence was a bit rich in light of his November 1 diatribe against the panacea mongers, but at least Harris did not use this letter to take another swipe at them. Instead, he dealt with Gelsenkirchen:

You ask why I did not attack Gelsenkirchen instead of Bochum. Gelsenkirchen is notorious from the point of view of the difficulty of finding and hitting the place, even in the best weather. It has been attacked times without number, and hardly a vestige of damage has ever been done to it. So much is this so that it has become a jest in Bomber Command that either there is no such place as Gelsenkirchen, or that it is marked wrong on the map. . . . I keep the most up to date photographs available of all the oil plants, and those taken on the 28th October of both the oil plants near Gelsenkirchen seemed to show no manufacturing activity.

Having stood his ground, Harris reverted to his emollient tone. "I am sorry," he wrote, "[that] you seem to think that I do not understand the importance of the oil war, because that is entirely wrong . . . [B]efore I had received your letter, I had already impressed upon my Staff the necessity for getting on with the oil as hard as we could whenever opportunity really served. I had in fact hauled them over the coals for not putting a specific part of the force that attacked Gelsenkirchen on the oil plants. Unfortunately that attack was laid on when I was taking a day off, otherwise it would have been done."[28]

Harris might have left it at that, but he couldn't resist a parting shot at the Air Ministry and, above all, the Ministry of Economic Warfare:

> It would be of interest to know how we arrive at so exact figures of German oil production. The form in which the information reaches me savours sometimes of the type of Admiralty paper which starts with a series of assumptions and works them in three places of decimals!

Harris's claims about Gelsenkirchen were disingenuous; he had in fact launched a successful raid on the Nordsten oil plant there on September 13–14, using only 102 aircraft.[29] It is also hard to credit the claim that his staff ignored his orders (a brave staff member that would be). Nonetheless, the letter seemed to keep Portal happy and Harris was able to get back to work. Over the next few days, he bombed Gelsenkirchen, Koblenz, Homburg, Harburg, and Dortmund. Clearly feeling Portal's pressure, three of these raids—Homburg, Dortmund, and Gelsenkirchen—were oil raids. Despite Harris's predictions to the contrary, both the Dortmund and the Gelsenkirchen raids were a success; a synthetic oil plant at Dortmund was severely damaged, and 514 aircraft bombed another plant at Gelsenkirchen before smoke obscured the target.[30] Harris didn't stop there, though. He couldn't leave an untouched city untouched, and 187 aircraft blasted Gelsenkirchen's center on November 6, adding another five hundred civilians to the growing death toll. The logs recorded a directive raid, and Harris got to destroy another city.[31] In some cases, where the targets were small, Harris could credibly make the case that he was applying the military principle of economy of force: after one hundred bombers or so had hit an oil target, the smoke from the bombs obscured it and the accuracy of subsequent bombers fell off dramatically. In other cases, such as the sprawling refineries in eastern Germany or Romania, this explanation strained credibility.

The November 6 raid on Koblenz destroyed 60 percent of the town's historic center, killed 104 people, and left 20,000 homeless. The city had been founded as a fortification in 1000, and grew up over the centuries as the seat of local monarchs and bishops. Its architecture was a mix of grand palaces and narrow, old-European streets. It had no industry to speak of.

As one city after another fell, Portal once again decided to respond. He could see, for only a fool could not, that Harris was making only a reluctant effort to bomb oil targets. But he felt limited by his own sense of decorum—it was not Portal's way to order his men around—and by the formal authority enjoyed by Harris. What was he to do? Portal had known Harris for many years and he knew better than anybody that challenging him head-on would only bring out the commander-in-chief's stubbornness. If it came to a full-out confrontation, Harris might threaten to resign; he had pulled this card before and there was nothing to stop him from doing so again. The last thing Portal needed, as Christmas approached and British troops were pushing toward Germany, was a high-profile resignation. All he could do was cajole.

Portal began by casting himself as Harris's patron in a world of hostile foes, one who needed to be properly armed if he was going to repel their assaults. "There is, of course[,] no question," Portal wrote, "but that the decision [about what to bomb] must lie with you alone. My concern, and my duty, however, is to satisfy myself and outsiders who may enquire, that your Command loses no opportunity of attacking the priority targets that are laid down in the directive. It is for this reason that I have felt bound to burden you with these enquiries." Thus covering his flank, Portal then adopted a tone that was more direct and (mildly) more damning than the one found in earlier missives. Probably recognizing the intrinsically subjective nature of the evidence, he stopped debating the merits of particular raids and raised the broader issue: if Harris was so committed to the oil offensive, why were so many bombs continuing to fall on cities and so few on oil?

> You have been good enough to state in full the factors which influenced you to go to Cologne rather than to the Ruhr, and to Bochum, rather than Gelsenkirchen. I must of course accept your decisions in these cases (but, may I say, with the hope that the daylight attack has laid the Gelsenkirchen bogey for ever). The issue [however] is a more fundamental one than

whether or not you could have made a better choice in these two individual cases. In the closing paragraphs of your letter of 1st November you refer to a plan for the destruction of the 60 leading German cities, and to your effort to keep up with, and even to exceed, your average of 2½ such cities devastated each month. I know that you have long felt such a plan to be the most effective way of bringing about the collapse of Germany. Knowing this, I have, I must confess, at times wondered whether the magnetism of the remaining German cities has not in the past tended as much to deflect our bombers from their primary objectives as the tactical and weather difficulties which you described so fully in your letter of 1st November. I would like you to reassure me that this is not so. *If I knew you to be so wholeheartedly in the attack on oil as in the past you have been in the matter of attacking cities, I would have little to worry about.*[32]

For the moment, Portal had plenty to worry about. He had been studying photographs and intelligence reports from spies within Germany since the summer, and they showed a worrying trend. Oil production had fallen off sharply in the summer months, but was ticking up again. Fine summer weather had made repeated attacks easier, and—exactly as Speer had predicted a year earlier—these had begun knocking the legs out from under German war production. By early November, less than 20 percent of RAF bombs were falling on oil targets, and Germany's industrial production was recovering, and quickly. Without throwing everything the Americans and the RAF had at oil, the campaign would not be effective. "The crux of the matter," Portal wrote, "is that German oil production has risen from [its] September level, and seems likely to go on rising unless we can make our attack more effective than it was throughout October. We have not been hitting oil hard enough, and we must devise means to ensure that we do hit it hard enough over the next few months."

The letter also directly addressed two claims made by Harris against bombing oil: that an operation had to go after the easiest target and that going after difficult oil targets would send Bomber Command casualties through the roof. In his November 6, 1944, letter, Harris had followed his sentence on agreeing with the "urgency and effectiveness of the oil plan" with these words:

It is my concern and constant anxiety to try to get the best overall effect out of the available sorties in the prevailing weather, and in that regard I cannot and should not, in my view, throw any opportunity of doing some-thing valuable with some better degree of certainty by trying to do something else which in the conditions prevailing at a particular moment I regard as being too chancy.[33]

This claim, wrote Portal, made oil bombing almost a logical impossibility: "You state that it is your constant anxiety to try and get the best *overall* effect from the effort available. Surely that would represent a falling away from the sharply defined policy of attacking oil." Harris defined "overall effect" as a function of the ease of the attack and its likelihood of success, and success was defined as the extent of destruction. Cities would almost always be easier to bomb than specific targets, so this calculus would almost always lead to the bombing of cities rather than oil. Given what the Allies knew by late 1944, Portal argued, "in my view our aims now should be to go for maximum effect on *oil* whenever a reasonable chance presents itself, even though this may be at the expense of an attack with greater certainty upon a lower priority target."[34]

In other words, since bombing oil produced more results than bombing cities, oil should be bombed even if it were more difficult. It was better to lose more planes to a useful oil raid than few to a pointless city raid. Portal might have added that when Harris had in the past believed a target was worthy, he was willing to assume greater risks to take it out: Cologne in the 1000-bomber raid, Berlin throughout 1943 and 1944, and, once he had signed on, the Sorpe, Eder, and Möhne dams.

Portal also directly addressed Harris's point about repeated attacks, allow-ing German defenses to concentrate, and the ensuing casualties among British bombers. "I must," he wrote,

make reference to the problem of concentrating on the Ruhr. From the statistics I have available, there is little evidence so far of our concentration in this area "putting the casualty rate up enormously." Since 1st September, our losses in the Ruhr area have averaged only 1.3% and these have been spread fairly evenly throughout the period. This rate is well below your average against some 42 of the major cities which has been 3.8% since January, 1942. There would seem no reason as yet for [deviating] in our attacks on the Ruhr.[35] On the contrary, it would surely be better to concen-trate against the Ruhr oil and the Ruhr now, before the enemy can solve his early warning difficulties. It will be time enough to change when heavy casualties do in fact materialize. We should if we can secure maximum effect on the Ruhr itself, and the quickest direct and indirect effect upon the Ruhr oil. Incidentally, I was delighted to see that you managed to attack the plant at DORTMUND last night without loss.

As Portal was no doubt thinking, Harris had frequently "tested" the casualty rate if he felt a campaign important. For instance, during the early Battle of Berlin, in August 1943, Harris launched three raids with high losses before delaying the campaign.

What Portal never did in these exchanges was order Harris to stop bombing cities. In this, he remained a product of Trenchard's bomber dream. The enthusiasm that had sustained him throughout 1942 had long faded. He stopped believing that bombing cities would win the war alone by the time of the Casablanca conference; by the end of the Battle of Berlin, he doubted that it would have much effect at all.[36] By the summer of 1944, there was enough evidence to conclude that area bombing was pointless. Yet, in his early November letter to Harris, he noted that "the destruction of Bochum as part of the Ruhr is of course very desirable." He also all but invited Harris to obliterate Gelsenkirchen ("a relatively undamaged built-up area [thrown] into the bargain").

It is impossible to know for certain what was going through Harris's mind as he read Portal's latest letter, but in all likelihood he recognized that he was running out of arguments. He decided instead to play for time. He did not bother to pen a reply for almost two weeks. Gladly responding to an American request for air support for the Army, Harris sent five hundred planes to destroy the medieval city of Düren. The bombing killed 3100 people, obliterated the city center, and left only 130 out of 6000 houses standing. The smaller towns of Heinsberg and Jülich were also destroyed that night.

Harris finally replied on November 24, 1944. It was one of many points during this months-long exchange at which he might have simply conceded that Portal was right, and carried on regardless. But that was not Harris's style. He had plenty of guile, but a visceral distaste for mendacity. He believed either that Portal was wrong on the casualty rate, or that his argument depended on him being wrong. Either way, he was not going to let Portal's arguments stand unquestioned.

Rather ironically, given his low regard for experts, he challenged Portal by summarizing four points from an Air Scientific Intelligence Report entitled "The Present Eclipse of the German Night Fighters." From it, Harris concluded that (i) Germany put an immense effort into the expansion and equipment of its night air defenses; (ii) British losses were kept in bearable limits only by attending to tactics such as "spoof" and diversionary tactics; and (iii) the retirement of the enemy to his own frontiers deprived him of much of his early warning system, making deception easier. The report, Harris continued,

> stresses the fact that our low losses up to the present are due not to our ability to fight and defeat the German defences, but to our success in evading them. [The report] points out that a quite small technical advance made by the Germans might, temporarily at least, reduce our powers of invasion. This would mean an immediate and large increase in our rate of loss, as our gunners, provided as they are with a poor view and deficient fire-power, cannot hope to deal effectively with the powerfully armed and heavily armoured German night fighters.[37]

It's probably a good thing that the letter wasn't shown to the Americans. It was a patronizing dismissal of the efforts made by the USSTAF to destroy the Luftwaffe. Their effort, Harris implied, had been pointless and only his skill at moving RAF bombers around Germany had saved them. Harris added one more argument against oil targets—bombing the same target is boring for crews—and sent the letter to Portal.

Portal took more than a week to respond. During that time, the bombing went on relentlessly. On November 27, the southern German city of Freiburg, which until then had remained untouched, was set alight. Fires tore through the narrow streets of the 875-year-old city. Within two hours, the heat and flames made it impossible for fire crews to reach the citizens, or to rescue those still in cellars.[38] When it was over, only a hollow shell of the old city remained and three thousand people were dead.

Over the course of November, Harris had dropped 60 percent of his bombs on cities, 24 percent on oil, and 9 percent on transportation. American raids at the same time made clear that there was nothing inevitable in this. The figures for the Eighth Air Force were 41 percent on oil, 33 percent on marshaling yards, and the rest mostly on ground support. For the Fifteenth Air

Force, they were 35 percent on oil and 51 percent on transportation.[39] Cities were not being destroyed because "weather made other targets impractical," but because Harris was disobeying orders.

December also opened with a city raid. On December 4, Harris sent 244 planes to Heilbronn, a 600-year-old city of 77,500 people and no industry. In just over 20 minutes, the RAF dropped 1249 tons of bombs on the city (40 percent incendiaries) and 170 tons of high explosives on the rail yard.[40] The city was decimated—every building in the old city was destroyed—and seven thousand people were killed, leveling the old city center.[41] The same night, Harris also bombed Karlsruhe, killing 375 people.[42] A September 26–27, 1944, attack had already carpet bombed the city center, leaving fifty dead. The two raids left only burned-out facades standing in the center, but some nearby houses and public buildings were intact. Harris would try one more time to flatten the city—on February 2, 1945—before leaving it alone.

From late November to mid-December, Harris also bombed Münster, Cologne, Neuss, Essen, Dortmund (twice), Bottrop, Osterfeld, Duisburg, Oberhausen, Osterfeld, Karlsruhe, Hallendorf, Hamm, and Hagen. A handful of these raids—on Kalk Nord railway yards in (obliterated) Cologne, on a tar and benzol plant in Dortmund, on a coking plant at Bottrop, and on steel-works in Hallendorf—were precision attacks. More than two thousand tons of bombs were dropped on Hagen, Karlsruhe, Essen, and Duisburg.

Two days after Heilbronn, Portal's letter arrived. Portal rejected outright Harris's argument about German air defenses and tolerable casualty rates. "While losses might go up on a particular raid, where German flak defences secured unexpected successes, the overall casualty rate was less than 1%." While this could, of course, change, "there is some force in the argument that we should exploit [Germany's] present confusion by making a maximum effort while it lasts."[43] He also rejected the argument, made in Harris's last letter, that a higher casualty rate was tolerable in 1943 but not in 1944. How, Portal asked, could Bomber Command give up the opportunity to press home a winning strategy? "In this, the culminating phase of the war we would not be justified in pulling our punches." The letter also reminded Harris—again—that oil and transportation were the *first* priorities.

Portal dismissed Harris's "boredom" argument. Morale could only benefit from bombing over a strategically important target under relatively safe conditions. Bombing a city was not like visiting one; they did not look radically different from the air. The excitement of the raid flowed from its danger, the flash of lights, fires, sound of flak. Most crews would happily do with less excitement in the form of incoming German fighters.

Portal might have left it at that. Instead—for reasons that are not at all clear—he handed Harris another lifeline. Apparently as a sop to the commander-in-chief's support for city bombing, he urged Harris to see the degrees of freedom the directives allowed him:

> When conditions are unlikely to be suitable for [visual] attacks on the specific targets, such as oil plants or railway centres, which is often the case in the winter, your directive makes provision for the attack of some twenty-four industrial centres throughout Germany, including Breslau, Dresden, Chemnitz and Munich. Such occasions might perhaps be exploited with the object of further increasing the enemy's uncertainty.
>
> For the present, therefore, I feel that neither the restrictions implicit in the directives, nor their effect in terms of increased losses are as serious as your letter suggests. Whether or not the enemy can overcome his present difficulties and inflict increasing losses upon us, only time can show; in such an event, you would have unlimited tactical licence under your directive to deal with the situation. For example, should it be *essential* for tactical reasons, in order to bomb Leuna, to send out considerable forces to attack one or two other targets not specifically mentioned in the directive, that would be acceptable. It would of course be better if you could achieve your diversionary effect by attacking targets mentioned in the directive, but this may not always be possible. There has never been any question of limiting your tactical freedom.

After fairly clearly demolishing the arguments Harris had presented against oil bombing, Portal balked. He invited Harris to reopen the already long debate about what was essential. He reminded Harris that there were plenty of cities that he could decimate as part of the Allied directive, and that in effect the Air Ministry would turn a blind eye when destroying a city not on the lists somehow served the directive. It was an open invitation. Harris would take it.

23

PORTAL PLEADS

Throughout the summer of 1944, Speer had been fighting to keep German production levels up in the face of the oil attack. Doing so required two related efforts: rushing to rebuild bombed oil refineries and synthetic oil plants and increasing fighter production.

On October 12, 1944, Speer was at a conference when Hitler took him aside. "You must not breathe a word of this to anyone." Hitler told him of plans to amass all available German forces for a large-scale offensive in the west. The idea was to assemble sixteen divisions of Wehrmacht soldiers on the Rhine, and in a surprise attack sweep through the Eifel and Ardennes, through Belgium and on to the Channel coast.[1] They would take Antwerp and from there circle and destroy American divisions. "For that," Hitler continued, "you must organize a special corps of German construction workers, one sufficiently motorized to be able to carry out all types of bridge building even if rail transportation should be halted. Stick to the organizational forms that proved their value in the western campaign of 1940."[2]

Speer, who had witnessed industrial production plummet in the face of repeated American oil attacks, replied, "But, my Führer, we scarcely have enough trucks left for such a task."

As ever, when Speer protested his technical limits, Hitler was dismissive. "Everything," he said, "must be put aside for the sake of this. This will be a great blow which must succeed."[3]

Hitler's confused vision drew on the early glories of the Blitzkrieg, the disaster of Stalingrad, his own crude Darwinian ideas, and the smoldering ruins of once-magnificent German cities. In an exchange with Speer about

Germany's losses, he said, "What does it all matter, Speer! I only laugh at them. . . . The enemy's advance is actually a help to us. People fight frantically only when the war reaches their own front doors. That's how people are . . . No city will be left in the enemy's hands until it is a heap of ruins! . . . It is those who are ruthless, not the cowards, who win! Remember this: it isn't technical superiority that is decisive. We lost that long ago." He made clear that Speer had no choice in sharing this vision: "I won't tolerate any opposition. . . . Anyone who disagrees with me now is going straight to the gallows! If the German people cannot understand me, I'll fight this alone. Let them go ahead and leave me! The reward only ever comes from history. Don't expect anything from the people!"[4]

Alfred Jodl presented his general plan to senior western commanders on November 3. To a man, they thought it hopeless. The Army had too few tanks, too little oil, and too few men to manage it. They could forget about taking Antwerp. At best, German divisions might reoccupy Aachen and use it as a base for a subsequent westward push.[5] More importantly, it would be suicide to decrease troop concentrations on the Eastern Front, where the Russians were likely preparing their own offensive. Jodl rejected these modest ambitions out of hand. The result had to be so stunning that it would "make the western powers ready to negotiate."[6]

Speer's task was to wrest enough fuel and materials from the Eastern Front to make the western counteroffensive possible. Speer thought the mission had little chance of achieving its objectives, but, if it was going to happen anyway, he had better be sure that it was as impressive as possible. Speer was a Nazi, and he still hoped to win the war. He got down to work.

He took a trip to the Ruhr, where he met Albert Vögler, a loyal Nazi, a Ruhr industrialist, and one of the most important munitions producers in the region. Speer was there in part to determine its ability to contribute to the Ardennes offensive, and he would later appoint Vögler his Ruhr plenipotentiary in charge of maintaining arms output. Speer was shocked to see the extent of destruction inflicted by Allied—above all, American—attacks on synthetic oil plants and transportation. On November 11, he wrote a report for Hitler. Speer told him that the Ruhr could no longer play its role in the Reich's industrial division of labor.[7]

Although he had been ordered to keep it top secret, Speer discussed the offensive in vague terms with Vögler, who had bluntly asked him, "When are we going to call it quits?" Speer replied that Hitler was staking everything on a last effort. In language that could have got him killed, Vögler asked, "But does he fully realize that after that we have to end it? We're losing too much of our substance. How will we be able to reconstruct if industry goes on taking such a beating even for a few months more?"

"I think," Speer replied slowly, "that Hitler is playing his last card and knows it, too."

Vögler flashed Speer an almost contemptuous look. "Of course it's his last card, now that our production is collapsing right, left and centre. Is this operation going to be directed against the east, to take off the pressure there?"

Speer said nothing.

"Of course," Vögler continued, "it will be on the eastern front. Nobody would be so crazy to try to hold back the enemy in the west."[8]

On December 16, 1944, mist hung over the Allied front along the Ardennes, running along the German border from Luxembourg in the south, through Belgium and into the Netherlands. Thick snow covered the ground. It was almost entirely silent. On the German side of the front, 30 divisions, 600 tanks, and 200,000 German troops were amassed. Most of the soldiers were boys—around fifteen or sixteen years old. Others were old men. They were waiting for the order to attack.

At 5:30 A.M., it came. At the northern end of the front, Sepp Dietrich's 6th SS Panzer Army launched a massive artillery barrage against American troops. By 8 A.M., all divisions had attacked. They hugely outnumbered the Americans, who had eighty thousand soldiers and four hundred tanks. The Germans also had the element of surprise. When the first sounds of gun and cannon fire were heard, the Americans dismissed it as friendly fire. It was only when they saw German soldiers moving through the forest that they realized they were under attack.

The Germans concentrated their attack on three positions: the north, center, and south of the front. In the north, the 6th SS Panzer Army pushed the Americans into Belgium, but they soon recovered and the Germans became bogged down in heavy resistance. In the south, Erich Brandenberger's 7th Army broke through American lines and pushed toward Luxembourg. After advancing for four miles, however, divisions of the U.S. VIII Corps blocked them, and held the new front.

In the center, the Americans were overrun. General Hasso von Manteuffel's 5th Panzer Army broke through. His tanks pressed forward in a deep cut of some sixty-five miles, making it within a few miles of the river Meuse.[9] Manteuffel surrounded two regiments of 106th Infantry Division. Almost eight thousand men surrendered to the Germans, the greatest American setback of the war in Europe. Manteuffel pushed on to encircle the entire 101st Airborne Division, and ordered its general, Anthony McAuliffe, to surrender. Defiant, McAuliffe gave a one-word reply: "Nuts." He scribbled the word on a paper, which was delivered to the Germans. They didn't know what it meant.

Spaatz was in Paris, at the USSTAF's new headquarters there, when he got word of the German counteroffensive. Wild rumors about Germans in Allied uniforms infiltrating the city circulated. Spaatz's deputy, Major General Hugh Knerr, recommended that the headquarters be locked down, streets around it blocked off, and sentry boxes set up. Spaatz didn't take this suggestion, but he was—as he later said—"caught off balance" by the German counterattack.[10]

He quickly recovered, however. Spaatz directed two of the Eighth's fighter groups to find proper Continental airfields on which to base themselves.[11] He put them under the direct command of Major General Hoyt S. Vandenberg, the young and handsome Maxwell Field graduate who had become commanding general of the Ninth Air Force in August. The rest of the U.S. bombing force—two-thirds of it—stayed west of the Rhine and awaited Spaatz's orders. On December 18 and 19, the Eighth braved atrocious weather in England to send out missions over the Ardennes, but equally foul weather shielded German troops from most of the bombing. On December 19, Harris—at Eisenhower's request—sent Lancasters out to bomb rail targets at Trier in foul weather. The bombers destroyed the targets, though stray bombs killed sixty Germans, including thirty nurses who died when a bomb penetrated their cellar.[12] Bomber Command's success was the exception, however, and for three days the Germans enjoyed the advantage.

It did not last. On December 23, a new ally—an area of high air pressure from Russia—came to the Americans' rescue. The thick clouds that had provided the Germans with essential cover cleared, leaving the troops exposed. Spaatz ordered an attack. On Christmas Eve, a vast armada of American bombers—made up of twenty thousand airmen—flew over the German troops and hammered them. The German formations were smashed; bridges, rail lines, and airfields were destroyed, and troops were limited to nighttime movement.[13] Panzer grenadier units could not reach the front, supplies and reserves could not be sent in by train, and even soldiers on bicycles found it impossible to get through wrecked railway towns.[14] On that day, the Eighth Air Force dropped more tonnage than it had on any other day during the war.[15]

On the ground, the steady drone of incoming bombers made the Germans' already miserable task impossible. Unknown to the Allies, Manteuffel's stunning advance was handicapped by a key shortage: oil. Speer was only able to secure enough oil to supply each tank for two to three days. After that, they simply stalled. The result was that Manteuffel's advance began to thin as it moved forward. In the north, the 6th SS Panzer Army's Joachim Peiper and his "*Kampfgruppe*" (a sort of ad hoc battalion with about eight hundred men) got as far as La Gleize in Belgium.[16] As they advanced, Peiper's men murdered more than one hundred American POWs and approximately eighty civilians. Once in La Gleize, the fuel ran out. Harassed by American bombers, they abandoned more than a hundred vehicles, including six tanks, in the town and made their way back to German lines on foot. At precisely this moment, Eisenhower was moving a quarter of a million men right into the thick of the fight.[17]

As the Americans launched their bombing raids, German Field Marshal Model announced that the offensive had "finally failed."[18] Hitler raged in front of his generals: "I have never in my life come to know the term capitulation." Germany would emerge victorious, or it would be "annihilated." The war would decide "the existence of the German people. . . . Elimination destroys such a race under certain circumstances forever."[19] An assistant of Hitler heard him say privately, "We may go down. But we shall take the world with us."[20] Hitler ordered the battle to continue.

On December 26, Patton broke through German lines. In one of the most thrilling rescue efforts of the war,[21] he had his Third Army race toward Bastogne where, encircled by the Germans, McAuliffe refused to surrender. The day after Christmas, Patton's troops entered the town.

One of those on the ground as the Allied bombers droned overhead was Albert Speer. However frustrated he may have been with Hitler's methods (and we will only ever have Speer's version of events), he remained wholly committed to winning the war. On December 16, the day the battle began, he had traveled from Berlin to a small Nazi headquarters in a hunting lodge near Bonn. From there, he joined the advancing troops, moving some two miles an hour in a car sandwiched between ammunition trucks. Throughout the first two weeks of the battle, he stayed on the front. On December 31, on his way to visit Sepp Dietrich, he passed through the site of a German attack on an American machine-gun position. Hundreds of young German soldiers lay dead on the ground, mowed down by the machine guns. Once at Sepp's headquarters on the Belgian border, the SS commander told him that the situation was hopeless. Air attacks had cut supply lines, and they were running out of ammunition. While the two men were talking, as if to provide proof of Sepp's conclusions, his headquarters were attacked by a low-flying bombing formation. He and Speer dived for cover amid the sound of howling and exploding bombs, their position lit up by the descending flares. "I was stunned," Speer wrote after the war, "by this scene of military impotence which Hitler's military miscalculations had given such a grotesque setting."[22] The obscenity did not end: Hitler ordered his troops to keep fighting.

That evening, airmen on German squadron bases were celebrating the arrival of 1945. "We danced, laughed, and drank," recalled Lieutenant Gunther Bloemetz, "until quite suddenly—on a gesture from the Kommandeur—the orchestra stopped playing."

"*Meine Herren*," the Kommandeur shouted, "we will check our watches. Take-off in fifty minutes."[23]

On Hitler's direct orders, every available German aircraft—some nine hundred, including both daytime fighters and nighttime bombers—launched a daring surprise raid on Allied airfields in Belgium, Holland, and northern France; the goal was to destroy the Allied Air Forces on the ground "in one stroke."[24] The Luftwaffe caught the Allies off guard and destroyed 450 planes, including 146 from Bomber Command.[25] But it lost much more: 400 engines, 237 pilots, 59 leaders, and the ability to fight on.

"The Luftwaffe received its death blow," Galland wrote after the war, "at the Ardennes offensive. In the unfamiliar conditions and with insufficient training and combat experience, our numerical strength had no effect. It was decimated while in transfer, on the ground, in large air battles . . . and was finally destroyed. In this forced action [the January 1, 1945, raids] we sacrificed our last substance."[26] The Americans' long war against the Luftwaffe—which had, like the villain in a bad horror movie, kept rising from the dead—had been definitively won. The German Air Force was finished, and with it went any hope of protecting German cities.

Hitler would make one last try—Operation Northwind, designed to break through U.S. lines in France, near Alsace—but it came to nothing. German troops advanced some twelve miles, then stopped. The Ardennes offensive was lost. As Speer put it after the war, because of transportation raids "the preparations for the Ardennes offensive were brought to a standstill . . . the attack was ordered to begin although the units had only one or two fuel supply units; the entire supplies of bridge-building equipment still lay in the rear areas, whilst the rest of the supply organization for the units was insufficient for the distant goal in view. . . . *Transport difficulties were decisive in causing the swift breakdown of the Ardennes offensive.*"[27] During January 1945, the Eighth launched thirty-two raids, the majority on marshaling yards. German troops killed nineteen thousand American soldiers—by far the highest death toll for any Second World War battle. Another twenty-three thousand were captured and forty thousand wounded. The scale of the blow temporarily destroyed Eisenhower's nerve and delayed another major American offensive against Germany by seven weeks.[28] The Germans were able to launch their counterattack, and to inflict such material and psychological damage so late in the war, because they could draw on Germany's remaining oil supplies.

Four days before the German counteroffensive on December 16, Harris wrote again to Portal, making yet another combination of his "I can't do it—it's not worth doing" arguments. Based on his staff's calculations, Harris concluded that knocking Germany's synthetic oil plants out of action, and keeping them there, would require 13 day raids of 200 aircraft and 18 night raids of 350 aircraft per month, or 56,500 sorties and 226,000 tons of bombs. Assuming the weather was clear on only three or four nights per month, Harris continued, it would be impossible to launch these night raids. Harris then switched arguments:

> You will recall that in the past M.E.W. experts have never failed to overstate their case on "panaceas" e.g. ballbearings, molybdenum, locomotives etc. . . . [A]fter the battle has been joined and [these] targets attacked, more sources of supply or other factors unpredicted by M.E.W. have become revealed. The oil plan has already displayed similar symptoms. The benzol plants were an afterthought. I am quite certain that there are dozens more benzol plants of which we are unaware and when and if we knock them all out I am equally certain we shall eventually be told by M.E.W. that German [industry] is continuing to run sufficiently for their purpose on producer gas, steam, industrial alcohol etc., etc.[29]

Five days after writing the letter, and one day after the Germans opened the Ardennes offensive, the RAF obliterated Ulm, leaving nothing of the old city and 707 people dead.

On December 22, as the German offensive was thinning and slowing due to lack of fuel, Portal replied.

> The essence of the immediate task before the Allied strategic bombers is to put out and keep out of action the 11 synthetic [oil] plants in Central Germany. These are producing 70% of the enemy's current supplies of aviation and motor spirit. There is no doubt in my mind that their immobilisation and the continued immobilisation of the remaining major producers would represent by far the greatest and most certain contribution that our strategic bombers could make to the achievement of an early decision in the German war. It is not expected by anyone that your Command can do this job by itself; neither can the US Eighth Air Force by itself. *Over the winter months it is essential, however, that no single opportunity is lost, whether by day or by night.*[30]

Portal urged Harris to view the bombing campaign in the overall context of the war, and to be sensitive to history's judgment. Were the Americans and the British to join in a coordinated campaign against oil, using every available opportunity to attack Germany's refineries,

> strategic bombing will go down to history as a decisive factor in winning this war. On the other hand, if by any weakening of determination or any reluctance to implement the policy which we have laid down our grip on the oil position is relaxed, the vast effort we have expended against oil will have been largely fruitless.

He then called Harris on the tension in his "I can't do it—it's not worth doing" arguments:

> I am profoundly disappointed that you still appear to feel that the oil plan is just another "panacea." Naturally while you hold this view you will be unable to put your heart into the attack of oil. Your letter gave me the impression that while you have somewhat reluctantly agreed to attack Politz and Leuna when occasion offers, you feel that this is all you should

be asked to contribute toward the attack of the all-important Central German plants. I must say I should have hoped that you would on the contrary be seeking opportunities to attack all or any of them whenever there is a chance of doing so, in order that the R.A.F. might play as large a part as possible in what is by far the most immediately profitable policy we have undertaken in this war.

The particular concern, even obsession, with cities and the related dismissal of all precision targets became a self-fulfilling policy. Harris did not believe in precision targets, attacked them halfheartedly, and then took the mixed results flowing from his less-than-total effort as evidence of the target's tactical irrelevance. "In your last paragraph," Portal wrote,

you again cast doubt on past estimates by the Ministry of Economic Warfare and by implication the whole principle of attacking a particular target system. You throw doubt also upon the soundness of our oil policy. If the attack of a particular target system is to be successful, it must be carried out as rapidly as possible and with the object of immobilising as many plants as possible in the system at the same time. Clearly we cannot expect to get very far if only half the plants are out of action at any one time. If we had tried harder in our attack on ball-bearings I have little doubt that full effects forecast by M.E.W. would have been achieved. I am glad to say that we have shown much more determination in the attack of oil, but if you allow your obvious doubts in this direction to influence your conduct of operations I very much fear that the prize may yet slip through our fingers. Moreover, it is difficult for me to feel that your staff can be devoting its maximum thoughts and energies to the accomplishment of your first priority task if you yourself are not wholehearted in support of it.[31]

With each exchange, Harris felt less and less inclined to soften his blows. He was offended by the suggestion that he did not follow orders and above all by the idea that his staff responded to his views rather than his orders. He penned a long letter to Portal—almost twice as long as the one sent to him. As he did, he became angrier: with the experts who knew nothing about bombing, with the Americans who had so long stood in the way of his campaign, with the Army for its many diversions, and with Portal, the erstwhile backer of city bombing. Harris dismissed out of hand the suggestion that his men might be affected by his views on strategic bombing, and his contempt for the MEW. Reacting to Portal's argument that only a small number of plants—fewer than twenty—were hit, Harris replied:

> I have certainly not overlooked the fact that the majority of output comes from the limited number of major plants. The point I tried to make clear was that I do not believe the M.E.W. know anything at all about the number of Benzol plants, or even oil plants for that matter. . . . I am certain that no feasible scale of destruction of oil plants and Benzol plants will vitally affect the carriage of essential supplies forward to their armies.[32]

As he crafted his reply, Harris reflected on the follies that had so often been held up as the final key to victory. Remember fighter jets?

> The attacks against the German fighter forces and industry last year are outstanding examples of the futility of panacea seeking. After all that vast effort against the German fighter industry the German fighter force finishes up at from two to two and half times as strong as when it started! . . . Nobody could say that every possible effort was not made, and brilliantly executed, in the best of conditions, to knock the German fighter forces on the ground and in their factories. But the enemy by concentrating his efforts and his great industrial abilities in countering the effects of these attacks rendered them virtually nugatory. All we have to show for it . . . is that we failed to achieve the aim. A failure both expensive and complete. If, over that long period of attacks on the German fighter industry, [U.S.] Eighth Bomber Command had instead joined with us in our area bombing, what vastly greater effects would not have been achieved on the enemy's war machine and will to war as a whole?

Remember ball bearings?

> You conclude saying that 5% or even 10% losses in successful attacks will be well worth while. Although that statement is by no means the equivalent, it reminds me much of a statement I once received from the Air Ministry that it was worth the virtual destruction of my force over a period of months, if we could knock out Schweinfurt. Where should we be now if I had agreed to that?

And now he was expected to believe that oil was the magic bullet. He wouldn't: "I am afraid that nothing will disillusion me of the view that the oil plan is, for reason[s] I have given above, and on many occasions elsewhere, another panacea." He would continue to attack oil—"It has always been my custom . . . to leave no stone unturned to get my views across, but, when the decision is made I carry it out to the utmost and to the best of my ability"—but doing so was pointless. "The basis," Harris wrote, "of the plan is wrong . . . and its pursuance is, and will prove to be, chimerical."

Harris used the letter to address Portal's argument that history would soon judge him. He turned it on its head. "The history of bombing," he wrote,

> throughout this war will, when it is all summed up, show our repeated lapses from that essential principle of war, the maintenance of an objective. Three years of bitter struggle have gone into our area blitzing. All Germany openly bemoans it as their worst trial. We know that on more than one occasion they have nearly collapsed under it. As the programme nears completion we chuck it all up—for a panacea.

The pursuit of these panaceas had already cost the Allies dearly. Just before D-Day, Harris had warned the Army that if Bomber Command lay off bombing Germany for five months, the country would recover all that was necessary for war production. "The aggregate of our diversions, on the railway plan, on helping the armies and now on oil, very far exceeds the five months' estimate." Referring to Ardennes, Harris added, "We need look no further for the cause of what happened in this last fortnight."

24

SPEER DESPAIRS, HARRIS THREATENS, PORTAL BLINKS

The year 1945 was two hours old when Speer arrived at Hitler's private, bombproof bunker hidden in a grassy valley near Bad Nauheim, about twenty miles north of Frankfurt. When he entered, he saw Martin Bormann, Hitler's doctors, and the lower-middle-class coterie—adjutants and secretaries—that made up Hitler's inner circle. They were drinking champagne, and Hitler himself, though entirely sober, was in a "grip of permanent euphoria."[1] Looking to the year ahead, he spoke of a quick recovery from past setbacks, of renewed glories, and of the *Endsieg*, the final victory. The circle met these prophesies in silence, some averting their eyes. Only Bormann, ever the sycophant, nodded furiously.

A day later, Bomber Command attacked Nuremberg. On the night of January 2, 1945, Bomber Command flattened the city's medieval center, killing two thousand people and leaving a hundred thousand homeless.

Two days later, Hitler, Keitel, Goebbels, and Bormann sat at a grand conference table. They were talking about the war. The only way to win it, Goebbels argued, was through mass conscription; everyone from the age of thirteen should be called up. Speer was incredulous. Allied attacks on oil and transportation were sapping Germany's remaining industrial strength. To rob it of workers would be suicide. "Total conscription," he argued, "would strike our remaining programs to such an extent that it would be equivalent to the total collapse of whole industries."

Goebbels turned to Hitler, and exploded in rage: "Then, Herr Speer, you bear the historical guilt for the loss of the war because of a few hundred thousand missing soldiers! Why don't you say yes for once! Think about it! It would be entirely your fault."

Everyone was stony silent. Hitler spoke: "Goebbels is right. We will win this war."

Speer saw no point in arguing. It was over; the war had been lost.

On January 6, Harris sent his bombers to destroy the center of Hanau. Munich's turn came the following night. More than six hundred Lancasters and a few Mosquitoes area bombed the center.[2] Incendiaries drenched the two cities, and Bomber Command suffered a low 2 percent casualty rate.

The day after the Munich raid, Portal wrote to Harris. His patience had worn thin, and he decided to speak truth to truculence. "In spite of your assertions to the contrary," Portal noted, "I believe your attacks on oil would be pressed home harder and more certainly if they were backed not solely by your sense of loyalty but by your enthusiasm as well."[3] He began by pointing out that Harris's raid on the oil plant at Politz involved only one-third of the total possible bombing force, and therefore he, Portal, was "not convinced by your argument that the prospect of damaging Politz would not have been increased had you despatched two or three times the force you did. The target is a large one . . ." He then went on to describe Harris's antipathy toward the MEW as "misplaced" and inimical to the war effort. The MEW did not choose the ball bearings and oil targets alone; economists' recommendations, agents' reports, and intelligence committees in both the United States and the United Kingdom all informed the decision.

> The adoption of these two policies was therefore backed by investigations which, as far as was humanly possible, covered all the ground and brought in all interests which were able to help. They were clearly not merely "panaceas enthusiastically put forward by the amateurish, ignorant, irresponsible and mendacious M.E.W." and it is an unworthy and inexcusable travesty of our conduct of the war to suggest that our policy is determined on that kind of basis.

His pen gaining flourish, Portal repeated and confronted the other claims made in Harris's letter. That he had done everything he could to destroy Germany's ball bearings factories:

You state that you are satisfied you achieved a "whole series of brilliantly executed attacks of an effectiveness that nobody would even have thought possible at the time when the ball-bearing plan was initiated." The facts scarcely seem to me to support your appreciation of your achievements.

That the American attacks on the German fighter force were futile:

Had the American forces joined with Bomber Command in bombing cities instead of fighter production, there is every possibility that the whole combined bomber offensive might have been brought to a standstill. It was only by a narrow margin that they gained the ascendency which virtually cleared the skies for "OVERLORD," the prerequisite condition for its launching, and obtained freedom to proceed to the attack of oil.

That area bombing would have proved decisive if the Americans had joined the campaign:

[The enemy's] counter measures would have prevented us from maintaining such a policy to the decisive point. We would have been forced to precision attack to maintain the air situation needed to continue the offensive at all. The Americans did this for themselves in 1943/1944 with a little help from Bomber Command. Under cover of the favourable air situation which was created "OVERLORD" was launched successfully, and the advance to the German frontier gave night bombing a new lease on life. But for this it is possible that the night blitzing of German cities would by now have been too costly to sustain upon a heavy scale. These factors must not be overlooked when considering the past and future results of area attacks.

Portal, the erstwhile backer of area bombing, ended the letter with a full—even passionate, if such a word can be used to describe such a gentlemanly character—embrace of precision attacks on oil:

We have determined to exploit our period of tactical freedom over Germany by the attack of the vital element in her war economy—oil. We have reduced their production to 30% of the pre-attack figure and her reserves are now virtually exhausted. . . . The completion of the oil plan lies so well within our capabilities that it can be pressured to a point at which the operational effectiveness of the German armies and air forces on all fronts will be decisively restricted; but to do this it is essential to hold firmly to this aim.

The energy, resource and determination displayed by the enemy in his efforts to maintain his oil production must be more than matched by our own determination to destroy it.

On January 16, Harris sent his bombers to attack the medieval city of Magdeburg. The historic core, with its churches, narrow streets, and elegant city hall, along with the *fin-de-siècle* northern suburbs were flattened and four thousand people were killed.[4] The bodies of thousands of women, children, and old men were piled up in the gutters. The same day, Portal and Spaatz issued Strategic Directive No. 3, making oil again the first priority followed by transportation. The category of "important industrial areas" to be attacked when weather demanded it was a distant third.

Having obliterated another four German cities, Harris answered Portal.[5] The jig was up. Portal would not accept his assurances that he was doing everything he could to implement the oil directive. Although January was the peak of his contribution to the oil campaign, only 30 percent of his bombs hit oil targets, while 40 percent fell on cities. Harris had little to gain in restraining his views. He let Portal know what he thought of precision targets:

All strategic targets of the panacea type are dependent on the assumption that the enemy has been fool enough to allow vital bottle-necks to persist even at this stage of the war. They are also dependent on the assumption that over a definite period of time, and quite a short time, those vital targets can all, or the major part of them, be destroyed before the enemy has time to disperse them, *and thereafter be kept destroyed.*[6]

Such a bombing effort would require most of the bombers and "*all* of the good weather." Even then the Germans would simply disperse their industries. "Small oil plants," Harris argued, "especially those suited for M.T. [motor transport] and jet fuels, can be erected inside ordinary farm, village, town and city housing" with ease. Finding, much less hitting, them would be impossible.

But above all, Harris concluded, destroying oil targets would not do any good anyway:

> On top of all this the final factor is that Germany wants so very little in the way of fuel *for the essentials with which to continue the fight defensively*. It is those last essentials which I know will be so extremely difficult to find, to deprive her of, and to keep her deprived of. It is not good knocking out 75% of something if 25% suffices for essentials.[7]

And doing so would further distract Bomber Command from the single most important aim of the bombing war:

> The main factor which I fear is the abandonment of priority for area attack[s] with all the vast harm they have done to the enemy war machine, in favour of a type of attack which *if it fails to achieve its objectives achieves nothing*. Nothing whatever. Worse than nothing. Because it largely relieves the enemy of his worst problem—industrial area bombing. *This we throw aside just as we near our long striven for goal of destroying the 50 leading industrial cities.*[8]

The oil plan, like all precision plans before it, "is another attempt to seek a quick, clever, easy and cheap way out. It will prove to be none of these things. If only because the enemy is neither a fool nor an incompetent. We will not deprive him of his last essentials in fuel. What we will succeed in doing will be largely to relieve Germany of her 'worst headache'—*the crescendo of industrial civil and morale destruction which is near intolerable to her war potential now and must soon, even in Gestapo-ridden Germany, react to her final undoing on every front, including the home front*. And that despite the fact . . . that the U.S. bombers have taken no serious part in area attacks."[9]

Given this, Harris was not prepared to follow his orders. "I will not willingly again lay myself open to the charge that the lack of success of a policy, which I have declared at the outset . . . not to contain the seeds of success, is after the event, due to my personal failure in not having really tried. That situation is simply one of heads I lose tails you win, and it is simply an intolerable situation."

If Harris were to remain in his position, he would do so to finish the job:

> The next three months will be our last opportunity to knock out the central and eastern industrial areas of Germany, viz. Magdeburg, Leipzig, Chemnitz, Dresden, Breslau, Posen, Halle, Erfurt, Gotha, Weimar, Eisenach and the rest of Berlin . . . These places are now the mainspring of German war production *and the culmination and consummation of three years' work depends upon achieving their destruction.* It is our last chance, and it would have more effect on the war than anything else. . . . But for all the diversions, necessary or otherwise, these places would nearly all be burnt out or blazing by now. That would have been the consummation of our three years' effort, and it would have been absolutely fatal for Germany.

If Portal was not prepared to accept this, then he had, Harris said in the letter's last lines, only one option. "I . . . ask you to consider whether it is best for the prosecution of the war and the success of our arms, which alone matter, that I should remain in this situation."

It was a defining moment in the bombing war. It was not the first time that Harris had threatened resignation. If Portal had called Harris's bluff, city bombing might have ended or at least been sharply reduced, and airplanes could have been redirected toward key oil and transportation targets. Tens of thousands of civilians would not have lost their lives, more than a dozen cities would have been spared, Germany might have capitulated earlier, and thousands of Allied lives might have been saved. Given Harris's record of disobeying orders and his insolence, there was every case for sacking him. Instead, Portal backed down. He wrote to Harris: "I willingly accept your assurance that you will continue to do your utmost to ensure the successful implementation of the policy laid down. I am very sorry that you do not believe in it, but it is no use my craving for what is evidently unattainable. We must wait until after the end of the war before we can know for certain who was right and until then I sincerely hope that you will continue in command of the [air] force."[10] It is hard to imagine a more feeble letter from a superior to a subordinate officer.[11]

25

AMERICAN AREA BOMBING

On February 3, 1945, Lieutenant John Welch, a co-pilot with the 457th Bombardment Group, was over Berlin. His plane was one of a thousand bombers flying across the capital. His aiming point was Friedrichstrasse station, a few minutes from Berlin's famous boulevard, the Unter den Linden, and from the Brandenburg Gate and the Reichstag. When Welch's plane reached the target, his bombardier released his load of 500-pound bombs on the station. "God help them," he whispered as the bombs hurtled toward their target.[1]

The station was crowded full of refugees fleeing the Russian advance. As the bombs rained down, people scurried into the tunnels. One was Herie Granberg, a Swedish newspaper correspondent. "The ground heaved," he wrote in a report smuggled out after the raid, "the lights flickered. It seemed the concrete walls bulged. People scrambled about like frightened animals."[2] Clouds of dust filled the tunnels.

Outside, it was worse. Those who did not make it into the station in time were slaughtered. Bombs exploded on or around them. Flying glass and metal fragments sliced through them. When the bombing stopped, Granberg climbed out of the tunnel to find dozens of people dead and dying in the square in front of the station.

The raid ravaged other areas of the stricken city. Large parts of Mitte (the center), Kreuzberg (south of the center and later the heart of West Berlin's counterculture scene), and Friedrichshain (working-class east Berlin) were reduced to rubble.[3] A vast column of smoke covered the central city. All utilities were knocked out. For days, delay-action time bombs exploded, shaking the ground.[4] The attack, wrote one Foreign Office official, "was the ultimate apocalypse, as far as Berlin is concerned . . . Never has the city looked so devastated . . . Rain and water from the melting snow bespatter its ruins with muck, and streams of filthy water flow through the streets."[5]

The raid was city and civilian bombing, pure and simple. "We were told today," a member of Welch's crew wrote in his diary, "that if we had any scruples about bombing civilians, it was hard luck for us because from now on we'll be bombing and strafing women, children, everybody."[6] More than a hundred thousand people were made homeless and at least three thousand civilians (probably many more, because the city was packed with millions of refugees) were killed, the largest single death toll for any raid on the capital. Two weeks after the raid, on February 17, German radio announced that the Wehrmacht was awarding the Order of the White Feather to Spaatz for "exceptional cowardice" in laying a "carpet of bombs" across a city "crowded with hundreds of thousands of refugees, principally women and children."[7] The Nazis' only award to those women and children was more suffering: "The homeless masses," Goebbels declared, "must share whatever new disaster may befall [the capital]."[8]

Such sympathy as the Germans received came from the aircrew. "Shacked women and children," wrote one bomb releaser on his airplane immediately after the raid. Another, a radio operator named James Henrietta, said much later, Berlin "bothered me for a long time. In fact, it still does. . . . I'm thinking we're bombing out a lot of people who maybe were helpless victims."[9]

The February raid on Berlin emerged from a complex set of first British, then American proposals set out over the early months of 1945. Both forces dusted off the THUNDERCLAP proposal of the previous summer. On January 12, the Russians launched their winter offensive. On January 25, the British Joint Intelligence Committee issued two reports on how best to assist the Russians. The first report argued that attacks on five targets would help the Soviet offensive.[10] The most important of them was oil. After oil, the committee recommended attacks on tank factories, on Berlin (to disrupt troop flows), and on German reinforcements moving from Italy or Hungary. It also recommended attacking sea mining operations in the Baltic. The second report—following the THUNDERCLAP proposals from the previous summer—looked exclusively at Berlin. It argued that attacks on Berlin should in no way interfere with oil or tank targets, and that destroying the regime would neither break Germany's will to resist nor lead to the downfall of the regime. Still, the massive bombing of the capital, as eastern Germany's main transportation hub and the home of millions of refugees, "would be bound to create great confusion, interfere with the orderly movement of troops to the front, and hamper the German military and administrative machine."[11]

Anyone who has worked in a large, complex organization will have noticed a curious tendency on the part of its officials to reinvent the wheel: ideas that were tried and failed in the past return. When they do, younger people who did not hear the original arguments or view the consequences of the decisions, or older people who did but forgot them, seize on these ideas and put them into practice. The "morale" argument was—by 1945!—tried, tested, and found to be thoroughly wanting. Yet, here it was again, repackaged only slightly as "confusion."

As often occurs in area bombing debates, other arguments were thrown in to provide further justifications. The 6th SS Panzer Army had, it was wrongly believed, left Belgium for the Eastern Front and would be passing through Berlin. Destroying the city would also demonstrate to the Soviets an American and British desire to help them, thus improving the Western Allies' hand at the upcoming Yalta conference.[12] Finally, though no one said it, bombing Berlin seemed—as it had almost from the start of the war—the right thing to do.

The next day, the Air Staff presented their views.[13] Oil targets should absolutely remain the first priority. Tank production could be attacked only if attacks on communications could be reduced. Mine laying would definitely produce dividends, but bombing German troop movements likely would not. As for Berlin, the Chiefs of Staff were doubtful that bombing would produce much in the way of results.

While these discussions were going on, Bottomley called Harris to hear his views. The commander-in-chief naturally loved the idea of bombing Berlin; such an attack was, he said, already "on his plate."[14] He recommended additional strikes on Chemnitz, Leipzig, and Dresden, as these cities were housing large numbers of refugees.[15] Harris was ready to blast Berlin "as soon as the moon had waned."

Churchill then entered the argument, with a predictably decisive effect. On the evening of January 25, he was preparing to have a drink with Harry Hopkins, President Roosevelt's envoy. Before he did, he called Sinclair. The prime minister had read the Joint Intelligence Committee's reports and asked Sinclair about the RAF's plans for "basting the Germans in their retreat from Breslau."[16]

Sinclair took Churchill's views to Portal the next day. Portal replied that oil targets should remain the first priority, but that attacks in support of the Russian advance could be the second. In some cases, though he did not explain which, city attacks might come first. That day, Sinclair passed this on to Churchill. "I feel strongly," Sinclair wrote on January 26, "that the best use of our heavy bombers at the present time lies in maintaining the attack upon German oil plants whenever weather permits. The benefits of these attacks are felt equally by the Russians and ourselves and *nothing should be allowed to interfere with them*. These opportunities might be used to exploit the present situation by the bombing of Berlin and other large cities in Eastern Germany such as Leipzig, Dresden and Chemnitz. . . . To achieve results of real value, a series of attacks would probably be required, and weather conditions at this time of year would certainly prevent these being delivered in quick succession. The possibility of these attacks being delivered on the scale necessary to have a critical effect on the situation in East Germany is now under examination."[17]

For Churchill, the response was too equivocal. He wanted it bombed immediately. "I did not ask you," he shot back on the same day, "about your plans for harrying the German retreat from Breslau. On the contrary, I asked whether Berlin, and no doubt other large cities in East Germany, should not now be considered especially attractive targets. I am glad that is 'under examination.' Pray report to me tomorrow what is going to be done."

Sinclair passed the prime minister's minute on to Bottomley, who issued orders to Harris. Bottomley attacked the Joint Intelligence Committee report and told Harris that in "the opinion of the Chief of Air Staff . . . it would not be right to attempt attacks on Berlin on the 'THUNDERCLAP' scale in the near future. He considers it very doubtful that an attack even if done on the heaviest scale with consequent heavy losses would be decisive. He agrees, however, that subject to the overriding claims of oil and the other approved target systems within the current directive, we should use available effort in one big attack on Berlin and related attacks on Dresden, Leipzig, Chemnitz or any other cities where a severe blitz will not only cause confusion in the evacuation from the East but will also hamper the movement of troops from the West."

"I am therefore," Bottomley concluded, "to request that subject to the qualifications stated above, and as soon as the moon and weather conditions allow, you will undertake such attacks with the particular object of exploiting the confused conditions which are likely to exist in the above mentioned cities during the successful Russian advance."[18]

A similar argument was developing on the other side of the Atlantic. Arnold, always impatient for results, was increasingly strident in his demand for action. He had just suffered his fourth heart attack and was driven by the realization that the war might finish him before he finished Germany. "With [our] tremendous striking power," he wrote to Spaatz, "it would seem to me that we should get much better and much more decisive results than we are getting now. I am not criticizing, because frankly I don't know the answer and what I am now doing is letting my thoughts run wild with the hope that out of this you get a glimmer, a light, a new thought, or something that will help us bring this war to a close sooner."[19] It was an open appeal for something dramatic. And brutal.

General Marshall was impatient as well. He wanted troops out of Europe and into the Pacific, and was prepared to try anything to get them there. Since the Germans had shown unexpected resistance, they had to be met with unexpected force. Just before Yalta, he met with Frederick Anderson and told him that he wanted Munich bombed (it would not be, at least not like Berlin), along with the cities in the Berlin-Leipzig-Dresden corridor. Eisenhower and Bradley signed on: there was no need to ask Roosevelt, as the president had for years called for hell's fury to be unleashed against Germany. In 1942, he told Congress that the Allies would hit Germany "from the air heavily and relentlessly. The people who bombed Warsaw, Rotterdam, London, and Coventry are going to get it."[20] On January 31, Bottomley radioed a message to Portal: oil would be the first priority, followed by Berlin, Leipzig, and Dresden.[21] With V-2 rockets raining down on London, few people disagreed with Roosevelt's sentiment.

Few, but not no one. When Spaatz presented the plan to Doolittle on January 30, Doolittle viewed it as what it was: terror bombing, which U.S. air forces had ruled out as immoral and pointless. He wrote back to Spaatz, urging him to reconsider. Doolittle pointed out that there "are basically no important, strictly military, targets in the area indicated." He dismissed the idea that Berliners could be terrorized into surrender. "The reactions of people of Berlin who have been bombed consistently will be very different from the people of London who have not experienced a heavy raid in years. Terror is inducted by the unknown. The chances of terrorizing into submission, merely by an increased concentration of bombing, a people who have been subjected to intense bombing for four years is extremely remote." Doolittle was doing nothing more than repeating the argument that Spaatz had himself made against THUNDERCLAP.[22] If Harris's obliteration campaign against Berlin hadn't worked in 1944, why would it work in 1945? But that was not all. There were other issues at stake, namely the Eighth Air Force's reputation and historical legacy.[23] "We will," Doolittle continued, "in what may be one of our last and best remembered operations regardless of its effectiveness, violate the basic American principle of precision bombing of targets of strictly military significance for which our tactics were designed and our crews trained and indoctrinated." Leave area bombing to those who believe in it: the British.[24] If the Americans had to take part in THUNDER-CLAP, Doolittle concluded, let them be assigned "precision targets of military significance." This appeal to conscience almost certainly had some impact, as Spaatz refused to even address it. "Hit Berlin," he wrote back, "whenever [weather] conditions do not indicate the possibility of visual bombing of oil targets but do permit operations to Berlin."

Doolittle, under a direct order, prepared every available bomber for a February 2 raid on Berlin. Heavy clouds over the capital led him to cancel it. That night, the weather was clearing. Doolittle knew what he had to do, but he tried once again to get Spaatz to change his mind. "Is Berlin still open to air attack?" he cabled Spaatz. "Do you want priority oil targets hit in preference to Berlin if they definitely become visual? Do you want [the center] of [the] city hit or definitely military targets, such as Spandau, on the Western outskirts?"[25] Spaatz called him within the hour and made it clear. He told Doolittle to bomb oil if he could do so visually; otherwise he had to bomb "Berlin—center of [the] city."[26]

When Doolittle's bombers were finished with Berlin, one of the dead was Roland Freisler, fanatical communist turned fanatical Nazi, representative at the Wannsee conference on the final solution, and president of the People's Court. He had sentenced Hans Scholl, Sophie Scholl, and Christopher Probst (all of Munich's White Rose anti-Hitler resistance movement) to death by guillotine. He had done the same to dozens implicated in the July 20, 1944, plot against Hitler. During the bombing, a collapsing beam crushed him. At the time of his death, Freisler was clutching the file of July 20 resister Fabian von Schlabrendorff.

Thousands of others killed were civilians.

On February 13, at 7:57 P.M., a single wooden airplane, a Mosquito, took off from a barren air base in Lincolnshire, in the north of England.[27] It joined 244 heavy, bomb-laden Lancasters in a formation on its way to Saxony.

At 10:06 P.M., radios crackled across the beautiful city of Dresden. The bombers were there.

At 10:13 P.M., the first Lancasters were over the bombing area, which took in the entire old city—its northern border just over the Elbe in the Neustadt and its southern border before the main station. The main station itself was outside the bombing area.

The bombing bays were opened. Thousands of high explosives hit the city center at once. Roofs were blown off, windows shattered. The interiors of churches, museums, palaces, and apartment blocks were exposed.

A few seconds letter, tens of thousands of four-pound incendiary bombs were dropped, landing in exposed corridors, concert halls, and living rooms. Beds, chairs, and paintings began to burn. The fires crossed the floors and climbed the walls. They exited the windows.

After fifteen minutes, the first wave of bombers left the city.

By 11 P.M., the firefighters were losing control of Dresden. The entire old city was in flames. In the cellars and air-raid shelters below, tens of thousands of civilians, including many refugees, cowered.

At 1:20 A.M., a second wave of bombers hit the city. They were meant to bomb the old city, but since it already was a raging inferno they dropped their bombs instead on the southern edges of the inner city, hitting the city's Great Garden where Dresdeners had sought refuge.

After the second bombing, the city was doomed. The fires leaped out of windows and open roofs. In the narrow streets of the city center, fires from buildings on either side, searching for oxygen, merged in the center, creating a ceiling of flames. It began to move toward the ground. The fires from the fourth, third, second, and ground floors joined in the center of the street. Still looking for oxygen, the flames moved through the streets at breathtaking speed.

As in Hamburg one and a half years earlier, hundreds of these fires converged in the center of the old city. They had nowhere to go but up. A great column of flames shot into the sky, setting off a process that created the firestorm. The column rose further, sucking in more air and gases. The process became self-fulfilling, and the fire climbed miles into the sky. Dresden was dying.

On the street, winds created by the firestorm reached ninety-five miles an hour. People struggled against them, went mad, and were sucked into the flames.

By 1:40 A.M., anyone left in the cellars was dead or dying.

It was not over, however. On February 14, the Eighth Air Force hit the city. Its aiming point—if a visual raid was possible—was the center of the city. Dresden was to be another Berlin. What they in fact bombed was the Friedrichstadt station and marshaling yards in the suburbs—to which inner city residents had fled the night before. "It was," historian Frederick Taylor wrote, "as if the enemy had anticipated the Dresdeners' every move, and then killed them like cattle cunningly driven into holding pens."[28] Or, at least twenty-five thousand of them.

The raid on Dresden was quickly followed by attacks on other cities. On the night of February 14, Bomber Command attacked the center of Chemnitz, near Dresden, with little success.[29] The railway was unscathed. In two days, Bomber Command had flown 1522 sorties and dropped 5256 bombs on the centers of German cities.[30] On February 15, the Americans—diverted by bad weather from oil attacks on Leipzig—made a second, unsuccessful, raid on Dresden's marshaling yards. Two weeks later, Harris sent his bombers to Pforzheim. The attacks of February 24–25 destroyed 83 percent of the city's built-up area and killed 17,600 people—20 percent of the city's population. "The whole place," Harris bragged at the next air commanders conference, "had been burned out. This attack had been what was popularly known as a deliberate terror attack." Bomber Command, he continued, "has now destroyed 63 German towns in this fashion."[31] A week later, on March 1, Harris sent 478 bombers to obliterate what was left of Mannheim.[32] The next day, 858 aircraft hit Cologne. A "carpet of bombs" spread right across the city, "the end of Cologne."[33] When the Americans took the cities four days later, they cleared more than four hundred bodies from the streets.[34]

After Berlin, just as the precision campaign that they had doggedly supported for years was on the threshold of success, the Americans succumbed to the self-fulfilling logic of terror bombing: if destruction fails to deliver victory, as it had in Berlin, its failure was answered with more destruction. Arnold wrote again to Spaatz and urged him to organize "widespread simultaneous attacks" by fleets of airplanes. Operation Clarion called for a "coordinated attack" against transportation targets by "all available American Air Forces."[35] Their target would not be Germany's rail nexuses or even large railway stations in major cities. Rather, it would be untouched transportation targets in "undefended or lightly defended targets": small towns and villages. Waves of bombers and fighters would, taking advantage of Allied air superiority, fly in low and cover the train stations—and much around them—with bombs and bullets. "The destruction of facilities with all means available, using bombs and machine guns and NAPALM where warranted." The absence of significant flak or fighter defense and low-altitude attacks would allow heavy and low-medium bombers to open up "tremendous machine gun power . . . for strafing." The aim in all of this? Morale, this time of railway workers: "As a result of continued pressure against transportation objectives, morale of railway employees is known to be infirm at best and it may well be that repeated attacks using all forces available will result in mass desertion from work."[36] The raid would "bring home the effects of the war upon German industry and people as no other method could do," pushing them perhaps "over the brink."[37]

When Spaatz passed the order on to Doolittle and Eaker, both objected. Oil targets should be bombed, not railway workers. If executed, Eaker wrote Arnold in an emotional letter, the plan would "absolutely convince the Germans that we are the barbarians they say we are, for it would be perfectly obvious to them that this is primarily a large scale attack on civilians . . . Of all the people killed in this attack over 95 percent of them can be expected to be civilians." As Spaatz had done over THUNDERCLAP, Eaker appealed to the Eighth's historical legacy: "We should never allow the history of this war to convict us of throwing the strategic bomber at the man in the street." Brigadier General Charles Cabell was blunter: "This is the same old baby killing plan of the get-rich quick psychological boys, dressed up in a new Kimono. It is a poor psychological plan and a worse rail plan."[38]

It went ahead anyway. On February 22 and 23, thirty-five hundred bombers and a thousand fighters prowled the territory of the Reich, bombing and strafing rail yards, train stations, bridges, grade crosses, motor vehicles, and canal barges.[39] American losses were light, totaling no more than a few bombers.[40] Anything that moved was a target. When the reports came in, the results were—or should have been—predictable: morale was not affected, transportation not significantly disrupted, and repair crews not overwhelmed. Many towns were hit heavily, including—to the Eighth's embarrassment—Stein am Rhein in Switzerland. But, as a U.S. air forces study concluded, the attacks were spread out too thinly over too great an area to have any decisive effect on German troop or goods movements.[41] It is not clear what the Americans were thinking when they launched Operation Clarion, or what they thought they would achieve. A concentrated raid or a series of raids would have had a greater impact—and killed fewer people. At a press conference, air force officials put the best face they could on it by stating that they could not destroy the morale of the Germans because it had already been destroyed.

On the day before Operation Clarion, Brigadier General George C. McDonald wrote an extraordinary letter to Anderson. McDonald was the USSTAF's intelligence director, with his fingertips on the latest information concerning German oil, fighter, and broader industrial production. "This [January 30] directive puts," he wrote, "the American Army Air Forces unequivocally into the business of area bombardment of congested civilian populations. . . . No intelligence available to this Directorate indicates that destruction of these three cities will decisively [a]ffect the enemy's capacity for armed resistance. . . . Nor can the elusive, if not illusionary target of morale justify the importance accorded these cities. The desideratum of morale attack is revolt. All authorities are agreed that the German people are powerless if not actually disinclined to revolt against the present controls." Referring obliquely to Arnold's (and to a lesser degree Spaatz's) frustrations with German resilience, McDonald added that, if the Eighth's previous bombing theory and practice had been proved ineffective, "we should face the issue squarely . . . abandon all other target priorities . . . and settle wholeheartedly to the extermination of populations and the razing of cities." McDonald followed the directive's claims to their logical conclusion: "If such a practice is sincerely considered the shortest way to victory, it follows as a corollary that our ground forces, similarly, should be directed to kill all civilians and demolish all buildings in the Reich, instead of restricting their energies to the armed Army."

In one line, McDonald cut to the heart of the contradiction of area bombing. On March 1, Spaatz ordered an end to terror bombing. He canceled the planned March 3 repeat of Operation Clarion and directed his troops to bomb oil targets and Germany's rail system, and to provide support to advancing Allied troops. A new directive stated in the strongest possible terms that only military targets were to be bombed. After three weeks, the American experiment in full-blown city bombing was over.

26

A CRESCENDO OF DESTRUCTION

In the first two weeks of March, Harris launched a series of raids under the transportation plan, but he used the same method: destroy the city and with it, ideally, the railway station.[1] At the end of 1943, he had argued that "the destruction of villages or even of small towns would contribute nothing to . . . destroying the whole organized system on which the German air effort depends."[2] That was now forgotten. On March 5, 683 aircraft dropped almost 2000 tons on the center of Chemnitz, devastating the old town and surrounding neighborhoods. The fires, which raged for hours, engulfed the railway station, but the Americans had already destroyed it two days earlier. On March 7–8, Dessau was ravaged by bombs, creating fires that were visible one hundred miles away. Three days later, Harris returned to the Ruhr. On March 11, more than one thousand aircraft bombed the center of Essen, causing great damage to the marshaling yards and the Krupp works. The next afternoon, a slightly larger force wrecked Dortmund. Five days later, it was Würzburg's turn.

On March 16, 1945, Herbert Oechsner, the illegitimate son of a working-class Würzburg mother, had snuck back to his city after being evacuated weeks earlier. He lived in Grombühl, a drab workers' suburb. His mother had many admirers, gave birth to two illegitimate children, and was rarely at home. His grandmother raised him and his one-year-old brother, Peter. On March 16, Herbert was playing at home.

A mile to the south, in a far more affluent part of town, Heinrich Giesecke was in his parents' apartment near the city's famous Cathedral. Giesecke's father had done well under National Socialism and could afford a large apartment in a desirable central street. In 1938, he had stood at the flat's front windows and watched Nazi thugs throw Jews and their belongings from the house across the street. It was Kristallnacht. On the night of Würzburg's destruction, he had just finished repairing the flat's windows, which had been blown out during an earlier raid.

A mile further southeast, Hans Heer, the fifteen-year-old son of a basket maker, was on his bed. He had drunk too much, and the room was spinning. Over his father's objections, Hans worked at a nearby airfield, where he met members of the passive resistance. His other friends, living in a school next to his house, were an equally unusual group of people in Nazi Germany: the blind.

Several blocks away, an eleven-year-old boy, Heinrich Weppert, was playing with toys given to him by his landlord. Weppert's life had improved under the Nazis. When Jews in a larger apartment in Heinrich's apartment block disappeared, Heinrich's family was able to move into it. The toys had been left by one of the deported Jewish children.

5 P.M., ENGLAND

Air marshals announced the targets: Nuremberg and Würzburg. Five Group had a distinguished history in the bombing war: its bombers had attacked Heilbronn, Darmstadt, Königsberg, Braunschweig, Munich, and Kassel, and it had been the leading and decisive component in the February 13, 1945, raid on Dresden.[3] At approximately 5 P.M., 501 Lancasters and 227 Mosquitoes prepared for takeoff.

The bombers did not take the most direct route. When they reached continental Europe, they followed a southeasterly course north of Reims toward the Vogesen mountains. From there, they went northeast, crossing the Rhine, by now the Western Front. At Crailsheim, a smaller formation of 223 bombers—212 Lancasters and 11 Mosquitoes—broke off from the main bombing stream and flew on to Würzburg; the rest headed toward what was left of Nuremberg. They would bomb southern Nuremberg, including the neighborhoods of Steinbühl, Lichtenhof, Galgenhoff, St. Leonhard, and the gasworks; 562 Germans and 35 foreigners, mostly forced laborers, would be killed.

At 9:20 P.M., the pathfinders flew over the red, peaked roofs of Würzburg. They dropped eighteen flares, which would guide the bombers over the town.

These were quickly followed by the green and red markers, the Christmas trees, whose slow descent lit up the Würzburg night.

A few minutes later, hundreds of bombers passed over the compact town and the bombs began to fall. In three waves, the RAF hammered Würzburg. The first wave dropped three hundred thousand four-pound incendiaries. They lit the place on fire.

The high explosives followed immediately. They landed in the area bounded by Neubaustrasse and Hoffstrasse, Theaterstrasse and Bahnhoffstrasse. They crashed through the roof of the Rathaus, the houses in the Domstrasse (hitting but not collapsing the roof of the Cathedral), and the rococo-stuccoed Falkanhause in the Marktplatz. Würzburg exploded.

By 9:30 P.M., ten minutes into the raid, every single street in the city was in flames. The houses in Spiegelstrasse, a few blocks north of the river, collapsed entirely; anyone who had not left the cellars died. At Würzburg's jewel, the Residence, the roof with its magnificent fresco over the grand staircase survived the bombardment, just as its architect, Neumann, had predicted in the 1740s (he offered to fire a battery of cannons in the Residence to prove that the ceiling would hold), but the incendiary bombs set the building alight. The fires tore through the south-wing apartments and the regal rooms. They climbed the walls and covered the ceilings, destroying everything. Many of the drapings and furniture had been moved after an earlier bombing, but the ornately decorated mirrors in the Spiegel room could not be. They shattered and fell. In the Green Room, the fires charred the walls and turned the green paint dark. The rococo-stuccoed ceiling of the White Room burned, and the roof collapsed.

In the Domstrasse, right in the center of the town, all of the houses were on fire. The flames from the two sides of the street met in the center and created a fire tunnel between the Cathedral and the Old Main Bridge. All of the buildings would by morning be empty shells. Only the tall, thin Rathaus (built on the base of a fourteenth-century house), its medieval tower, and the adjacent buildings would be restored. The Cathedral itself survived the bombing (the roof would collapse a year later), but a high explosive crashed through the southeastern side. The fires consumed the gilded altar, and Riemenschneider's Madonna. A few streets away at the Marktplatz, more of Riemenschneider's sculptures, which graced the spires of the Gothic Mary Chapel, were destroyed or damaged by the bombs.

The bombers had crossed the city in seventeen minutes. The raid was over. They had not lost a single airplane.

8 P.M., ON THE GROUND

Radio stations across the city were interrupted. A voiced announced, "A large formation is heading toward our city. Seek shelter immediately!"[4] An entire city stood up. People grabbed their children, relatives, and suitcases, and made for the cellars.

Herbert was in his apartment when he heard the alarm. He ran up the hill to a neighbor's *Schrebergärten*, plots of land with small shacks created so that the working classes would have green space. He arrived at an old shack housing a table and several chairs. He was the first to arrive and claimed a chair. A few minutes later, the rest of his family, the plot's owner, and a sixth person, a woman from Herbert's neighborhood, arrived. They sat and waited. A few minutes later, Herbert looked out a window facing north and saw the Christmas trees cascading down over the city. Then the bombing began. Herbert heard a man shout, *"Würzburg brennt!* Würzburg is burning!"* He heard the whistle of a high explosive and, then, nothing.

A bomb landed not far from the shack, blowing a crater into the ground. The air pressure flattened all of the garden houses, killing most of the people inside them instantly. When the hospital attendants arrived, they saw a field littered with bodies, and began the gruesome task of piling them up for transport. Then, one of the orderlies noticed something: a small body moving among the corpses. It was Herbert. They left to find a stretcher, or its equivalent. By the time they returned, he had vanished.

Only half-conscious, he had started climbing up the hill, only coming to once he was well away from the bomb site. He continued to move away from the heat, following the vine-draped, taut wires up the hill. Some three hundred feet away, there was a sports ground used as an assembly point. As he approached it, he was spotted by two people at the northern gate. Herbert collapsed, and he was taken to a small dressing room. He asked after his family but no one knew of them or their fate. He dropped in and out of consciousness, though he did not know for how long, and was taken to the university psychiatric clinic on the Füchsleinstrasse, which was used as an SS hospital. He spent a week in a dark cellar without medical attention. Kindly slave laborers gave him bread and moistened sugar. Several days later, an ambulance drove him to a mental hospital at Lohr am Main. American fighter pilots were rumored to spray the roads with machine-gun fire by day, so the driver took safer back roads.

Herbert's grandmother and brother had burned to death; she had pulled the child into her, and the two had melted together. She was so badly burned that she could only be recognized by the pattern of her knitted vest, burned into her skin. His mother suffered severe burns on the lower half of her body and was evacuated. No one ever heard of her again.[5]

8 P.M., CENTRAL WÜRZBURG

Heinrich Giesecke had spent the day at his great-aunt's. The windows and doors to her flat had been blown out in a previous raid, and Heinrich spent the day making the apartment habitable. He returned home relatively late. When the pre-alarm rang out, he, his brother, and his mother were in the apartment. They left their flat, rushed to the Domstrasse, and headed out of the city. As they were crossing the Old Main Bridge, the full alarm rang out; they heard the planes overhead and saw the pathfinders' markers. It was time to run. When they reached the cellar, there was only standing room.

In the cellar, Heinrich heard a whistle, saw a flash of light, and then heard an explosion. And again, and again. Within a few seconds of the first bombs, one landed near the cellar's exit; dust, plaster, and soil exploded into the cellar, wounding those near the door. The lights went out. People in the cellar huddled closer together. After an explosion, they screamed. Heinrich noticed that something was burning; the air became warm and there was water in the cellar. One of the city's main pipes had burst; they had to leave.

Heinrich threw a blanket around his mother, brother, and himself. They came out of the emergency exit and jumped through the flames. They climbed a burning rubble mound, slipped past two houses, and made for the steps of the Tellsteige (leading up to the old fortress looking over the city). The steps themselves were burning. From there, Heinrich looked back at Würzburg. It was an inferno: every roof was on fire, and the smoke and flames covered the buildings right to the Main River. The fires sucked in oxygen, and Heinrich and his family had to push against the wind to avoid falling down the stairs. They stayed there for the rest of the night and watched their city burn.

8 P.M., SOUTHEAST WÜRZBURG

When the first alarm went off, Hans Heer was lying on his bed in his parents' third-floor flat. One of the partially sighted residents from the school for the blind had brought some wine back from a nearby vineyard, and Hans had drunk too much. He felt so ill that he told his father to leave him in the apartment until the air-raid sirens stopped. He then heard an official warning: "A large formation is heading toward our city. Seek shelter immediately!" His father frantically rang the doorbell; Hans needed no encouragement. He hit the floor running, and hurried with his father into the air-raid shelter. He thought, *Jetzt ist Würzburg daran* (It's Würzburg's turn). The director of the school for the blind, two nuns, and all of the school's residents were in the shelter under his father's workshop, rather than in the cellar of the four-story house. Hans's father thought it much better. If the building took a direct hit, they would die instantly. If a high explosive landed near the building and flattened it, there would be less rubble out of which to climb. Either way, the cellar would not become their coffin. In the thirty-square-yard room, they sat and waited for the bombs to fall.

When one of the first high explosives landed, the air pressure bent the shelter's large steel door. The sounds of exploding bombs and shattering buildings became louder. Everyone in the cellar began to pray, reciting a particular Franken devotion to the Virgin Mary: "*Maria breit den Mantel aus, mach Schirm und Schild für uns daraus, lass uns darunter sicher stehen, bis alle Feinde vorüber gehen* [Mary, make your coat a shield, and let us seek shelter under it, until the enemy has passed over us]."

When the bombing seemed to be subsiding, Hans's father stepped out of the shelter. Everywhere there was fire, and the workshop itself was consumed by flames. He ordered everyone out. Rubble was strewn in front of the shelter's exit, and Hans, his father, and the school director had to help the blind over it. One by one, they brought them out into the yard, with fires all around them. After the last person was out, the workshop collapsed. They were in the garden behind the school; it was large, and surrounded by an eight-foot wall. It sheltered them from the winds that, driven by the fire, raged through the dying city. There were two reservoirs in the garden, and nuns went back and forth dousing the school residents and everyone else with water. At 11 P.M., they heard an explosion: Hans's house collapsed. They decided they had to get out of the city. They followed Hans's father, a beneficent Pied Piper, single file, each holding another's hand, out of the burning town. They crossed a railway embankment nearby, walked along Fichtestrasse and Kantestrasse, which lead south out of the city, finally finding a vineyard shed. They stayed there until the morning.

8 P.M., THE WEPPERTS' APARTMENT

When the first alarm went off, Heinrich Weppert, his parents, and his great-aunt rushed to the cellar; their confidence in Würzburg's immortality had been destroyed by earlier raids. Heinrich's cousin was with them. She was from Nuremberg, and she mocked them for running to the cellar; compared to the bombing in Nuremberg, she said, the raids on Würzburg were nothing. She stayed upstairs, but changed her mind before the first bombs fell.

In a scene that was repeated across the city, the first bombs knocked the cellar lights out. There were twenty people cowering in the cellar, and they pulled blankets over their heads for comfort and to shield themselves from falling dust. Heinrich climbed into his mother's arms and stayed there during the first wave of bombing. As it seemed to let up, his father left the cellar to see what had happened. When he returned, he was ashen. The entire city, he said, was on fire, and there was no point in even trying to extinguish the flames. After hastily retrieving a few items from their apartment, he ordered the family to get out. Even his normally truculent cousin did not resist, and their neighbor followed them out. They arrived in the street relatively early, before the fires had reached their peak, and they ran down it, past the Gieseckes' house and toward City Hall. They turned to the Main River, but the narrow passage leading to the Old Main Bridge was by then blocked by flames. His father took them back toward the center, but they were blocked by a great rush of people fleeing the city. They turned into the Augustiner-strasse, which led out of the city. Heinrich's father knew the cellars were linked through a series of passages that would be safer than the street. He was right: a short while later, the fires reached deadly temperatures and all of the houses collapsed. His father led them into the first house's cellar, followed by his mother, aunt, Heinrich himself, his cousin, and the neighbor. As they left the first house for the second, the cellar roof gave, killing the neighbor instantly.

They made it out of the houses in the Augustinerstrasse, through an arch-way and directly to the Main. His father led them down to the riverbanks and followed the water. Houses collapsed around them, spraying debris onto the banks and into the river. When they reached the Löwenbrücke, they climbed the small steps onto the bridge. There was a great crowd of people on it; in its center was a burned-out tram, and the tramlines had fallen onto the bridge. The crowds were convinced that the lines were still live, and each person gingerly stepped over them, grinding progress to a halt. When they finally reached the other side of the bridge, they saw an old maternity hospital that had been transformed into a military one. It was on fire, and the staff were throwing wounded soldiers, often with missing limbs, down to the street. Those running past were ordered to stop and help, but they ignored the command.

Heinrich's group moved past buildings that continued to burn, but less intensely as they continued away from the city. Once they passed Heidingsfeld, they met a driver from the fire service who agreed to bring them to Reichenberg, where Heinrich's uncles lived. Reichenberg was full of refugees eager to tell their stories, but Heinrich only wanted sleep. The uncles divided the family between them; it was finally over.

9:20 P.M., WÜRZBURG

The city was an inferno. In the Ursulinengasse, a few minutes from the central Domstrasse, one woman took the fateful decision to leave the cellar in time and ran with her two children for the safety of the river or the country. As she did, she lost her grip on them, and the crowd crushed them.[6] Gusti Schmitt was a young girl fleeing the city with her parents. As she climbed out of her cellar into the street, she saw a woman run past holding a burning package; another man tried to wrest it from her and she screamed, "It's my child!" A few blocks later, she passed the school turned military hospital. A wounded patient's bandages caught fire; he threw himself through the window, ran down the street, and died.[7] As in countless other cities, split-second decisions meant the difference between life and death. A wounded soldier, Karl-Heinz Wirsing, decided to seek shelter in neither the Domstrasse nor his military hospital, which was behind the Cathedral.[8] He instead took the far more risky route across the Main, and was let into a shelter near the Marienberg as the bombs were falling. It saved his life: no one came out of the Domstrasse or the Paradeplatz shelters alive.

The fires themselves tore through the streets, consuming everything in their path. The floors and roofs burned, and collapsed. In the center, near the Domstrasse, almost all of the houses collapsed, leaving only mounds of rubble and sand. Everywhere else, only the facades survived. Thirty-five churches, all of the museums and monuments, the Residence, Rathaus, and the Marienberg were destroyed.

The destruction of more than a millennium of architectural and cultural history took just over fifteen minutes. It was little more than a footnote in the bomber war; on that night alone, five other towns were bombed.[9] The Night Raid Report devoted five lines to Würzburg's obliteration. It noted that the "intention was to complete the destruction of the built up area and associated industries and rail facilities," a task that was "practically completed."[10] The report failed to mention that the Americans had already destroyed the railway on February 21, and that there were no industries of significance in the city.

The day after the attack, Hans Heer learned that his mother and sister were safe. His aunt, however, was not: her two-story house had collapsed over her cellar, and trapped her and everyone else inside. Across the city, the task of gathering the bodies began.

27

DOUBTS

On March 6, 1945, ten days before the destruction of Würzburg, Richard Rapier Stokes, a decorated First World War hero and devout Catholic, stood up in the House of Commons. He read from the *Manchester Guardian*: "Tens of thousands who lived in Dresden are now burned under its ruins. Even an attempt at identification of the victims is hopeless. What happened on that evening of February 15? There were 1,000,000 people in Dresden, including 600,000 bombed-out evacuees and refugees from the east. The raging fires which spread irresistibly in the narrow streets killed a great many from sheer lack of oxygen." Stokes went on to quote from the February 17 dispatch of Associated Press reporter Howard Cowan: "Allied Air Chiefs have made the long-awaited decision to adopt deliberate terror bombing of German population centres as a ruthless expedient to hasten Hitler's doom. More raids such as those carried recently by heavy bombers of the Anglo-American Air Forces on residential sections of Berlin, Dresden, Chemnitz and Cottbus are in store for the Germans for the avowed purpose of heaping more confusion on Nazi road and rail traffic and to sap German morale." Cowan's source was an "off-the-record" SHAEF press briefing in Paris by C. M. Grierson, an RAF intelligence officer (a confirmation, it seemed, of Spaatz's and Kuter's fears).[1] Grierson described air force plans to bomb large population centers and, afterward, to block relief supplies.[2]

Grierson's statement, Stokes continued, was widely broadcast in America and in Germany, but not in the United Kingdom. "Is terror bombing," Stokes demanded of the government, "now part of our policy? If so, why was this declaration from S.H.A.E.F. issued for publication and then suppressed? If it is not part of the policy, why was the statement handed out at all? And why is it that the British people are the only people who may not know what is done in their name? . . . I think we shall live to rue the day we have done this and that . . . it will stand for all time as a blot upon our escutcheon."[3]

About this time, Violet Bonham-Carter, the daughter of First World War Prime Minister Asquith and graduate of a Dresden finishing school, marched up to 10 Downing Street and demanded to speak with Churchill. The young Churchill had been a Liberal Cabinet minister under her father. She rounded on the prime minister, who quietly took it in, for the bombing of Dresden.[4]

While the storm was brewing, Harris continued his work. In March 1945, the month of Würzburg's destruction, Harris dropped sixty-seven thousand tons of bombs on Germany. It was the largest monthly tonnage ever dropped on the country, and only slightly less than the total dropped between 1939 and 1941.[5] All of the cities listed in Harris's November 1 appeal to Portal had been heavily bombed and most thoroughly destroyed. In the last weeks of the war, Harris returned to the Ruhr. Essen was blasted for the last time and, on March 12, eleven hundred RAF bombers dropped five thousand tons of bombs on Dortmund, wiping what was left of that city off the map. Four days later, it was Würzburg's turn. From March 1 to 27, Harris area bombed thirteen cities with more than a thousand tons of bombs on each raid. During the same period, the Eighth Air Force dropped 40 percent of its bombs on rail targets, 13 percent on oil, and the rest on jet, vehicle, tank, and U-boat production. The Fifteenth Air Force dropped 60 percent of its bombs on marshaling yards and 25 percent on oil. March 1945 was the peak of the bombing offensive.

On March 28, 1945, Churchill penned a memorandum for General Ismay, his Chief of Staff. "It seems to me," wrote the prime minister,

> that the moment has come when the question of bombing of German cities simply for the sake of increasing the terror, though under other pretexts, should be reviewed. Otherwise we shall come into control of an utterly ruined land. . . . I am of the opinion that military objectives must henceforward be more strictly studied in our interests rather than that of the enemy.
>
> The Foreign Secretary has spoken to me on this subject, and I feel the need for more precise concentration upon military objectives such as oil

and communications behind the battle-zone, rather than on mere acts of terror and wanton destruction, however impressive.[6]

The war was coming to an end, and Churchill-the-commander was giving way to Churchill-the-historian. The prime minister was capable of great emotion, and he did feel genuine regret over Dresden's destruction. The memo was nonetheless a calculated effort to distance himself from a bombing war that he had long, if somewhat erratically, supported.

And it infuriated Harris. Bottomley had sent him the note the next morning. The allegations of terror were an "insult to both the Air Ministry's bombing policy and to the way Bomber Command had executed it." The destruction of German cities had fatally weakened the enemy and only it was allowing the armies such an easy walk across Germany. Unless it could be clearly shown that bombing would neither shorten the war nor save Allied lives, it had to continue. Playing off Bismarck's line that eastern Europe was "not worth the bones of a Pomeranian grenadier," Harris wrote: "I do not regard the whole of the remaining cities in Germany as worth the bones of a single British grenadier." Then, all guns blazing, Harris heaped contempt on those who were, possibly strategically, becoming sentimental about Dresden: "The feeling, such as there is, over Dresden could be easily explained by a psychiatrist. It is connected with German bands and Dresden shepherdesses. Actually, Dresden was a mass of munitions works, an intact government center, and a key transportation center. It is now none of those things."[7]

Harris's description of Dresden was hardly an accurate one, but he nonetheless had a point. Dresden was no different from dozens of other German cities that had been destroyed. It had dozens of small industries and—more importantly—it was part of a central rail system linked with Berlin and Leipzig.[8] A precision raid on the rail yards would have been logical and consistent with the transportation plan.[9] But the raid was not a precision attack; it was an obliteration raid. And it echoed around the world not simply because of the city's exceptional beauty, though that was certainly part of it. The destruction of Dresden was a window onto the broader area bombing campaign. It brought home to people in a way that dozens of euphemism-ridden official reports could not, what the RAF had been doing to Germany since Hamburg and particularly since 1944. It was a raid like any other, not a "raid too far," and for this reason it was the beginning of the end of Harris.

Harris's angry reply eventually harmed him more than Churchill, but in the short term it did its job. Churchill withdrew the memo and issued a more anodyne version on April 1:

> It seems to me that the moment has come when the question of the so called "area bombing" of German cities should be reviewed from the point of view of our own interests. If we come into control of an entirely ruined land, there will be a great shortage of accommodation for ourselves and our Allies; and we shall be unable to get housing materials out of Germany for our own needs. . . . We must see to it that our attacks do not do more to harm ourselves in the long run than they do to the enemy's immediate war effort. Pray let me have your views.

Ten days later, Harris was at the SHAEF conference. There, he proposed another raid, this time on Potsdam. The seat of Frederick the Great and home of some of the finest architecture in Germany had made it to that point in the war largely untouched. Under Harris's plan, bombing would destroy the city's rail facilities and military barracks. Tedder thought there wasn't much point; they weren't important enough to justify even a precision raid. What's more, Soviet High Command, which was closing in on Berlin, might have a view on the matter. Tedder told Harris to clear it with the Chief of Air Staff.

On April 12, Spaatz and Bottomley, after consulting Tedder, issued Strategic Directive No. 4, the final one of the war. It placed aid to the land campaign at the top, followed by oil, enemy communications, the Luftwaffe, and U-boats. The catch-all category of "important industrial areas" was not listed.

Two nights later, without consulting Portal, Bomber Command bombed central Potsdam. Almost two thousand tons of bombs flattened the old city center and killed as many as five thousand people.[10]

One hundred and twenty-five miles to the south, in Dresden, communications were still functioning. Despite the raids, Dresden's railway stations were still running. In the largest single raid launched on the city (counting the two British raids in February separately), the Americans attacked them. At a cost of four to five hundred civilian lives, they took these targets out for good.

28

AS THE LAST BOMBS FELL

On March 15, 1945, a day before the raid on Würzburg, Richard Peck, Assistant Chief of Air Staff, wrote a memorandum to the Under Secretary of State: "You will remember the great anxiety on the part of the C-in-C Bomber Command [Harris] that the public should be reminded at the time of the entry of our armies into the great German industrial cities that these have been devastated by Bomber Command."

Two weeks later, on March 30, 1945, an American GI named Tony Vaccaro crossed the Rhine at Wesel.[1] The city had been bombed so many times that it looked like the face of the moon; in the center, not even the outline of the street plan remained. Vaccaro, like many GIs, was first awed, then dismayed. He began taking photos, and his and many others were sent out of Germany. As they arrived in Britain, criticism grew.

The government was all too happy to forget the bombings. On May 9, 1945, Arthur Harris waited for his and Bomber Command's invitation to the ceremonies at which Germany's surrender was formally accepted. None came, and on May 12 he wrote to Portal in protest. The next day, Churchill gave his VE speech to the nation. The prime minister spoke of the early days of the war, the Battle of Britain, the Blitz, the importance of Northern Ireland, the work of the Royal Navy and the Merchant Navy in the crucial Battle of the Atlantic, the entry into the war of Russia, Japan, and the USA, the liberation of France, the defeat of the V-weapons campaigns, the invasion of the Continent, and the postwar world. With the exception of a vague reference to bomb damage in Berlin, the bomber offensive got not a single mention.

Harris waited for some other recognition for his role in defeating Germany. It did not come. The British government excluded Bomber Command from the honors liberally handed out. It was denied a campaign medal. Clement Attlee, Churchill's successor as prime minister, thought little of Harris. He denied him a peerage (Harris alone among major British war leaders failed to secure one) and Churchill declined to intervene.[2] Harris was given no offer of further employment, and he departed for South Africa at the end of 1945, making no effort to hide his bitterness about how he and his men had been treated.

Harris rushed his memoirs into print in 1947, but they did nothing to rescue his plummeting reputation. His inability to be anything but brutally honest damaged it further. He made no apologies for civilian deaths or cultural losses, defended area bombing as "comparatively humane," and argued that if he had only had more bombers he would have single-handedly defeated the Germans. The United Kingdom's most prestigious military institute refused to review Harris's book in its *Journal of the Royal United Services Institute*. Harris was finished. He spent the next eight years in South African obscurity, running a shipping company. He returned to England in 1953, retiring in Goring-on-Thames. He spoke little and his neighbors knew nothing of his wartime activities. To the end, he retained the support and loyalty of his men.

Speer and Göring turned themselves in, and both were tried for war crimes at Nuremberg. Göring was sentenced to death by hanging, but—it is believed—his American guard gave him enough cyanide to kill himself. Milch was convicted of war crimes (against prisoners of war and slave laborers) and sentenced to life in prison. The Americans later reduced this to fifteen years, and he was released in 1954. He wrote a book on the Luftwaffe and made a living advising industry. Galland did rather better, enjoying a long career in aviation that began with lectures to the RAF on tactics.

Speer was sentenced to twenty years' imprisonment and was released in 1966. He spent most of the postwar period trying to justify his role in the Nazi regime, and denying his knowledge of the worst Nazi crimes. Only near the end of his life did he effectively admit to Gitta Sereny that he knew, at the time, that the Jews of Europe were being murdered in the millions. Had he said so at Nuremberg, he would have been hanged.[3]

Churchill lost the 1945 election to Attlee, but—ever the master of the historical record—managed to escape ignominy for carpet bombing. After ordering the destruction of Dresden, his strategic memo of April 1, 1945, is still cited as evidence of Churchill's opposition to bombing civilians.

On the other side of the Atlantic, Eaker, Arnold, and Spaatz fared much better. Eaker and Spaatz were promoted, retired with honors, and enjoyed successful postwar careers. President Truman personally signed a bill making Arnold the air force's only permanent general. Across the United States, roads, schools, airports, and bases bear these men's names. They felt they had little to regret about the war over Germany, but—unlike Harris—came close to admitting that they did. Near the end of his life, Spaatz looked back on American bombing: "We never had as our target in Europe anything except a military target—except Berlin."[4]

The aircrew who, against the odds, survived headed home. Lasting friendships between comrades—and also between former enemies—formed after the war. For only an airman, whether German, American, Canadian, or British, could understand what it really had been like. There were moments when this had been clear even in pitched battle. After a bombing run, a German fighter was closing in on a B-17 from the 348th Squadron, 99th Bomb Group, machine-gun fire blasting at the bomber's wings and cockpit. Jules Horowitz, the pilot, reached for the flare gun in the ceiling of the cockpit to shoot at the fighter. Jules forgot to turn off the gun's safety, and the fighter simply missed. When the fighter saw Jules' hand in the air, from about forty feet, he thought he was waving; the German waved back.[5] After the war, the contact was more than fleeting. On the fiftieth anniversary of the October 1943 Schweinfurt raid, two Germans, Dr. Helmut Katzenberger and Vomar Wilckens, attended the reunion in New Orleans of the Second Schweinfurt Memorial Association (SSMA) to give a presentation on the raid. In 1996, the SSMA members invited more of their former enemies to the reunion in Las Vegas. They included Georg Schaefer, whose grandfather founded one of the targeted ball bearings factories and who worked in a flak battery in Schweinfurt. At the Americans' suggestion, a joint American–German war memorial was erected at the site of an air-raid shelter in Schweinfurt. The city's mayor was there, telling the American aircrew that Schweinfurt is "your home."

After the last bomb had fallen, the civilians set about rebuilding their lives. Gerhard Lange was dispatched to England, where he boarded with a family that showed him a kindness that brought tears to his eyes sixty years later. He tried to return to Hamburg, but found the bombed shell of his city intolerable. He emigrated to Australia in the early 1950s and returned to Hamburg to retire. Elfriede Bock, Werner Wendland, and Ernst-Günther Haberland all stayed in Hamburg, with Werner and Ernst-Günther returning to their old neighborhood.

In Würzburg, Heinrich Giesecke, Hans Heer, and Heinrich Weppert all stayed in the city. Hans became a teacher, while Heinrich set up his own business. Herbert took the English book he found in the rubble as a cue, and left Germany, ending up in Australia. To this day, he returns to Würzburg every summer.

In the United Kingdom, the initial euphoria partially gave way to the cold realities of the postwar years. Rations and general austerity lasted into the 1950s, when the economy finally picked up and Britons enjoyed growth and rising standards of living, though both were notably behind Germany and the rest of northwestern Europe until the 1980s.[6] Some rebuilding began right away. Plans for reconstructing the House of Commons were drawn up in January 1945, but the task was not completed until October 1950. The Commonwealth provided the furniture for the new Chamber—Australia provided the Speaker's Chair; Canada, the table; and South Africa, the three clerks' chairs.[7] India and Pakistan gave the entrance doors. Over the next decade, other architectural wonders—Westminster Abbey, the Inns of Court, and the Temple Church—were restored to their former glory. The Queen's Hall—home of the Proms—was never rebuilt.

The story was a less happy one for many London neighborhoods. The planning mania of the postwar years led local councils to flatten whole neighborhoods and replace them with soulless public housing. Vast swathes of Elephant and Castle, Southwark, and other working-class neighborhoods were blighted by cheap concrete tower blocks.

The story was similar outside London. Coventry was rebuilt along modernist lines. Today, its most beautiful structure is probably the burnt-out cathedral, left untouched as a memorial to the war. In Birmingham, the result was worse still: the old core, with its solid public architecture, was torn out and replaced with freeways, tunnels, and towers.

For all of the destruction and all of the mistakes, England was too old and the bombing too limited for the character of the country to be radically changed. London is much more like its prewar self than Berlin is, and the list of beautiful towns in England is long. Like Germany, however, the most untouched architecture is to be found outside the cities, in the villages left alone by both bombers and planners.

For Germany, the task of rebuilding was mammoth, almost overwhelming. Many people thought the country could never recover. Allied bombing had killed almost 600,000 people.[8] Sixty cities were destroyed and another hundred were damaged. Before the war, Germany had dozens of Europe's finest cities; today, it has a handful. Well over a thousand churches and museums burned to the ground. The medieval centers of Frankfurt, Ulm, Aachen, Würzburg, Cologne, and Nuremberg were simply wiped off the face of the earth. A millennium of Europe's finest architecture and culture were gone. Twenty million books had been burned. The destruction often took no longer than an average coffee break.

The cities were nonetheless rebuilt, often at breakneck speed. Some—Frankfurt, Cologne, and Darmstadt—decided to embrace modernity. Others, often but not always the more conservative ones, rebuilt their cities according to original plans. Nuremberg was partially rebuilt in prewar style, and its famous old city (*Altstadt*) was restored to at least some of its former glory. Munich also bears much resemblance to its old self. A few of Würzburg's most important buildings—the City Hall, some of the churches, and above all the palace—were restored, but the rest of the city dates obviously to the 1950s. It looks its best from the hills above, where the red rooftops evoke the prewar city. In Hamburg, much of the old city— the narrowest lanes and tiny courtyards—is gone, but the administrative and commercial center— around the City Hall—was sensitively rebuilt, and today Hamburg resembles the prewar city. The St. Nicholas church—which was in the center of the aiming point on July 28, 1943—was left in ruins, a memorial to the horrors of war.

Bombing in part brought these horrors home to the German people. It is often said that they were spared horror during the First World War (as if mass starvation and the loss of a generation of sons are not horrors), and that bombing thus played a role in the pacification of postwar Germans. It might have, but bombing was hardly needed. Seven million dead, occupation, division, more than ten million people expelled, Soviet prisoner of war camps, and mass rapes in the Soviet sector would have made it clear to the Germans that war had consequences. It was, in any event, not certain that these experiences and bombings would turn the Germans into pacifists. They could have as easily been the foundation for a new bitterness among the German people and the anchor for efforts to minimize Germany's own crimes. That they did not (despite a few Germans' and non-Germans' best efforts) was due to insistence on the part of both the Allies and the Germans themselves that the German people understood their history, and their responsibility.

29

CONCLUSION

By May 1945, the bombing war was over. Almost two million tons of bombs had been dropped on Germany; more than sixty cities had been destroyed and hardly a town or village in the Reich had escaped the bombs. Bombing had left 583,000 people in Germany and 80,000 aircrew dead. From the moment the last bomb fell, the bombing campaign has been surrounded by controversy—always lively, sometimes hysterical. At its center lie two overlapping but not identical questions: were the bombings justified, and did they work? Answering the first question depends on the answer to a third question: justified against which standard? Whether the bombing could be justified depends inevitably on one's theory of war. According to some absolutist positions, waging war—intentionally or accidentally—against civilians is never justified. By this standard, neither the American nor the British bombing of Germany could at any point be justified. At the other extreme, the whole point of bombing is to terrorize, make homeless, maim, and kill civilians. President Roosevelt came close to such a view of bombing when he said that "too many people here and in England hold to the view that the German people as a whole are not responsible for what has taken place—that only a few Nazi leaders are responsible. That unfortunately is not based on fact. The German people as a whole must have it driven home to them that the whole nation has been engaged in a lawless conspiracy against the decencies of modern civilization." Of course, there were many ways to do this short of killing them, but this seems to be what Roosevelt had in mind: in 1942, he called for the Allies to hit Germany "from the air heavily and relentlessly." The people who "bombed Warsaw, Rotterdam, London and Coventry are going to get it."[1] Bombing, in his view, would accomplish that.

Most people place themselves between these two extremes. Only a few moral absolutists believe that bombing would not be worth the death of a single German civilian, still fewer that the Germans should not suffer at all for what they did. Similarly, only a few extremists would hold the view that all German civilians were fair targets and that Allied soldiers should have gone from house to house mowing them down in the millions. Those in the middle contend that it would be acceptable if *some* civilians died, but only if their deaths substantially aided the outcome of the war. This is necessarily an indeterminate standard—no one can say exactly how many deaths were acceptable. For my part, I would argue that even the level of destruction and death meted out at Hamburg would have been justified if it had led to a quick and immediate end to the war.

With this view, it is possible to justify the area bombing campaign—against Rostock, Lübeck, Cologne, and a few other cities—up to the end of 1943. From then it was clear—and increasingly so—that area bombing was not delivering the goods. The RAF's switch from precision bombing to area bombing in 1942 was based on more than the fact that precision bombing was, this early in the war, difficult. After all, they might have stopped bombing altogether, saving the lives of both Allied aircrew and German civilians. It was instead based on the theory that area bombing would deliver results. Before Hamburg, this was an untested theory; at Hamburg, the theory was fully tested. The raid achieved a level of destruction that was unmatched until then, and only matched again in early 1944. The statistics were and are staggering: 40,385 buildings were obliterated, including 60 percent of Hamburg's residential accommodation; 3785 industrial plants were destroyed, as were 7190 small businesses, two-thirds of the city's retail stores, 83 banks, 379 office buildings, 112 Nazi party offices, 13 public utility premises, 22 transport premises, 76 public offices, 80 military installations, 12 bridges, 24 hospitals, 277 schools, 58 churches, 77 cultural institutions (operas, cinemas), and one zoo. Perhaps most impressive were the human consequences: 42,000 died, and another million fled the city. The extent of death and destruction exceeded that of Dresden. Little wonder (though these figures probably exceeded even Harris's hopes) that champagne bottles were cracked open at High Wycombe.

If any area raid were to knock the Germans out of the war, it would have been Hamburg. There is no question that the bombing slowed the place down.

By the end of 1943, 35 percent of the city's workforce was not turning up at work, and production was at 82 percent of its pre-bombing level. The problem was that most of the workers who left Hamburg found jobs elsewhere (making Hamburg's loss some other city's gain, and sparing the overall German economy). The U.S. official history estimates that the production loss for Hamburg, which suffered the most devastating raid of the entire war, was 9 percent of a month's production spread over eleven months following the attack.[2] As the official British history concluded after the war, the area bombing of Hamburg "had only an irritant effect on German production." The much smaller raids, late in the war, on Hamburg's transportation links with the Ruhr had a much greater effect on production.

Area bombing—working "on the principle that in order to destroy anything it was necessary to destroy everything"[3]—simply failed to deliver the results that Harris and its other supporters promised. Given Britain's isolation during 1941–1942, the specter of a Nazi-dominated Europe, and the pre-1943 inability to bomb with any measure of precision, the choices were area bombing or nothing. But, as bombing became more intense and more destructive of lives and property, the argument against it became stronger with each passing day.

Area bombing not only failed to win the war, it probably prolonged it. Supporters of Bomber Command are very keen to quote Speer's observation that bombing opened a "second front" right over Germany. They are less keen to quote his observations on area bombing—"pointless"—or to examine his views on bombing in greater detail. The Americans interrogated Speer on May 15, 1945, asking him about the effects of the different bombing campaigns. His answers were unequivocal. He was asked: "Which, at various periods of the war, caused most concern; British or American heavy bomber attacks, day or night attacks; and why?"[4] Speer replied, "The American attacks which followed a definite system assault on industrial targets, were by far the most dangerous. It was in fact these attacks which caused the breakdown of the German armaments industry." He said exactly the same thing to British interrogators. At three points, a limited number of precision bombing raids—on ball bearings and on the dams in 1943, and on oil and transportation in 1944–1945—almost brought Germany to its knees. After both the ball bearings and the dam raids, Speer waited in fear for repeat attacks. That they did not come was in large part thanks to Harris. This conclusion is not based on hindsight. In March 1943, the Committee of Operations Analysts (COA), a group of civilian experts convened in December 1942, issued a report. Using words that Speer himself might have written, the COA concluded that it was "better to cause a high degree of destruction in a few really essential industries or services than to cause a small degree of destruction in many industries."[5] The COA recommended precision attacks on industries suffering bottlenecks: ball bearings, propellers, tires, and engines. It deferred a decision on oil until more information was available. A year later, on June 21, 1944, it called for direct attacks on the aircraft industry, oil, and ball bearings.[6]

The oil and transportation raids played a direct role in Germany's post-summer 1944 implosion. They were kept on the agenda by the Americans, pushed for heavily by Spaatz and Tedder, and opposed by Harris. They were only possible, as the Americans well knew, because of another type of precision bombing: the destruction of the Luftwaffe. Despite repeated pleas that Harris join the fight, the destruction of the Luftwaffe was an American achievement.[7] Over the course of the war, the bombing that damaged Germany most was American.

American efforts are often equated for moral and strategic purposes with the RAF, perhaps because a number of writers have recoiled from the idea that there was a clear and sharp distinction between the American and the British bombing campaigns. They are right to do so. Much precision bombing involved casualties, and in some cases—when there was extensive cloud cover— "precision" bombing was little more than a hope and a prayer. Until 1944, radar could help pilots find cities covered in cloud but not specific targets within cities. Because they weren't sure they would hit their targets in cloud cover, the Americans regularly used a high percentage of incendiaries (60 percent to 40 percent high explosives during the February 14, 1945, raid on Dresden, a typical mix for a city raid) in the hope that a wider circle of destruction would take out the target.[8] An unknown number—but certainly one in the thousands—of civilians were killed that day. During the transportation plan, bombing the railway station in the center of the city inevitably meant destroying the area around it. If the city were small enough, bombing would destroy the entire town. And in several cases—over Münster in October 1943 and Berlin and Dresden in February 1945—the Americans area bombed intentionally. In the same vein, although Harris always opposed precision attacks, many British bombs fell on precision targets, often very effectively.

That it is difficult to draw clear and complete distinctions between American and British bombing is true. This does not mean that none can be drawn.

The differences between American and British bombing narrowed over the course of the war, but they never disappeared. The first point concerns precision bombing. It is at times argued that Bomber Command did not have the luxury of precision bombing by 1943.[9] This is not true. The dambuster raids showed that Bomber Command was capable of the most impressive precision—to within a few inches. It was rather that precision bombing of this sort remained weather-dependent and exacted a heavy toll—up to 20 percent of a bombing force. Both factors meant that there could only be a limited number of such raids before there were no more bombers—or aircrew—to carry out the bombing. The question for both the Americans and the British was thus: is it better to lose more aircrew on a given raid but to bomb less overall? The Americans answered yes, accepting a casualty rate on a given raid of approximately double that of the British—10 percent—but bombing less.

The second point concerns intention. Before 1945, Spaatz tried whenever possible to avoid killing German civilians; Harris killed them deliberately and with equanimity. Even on the worst winter days in 1943 and 1944, when the Americans "blind bombed" in the heaviest of clouds, they were trying to hit and destroy military targets. They just sometimes weren't that successful at it. Sometimes, but not always. After Harris's September 1944 obliteration raid on Darmstadt failed to reduce production (it was fully restored within a month), the Americans knocked the city's suburban industries out in December, with little loss of life or civilian property.[10] For Harris, the whole point of bombing was to destroy cities, and technological developments were only useful insofar as they aided this eliminationist project. The history makes this clear. One study concludes that by 1945 the United States had "reverted from its selective bombing doctrine to the Douhetian principles of mass attack and terror."[11] Yet, beyond the February 1945 raids, it does not specify any significant cities destroyed. The numbers speak for themselves. Looking at the whole war, one German study deliberately opts for a low estimate of German casualties: 400,000.[12] Of these, it estimates that 75 percent were killed by the RAF, 25 percent by the USAAF. Another author concludes that the RAF killed hundreds of thousands, the USAAF tens of thousands.[13] No one can know for certain, but the figures roughly track the official statistics. Over the course of the war, the RAF dropped 48 percent of its bombs on towns; the Eighth Air Force dropped somewhere between 6 and 13 percent (the lower figure includes bombs aimed at cities; the higher those that hit them anyway).[14] From January 1942, 56 percent of Bomber Command sorties targeted city centers.[15]

One-half of Bomber Command's bomb load—some 500,000 tons of bombs—was dropped on heavily populated city centers. If Harris had had his way, the figure would have been a million tons.

Harris himself bemoaned in 1945 "the fact that the U.S. bombers have taken no serious part in area attacks."[16] Except for Berlin in 1945 (where different weather, defenses, and street plans might have led to a firestorm), there is no Hamburg, Pforzheim, or Darmstadt that can be attributed to American bombing.[17] The city the Americans bombed most was Vienna. Much of this was H2X bombing,[18] but the city came out of the war far more intact than comparable German cities. At Hamburg, the Americans—who tried to bomb the shipyards through the smoke created by the RAF attack—were responsible for less than 1 percent of the civilian casualties.[19] Berlin excepted, American bombing of cities was viewed as a matter of last rather than first resort, and the city bombing that did occur lacked the eliminationist intent driving the RAF's campaign. Visit Vienna, visit Darmstadt, and compare. If Bomber Command killed three civilians for every one killed by the USAAF, it is incredible that observers suggest there was little difference between the two campaigns. There was all the difference.

To the end, the American campaign was affected by a concern for the moral implications of bombing. Many writers deny this, and Spaatz, Doolittle, and Eaker were keen after the war to disassociate themselves from the taint of morality. It's clear why: expressing moral concerns over women and children was at best unstrategic; at worst, it was unmanly. It is nonetheless impossible to read Eaker's impassioned plea to Spaatz over Operation Clarion, Doolittle's eleventh-hour attempts to save the center (and the residents) of Berlin, or McDonald's February 21, 1945, denunciation of area bombing without seeing a deep and abiding moral concern.

In a similar vein, the Americans also made a number of specific efforts to protect Europe's cultural heritage. Stimson, who viewed the war as a defense of European culture and values against fascist barbarism, took a direct interest in safeguarding cultural monuments. John McCloy of the War Department personally appealed to Roosevelt to save Rothenburg ob der Tauber, and he flew in person to American Army headquarters in Germany to secure Army support. His efforts paid off, and the city was spared. In August 1943, President Roosevelt agreed to the creation of the American Commission for the Protection and Salvage of Artistic and Historic Monuments in Europe. One can only imagine Harris's reaction to an equivalent British body. Working closely with a very cooperative U.S. Army, the Commission drew up maps of cities and monuments that were to be spared by the invading U.S. forces. Florence, Rome, Venice, and Tocello were never to be bombed without express authority. General Eisenhower sent his air force officers these instructions:

> If we have to choose between destroying a famous building and sacrificing our own men, then our lives count infinitely more and the buildings must go. But the choice is not always so clear-cut as that. In many cases the monuments can be spared without any detriment to operations. Nothing can stand against the argument of military necessity . . . but the phrase "military necessity" is sometimes used where it would be more truthful to speak of military convenience or even of personal convenience. I do not want it to cloak slackness or indifference.[20]

That Italy today remains a land of endless architectural and cultural wonder owes something to American care and American constraint. When Athens was prepared to see Europe burn, Sparta spared it.

The question is why this moral concern was less fully extended to the Japanese, whose cities were firebombed (with the exception of Kyoto) and then hit with nuclear bombs. Or to the Jews. The Allies could have tried to use the air forces to hinder the genocide later in the war—from the summer of 1944. It is true that, by then, 95 percent of what would come to be called the Holocaust was over. It's also not clear that such an attempt would have succeeded.[21] But the fact remains that the Allies never tried.

That they did not casts cold water on the suggestion that the Holocaust in some way justifies or mitigates the bombing campaign. It does not. It is possible to reflect at an abstract level on whether civilian bombing might be just punishment for genocide, but it can be no part of a real-world historical explanation for the justification of the campaign. No RAF official, politician, or official document mentions the Holocaust as a justification for bombing. Whatever the bombing war was about, it was not about saving Jews. After the war, the genocide certainly meant that people had less pity for German suffering, and this is no surprise. It is grating to read early postwar publications that bemoan in self-pitying tones the destruction of German cities without mentioning anti-Semitism, or the harassment, persecution, and eventual deportation and murder of the Jews.[22] But this reaction does not change the argument: the Holocaust is neither an explanation nor a justification for the bombings.

It also casts cold water on another popular idea: that area bombing saved Jewish lives (for example, Victor Klemperer, a Jew, was saved by the bombing of Dresden; he was about to be deported). Indiscriminate area bombing killed more hidden Jews and foreign slave laborers than it spared. Neither Jews nor foreign workers were allowed into shelters. In a single 1943 raid on Berlin, eighteen forced laborers died when a house collapsed in the Joachimsthaler Strasse.[23] A raid on Dora in the same year killed five hundred. By the end of the war, Allied bombing had killed thirty-two thousand foreign civilians and prisoners of war.[24] Their deaths were unintentional and very much regretted, but, in the light of them, one cannot pretend that the few Jews and POWs who were saved (or even heartened) by bombing justified the campaign.

The failure of area bombing to deliver any clearly measurable results has led its sympathizers to emphasize its secondary effects. Bombing did not win the war directly—as no one but its advocates said it would—but it had important indirect effects. The defense of the Reich against bombing forced a diversion of resources from the rest of Germany's war effort:

> By 1944, some two million soldiers and civilians were engaged in ground anti-aircraft defence. This was more than the total employed in the whole of the aircraft industry. A large quantity of war material was produced specifically for defence against bombing. Speer estimated that 30 per cent of total gun output and 20 per cent of heavy ammunition in 1944 was intended for anti-aircraft defences. Some 50 per cent of electro-technical production and 33 per cent of the optical industry was devoted to radar and signals equipment for anti-aircraft installations, starving the front of essential communications resources. In addition, material had to be diverted from new capital investments to satisfy the demands for repairs to damaged factories and communications.[25]

These secondary effects were not unknown to the bombers at the time; indeed, British propaganda often emphasized them, as did Harris himself after the war.[26] The "manpower" transfer is sometimes exaggerated: many of those manning the flak and searchlights were teenagers or women, who were of questionable use at the front (though that did not stop Hitler from sending 200,000 youngsters there).[27] There can be no doubt, though, that the task of defending Germany required massive amounts of resources that could not by definition be used elsewhere.

How important was this transfer? It clearly did not put a halt to German industrial production, which increased right up to September 1944, when it began to fall off sharply. As this fall coincided with the possibly more important loss of resources in liberated territories, it is hard to quantify bombing's precise contribution. But German industrial production might well have been higher still without the transfer. The president of Focke-Wulf, the aircraft manufacturer, thought the transfers might have had some effect but were not "in any sense decisive."[28] Richard Overy, who popularized the argument, concludes—conservatively and sensibly—that the transfer created a ceiling to German war production: "the important consequence of bombing was not that it failed to stem the increase in arms production, but that it prevented the increase from being very considerably greater than it was."[29]

It is an intriguing argument, but it is impossible to prove. It is inherently difficult to explain why something wasn't rather than why it was. Moreover, we can't ask how the war would have developed for the Germans if they'd had the planes, guns, and people used for defense on the front *without* asking how the war would have developed for the Allies if they'd had the planes, guns, and people used to bomb Germany over the Atlantic, in the Mediterranean, or in the Pacific. How would the war have developed if the huge resources expended on bombing were spent on winning the Battle of the Atlantic or backing up an earlier invasion of the Continent?

It is only possible to answer such questions roughly. During the war, Britain and America produced 456,299 airplanes; Germany produced 117,791. In 1944, when Allied bombing was at a peak, Britain and America had 3.5 million workers in the aircraft industry; in 1941, when German bombing was at a peak, it had 1.85 million. Germany spent large amounts of resources on radar and optical equipment in defending German cities; the Allies spent large amounts of money on radar and radar-jamming equipment in bombing them. The two clear "debits" against the Germans are absenteeism (which affects the bombed, not the bomber) and flak production. Taking the last, there is no flak without bombs: the large German output on flak has to be set against the large Allied output on bombs. Absenteeism, for its part, could be problematic, but as the U.S. official history emphasizes, it had little effect: absenteeism was highest among women (who generally were not directly involved in German industrial production), absentee workers were often replaced with forced laborers, and absentee workers found jobs in other German cities.[30] These statistics do not fully compare like with like, and can only provide a rough picture. It is nonetheless one that gives us no reason to believe that the resource transfers needed to protect German cities were significantly greater in absolute terms than the resource transfers needed to bomb them. Resource transfers on both sides to some degree canceled each other out,[31] though it is likely that the larger American economy bore this transfer more easily than did the German one.

More importantly, most, if not all, of the resource transfers created by bombing could have been created by precision bombing alone, with no recourse to area bombing. During the war itself, the Americans recognized and exploited the diversionary effects on precision bombing.[32] This fact explains why Speer, during his Allied interrogation, said both that area bombing had an insignificant effect on the outcome of the war *and* that bombing led to the resource transfers mentioned by Overy (indeed, the two statements are a few paragraphs apart in the transcript).[33] Intense, targeted precision bombing raids wreaked havoc with German industrial production, and defense of industrial targets was a mammoth task. A countrywide precision bombing campaign of the sort achieved during the transportation plan would have required a massive, coordinated German defense. The Americans recognized this early on, as they tried to develop the capability to bomb aircraft industry in the Augsburg area. Doing so weakened the Luftwaffe and made "the Germans split their defences as well as their radar control by compelling them to protect from attacks from the south *and* [the] north."[34] At the same time, the effects of bombing Germany's resource base were even more detrimental for the fronts than the transferred men and material. As Speer put it, "In the Luftwaffe, the shortage of liquid fuel became insupportable as from September 1944 onwards, since as from that date the allocation was cut down to 30,000 tons a month, whereas the monthly requirements amounted to between 160,000 and 180,000 tons. So far as the Army was concerned, the shortage of liquid fuel, which in this case was also due to supply difficulties, first became catastrophic at the time of the winter offensive of 16 December 1944 and this was substantially responsible for the rapid collapse of the German defensive front against the Russian breakout from the Baranovo bridgehead. There were approximately 1500 tanks ready for action but these lacked sufficient supporting equipment (*Versorgungssätze*) and were consequently immobilized."[35] These were, of course, the oil raids that Portal urged and Harris ridiculed. After 1943, as precision improved, as daylight bombing became (thanks to fighter escorts) safer, and as area bombing failed to deliver on its promises, there was less and less reason to bomb German cities. Yet these were precisely the years during which the area bombing campaign reached its merciless climax.

The failure of area bombing has led some to dismiss Bomber Command's role in the war. This too is a mistake, as area bombing was only part of what Bomber Command did. Throughout the war, it also devoted substantial resources to mine-laying and to strategic attacks on ships, harbors, transportation, and oil targets. In 1942, the year of the Rostock, Lübeck, and Cologne raids, some 50 percent of Bomber Command's efforts went into naval targets.[36] Some of this precision bombing led to significant and morale-boosting precision attacks—the maiming of the *Scharnhorst* and *Gneisenau* battleships, and of course the dambuster raids—and at the end of the war the attacks on oil did much to undermine the Nazi regime. It is unquestionably the case that without these attacks, and above all without the late 1944 attacks on oil, the war would have lasted longer than it did and still more people would have died. The problem is that all of these attacks were undertaken only reluctantly, with less force, and less often than they could have been.

This last claim might raise some eyebrows. Harris claimed, as have his supporters, that he hit oil whenever he could. The difficulty for Portal in 1944–1945 is that Bomber Command was attacking oil targets, and—when it did—generally with impressive results. Throughout 1944 and 1945, Bomber Command dropped many tons of bombs on oil targets: four thousand in October 1944, fifteen thousand in November, six thousand in December, ten thousand in January 1945, sixteen thousand in February, twenty-one thousand in March, and six thousand in April.[37] The question was whether they couldn't do more.

The Chiefs of Staff thought so. After the war, a "Technical Sub-Committee on Axis Oil" concluded that Harris might have bombed oil on seven additional nights and three days in the last months of 1944.[38] This report refers to ten *additional* attacks. The RAF might also have accompanied the Americans on their bombing raids or followed up on them. This would have sharply increased the number of RAF bombs falling on oil targets and wrecked much greater damage. Again, as German oil production was teetering on the brink of collapse, increased damage on a few more raids might have proved decisive. As Speer told his interrogators in May 1945, "You have to understand that such a concentration of bombers which was almost daily over Germany and with only one target you could have brought about the collapse of Germany within eight weeks so that further resistance would have been impossible either in the east or in the west. . . . For instance, in the attacks on the chemical plants only a part of the bomber formation attacked the chemical plants. As far as I know only 20 to 30 percent of the bombers. Had you concentrated 100 percent instead of 20 percent, reconstruction would have been impossible. No labor would have entered plants because of the continued bombing. In that case the war would have ended within 6 to 8 weeks."[39] Harris frequently sent massive bombing formations into the air, but otherwise his strategy was the opposite of Speer's suggestion: one area target after another, spread over the whole country.

There are other reasons for thinking that eight weeks was not the upper limit. As the official British narrative noted, the Ruhr valley contained large numbers of benzol plants, on which the Wehrmacht increasingly had to rely as eastern supplies of oil vanished to retreat and bombing.[40] The Ruhr was easier to reach than eastern Germany, and Harris hit it many times throughout 1944–1945. As Portal himself noted, it is hard to believe that weather conditions varied so much in this compact corner of Germany. Finally, the statistics again give the lie to Harris's argument, and that of his apologists: over the course of the war, the Americans made 347 separate oil strikes; the British made 158 (including oil strikes made in the early years of the war). As weather did not distinguish between Americans and Britons,[41] it is difficult to see how Harris could have been doing, as he claimed, his best.

Oil was the most important precision target. As Speer put it, "The planned assaults on the chemical industry which began on 12th May 1944 caused the first serious shortages of indispensable basic products and therefore the greatest anxieties for the future conduct of the war. . . . I had the impression that these attacks were to mark the beginning of the long expected and long feared series of planned attacks upon [the] industrial economy and moreover upon a sphere which owing to its complicated structure was particularly difficult to restore and impossible to decentralize. In actual fact, this type of attack was *the most decisive factor in hastening the end of the war*."[42]

It was not, however, the only one. Attacks on transportation—railway stations, bridges, roads—were complementary to the oil campaign in that they further disrupted the movement of oil and made repairs to damaged equipment more difficult. They also interfered with the movement of coal and finished goods, entirely disrupting the planned economy that Speer had used to achieve his production "miracle."[43] Finally, they severely affected troop movements. "In May and June 1944," Speer noted, "the concentrated day and night attacks on the Ruhr transport and communications system first began to cause most serious anxieties about future developments, since supplies to industry in the rest of the Reich of the numerous products of the Ruhr, ranging from coal to single items, were bottled up in the Ruhr."[44] During 1945, the U.S. Eighth Air Force dropped 50 percent of its bombs on transportation targets; the figure for the RAF was 13 percent.[45] There continues to be debate about whether attacks on oil or transportation did more to undermine the German economy; there can be no debate that these precision targets were far more important than cities.

And then there was the Luftwaffe, which the Americans alone destroyed. Had they not done so, no bombing war of any sort would have been possible. The particular genius of the American strategy was combining offense and defense into a single, mutually supportive strategy. The British had viewed the two as separate and competing.[46] Harris sought throughout the war complete independence for Bomber Command and often expressed frustration at the constraints placed on him and his Command. Fighter Command and Bomber Command remained separate organizations, and they were jealous of each other's prestige and power.

Harris was in many ways an impressive commander, almost a great one. He was decisive and tenacious, and generated complete loyalty from his men. He was one of them. He was a product of Bomber Command, defended it uncompromisingly, and gave the world the impression that more than anything else he loved his men. They affectionately referred to him as "Butcher" Harris, because he killed them—not the Germans—in the hundreds. Harris equally affectionately called them "my lags" (criminals). The men loved him as much as he loved them. He accomplished this while doing nothing to court popularity. Sidney Thomas ("Tom") Wingham, wing commander with 102 Squadron, recalled a rare visit by Harris. The Polish contingent exploded in applause, table banging, and cheers when they saw Harris. The commander-in-chief did not smile; he looked directly at them and, saying nothing, nodded sharply, turned on his heels, and left the room.[47]

These characteristics allowed Harris to serve Bomber Command well. He was steadfast in his refusal to see the organization folded into the other two main military wings; he fought tirelessly for more and better planes and for improved pay and conditions for his men; and he managed to maintain throughout the war morale among a group of volunteers whose chances of survival over a tour stood at around 50 percent.

Harris was in many ways almost a revolutionary. The thousand-bomber raid seemed impossible before 1942; by the end of the war, it was commonplace. Like many revolutionaries, his actions were driven by ideology. Harris's commitment to area bombing was total, and he was at best blind and at worst hostile to any evidence challenging it. When area bombing did not work, and when intelligence reports suggested it could not work, Harris found himself backed into a corner. He could only respond by denying the evidence (hence his invectives against experts) and by calling for more bombing. As technological developments and industrial production made bombing more effective and more deadly, the result was ever more death and destruction. By the end of the war, Harris had made the complete obliteration of German cities the end goal. The bombing of German cities—originally adopted because all other options were impossible or unpalatable and because it promised to save lives—had become an end in itself, one that appeared to be something like indiscriminate slaughter.

It is important to recognize that, while the start of the area campaign was probably inevitable given Britain's position in 1941–1942, its end was not. It is not the case that once area bombing started, it couldn't be stopped.[48] On a general level, the public strongly supported bombing. This is no surprise; in war, governments and armed forces enjoy strong support unless they do something to squander it. The public on both sides of the Atlantic no doubt accepted that civilians would be casualties of war. But throughout the war, both American and British governments were mindful of a public reaction against the deliberate and indiscriminate killing of civilians; it was this concern that so frustrated Harris. If the public had been gung ho about city bombing, there would have been no reaction to Cowan's February 17 dispatch on it. It would have been routine. As it was, civilian and military leaders on both sides of the Atlantic scrambled to deny it. When Cecil King, a senior executive at the *London Daily Mirror* (tabloids, whatever else they are, are tuned in to the public mood), heard of the dispatch, he exclaimed, "This is entirely horrifying . . . it gives official proof for everything Goebbels ever said on the subject."[49] Public opinion would probably have recoiled at the idea of an end to all bombing, but it would hardly have reacted to the closing of an area bombing campaign that the government only half-admitted was occurring.

This is not to lay everything at Harris's door. He did not invent area bombing; he was not the first in the RAF to endorse it officially, Portal was. Under Portal's lead, the Air Staff gave it support, seeing the killing of skilled workers as one of its chief advantages, throughout 1942 and, in a more qualified way, much of 1943.[50] All along the way, Harris had strong if erratic support from Churchill. Many other high-level officials were prepared to turn a blind eye. This, however, is as far as it can go.

Harris was not behind the February 1942 directive initiating the era of carpet bombing.[51] The initiative was drafted by the Directors of Bomber Operations and approved by the Cabinet. Harris, however, interpreted it in a matter that strayed from its authors' intentions. In his dispatches, published after the war, he gave the misleading impression that the phrase "to focus attacks on the morale of the enemy civilian population and, in particular, on the industrial workers" was the unalterable foundation of the directive.[52] It was not. Air Staff saw the directive not as an immutable principle that would guide air force policy throughout the war regardless of circumstances. It was rather to be a *temporary* policy, justified by the lack of tactical alternatives, pursued until precision bombing was possible. As Air Commodore Bufton, Co-Director of Bomber Operations during Harris's tenure, put it: Harris's "interpretation was correct for the period immediately following the issue of the directive, but it does not, in my view, *as the person who drafted the directive originally*, embrace the whole intention of the Air Staff at that time. The intention was *always* to return to the bombing of precise targets as quickly as [the] tactical capabilities of the bomber force would permit."[53] This is not retrospective memory: the directive itself makes clear that area bombing was to be a temporary expedient: once Gee was introduced, it should allow "for effective attacks on *precise* targets."[54] As the directive also repeated the Air Staff view that the Germans would jam Gee within six months, precision bombing was expected, and implicitly demanded, following that period.[55]

Although Harris often complained that he faced constant interference, he enjoyed an inordinate amount of autonomy. Subject to loose and malleable official instructions, he chose in most cases what to bomb and how to bomb it. The Air Ministry would not know a target until a few hours before it was attacked and he was no better at keeping his American allies informed in advance either.[56] This sovereignty flowed in part from the nature of the RAF command structure. As Tedder put it in a 1931 RAF Staff College lecture, "In war, owing to the need for rapid decision to meet rapidly changing conditions, it is important to relieve the Commander as much as possible—to leave him free to devote himself entirely to purely operational matters."[57] By contrast, the Chief of Air Staff—Portal's job—was weak and ambiguous. "The main argument against the Chief of Staff," Tedder wrote, "is that he is apt either to be a post office, a bottleneck which will only serve to slow up the working of the staff machinery, or else to become the power behind the throne—a second, but shadow commander with all the power and without the responsibility."[58] The same was true in the United States. Throughout the war, Arnold, with his usual lack of tact, urged Spaatz to be more bloodthirsty. In August 1944, he accused Doolittle of being "afraid of the Hun"; a few months later, he implied that Spaatz and his men lacked "a desire to kill Germans."[59] Arnold could put immense pressure on Spaatz, and there were times—such as over Berlin in February 1945—that the commander relented. But it was Spaatz who took the ultimate decisions.

After Casablanca, the directives made city bombing the lowest priority (though they did allow it); Harris made it the first priority. POINTBLANK had left the door open to destroying cities, mainly to appease Harris, but the cities he selected for destruction had—almost brazenly—nothing to do with POINTBLANK. A September 1943 Air Ministry memorandum urging the destruction of Augsburg, Brunswick, Gotha, Kassel, and Leipzig as centers of the German aircraft industry expressed mystification over the fact that Harris was attacking Hamburg, Berlin, Nuremberg, and Mannheim.[60] A few months later, the Air Staff ordered Harris to leave Berlin and Germany's other big cities alone and to attack smaller cities with a high concentration of POINTBLANK-relevant industries.[61] Harris refused. By this point in the war, the Air Staff were in favor of precision bombing. "The difference in view between the Air Staff and Bomber Command," an official wrote in January 1944, "may, I think, be accurately described by saying that the Air Staff advocate throwing the weight of Bomber Command around the weak places in the German structure, whereas [Harris] believes more in piling the maximum on to the structure as a whole."[62]

Harris dismissed and did everything he could to block the precision bombing campaigns—against ball bearings, oil, the Luftwaffe, and transportation—that did so much damage to the German cause. These facts come out at many points in the history. What's striking about the Harris–Portal exchange in 1944–1945 is the accuracy of Portal's assertions (about the state of the German economy, about the shortage of oil, about the importance of destroying the Luftwaffe, about the need to overwhelm the choke points in German industry through repeated attacks, and about the complementary nature of oil and transportation attacks) and the inaccuracy of Harris's arguments (about oil's irrelevance, about the time wasted on the Luftwaffe, about the role of city bombing in aiding the armies' advance on Europe, and about the problems caused by city bombing for the Germans). In a rare admission of failure, Harris conceded after the war that the oil campaign had been "a complete success," but added: "I still do not think it was reasonable, at the time, to expect that campaign would succeed; what the Allied strategists did was to bet on an outsider, and it happened to win the race."[63] And yet the supporters of the oil and transportation plans, in Britain and in America, based their conclusions on the work of the Committee of Operations Analysts, the Ministry of Economic Warfare, the Joint Intelligence Committee, and multiple intelligence reports. Throughout the war, Harris insisted on claims that proved to be wrong. He insisted that area bombing would force the Germans to capitulate; it didn't. He insisted that the precision bombing wouldn't work; the Americans made it work. He insisted that going after the Luftwaffe was pointless; doing so made the bombing war possible. He insisted that oil, transportation, and ball bearings were irrelevant; they were either decisive (oil, transport) or could have been (ball bearings). Harris insisted on a strategy that failed and that cost the lives of hundreds of thousands—British, American, and Canadian, as well as German. Historians should try to understand the position Harris was in and the reasons behind his actions; equally, however, they should hold him responsible for those actions. After flattening dozens of cities and killing hundreds of thousands of civilians, Harris should be held to account and not simply be forgiven for making a "bad call." That said, in the Anglo-American system of governance, the supremacy of civilian control over military is sacred. Churchill could have stopped area bombing and he did not; indeed, near the end of the war, he urged it on.

One final issue remains to be considered because it is raised so often: whether or not bombing was a war crime. In an already emotional debate, no question has generated more emotion. The issue is both clear and confused. It is clear insofar as the one generally accepted guide to war crimes is found in the

Nuremberg Principles, articulated during the Nuremberg trials and adopted by the United Nations in 1950. Principle VI defines as a war crime the "wanton destruction of cities, towns, or villages, or devastation not justified by military necessity." Under the principles, a war crime is such whether it was committed before or after the Second World War, a fact that makes Harris's technically correct claim that the laws of warfare did not cover bombing less compelling than it might seem. If the area bombing campaign constituted "wanton destruction," it was a war crime. The issue is confused in that the debate over whether the bombing was "wanton" or "justified" will continue.

It is often said that total war justified the area bombing of Germany. This is doubtful. Whereas total war—understood as the erasure of the distinction between a soldier and a civilian—with all of its unspeakable human consequences, existed between the Germans and the Soviets, there is a case for suggesting that it never did between Germany and the Western Allies. Total *mobilization*, yes (if latterly in Germany and never in America); total war, no. When Allied soldiers or airmen fell into German captivity, they were—in the main—treated decently, in line with the Geneva Convention. When Allied aircrew found themselves attacked by angry civilians or the SS, the Wehrmacht (unless it arrived too late) protected them. The same was of course true on the other side. And, finally, when the Allied armies invaded Germany, they did not—as total war would predict—go from house to house spraying civilians with machine-gun fire. On the contrary, they took every reasonable effort to minimize civilian casualties. Had there been total war, none of this would have happened. And this means that the war did not—as some would have it—entirely erase the distinction between a soldier and a citizen (though it may have blurred it), making both targets for the bombing war.

Moral clarity has two sides to it: it gives the Allied war aims moral purpose and it defines the limits within which those aims are pursued. Germany unilaterally launched a war that brought untold death, destruction, and suffering to tens of millions of people around the globe. The defeat of Germany was both a geopolitical and a moral necessity, and the Allies were right to mobilize all of their resources in achieving this goal. It was inevitable that ordinary Germans would find themselves the victims of events. None of this, however, can justify the degree of death and destruction meted out by Harris and tolerated (if intermittently) by Churchill.

Recognizing this fact in no way tarnishes the Allies' victory or the honor of the young men who did what they could to ensure it. Judging area bombing is not the same thing as judging the young aircrew who were serving their country and following orders. Those who suggest that these men should have refused to fly should be more hesitant about condemning from the security of peace those who made decisions in the chaos of war. The loss of some eighty thousand of them, most still boys, is one of the great tragedies of the war. Indeed, one oft-overlooked element of the bombing war is the extent to which both Allied aircrew and German civilians had much in common: during a raid, they were both in a desperate struggle for survival. Equally, however, the need to defeat Germany cannot provide a blanket justification for what in the end became a massacre. It cannot change the fact that area bombing was a moral and strategic failure, whether or not it was a war crime. We cannot shy away from this conclusion out of a fear of giving succor to the far right or of offending Royal Air Force or Royal Canadian Air Force aircrew. On the contrary: the freedom to write and speak the truth is what the aircrew were fighting for.

ACKNOWLEDGMENTS

I have many people to thank for their help in the writing of this book. My first debt is to my agent, Andrew Lownie for backing this book and for providing many invaluable comments along the way. Thanks also to John Pearce and Bruce Westwood, of Westwood Creative Artists, for taking great interest in the book.

My New American Library editor, Mark Chait, has been the ideal critic and supporter. He read the manuscript with a keen eye, and with polite but unwavering determination encouraged me to keep to the story.

I am immensely grateful to the dozens of individuals—American, British, and German, soldier and civilian—whom I interviewed or who wrote to tell me of their experiences during the war. Inevitably, I could only include explicitly a fraction of these harrowing and often moving accounts, but all were immensely helpful to me. In this vein, I am particularly grateful to Sidney "Tom" Wingham, who agreed to be interviewed and who invited me to a July 2003 reunion dinner for 102 Squadron, Bomber Command; to Oktavia Christ of the *Volksbund Deutsche Kriegsgräberfürsorge* in Hamburg, who arranged the interviews that form the core of the first chapter; and to Hans Weppert of Würzburg, who allowed me to speak and solicit witnesses at one of his seniors association's meetings. Adrian Fort, author of the highly regarded biography of Cherwell, very kindly met me for coffee in Oxford, where we spoke about Cherwell's role in the air war. Thanks also go to Jack Pragnell, who had me to his house for lunch, and for hours of fascinating conversation about his time in Bomber Command. I also owe a debt to the current owner of Springfield, who very kindly showed me around the house.

I owe a great debt to the archivists at the National Archives, Kew; the Royal Air Force Museum, London; the Bundesarchiv, Koblenz and Berlin; the Library of Congress, Washington, DC; and city archives in Hamburg, Lübeck, Würzburg, Cologne, and Berlin.

My thanks also to the librarians and staff at Nuffield College, Oxford, and Christ Church, Oxford, for providing access to, respectively, the Cherwell and Portal papers. The head porter at Christ Church was kind enough to show me Portal's and Cherwell's rooms at my old college, and to my juvenile delight I learned that the room I had occupied as a research fellow had been Cherwell's drawing room. That day, Jonathan Wright (my former teacher and colleague) and Paul Kent met me to talk of Cherwell's time at Christ Church, and Mr. Kent sent me information afterward. My thanks go to both of them.

For research assistance, I am grateful to Guy Tourlamain, Jonas Nahm, André Ghione, Patricia Greve, Margaret Haderer, Farzin Yousefian, and Aleksander Jeremic. Dr. Janet Hyer, Aleksander Jeremic, and Cliff Vanderlinden read the entire manuscript, and I am immensely grateful for their many comments. In this vein, particular thanks go to Dr. Richard G. Davis, one of the world's greatest experts on the history of air power, for reading and commenting on the manuscript.

For financial support, my thanks go to the British Academy, Merton College, Oxford, Queen Elizabeth House, Oxford, the University of Newcastle, and the University of Toronto's Joint Initiative in German and European Studies and Department of Political Science.

Many other people have taken time to discuss the arguments put forward in this book: Robert Falkner, Simon Green, Atina Grossmann, Jeffrey Kopstein, Michael Bodemann, Timothy Garton Ash, Desmond King, Margaret MacMillan, Rainer Ohliger, Clifford Orwin, Derek Penslar, Rebecca Wittmann, Peter Pulzer, and Robert Austin. Particular thanks also go to Timothy Cashion, who gave up hours of his time during his stay in Toronto to hear about the book's fitful progression and who, very much in character, made trenchant comments. I am very grateful to him.

Finally, my thanks go to my wife, Katja, for putting up with my monster of a personality when the writing was not going well (it generally wasn't) and for putting up with endless lectures on the history of bombing.

NOTES

Chapter 1: The day Hamburg died

1 M. Gretzschel (2003). "Hamburg im Feuersturm." *Hamburger Abendblatt*. Hamburg: 1–2, 2.

2 Quoted in Martin Middlebrook, *The Battle of Hamburg* (London: Cassell & Co., 2002), 275–276.

Chapter 2: The Blitz: Bombing civilians and destroying houses

1 Story and quotation from Philip Ziegler, *London at War 1939–1945* (Toronto: Alfred A. Knopf, 1995), 113.

2 Stories from Ziegler, *London at War*, 113–117.

3 Richard Overy, *The Battle of Britain* (London: Penguin, 2000), 83.

4 Overy, *The Battle of Britain*, 79.

5 Overy, *The Battle of Britain*, 79.

6 Overy, *The Battle of Britain*, 79.

7 Keith Lowe, *Inferno: The Devastation of Hamburg, 1943* (London: Penguin, 2007), 57.

8 Lowe, *Inferno*, 57.

9 Peter Hennessy, *Never Again: Britain 1945–1951* (London: Vintage, 1993), 35.

10 On this, see Richard Overy, *The Air War 1939–1945* (Washington, DC: Potomac Books, 2005), 31–32.

11 Overy, *The Air War*, 34.

12 Richard Overy, *Why the Allies Won* (London: Pimlico, 1996), 133.

13 Denis Richards, *Portal of Hungerford* (London: Heinemann, 1977), 122.

14 Max Hastings, *Bomber Command* (London: Pan Books, 1999), 65.

15 Details from Hastings, *Bomber Command*, 71–72.

16 Hastings, *Bomber Command*, 74.

17 Quoted in Richards, *Portal of Hungerford*, 163.

18 Hastings, *Bomber Command*, 95. Quotations from this page.

19 Quoted in Hastings, *Bomber Command*, 98.

20 Quoted in Hastings, *Bomber Command*, 97.
21 Portal papers, File 2, Development and Employment of the Heavy Bomber Force, Memorandum from Portal to Churchill, September 22, 1941 [sent to Churchill on September 25].
22 Portal papers, File 2, Minute from Portal to Churchill, September 25, 1941.
23 Portal papers, File 2, Personal Minute from Churchill to Portal, September 27, 1941.
24 Quoted in Richards, *Portal of Hungerford*, 189–190.

Chapter 3: Bomber Harris takes over
 1 I owe this insight to Frederick Taylor.
 2 Quoted in Henry Probert, *Bomber Harris: His Life and Times* (London: Greenhill Books, 2001), 60.
 3 Probert, *Bomber Harris*, 61.
 4 Probert, *Bomber Harris*, 77.
 5 Probert, *Bomber Harris*, 122.
 6 Probert, *Bomber Harris*, 123.
 7 Gerard J. De Groot, *Liberal Crusader* (New York: New York University Press, 1993), 186.
 8 Hastings, *Bomber Command*, 134.
 9 Quoted in John Colville, *The Fringes of Power* (New York: W.W. Norton and Company, 1985), 311.
10 Maurice Cowling, *The Impact of Hitler: British Politics and British Policies, 1933–1940* (Chicago: University Chicago Press, 1977), 215.
11 *Parliamentary Debates (Commons)*, February 25, 1942. Copy in PRO AIR 8/619.

Chapter 4: The Americans
 1 Details from Thomas S. Coffey, *Hap: Military Aviator* (New York: Viking Press, 1982).
 2 Richard G. Davis, *Henry (Hap) Arnold: Military Aviator* (Washington, DC: Air Force History and Museum Program, 1997), 1.
 3 Davis, *Henry (Hap) Arnold*, 2.
 4 Coffey, *Hap*, 40.
 5 Coffey, *Hap*, 92.
 6 Ronald Schaffer, *Wings of Judgment: American Bombing in World War II* (New York: Oxford University Press, 1985).
 7 James Parton, *"Air Force Spoken Here": General Ira Eaker and the Command of the Air* (Bethesda, MD: Adler & Adler, 1986).
 8 Details on Mitchell drawn from Donald L. Miller, *Masters of the Air: America's Bomber Boys Who Fought the Air War against Nazi Germany* (New York: Simon and Schuster, 2006), 30.
 9 Schaffer, *Wings of Judgment*, 25.
10 Carl Spaatz papers, Interview with James Parton by S.H. Stackpole, November 28, 1943.

11 Major Craig R. Edkins, *Anonymous Warrior: The Contributions of Harold L. George to Strategic Air Power* (Montgomery, AL: Air Force University, 1997).

12 Schaffer, *Wings of Judgment*, 32.

13 Carl Spaatz papers, Box I: 135, Interview with Brig. General H.S. Hansell by Dr. Bruce C. Hopper, October 5, 1943.

14 Miller, *Masters of the Air*, 39.

15 Carl Spaatz papers, Box I: 135, Interview with Brig. General H.S. Hansell by Dr. Bruce C. Hopper, October 5, 1943.

16 Miller, *Masters of the Air*, 39.

17 Carl Spaatz papers, Box I: 135, Interview with Brigadier General O.A. Anderson, November 10, 1944, 19–20.

18 Haywood S. Hansell, *The Strategic Air War against Germany and Japan: A Memoir* (Washington, DC: Office of Air Force History, United States Air Force, 1986), 13.

19 On this, see John Keegan, We Wanted Beady-Eyed Guys Just Absolutely Holding the Course, *Smithsonian Magazine*, 14, 5 (1993).

Chapter 5: Building the mighty Eighth

1 Quoted in Coffey, *Hap*, 182.

2 Quoted in Miller, *Masters of the Air*, 45.

3 Schaffer, *Wings of Judgment*, 5–6.

4 Quoted in Schaffer, *Wings of Judgment*, 15.

5 Quoted in Coffey, *Hap*, 232.

6 Quoted in Coffey, *Hap*, 233.

7 Carl Spaatz papers, Box I: 135, Interview with Brig. General H.S. Hansell by Dr. Bruce C. Hopper, October 5, 1943.

8 Carl Spaatz papers, Box I: 135, Interview with Brig. General H.S. Hansell by Dr. Bruce C. Hopper, October 5, 1943.

9 Carl Spaatz papers, Box I: 135, Interview with Brig. General H.S. Hansell by Dr. Bruce C. Hopper, October 5, 1943.

10 Carl Spaatz papers, Box I: 135, Interview with Brig. General H.S. Hansell by Dr. Bruce C. Hopper, October 5, 1943.

11 Quoted in Richard G. Davis, *Carl A. Spaatz and the Air War in Europe* (Washington/London: The Smithsonian Institute, 1992), 41.

12 See Davis, *Carl A. Spaatz and the Air War in Europe*, chapter 2.

13 Hastings, *Bomber Command*, 125.

14 Quotations from Coffey, *Hap*, 228.

15 Coffey, *Hap*, 228.

16 Quoted in Coffey, *Hap*, 230.

17 Quoted in Coffey, *Hap*, 234.

18 Coffey, *Hap*, 234.

19 Coffey, *Hap*, 251.

20 Quoted in Coffey, *Hap*, 252.

21 Quoted in Parton, *"Air Force Spoken Here,"* 129–130.

22 I am grateful to the current owner of Springfield for showing me around the house and pointing this detail out to me.

23 Parton, *"Air Force Spoken Here,"* 134.

24 Parton, *"Air Force Spoken Here,"* 141.

25 Parton, *"Air Force Spoken Here,"* 141.

26 Parton, *"Air Force Spoken Here,"* 143.

Chapter 6: Burn, Germany, burn

1 Statistic from Robin Neillands, *The Bomber War: Arthur Harris and the Allied Bomber Offensive 1939–1945* (London: John Murray, 2001), 110.

2 Neillands, *The Bomber War,* 111–112.

3 On this, see Hastings, *Bomber Command,* 146.

4 Harris papers, Buft 3/27, Letter from Harris to VCAS, April 29, 1942.

5 Lutz Wilde, *Bomber gegen Lübeck: Eine Dokumentation der Zerstörungen in Lübecks Altstadt beim Luftangriff im März 1942* (Lübeck: Verlag Schmidt-Römhild, 1999), 13 [consulted in Lübeck city archives, L II 2995].

6 Hans-Günter Feldhaus, *Nun zu guterletzt* (Lübeck: Druckerei Wulf, 2003), 104.

7 Details on timing from *Archiv der Hansestadt Lübeck*, Materialsammlung zum Luftangriff 1942—Flakuntergruppe Lübeck 1–6, file 6, "Erfahrungsbericht über den Grossangriff auf Lübeck in der Nacht vom 28. zum 29. 3 1942." The author, the Division Commander for Flak Abteiling 161, Herr Major Schreiber (later Landessuperintendant in Lübeck), noted the new strategy: *"Der Grossangriff auf Lübeck scheint in dieser Art erstmalig in Deutschland geflogen zu sein, and zwar hinsichtlich massierten Einsatzes kriegserfahrener Piloten auf ein räumlich engbegrenztes Ziel mittel alterlicher Bauart nach genau festgelegtem Angriffsplan mit geschicktester Taktik und rücksichtlosem Einsatz. Der Gegner versuchte im Anflug zu täuschen."*

8 *Archiv der Hansestadt Lübeck*, Materialsammlung zum Luftangriff 1942—Flakuntergruppe Lübeck 8–22, 17, "Batterie Chronik der 2. Schwere Flak Abt. 161," 52.

9 Details from report by Renate Brockmüller, Lübeck, undated (Spring 2007).

10 Details from Wilde, *Bomber gegen Lübeck*, 15–16.

11 Wilde, *Bomber gegen Lübeck*, 15.

12 Hans Schönherr, *Lübeck—Aufbau aus dem Chaos* (Lübeck: GMBH Buchverlag Lübeck, 1962), 9.

13 J. Friedrich, *Der Brand: Deutschland im Bombenkrieg 1940–1945* (Munich: Ullstein Heyne, 2002). For photos of St. Mary's interior following the bombing, see *Archiv der Hansestadt Lübeck*, HS 1192, "Aufnahmen über Zerstörungen durch den Luftangriff auf Lübeck in der Nacht zum 29. März 1942."

14 *Archiv der Hansestadt Lübeck*, Materialsammlung zum Luftangriff 1942—Flakuntergruppe Lübeck 1–6, File 6, "Erfahrungsbericht über den Grossangriff auf Lübeck in der Nacht vom 28. Zum 29. 3 1942."

15 *Archiv der Hansestadt Lübeck*, Materialsammlung zum Luftangriff 1942—Flakuntergruppe Lübeck 1–6, File 6, "Erfahrungsbericht über den Grossangriff auf Lübeck in der Nacht vom 28. zum 29. 3 1942."

16 Hastings, *Bomber Command*, 150.

17 *Archiv der Hansestadt Lübeck*, "Britischer Luftüberfall auf Lübeck" (collected newspaper clippings), story entitled "Lübecks Flak kämpfte wie Helden."

18 *Archiv der Hansestadt Lübeck*, "Britischer Luftüberfall auf Lübeck" (collected newspaper clippings), story entitled "Lübecks Herzen stärker als Englands Bomben."

19 *Archiv der Hansestadt Lübeck*, "Britischer Luftüberfall auf Lübeck" (collected newspaper clippings), story entitled "Schnelle Hilfe auf allen Gebieten."

20 *Archiv der Hansestadt Lübeck*, "Britischer Luftüberfall auf Lübeck" (collected newspaper clippings), story entitled "Sie sind gefallen wie Soldaten in der Schlacht."

21 *Archiv der Hansestadt Lübeck*, "Britischer Luftüberfall auf Lübeck" (collected newspaper clippings), stories entitled "Ein neues Lübeck wird erstehen," "Lübeck wird wieder sein altes Gesicht erhalten," and "Wie Lübeck die Nacht zum Palmsonntag erlebte."

22 *Archiv der Hansestadt Lübeck*, eyewitness report by Günther Becker, May 30, 1942.

23 Jörg Friedrich, *The Fire: The Bombing of Germany 1940–1945* (New York: Columbia University Press, 2006), 71.

24 Quoted in Parton, *"Air Force Spoken Here,"* 147.

25 Adrian Fort, *Prof: The Life of Frederick Lindemann* (London: Jonathan Cape, 2003), 43–45.

26 Cherwell papers, Nuffield College, Oxford, A 14/f4, Letter to Lindemann, November 2, 1932.

27 Roy Harrod, *The Prof: A Personal Memoir of Lord Cherwell* (London: Macmillan, 1959), 74. Emphasis in the original.

28 For the full story, see Fort, *Prof*, 246–248.

29 Fort, *Prof*, 247.

30 Fort, *Prof*, 247.

31 Fort, *Prof*, 247.

32 Portal papers, File 2, Memorandum from Cherwell to Churchill, March 30, 1942.

33 For the details of Churchill's routine, I draw on M. Gilbert, *Churchill: A Life* (New York: H. Holt, 1991); R.A. Hough, *Winston and Clementine: The Triumph of the Churchills* (New York: Bantam Books, 1991); R. Jenkins, *Churchill* (London: Macmillan, 2001).

34 Carl Spaatz papers, Box I: 136, Interview with Sir Henry Tizard by Maj. James Lawrence, November 15, 1944.

35 Quoted in Hastings, *Bomber Command*, 152 [2nd ed., 1981].

36 Quoted in Hastings, *Bomber Command*, 153.

37 Lord Zuckerman, *From Apes to Warlords* (London: Hamish Hamilton, 1978), 139–146 [Zuckerman's autobiography].

38 Quoted in Maurice W. Kirby, *Operational Research in War and Peace—The British Experience from the 1930s to 1970* (London: Imperial College Press, 2003), 141. Emphasis added.

39 Both quoted in Hastings, *Bomber Command*, 153 [2nd ed.].

Chapter 7: Killing the Boche

1 Quotations and two previous paragraphs taken from Parton, *"Air Force Spoken Here,"* 148.

2 Parton, *"Air Force Spoken Here,"* 148.

3 Parton, *"Air Force Spoken Here,"* 158.

4 Friedrich, *Der Brand*, 183–184; Hans-Werner Bohl, Bodo Keipke, and Karsten Schröder (eds.), *Bomben auf Rostock* (Rostock: Konrad Reich Verlag, 1995).

5 Harris papers, Buft 3/27, A.I.3 (c) (Air Liaison), Air Attack by Fire, October 17, 1941.

6 Harris papers, Buft 3/27, Letter from Freeman to Harris, April 27, 1942.

7 Churchill College, Buft 3/27, Letter from Harris to Freeman, VCAS, April 29, 1942.

8 Anthony Furse, *Wilfred Freeman: The Genius behind Allied Survival and Air Supremacy 1939 to 1945* (Kent: Spellmount, 1999), 204.

9 Furse, *Wilfred Freeman*, 150.

10 Arthur Harris, *Bomber Offensive* (London: Collins, 1947), 107–109.

11 Neillands, *The Bomber War*, 120.

12 Hastings, *Bomber Command*, 150.

13 Eric Taylor, *Operation Millennium: "Bomber" Harris' Raid on Cologne, May 1942* (London: Robert Hale, 1987), 45.

14 Quoted in Taylor, *Operation Millennium*, 46–67.

15 Charles Messenger, *Cologne: The First 1000-Bomber Raid* (London: Ian Allan Ltd., 1982), 40.

16 Messenger, *Cologne*, 40.

17 The last three sentences are taken (though not directly quoted) from D. Saward, *The Bomber's Eye* (London: Cassell, 1959), 381.

Chapter 8: Cologne

1 Taylor, *Operation Millennium*, 83.

2 Taylor, *Operation Millennium*, 84.

3 Story related by Hastings, *Bomber Command*, 151–152.

4 Story related by Sweetman in Harris, *Bomber Command*, 81.

5 *"Wenn sich Sekunde an Sekunde, Minute an Minute reihen, die wie eine Ewigkeit erscheinen, wächst die Angst ins Unermeßliche."*

6 Friedrich, *The Fire*, 73.

7 Quotations from Parton, *"Air Force Spoken Here,"* 160.

8 Miller, *Masters of the Air*, 58.

9 Quoted in Miller, *Masters of the Air*, 59.

Chapter 9: Göring and Speer

1 Richard Overy, *Göring: The "Iron Man"* (London: Routledge, 1984), 232.

2 Quoted in Overy, *Göring*, 234.

3 Overy, *Göring*, 232.

4 Roger Manvell, *Der Reichsmarschall: Aufstieg und Fall des Hermann Göring* (Rastatt: Pabel-Moewig Verlag, 1983), 81.

5 Quoted in Overy, *Göring*, 237.

6 Lord Halifax, personal diary, Halifax papers, Borthwick Institute, York University, PRO File Fo.371/20736.

7 Overy, *Göring*, 25.

8 Werner Maser, *Hermann Göring—Hitlers janusköpfiger Paladin* (Berlin: Quintessenz Verlag, 2000), 253–59.

9 Overy, *Göring*, 128.

10 Stefan Martens, *Herman Göring—Erster Paladin des Führers und Zweiter Mann im Reich* (Paderborn: Ferdinand Schöningh, 1985), 16.

11 Overy, *Göring*, 181.

12 Maser, *Hermann Göring*, 377.

13 Matthias Schmidt, *Albert Speer—Das Ende eines Mythos* (Bern: Scherz Verlag, 1982), 36.

14 Dan Van Der Vat, *Der gute Nazi* (Berlin: Henschel, 1997), 50.

15 Joachim Fest, *Speer: The Final Verdict* (London: Weidenfeld & Nicolson, 2001), 14.

16 Schmidt, *Albert Speer—Das Ende eines Mythos*, 43.

17 Fest, *Speer*, 30.

18 Van Der Vat, *Der gute Nazi*, 50.

19 Quoted in Fest, *Speer*, 47.

20 Van Der Vat, *Der gute Nazi*, 78–80.

21 Fest, *Speer*, 56.

22 Schmidt, *Albert Speer—Das Ende eines Mythos*, 62.

23 Quoted in Fest, *Speer*, 111.

24 Fest, *Speer*, 116.

25 Susanne Willems, *Der entsiedelte Jude—Albert Speers Wohnungsmarktpolitik für den Berliner Hauptstadtbau* (Berlin: Edition Hentrich, 2002), 80–84.

26 Fest, *Speer*, 116.

27 Ian Kershaw, *Hitler: 1936–1945. Nemesis* (London: Penguin, 2000), 502.

28 Fest, *Speer*, 128.

29 Fest, *Speer*, 128.

30 Martin Gilbert, *Auschwitz and the Allies* (New York: Holt, Rinehart and Winston, 1981), 13.

31 Gilbert, *Auschwitz and the Allies*, 15.

32 Gilbert, *Auschwitz and the Allies*, 15.

33 Gilbert, *Auschwitz and the Allies*, 18. On Germany's genocide, as well as the SS's *Generalplan Ost*, involving the expulsion of more than thirty million east Europeans, see Adam Tooze, *The Wages of Destruction: The Making and Breaking of the Nazi War Economy* (New York: Viking, 2006), chapter 14.

34 Van Der Vat, *Der gute Nazi*, 155–156.

Chapter 10: Churchill, Roosevelt, and the future of bombing

1 Quoted in Parton, "*Air Force Spoken Here*," 215.

2 W. Churchill, *Memoirs of the Second World War: an abridgement of the six volumes of the Second World War, with an epilogue by the author on the postwar years written for this volume* (Boston: Houghton Mifflin, 1959), 667.

3 W.A. Harriman and E. Abel, *Special Envoy to Churchill and Stalin, 1941–1946* (New York: Random House, 1975), 180.

4 R.D. Murphy, *Diplomat Among Warriors* (Garden City, NY: Doubleday, 1964), 165.

5 Murphy, *Diplomat Among Warriors*, 165.

6 Harriman and Abel, *Special Envoy to Churchill and Stalin, 1941–1946*, 181.

7 Churchill, *Memoirs of the Second World War*, 667.

8 Churchill, *Memoirs of the Second World War*, 667.

9 Murphy, *Diplomat Among Warriors*, 165.

10 W.F. Kimball, *Forged in War: Roosevelt, Churchill, and the Second World War* (New York: W. Morrow, 1996), 184.

11 Harriman and Abel, *Special Envoy to Churchill and Stalin, 1941–1946*, 182–183.

12 Quoted in Hastings, *Bomber Command*, 184.

13 G.L. Weinberg, *A World at Arms: A Global History of World War II* (Cambridge/ New York: Cambridge University Press, 2005), 380–381.

14 PRO 14/3507, Letter from Harris to the prime minister, June 17, 1942.

15 Quoted in Parton, *"Air Force Spoken Here,"* 218.

16 Carl Spaatz papers, Box I: 136, Interview with James Parton by Captain H.S. Stackpole, November 28, 1943.

17 Carl Spaatz papers, Box I: 136, Interview with James Parton by Captain H.S. Stackpole, November 28, 1943.

18 Quotations and paragraph from Parton, *"Air Force Spoken Here,"* 221.

19 Quotations and previous paragraph from Parton, *"Air Force Spoken Here,"* 220.

20 Quoted in Parton, *"Air Force Spoken Here,"* 222.

21 Quoted in Parton, *"Air Force Spoken Here,"* 222.

22 Murphy, *Diplomat Among Warriors*, 167.

23 Murphy, *Diplomat Among Warriors*, 168.

24 Churchill, *Memoirs of the Second World War*, 675.

25 PRO AIR 19/189, "Combined Chiefs of Staff: The Bomber Offensive from the United Kingdom," January 21, 1943.

26 Hastings, *Bomber Command*, 184.

27 J. Alwyn Phillips, DFM, *The Valley of the Shadow of Death* (Chippenham, Wiltshire: Antony Rowe Ltd., 1992).

28 Sir Charles Webster and Dr. Noble Frankland, *The Strategic Air Offensive against Germany 1939–1945*, Vol. I (London: HMSO, 1961), 145.

29 See PRO AIR 20/4832, Letter from Bufton to ACAS (Ops), May 27, 1943, in which Bufton suggests that Harris be reminded that "only a proportion of the night bombing effort can be employed effectively" against Luftwaffe targets.

Chapter 11: The Ruhr

1 Franz-Josef Brüggemeier, *Leben vor Ort—Ruhrbergleute und Ruhrbergbau 1889–1919* (Munich: C.H. Beck, 1984), 42.

2 Brüggemeier, *Leben vor Ort—Ruhrbergleute und Ruhrbergbau 1889–1919*, 48–49.

3 Lynn Abrams, Zur Entwicklung einer kommerziellen Arbeiterkultur im Ruhrgebiet (1850–1914). In Dagmar Kift (ed.), *Kirmes-Kneipe-Kino: Arbeiterkultur im*

Ruhrgebiet zwischen Kommerz und Kontrolle (Paderborn: Schöningh Verlag, 1992), 41–47.

4   Police report, "Der Angriff," sent to the author by H. Pavis, April 2007.

5   "Die Nacht als Essen unterging," *NRZ: Zeitung für Essen*, March 6, 1993.

6   Bashow, *No Prouder Place.*

7   Details from Hastings, *Bomber Command*, 225–227 and 203.

8   Quoted in Probert, *Bomber Harris*, 254.

Chapter 12: Busting dams

1   Albert Speer, *Inside the Third Reich* (London: Picador, 1996), 384.

2   And, as such, are well known. This account draws mostly on Neillands, *The Bomber War*, chapter 10.

3   Quoted in Probert, *Bomber Harris*, 254.

4   Bashow, *No Prouder Place*, 156.

5   Bashow, *No Prouder Place*, 156.

6   Hopgood's story and Fraser's quotation can be found in Tamara Stecyk, "A Dambuster's Daughter," at http://www.lancastermuseum.ca/s,dambustersdaughter .html (viewed February 28, 2007).

7   Neillands, *The Bomber War*, 232.

8   Spencer Dunmore, *Above and Beyond: The Canadians' War in the Air, 1939–1945* (Toronto: McClelland & Stewart, 1996), 258.

9   Speer, *Inside the Third Reich*, 384.

10   Speer, *Inside the Third Reich*, 384.

11   PRO AIR 19/189, Letter from Portal to Churchill, October 15, 1943.

12   Quoted in Vera Brittan, *Stop Massacre Bombing* (New York: The Fellowship of Reconciliation, 1944), 61.

13   Details from eyewitness report by Hermann-Josef Baum, February 14, 2007.

14   *Heranziehung von Schülern zum Kriegshilfseinsatz der deutschen Jugend in der Luftwaffe*, February 15, 1943 (sent to author by Hermann-Josef Baum).

15   Speer, *Inside the Third Reich*, 383–384; on coal's importance, see Alfred C. Mierzejewski, *The Collapse of the German War Economy, 1944–1945* (Chapel Hill, NC: University of North Carolina Press, 1988), chapter 2.

16   Speer, *Inside the Third Reich*, 383.

17   Probert, *Bomber Harris*, 339.

18   PRO 14/3507, Letter from Harris to the prime minister, June 17, 1942.

19   Gerhard E. Sollbach (ed.), *Hagen—Kriegsjahre und Nachkriegszeit 1939–1948* (Hagen: Verlag Dierk Hobein, 1995).

Chapter 13: England, July 27, 1943: "Let us open the window"

1   Friedrich, *The Fire*, 25.

2   One room of which was occupied, as it happened, by the author some sixty years later.

3   R.V. Jones and William S. Farren, "Henry Thomas Tizard, 1885–1959." In *Biographical Memoirs of Fellows of the Royal Society*, Vol. 7, 313–348, 330–331.

4 Jones and Farren, "Henry Thomas Tizard, 1885–1959," 329–300.
5 Friedrich, *The Fire*, 25–26.
6 Jones and Farren, "Henry Thomas Tizard, 1885–1959," 329–300, 333.
7 Friedrich, *The Fire*, 25–26.
8 Hastings, *Bomber Command*, 129.
9 Hastings, *Bomber Command*, 205.
10 RAF, Memo from Arthur Harris on "Window," May 31, 1942, H 35.
11 Hastings, *Bomber Command*, 205.
12 Hastings, *Bomber Command*, 259.

Chapter 14: To destroy Hamburg

1 The details in this paragraph are taken from Lowe, *Inferno*, 78–80.
2 Quoted in Kevin Wilson, *Bomber Boys* (London: Weidenfeld & Nicolson, 2005).
3 Details in this paragraph from Lowe, *Inferno*, 80–81.
4 PRO AIR 25/257.
5 Lowe, *Inferno*, 83.
6 Lowe, *Inferno*, 93.
7 Details from Friedrich, *The Fire*, 30–31.
8 Details from Lowe, *Inferno*, 95–96.
9 Lowe, *Inferno*, 94.
10 Quoted in Lowe, *Inferno*, 95.
11 PRO AIR 14/3410, Bomber Command Night Raid Report No. 383, July 24–25, 1943, 398–400.
12 Heute vor 60 Jahren in Hamburgs Zeitungen, *Hamburger Abendblatt*, July 22, 2003, 12.
13 Middlebrook, *The Battle of Hamburg*, 137.
14 728 of 791 despatched. PRO AIR 14/3410, Bomber Command Night Raid Report no. 383, July 24–25, 1943, 398–400.
15 N. Longmate, *The Bombers: The RAF Offensive against Germany* (London: Hutchinson, 1983), 266.
16 Quoted in Bashow, *No Prouder Place*, 175.
17 Lowe, *Inferno*, 97.
18 With the exception of the fourth wave, during which seventy planes bombed the city.

Chapter 15: Under the bombs

1 This paragraph is based on an interview with Karl Alfeis Heinz, Hamburg, July 31, 2003.
2 Interview with Hans Pauels, May 2007.
3 The following two stories are taken from Martin Middlebrook, who interviewed the witnesses in the 1970s.
4 Others had more luck. Hamburg's firemen donned gas masks and protective glasses, and fought their way through the fiery streets near the firestorm. In the Kiebitzstrasse, one fireman looked into a house engulfed by flames from the roof to the basement. In it were a sixty-five-year-old man and a fifteen-year-old boy

struggling to rescue an incapacitated man of some forty-eight years of age. With the help of a two-wheeled pram, they made it. Staatsarchiv Hamburg (undated), Bericht über meine Tätigkeit in der Angriffsnacht vom 26/27.7.1943, A 10–1 Nr. 110.

5 Staatsarchiv Hamburg (undated), Dr. Zaps, Oberst der Feuerschutzpolizei, Bericht über die Erfahrungen des FE-Dienstes bei den Luftangriffen auf Hamburg in der Zeit vom 24.7/3.8.1943, 333–3 I Feuerwehr I, Hamburg.

6 J. Nyary, Die Nacht, in der 35000 Menschen starben, *Hamburger Abendblatt*, July 26–27, 1943, 16.

7 Staatsarchiv Hamburg (undated), Dr. Zaps, Oberst der Feuerschutzpolizei, Bericht über die Erfahrungen des FE-Dienstes bei den Luftangriffen auf Hamburg in der Zeit vom 24.7/3.8.1943, 333–3 I Feuerwehr I, Hamburg.

Chapter 16: Speer's nightmare

1 Fest, *Speer*, 135–137.

2 Fest, *Speer*, 138.

3 Fest, *Speer*, 138.

4 On the *Zentrale Planung*, see Tooze, *The Wages of Destruction*, 559.

5 Speer, *Inside the Third Reich*, 389.

6 Speer, *Inside the Third Reich*, 388.

7 Adapted from Speer, *Inside the Third Reich*, 389.

8 Staatsarchiv Hamburg (undated), Dr. Zaps, Oberst der Feuerschutzpolizei, Bericht über die Erfahrungen des FE-Dienstes bei den Luftangriffen auf Hamburg in der Zeit vom 24.7/3.8.1943, 333–3 I Feuerwehr I, Hamburg.

9 Mierzejewski, *The Collapse of the German War Economy*, chapter 1.

10 Details on the Schweinfurt-Regensburg raids taken from M. Middlebrook, *The Schweinfurt-Regensburg Mission* (London: Allen Lane, 1983).

11 Martin Middlebrook, *The Berlin Raids: RAF Bomber Command Winter 1943–44* (London: Cassell Military Paperbacks, 2000), 6–7.

12 Quoted in Schaffer, *Wings of Judgment*, 68.

13 PRO AIR 19/189, Letter to Portal, September 25, 1943.

14 Schaffer, *Wings of Judgment*, 18.

15 Curtis LeMay, *Mission with LeMay* (New York: Doubleday, 1965), 425.

16 Schaffer, *Wings of Judgment*, 66.

17 Carl Spaatz papers, Box I: 136, Interview with Colonel Curtis LeMay by Dr. Bruce C. Hopper, September 7, 1943, 21.

18 Quoted in Middlebrook, *The Schweinfurt-Regensburg Mission*, 174.

19 Interview with Wilbur Klint, August 24, 2007.

20 Quoted in Middlebrook, *The Schweinfurt-Regensburg Mission*, 198.

21 Quoted in Middlebrook, *The Schweinfurt-Regensburg Mission*, 201.

22 Parton, *"Air Force Spoken Here,"* 311.

23 PRO AIR 19/189, "Most Secret. Increased importance of Schweinfurt as an Objective for RAF Bomber Command," December 12, 1943, and Letter from Bottomley to Harris, December 17, 1943.

24 PRO AIR 19/189, Letter from Bottomley to Harris, December 23, 1943.

25 Portal papers, Letter from Harris to Portal, January 18, 1945, 3g.

26 PRO AIR 19/189, Letter from Harris to Bottomley, December 28, 1943.

27 He had been doing so since 1942. See PRO AIR 14/3507, Letter from Harris to the prime minister, May 2, 1942. It is Harris's response to Churchill's questions on (a) why he bombed Augsburg and (b) why he didn't bomb Schweinfurt.

28 Wilson, *Bomber Boys*, 312.

29 Speer, *Inside the Third Reich*, 390.

30 Speer, *Inside the Third Reich*, 391.

31 Speer, *Inside the Third Reich*, 391.

32 Speer, *Inside the Third Reich*, 390.

33 Quoted in Coffey, *Hap*, 321.

34 Coffey, *Hap*, 321.

35 Coffey, *Hap*, 321.

36 Details and quotations from Parton, *"Air Force Spoken Here,"* 303.

37 The original text, as was the style at the time, is written in third-person past tense. I have put it into the present tense for ease of reading.

38 Emphasis added.

39 Details from Parton, *"Air Force Spoken Here,"* 305–306.

40 Parton, *"Air Force Spoken Here,"* 306.

41 Coffey, *Hap*, 322.

42 Parton, *"Air Force Spoken Here,"* 313.

43 Quoted in Coffey, *Hap*, 322.

44 Details and quotations from Speer, *Inside the Third Reich*, 396–399.

45 Quoted in Speer, *Inside the Third Reich*, 396.

46 Details from Speer, *Inside the Third Reich*, 396–399.

47 Speer, *Inside the Third Reich*, 391.

48 Ira Eaker papers, Library of Congress, Washington, DC, Box I: 17, "Text of Cable—Eaker to Arnold," October 15, 1943.

49 Ira Eaker papers, Library of Congress, Washington, DC, Box I: 17, "Text of Cable—Eaker to Arnold," October 15, 1943.

50 Speer, *Inside the Third Reich*, 391. In a bizarre passage, Robin Neillands argues that the October 14 raid achieved "nothing" and that "very few bombs hit the target." As he provides no citations, it is impossible to know how he arrived at this conclusion, but it is clearly false.

51 Ira Eaker papers, Library of Congress, Washington, DC, Box I: 17, "Text of Cable—Eaker to Arnold," October 15, 1943.

52 Speer, *Inside the Third Reich*, 391.

53 PRO AIR 19/189, "Most Secret. Increased importance of Schweinfurt as an Objective for RAF Bomber Command," December 12, 1943, and Letter from Bottomley to Harris, December 17, 1943: "It is suggested that a night area attack on Schweinfurt be made by the main force of Bomber Command . . . A successful attack would undoubtedly justify great efforts to secure destruction of this target, and would constitute a major contribution to the success of the Combined Bomber Offensive Plan."

54 Quoted in Ian L. Hawkins, *The Munster Raid: Before and After* (Trumbull, CT: FNP Military Division, 1999), 72.

Chapter 17: The Battle of Berlin

 1 Details from Middlebrook, *The Berlin Raids*, 8–9.
 2 Middlebrook, *The Berlin Raids*, 7.
 3 Middlebrook, *The Berlin Raids*, 7.
 4 Middlebrook, *The Berlin Raids*, 8–9.
 5 Stories and quotations from Middlebrook, *The Berlin Raids*, 53–55.
 6 Interview with Werner Schenk, August 24, 2007.
 7 Interview with Günther Ackerhans, July 13, 2007.
 8 Peter Spoden's story and quotations from Middlebrook, *The Berlin Raids*, 51–53.
 9 Neillands, *The Bomber War*, 239.
10 Middlebrook, *The Berlin Raids*, 16.
11 Middlebrook, *The Berlin Raids*, 16.
12 Neillands, *The Bomber War*, 239.
13 Middlebrook, *The Berlin Raids*, 16–17.
14 Portal papers, Letter from Harris to Churchill, November 3, 1943.
15 Friedrich, *The Fire*, 100.
16 Longmate, *The Bombers*, 288.
17 S. Cox, Introduction. In A. Harris, *Despatch on War Operations 23rd February, 1942 to 8th May, 1945* (London: Frank Cass, 1995), xxi.
18 PRO AIR 19/189, Letter from W.A. Coryton, ACAS (Ops) to Portal, November 5, 1943.
19 Neillands, *The Bomber War*, 290.
20 Martin Middlebrook, *The Bomber Command War Diaries* (New York: Viking, 1985), 477.
21 Middlebrook, *The Bomber Command War Diaries*, 482–483.
22 Hastings, *Bomber Command*, 257.
23 Longmate, *The Bombers*.
24 Longmate, *The Bombers*, 298.
25 Hastings, *Bomber Command*, 268.
26 See Neillands, *The Bomber War*, 301.

Chapter 18: What the British knew

 1 *Times*, Bomb Damage at Essen, March 21, 1942, 3.
 2 Quoted in the *Times*, Bomb Havoc in Germany: Sir Sinclair's Forecast, Ruthless Attacks, August 24, 1942, 2. Similarly, after Cripps's February 25, 1942, speech, Sinclair told a Bristol audience that the "one force which can and will strike hard blows this year and at the very heart of Germany is the Royal Air Force. . . . [When the weather improves] Bomber Command will be ready to carry into Germany destruction on a greater scale than your own beautiful city suffered a year ago." PRO 8/619, "We Must Take Germany by the Throat—and Start in 1942," February 28, 1942.

3 *Times*, RAF Targets in Germany: Comparison of Bombing Damage, January 1, 1943, 8.

4 *Times*, Effects on Bombing Inside Germany: New Propaganda Note, June 21, 1943, 8.

5 Schaffer, *Wings of Judgment*, 69.

6 Schaffer, *Wings of Judgment*, 69.

7 *Daily Sketch*, U-Boat Yard Blazes Night and Day, March 30, 1942.

8 *Times*, Big-Scale Air Offensive Fortresses Bomb Germany, Record RAF Raid on Hamburg. Hamburg Smoke at 24,000 feet, Fires Seen 200 Miles Away, July 29, 1943.

9 PRO AIR 19/189, Letter from William Cantaur to Sinclair, July 9, 1943.

10 PRO AIR 19/189, Letter from Sinclair to the Archbishop of Canterbury, July 19, 1943.

11 *Times*, Fortresses Bomb Germany, Gelsenkirchen and Bonn, Over 20 Fighters Down, August 13, 1943.

12 Jana Flemming, Der Bombenkrieg im Meinungsbild der britischen Öffentlichkeit 1940–1944. In Bernd Heidenreich and Sönke Neitzel (eds.), *Der Bombenkrieg und seine Opfer* (Wiesbaden: Hessische Landeszentrale für politische Bildung, 2004), 21.

13 Jana Flemming, Der Bombenkrieg im Meinungsbild der britischen Öffentlichkeit 1940–1944, 21.

14 Air Commodore Howard Williams, 74,000 Tons of Bombs on Nazis in 100 days, *Daily Telegraph*, October 21, 1943. Copied from PRO AIR 2/7852.

15 PRO AIR 2/7852, Letter from Arthur Harris to the Under Secretary of State, Air Ministry, October 25, 1943.

16 Emphasis added.

17 PRO AIR 2/7852, Letter from Arthur Harris to the Under Secretary of State, Air Ministry, October 25, 1943.

18 PRO AIR 19/189, Letter from A.W. Street to Harris, October 28, 1943.

19 PRO AIR 2/7852, Minute from the Deputy Chief of the Air Staff, Norman Bottomley, to Richard Peck, November 5, 1943.

20 PRO AIR 2/7852, Letter from A.W. Street to Arthur Harris, December 15, 1943.

21 Emphasis in the original.

22 PRO AIR 2/7852, Letter from Harris to the Under Secretary of State, Air Ministry, December 23, 1943.

23 PRO AIR 2/7852, Letter from Harris to the Under Secretary of State, Air Ministry, December 23, 1943.

24 PRO AIR 2/7852, Letter from Air Ministry to Harris, undated.

Chapter 19: Taking out the Luftwaffe

1 Quoted in Davis, *Carl A. Spaatz and the Air War in Europe*, 300.

2 Carl Spaatz papers, Box I: 135, Major General Orvil Anderson, Chief, Strategic Bombing Survey, interviewed by Historical Section, USSTAF, August 22, 1945, 9.

3 Ira Eaker papers, Library of Congress, Washington, DC, Box I: 17, "Text of Cable—Eaker to Arnold," October 15, 1943.

4 Miller, *Masters of the Air,* 247.

5 Carl Spaatz papers, Box I: 137, "Jockey Committee: Its History and Functions," undated.

6 PRO AIR 19/189, Letter from Portal to ACAS (Ops), June 10, 1943.

7 PRO AIR 19/189, Letter from A.W. Street to Portal, October 31, 1943.

8 Miller, *Masters of the Air,* 254.

9 Davis, *Carl A. Spaatz and the Air War in Europe,* 303.

10 Details on Leigh-Mallory from Davis, *Carl A. Spaatz and the Air War in Europe,* 310–312.

11 Quoted in Davis, *Carl A. Spaatz and the Air War in Europe,* 318.

12 Neillands, *The Bomber War,* 290.

13 See clippings in Carl Spaatz papers, Box I: 75.

14 Quoted in Davis, *Carl A. Spaatz and the Air War in Europe,* 318.

15 Miller, *Masters of the Air,* 257.

16 On this, see Davis, *Carl A. Spaatz and the Air War in Europe,* 321.

17 Davis, *Carl A. Spaatz and the Air War in Europe,* 257.

18 Carl Spaatz papers, Box I: 169, "Materiel behind the 'Big Week,'" April 25, 1944.

19 Carl Spaatz papers, Box I: 153, Notes on the Weather Aspects of Strategic Air Force Operations During the Period 20–25 February, 1944.

20 Details from Davis, *Carl A. Spaatz and the Air War in Europe,* 260.

21 Miller, *Masters of the Air,* 256.

22 Miller, *Masters of the Air,* 260.

23 Quoted in Davis, *Carl A. Spaatz and the Air War in Europe,* 323.

24 Carl Spaatz papers, Box I: 169, "The Big Week."

25 Quoted in Davis, *Carl A. Spaatz and the Air War in Europe,* 323.

26 Quoted in Davis, *Carl A. Spaatz and the Air War in Europe,* 323.

27 Speer, *Inside the Third Reich* (1970 ed.).

28 Robert N. Proctor, *Racial Hygiene: Medicine under the Nazis* (Cambridge: Harvard University Press, 1988), 220.

29 Quoted in Fest, *Speer,* 202.

30 Quotations from Fest, *Speer,* 203.

31 Quoted in Speer, *Inside the Third Reich* (1970 ed.), 332.

32 Quoted in Speer, *Inside the Third Reich* (1970 ed.), 332.

33 Quoted in Miller, *Masters of the Air,* 272.

34 Quoted in Miller, *Masters of the Air,* 274.

35 Miller, *Masters of the Air,* 274.

36 Miller, *Masters of the Air,* 274–275.

37 Fest, *Speer,* 213.

Chapter 20: Germany's Achilles' heel

1 Royal Air Force Museum, *The Liberation of Northwest Europe,* Vol. I (London: Royal Air Force Museum Archives), 142.

2 Royal Air Force Museum, *The Liberation of Northwest Europe*, Vol. I, 145.

3 Royal Air Force Museum, *The Liberation of Northwest Europe*, Vol. I, 142.

4 Royal Air Force Museum, *The Liberation of Northwest Europe*, Vol. I, 147.

5 A view that had not changed in more than fifteen years: "The Air Force does not," he said in the late 1920s, "aim to win wars by itself—nor do any of the other services." Royal Air Force Museum, Tedder papers, B 270, Lecture on "Air Power," February 2, 1928.

6 Quoted in Davis, *Carl A. Spaatz and the Air War in Europe*, 349.

7 Details of the meeting from Davis, *Carl A. Spaatz and the Air War in Europe*, 350–353.

8 Quoted in Davis, *Carl A. Spaatz and the Air War in Europe*, 350.

9 PRO AIR 41/66, RAF Narrative, *The Liberation of Northwest Europe*, Vol. I, 154.

10 Quoted in Probert, *Bomber Harris*, 291–292.

11 Carl Spaatz papers, Telegram from Spaatz to Cabell, March 17, 1944.

12 Quoted in Probert, *Bomber Harris*, 291.

13 Middlebrook, *The Bomber Command War Diaries*, 479.

14 Middlebrook, *The Bomber Command War Diaries*, 479.

15 Probert, *Bomber Harris*, 291.

16 Davis, *Carl A. Spaatz and the Air War in Europe*, 353.

17 Carl Spaatz papers, Box I: 136, Interview of General Carl Spaatz by Dr. Bruce C. Hopper, Historian USSTAF, May 20, 1945, 14–15.

18 Quoted in Davis, *Carl A. Spaatz and the Air War in Europe*, 353.

19 Davis, *Carl A. Spaatz and the Air War in Europe*, 354.

20 Parton, *"Air Force Spoken Here,"* 385.

21 Davis, *Carl A. Spaatz and the Air War in Europe*, 386.

22 Richard G. Davis, Spaatz, *Air Force Magazine* (December 2000), 66–73, 72.

23 PRO AIR 8/1229, Extract of Minutes of C.O.S (44) 20th Meeting (o), "Operation Crossbow"—retaliation with gas.

24 PRO AIR 8/1229, War Cabinet, Chiefs of Staff Committee, "Operation Crossbow. Report by the Vice Chiefs of Staff," December 8, 1944.

25 Davis, *Carl A. Spaatz and the Air War in Europe*, 391.

26 Adolf Galland, *The First and the Last: The Rise and Fall of the German Fighter Forces, 1938–1945* (New York: Buccaneer Books, 1954), 209.

27 Galland, *The First and the Last*, 208.

28 Speer, *Inside the Third Reich*, 468.

29 Speer, *Inside the Third Reich*, 469.

30 Davis, *Carl A. Spaatz and the Air War in Europe*, 398.

31 Quoted in Miller, *Masters of the Air*.

32 Details and quotations in the next three paragraphs from Speer, *Inside the Third Reich*, 469–471.

33 Adapted from Speer, *Inside the Third Reich*, 470.

34 Speer, *Inside the Third Reich*, 470.

35 Wesley Frank Craven and James Lea Cate, *The Army Forces in World War II, Volume III: Argument to V-E Day* (Chicago: University of Chicago Press, 1951), 178.

36 Speer, *Inside the Third Reich*, 471.

37 Galland, *The First and the Last*, 208.

38 Galland, *The First and the Last*, 208.

39 Fest, *Speer*, 219.

40 Miller, *Masters of the Air*, 272.

41 Quoted in Galland, *The First and the Last*, 218.

42 Mierzejewski, *The Collapse of the German War Economy*, 185.

Chapter 21: Oil and baby killing

 1 Quoted in Davis, *Carl A. Spaatz and the Air War in Europe*, 399.

 2 Sir Charles Webster and Noble Frankland, *The Strategic Offensive against Germany 1939–1945*, Vol. 3 (London: HMSO, 1961), 47.

 3 F.H. Hinsley, *British Intelligence*, Vol. 3, part 2 (London: HMSO, 1988), 502–503.

 4 Details from Webster and Frankland, *The Strategic Offensive against Germany 1939–1945*, Vol. 3, 47.

 5 Webster and Frankland, *The Strategic Offensive against Germany 1939–1945*, Vol. 3, 47.

 6 Figures from M. Hastings, *Armageddon: The Battle for Germany 1944–45* (London: Macmillan, 2004), 348–349.

 7 Carl Spaatz papers, Library of Congress, Washington, DC, Box I: 135, Verbatim translation of personal report made by Speer to Hitler, June 30, 1944, 3. Emphasis in original.

 8 Both quoted in Davis, *Carl A. Spaatz and the Air War in Europe*, 442.

 9 War Cabinet, Joint Intelligence Sub-Committee, Effects of the Bombing Offensive on the German War Effort, Report by the Joint Intelligence Committee (JIC [44] 241), June 13, 1944.

10 Details from Robert L. Beir, *Roosevelt and the Holocaust* (Fort Lee, NJ: Barricade, 2006), 246.

11 Gilbert, *Auschwitz and the Allies*, 190.

12 Gilbert, *Auschwitz and the Allies*, 232; David S. Wyman, *The Abandonment of the Jews: America and the Holocaust, 1941–1945* (New York: The Free Press, 1984), 290.

13 David S. Wyman, Why Auschwitz Was Never Bombed, *Commentary*, 65, 5 (1978), 37–46, 38; Gilbert, *Auschwitz and the Allies*, 232.

14 Gilbert, *Auschwitz and the Allies*, 233.

15 Quoted in Beir, *Roosevelt and the Holocaust*, 247–248.

16 Wyman, *The Abandonment of the Jews*, 290.

17 Gilbert, *Auschwitz and the Allies*, 238.

18 Gilbert, *Auschwitz and the Allies*, 339.

19 Richard G. Davis, *Bombing the European Axis Powers: A Historical Digest of the Combined Bomber Offensive, 1939–1945* (Maxwell, AL: Air University Press, 2006), 407–408.

20 Davis, *Bombing the European Axis Powers*, 406.

21 Miller, *Masters of the Air*, 323.

22 Davis, *Bombing the European Axis Powers*, 403.

23 Miller, *Masters of the Air*, 324.

24 Details of this paragraph from Gilbert, *Auschwitz and the Allies*, chapter 28.

25 Quotations from Gilbert, *Auschwitz and the Allies*, 270.

26 Quotations from Gilbert, *Auschwitz and the Allies*, 272.

27 Quotations from Gilbert, *Auschwitz and the Allies*, 279.

28 Quotations from Gilbert, *Auschwitz and the Allies*, 285.

29 Quoted in Beir, *Roosevelt and the Holocaust*, 248.

30 Quoted in Beir, *Roosevelt and the Holocaust*, 251.

31 Gilbert, *Auschwitz and the Allies*, 301.

32 Gilbert, *Auschwitz and the Allies*, 309.

33 Wyman, *The Abandonment of the Jews*, 300.

34 Gilbert, *Auschwitz and the Allies*, 303.

35 Wyman, *The Abandonment of the Jews*, 300.

36 Miller, *Masters of the Air*, 327.

37 Quoted in Miller, *Masters of the Air*, 327.

38 Letter from Shalom Lindenbaum to Martin Gilbert, June 13, 1980, quoted in Gilbert, *Auschwitz and the Allies*, 311.

39 PRO 14/3507, Letter from Harris to the prime minister, June 17, 1942.

40 PRO AIR 8/1229, Flying Bomb Statement by the prime minister, undated. Also see PRO AIR 8/1229, Attack on German Civilian Morale, August 1, 1944.

41 PRO PREM 3/4/2, Minute from Portal to Churchill, June 20, 1944.

42 PRO AIR 8/1229, Minute VCAS 1803, VCAS to CAS, subj: Crossbow, July 2, 1944.

43 PRO AIR 8/199, War Cabinet, Chiefs of Staff Committee, "Crossbow": Question of Retaliation, July 5, 1944.

44 PRO AIR 19/189, Letter to CAS, December 29, 1943.

45 PRO AIR 8/1229, Bombing of German Towns in Retaliation for Flying Bomb Attacks: Appendix A, July 1, 1944.

46 PRO AIR 8/1229, Bombing of German Towns in Retaliation for Flying Bomb Attacks, July 1, 1944.

47 PRO AIR 8/1229, Minute VCAS 1803, VCAS to CAS, subj: Crossbow, July 2, 1944.

48 PRO AIR 8/1229, "Crossbow": Question of Retaliation, July 5, 1944.

49 It is possible, but impossible to prove, that his reading of the Auschwitz protocols may have influenced his belligerent attitude. I owe this point to Richard Davis.

50 Davis, *Carl A. Spaatz and the Air War in Europe*, 433.

51 PRO AIR 8/1229, Note from Portal to Deputy Chief of Air Staff, July 5, 1944.

52 PRO AIR 8/199, War Cabinet, Chiefs of Staff Committee, "Crossbow": Question of Retaliation, July 5, 1944.

53 PRO AIR 8/199, War Cabinet, Chiefs of Staff Committee, "Crossbow": Question of Retaliation, July 5, 1944.

54 PRO AIR 20/4831, Operation Thunderclap, undated.

55 Schaffer, *Wings of Judgment*, 75.

56 Quotations from Schaffer, *Wings of Judgment*, 78.

57 Davis, *Carl A. Spaatz and the Air War in Europe*, 438.

58 Details in this paragraph from Webster and Frankland, *The Strategic Offensive against Germany 1939–1945*, Vol. 3, 50.

59 Andreas Förschler, *Unser Stuttgart geht unter: Die Bombenangriffe im Juli und September 1944* (Wiesenthal: Wartberg Verlag, 2004), 25–36.

60 PRO AIR 8/1229, War Cabinet, Chiefs of Staff Committee, An Attack on German Civilian Morale, Memorandum by the Chief of Air Staff, August 1, 1944. Also see PRO AIR 20/4831, Attack on German Civilian Morale, July 17, 1944.

61 PRO AIR 20/4831, COS (44) 650 (O), Attack on German Civilian Morale, August 2, 1944.

62 PRO AIR 20/4831, Operation Thunderclap, undated.

63 PRO AIR 8/1229, Attack on German Civilian Morale, August 1, 1944.

64 PRO AIR 20/4831, Draft D.B.Ops comments on Attack on the German Government Machine, Outline Plan by Joint Planning Staff J.P (44)203(O). Revised preliminary draft, August 15, 1944.

65 Hastings, *Bomber Command*, 301.

66 Miller, *Masters of the Air*, 412.

67 Miller, *Masters of the Air*, 412.

68 Carl Spaatz papers, Box I: 153, Letter from Maj. General L.S. Kuter to Maj. General Frederick L. Anderson, August 15, 1944.

69 Carl Spaatz papers, Box I: 153, Letter from Maj. General L.S. Kuter to Maj. General Frederick L. Anderson, August 15, 1944.

70 Carl Spaatz papers, Box I: 135, Interview with Brig. Gen. Cabell, July 9, 1944.

71 Quoted in Schaffer, *Wings of Judgment*, 83.

72 Carl Spaatz papers, Diary, Box I: 15, Letter from Spaatz to Arnold, August 21, 1944.

73 Schaffer, *Wings of Judgment*, 61–62.

74 Carl Spaatz papers, Box I: 135, Memorandum from Arnold to General F.L. Anderson, September 12, 1944.

75 Carl Spaatz papers, Box I: 153, C.P. Cabell, Attacks for Demoralization of the German People, June 26, 1944.

76 Carl Spaatz papers, Box I: 153, Plan for Systematically Attacking Morale within Germany, September 18, 1944.

77 PRO AIR 8/1229, Minute from the prime minister to the Chiefs of Staff, August 23, 1944.

78 Carl Spaatz papers, Diary, Box I: 15, Daily Summary of Intelligence, August 18, 1944.

79 Webster and Frankland, *The Strategic Offensive against Germany 1939–1945*, Vol. 3, 50.

80 Carl Spaatz papers, Subject File 1929–1945, Memo from Anderson to director of operations, July 21, 1944.

81 Davis, *Carl A. Spaatz and the Air War in Europe*, 435.

82 Details from Walter Gilbert's journal, sent to the author by his granddaughter, Michelle L. Gilbert, September 13, 2007.

83 Davis, *Carl A. Spaatz and the Air War in Europe*, 443.

84 Details in the next remaining paragraphs from Speer, *Inside the Third Reich*, 546–547.

85 Speer, *Inside the Third Reich*, 547.

86 Tooze, *The Wages of Destruction*, 560.

Chapter 22: Harris's and Spaatz's orders

1 Davis, *Carl A. Spaatz and the Air War in Europe*, 511.

2 Hastings, *Armageddon*, chapter 2.

3 Davis, *Carl A. Spaatz and the Air War in Europe*, 512.

4 See the thoughtful discussion by Hastings, *Armageddon*, chapter 3.

5 Hastings, *Armageddon*, 99.

6 Hastings, *Armageddon*, 99–100.

7 Quotation and paragraph from Miller, *Masters of the Air*, 364–365.

8 Neillands, *The Bomber War*, 338.

9 Details on the bombing from Peter Engels, Darmstadts Zerstörung aus der Luft. In Bernd Heidenreich and Sönke Neitzel (eds.), *Der Bombenkrieg und seine Opfer* (Wiesbaden: Hessische Landeszentrale für politische Bildung, 2004), 47–57. Also see Hastings, *Bomber Command*.

10 Quoted in Engels, Darmstadts Zerstörung aus der Luft, 47–57.

11 Miller, *Masters of the Air*, 439.

12 Neillands, *The Bomber War*, 338.

13 PRO AIR 14/3507, Letter from Harris to Churchill, September 30, 1944. See also PRO AIR 20/4832, Weekly GAF Priority Signal, August 31, 1944, and A Counter Air Force Program for the Period from Now until the German Collapse, [U.S. Embassy], October 24, 1944.

14 Davis, *Bombing the European Axis Powers*, 437.

15 Middlebrook, *The Bomber Command War Diaries*, 602.

16 Figures from Davis, *Bombing the European Axis Powers*, 466–470.

17 Quoted in Davis, *Bombing the European Axis Powers*, 446.

18 Portal papers, Harris correspondence 1944, No. 32, Letter from Harris to Portal, November 1, 1944.

19 Tami Davis Biddle, *Rhetoric and Reality in Air Warfare* (Princeton, NJ: Princeton University Press, 2002), 248.

20 LTR, Spaatz to Arnold, November 5, 1944, Spaatz papers, Diary. Quoted in Davis, *Carl A. Spaatz and the Air War in Europe*, 519.

21 Davis, *Carl A. Spaatz and the Air War in Europe*, 519.

22 PRO AIR 20/4832, Memorandum by Wing Commander D.S. Allen, October 26, 1944.

23 Details in the next two paragraphs from Davis, *Carl A. Spaatz and the Air War in Europe*, 521.

24 Middlebrook, *The Bomber Command War Diaries*, 612.

25 Middlebrook, *The Bomber Command War Diaries*, 613.

26 Portal papers, Letter from Portal to Harris, November 6, 1944, 32a.

27 Stadtarchiv Solingen, *Solingen im Bombenhagel: 4. und 5. November 1944* (Wiesenthal: Wartberg Verlag, 2003).

28 Portal papers, Letter from Harris to Portal, November 6, 1944, 32g.

29 Middlebrook, *The Bomber Command War Diaries*, 583; Neillands, *The Bomber War*, 326–327.

30 Middlebrook, *The Bomber Command War Diaries*, 614.

31 Thus, the December 6–7 raid on Giessen allocated 87 aircraft to the railway yards

but 168 to the town center, and the December 21–22 raid only devoted one-third of the bombing force to Ploesti; the other two-thirds bombed Cologne and Bonn.

32 Portal papers, Letter from Harris to Portal, November 12, 1944, 32c. Emphasis added.

33 Portal papers, Letter from Portal to Harris, November 6, 1944, 32g.

34 Emphasis in the original.

35 "Designating" in the original, likely a typo.

36 Biddle, *Rhetoric and Reality in Air Warfare*, 247.

37 Portal papers, Letter from Harris to Portal, November 24, 1944.

38 Ulrich P. Ecker, *Freiburg 1944–1994: Zerstörung und Wiederaufbau* (Freiburg: Stadtarchiv, 1994).

39 Figures from Davis, *Bombing the European Axis Powers*, 467.

40 Herbert Bläsi and Christhard Schrenk, *Leben und Sterben einer Stadt* (Heilbronn: Stadtarchiv Heilbronn, 1995), 85.

41 Middlebrook, *The Bomber Command War Diaries*, 627.

42 Details from Erich Lacker, *Zielort Karlsruhe: Die Luftangriffe im Zweiten Weltkrieg* (Karlsruhe: Badenia Verlag, 1996).

43 Portal papers, Letter from Portal to Harris, December 6, 1944, 36a.

Chapter 23: Portal pleads

1 Ian Kershaw, *Hitler, 1889–1936: A Study in Hubris* (London: W.W. Norton & Company, 1998), 741.

2 Speer, *Inside the Third Reich*, 555.

3 Speer, *Inside the Third Reich*, 556.

4 Quoted in Fest, *Speer*, 239.

5 Kershaw, *Hitler, 1889–1936*, 742.

6 Kershaw, *Hitler, 1889–1936*, 742.

7 Alfred C. Mierzejewski, When Did Albert Speer Give Up? *Historical Journal*, 31, 2 (1988), 391–397.

8 Quotations from Speer, *Inside the Third Reich*, 556.

9 Kershaw, *Hitler, 1889–1936*, 742.

10 Davis, *Carl A. Spaatz and the Air War in Europe*, 532.

11 Davis, *Carl A. Spaatz and the Air War in Europe*, 532.

12 Probert, *Bomber Harris*, 314.

13 Fest, *Speer*, 239.

14 Miller, *Masters of the Air*, 373.

15 Miller, *Masters of the Air*, 372.

16 Hastings, *Armageddon*, 271.

17 Miller, *Masters of the Air*, 372.

18 Speer, *Inside the Third Reich*, 240.

19 Quotations from Kershaw, *Hitler, 1889–1936*, 744.

20 Quoted in Fest, *Speer*, 240.

21 Miller, *Masters of the Air*, 372.

22 Speer, *Inside the Third Reich*, 560.

23 Quotations from Miller, *Masters of the Air,* 373.

24 Galland, *The First and the Last,* 243.

25 Miller, *Masters of the Air,* 374.

26 Galland, *The First and the Last,* 243.

27 Carl Spaatz papers, Box I: 135, Combined Intelligence Objectives Sub-Committee: Interrogation of Albert Speer—Former Minister for Armaments and War Production, 5, 14, Library of Congress, Washington, DC. Emphasis in original.

28 Hastings, *Armageddon,* 276.

29 Portal papers, Letter from Harris to Portal, December 12, 1944.

30 Emphasis added.

31 Portal papers, Letter from Portal to Harris, December 22, 1944.

32 Portal papers, Letter from Harris to Portal, December 28, 1944.

Chapter 24: Speer despairs, Harris threatens, Portal blinks

1 Speer, *Inside the Third Reich,* 560.

2 Middlebrook, *The Bomber Command War Diaries,* 649.

3 Portal papers, Letter from Portal to Harris, January 8, 1945.

4 Friedrich, *The Fire,* 306. Alfred Heidelmayer gives a higher, and probably exaggerated, figure of sixteen thousand. See Heidelmayer, Magdeburg 1945: Zwischen Zerstörung und Kriegsende. Ein Bericht. In Matthias Puhle (ed.), *Dann färbte sich der Himmel blutrot . . .* (Magdeburg: Grafisches Zentrum, Calbe, 1995) [Exhibition in the Museum for Cultural History, Magdeburg, January–May 1995].

5 Portal papers, Letter from Harris to Portal, January 18, 1945. On January 9, probably before receiving Portal's January 8 letter (it addresses none of the points Portal raised), Harris sent him a letter concerning the shortage of high explosives. See Portal papers, Letter from Harris to Portal, January 9, 1945; for the reply, Letter from Portal to Harris, January 27, 1945.

6 Emphasis in the original.

7 Emphasis in the original.

8 Emphasis added to the last sentence.

9 Emphasis added.

10 Portal papers, Letter from Portal to Harris, January 20, 1945.

11 Hastings, *Armageddon,* 352.

Chapter 25: American area bombing

1 Quoted in Miller, *Masters of the Air,* 424.

2 Quotations and story from Miller, *Masters of the Air,* 424–425.

3 On the last, see Erik Smit et al., *3. Februar 1945: Die Zerstörung Kreuzbergs aus der Luft* (Berlin: Kunstamt Kreuzberg, 1995).

4 Miller, *Masters of the Air,* 425.

5 Hans-Georg von Studnitz, *While Berlin Burns* (London: Weidenfeld and Nicolson, 1964), 243.

6 John Briol, *Dead Engine Kids: World War II Diary of John J. Briol, B-17 Ball Turret Gunner* (Rapid City, SD: Silver Wings Aviation, 1993), 181.

7 Quoted in Miller, *Masters of the Air,* 427.

8 Quoted in Miller, *Masters of the Air,* 427.

9 Quotations from Miller, *Masters of the Air,* 427.

10 PRO AIR 41, The RAF in the Bombing Offensive against Germany (official narrative), Vol. VI, 198.

11 PRO AIR 41, The RAF in the Bombing Offensive against Germany (official narrative), Vol. VI, 198.

12 Miller, *Masters of the Air,* 413.

13 PRO AIR 41, The RAF in the Bombing Offensive against Germany (official narrative), Vol. VI, 198–199.

14 Webster and Frankland, *The Strategic Offensive against Germany 1939–1945,* Vol. 3, 100.

15 PRO AIR 41, The RAF in the Bombing Offensive against Germany (official narrative), Vol. VI, 199.

16 Webster and Frankland, *The Strategic Offensive against Germany 1939–1945,* Vol. 3, 101.

17 Quoted in Dudley Saward, *Bomber Harris: The Story of Marshal of the Royal Air Force, Sir Arthur Harris* (Garden City, NY: Doubleday, 1985), 283. Emphasis added.

18 Quotations from Frederick Taylor, *Dresden: Tuesday, February 13, 1945* (London: Bloomsbury, 2004), 185–186.

19 Quoted in Miller, *Masters of the Air,* 415.

20 Carl Spaatz papers, Box I: 40, Telegram from Doolittle to Spaatz, January 30, 1945.

21 Davis, *Bombing the European Axis Powers,* 493.

22 Miller, *Masters of the Air,* 416.

23 Miller, *Masters of the Air,* 416.

24 Miller, *Masters of the Air,* 419.

25 Carl Spaatz papers, Box I: 41, Telegram from Doolittle to Spaatz, February 2, 1945.

26 Carl Spaatz papers, Box I: 41, Telegram from Doolittle to Spaatz, February 2, 1945. Spaatz's handwritten note about the telephone conversation can be found at the bottom of the telegram.

27 Details of the raid found in Taylor, *Dresden,* chapters 19–22.

28 Quoted in Miller, *Masters of the Air,* 433.

29 PRO AIR 41, The RAF in the Bombing Offensive against Germany (official narrative), Vol. VI, 225.

30 PRO AIR 41, The RAF in the Bombing Offensive against Germany (official narrative), Vol. VI, 225.

31 Quoted in PRO AIR 41, The RAF in the Bombing Offensive against Germany (official narrative), Vol. VI, 225; Davis, *Bombing the European Axis Powers,* 531.

32 PRO AIR 41, The RAF in the Bombing Offensive against Germany (official narrative), Vol. VI, 225.

33 Middlebrook, *The Bomber Command War Diaries,* 673.

34 Middlebrook, *The Bomber Command War Diaries,* 673.

35 Carl Spaatz papers, Box I: 170, General Plan for Maximum Effort Attack against Transportation Objectives, December 17, 1944.

36 Miller, *Masters of the Air*, 441.
37 Carl Spaatz papers, Box I: 170, General Plan for Maximum Effort Attack against Transportation Objectives, December 17, 1944.
38 Quoted in Schaffer, *Wings of Judgment*, 92.
39 Carl Spaatz papers, Box I: 40, Telegram from Eaker to Spaatz, February 22, 1945.
40 Carl Spaatz papers, Box I: 40, Telegram from F.L. Anderson to Spaatz, February 22, 1945.
41 Carl Spaatz papers, Box I: 170, Headquarters, United States Strategic Air Forces in Europe, Office of the Director of Intelligence, Study of Results Achieved by Operation Clarion, undated.

Chapter 26: A crescendo of destruction

1 Details of raids taken from PRO AIR 41, The RAF in the Bombing Offensive against Germany (official narrative), Vol. VI, 225–226.
2 PRO AIR 19/189, Letter from Harris to Bottomley, December 28, 1943.
3 D.W. Rockenmaier, *Als vom Himmel Feuer fiel: So starb das alte Würzburg* (Würzburg: Fränkische Gesellschaftsdruckerei, 1995).
4 A loose translation of *"Starker Kampfverband im Anflug auf unsere Stadt. Luftschutzmässiges Verhalten ist dringend erforderlich!"*
5 Herbert Oechsner heard two stories about his mother's fate. This version was told to him at the time by someone at the clinic, possibly an orderly. Decades later, he met the daughter of a woman who was at the scene, and she claimed that his mother was among the bodies. Mr. Osner regards her account as somewhat unreliable and, given the difficulty in recognizing the bodies at the time, the woman may have mistaken someone else for his mother.
6 K.F. Bauer, *Würzburg im Feuerofen* (Würzburg: Echter Verlag, 1985), 20.
7 K.M. Höynck and E. Schellenbeger (eds.), *Erinnerungen an Würzburgs Schicksalstag und das Ende des Krieges* (Würzburg: Bayerischer Rundfunk, 2005), 26.
8 The next two sentences are based on a report by Karl-Heinz Wirsing, mailed to the author on June 17, 2005.
9 C. Kucklick, *Feuersturm: Der Bombenkrieg gegen Deutschland* (Hamburg: GEO, 2003).
10 PRO AIR 14/3412, Bomber Command Night Raid Report No. 867, March 16–17, 1945.

Chapter 27: Doubts

1 Schaffer, *Wings of Judgment*, 99.
2 PRO AIR 41, The RAF in the Bombing Offensive against Germany (official narrative), Vol. VI, 202.
3 *Parliamentary Debates (Commons)*, vol. 408, March 6, 1945.
4 Story found in Taylor, *Dresden*, 364.
5 Taylor, *Dresden*, 373.
6 PRO CAB 121/3, Bombing Policy in Europe, March 28, 1945.
7 Quoted in Probert, *Bomber Harris*, 322.
8 On this, see Taylor, *Dresden*.

9   On this, see Miller, *Masters of the Air,* 436.

10   Middlebrook, *The Bomber Command War Diaries,* 696.

Chapter 28: As the last bombs fell

1   Tony Vaccaro, *Entering Germany 1944–1949* (Cologne: Taschen, 2001).

2   A.J.P. Taylor, *English History: 1914–1945* (Oxford: Oxford University Press, 1992), 592.

3   Gitta Sereny, *Albert Speer: His Battle with the Truth* (London: Knopf, 1995), 708. Also see Volker Ullrich, Speers Erfindung, *Die Zeit,* May 4, 2005.

4   Quoted in Miller, *Masters of the Air,* 420.

5   Jules Horowitz, My Air War: North Africa–Italy (unpublished diary). I am grateful to Mr. Horowitz for sending this to me.

6   See Tony Judt, *Postwar: A History of Europe since 1945* (New York: Penguin Press, 2005), 354–359.

7   Gavin Mortimer, *The Longest Night: The Bombing of London on May 10, 1941* (New York: Berkley Caliber, 2005), 320.

8   In 1962, the West German Ministry for expellees, refugees, and those suffering war damage arrived at a death toll of 593,000, including 410,000 resident German civilians, 32,000 foreign civilians or prisoners of war, 23,000 members of the German Army or police, and 128,000 German refugees from the eastern territories. Gunnar Heinson, *Lexikon der Völkermorde* (Hamburg: Rowohlt Tb, 1998), 115. These estimates include the lower 35,000 figure for Dresden.

Chapter 29: Conclusion

1   Both quotations from Miller, *Masters of the Air,* 416.

2   The Economic Effects of the Air Offensive against German cities, *The United States Strategic Bombing Survey* (New York: Garland Publishing, 1976), 9.

3   Webster and Frankland, *Strategic Air Offensive against Germany 1939–1945,* Vol. 3, 44.

4   Carl Spaatz papers, Box I: 135, Combined Intelligence Objectives Sub-Committee: Interrogation of Albert Speer—Former Minister for Armaments and War Production, 5, 14, Library of Congress, Washington, DC, 7.

5   Carl Spaatz papers, Box I: 146, COA Memorandum for Lt. General Arnold, March 8, 1943.

6   Carl Spaatz papers, Box I: 145, Revision of Basic Study "Report of the Committee of Operations Analysts," March 8, 1943.

7   See for instance PRO AIR 19/189, Letter from A.W. Street to Portal, October 31, 1943, and Minute from Chief of Air Staff, February 7, 1944.

8   Miller, *Masters of the Air,* 438.

9   Lowe, *Inferno,* 333.

10   Miller, *Masters of the Air,* 439.

11   Schaffer, *Wings of Judgment,* 103.

12   Helmut Schnatz, Die Zerstörung der deutschen Städte und die Opfer. In Bernd Heidenreich and Sönke Neitzel (eds.), *Der Bombenkrieg und seine Opfer* (Wiesbaden: Hessische Landeszentrale für politische Bildung, 2004).

13 Davis, *Bombing the European Axis Powers*, 575.

14 *The Strategic Air War Against Germany 1939–1945: Report of the British Bombing Survey Unit* (London: Frank Cass, 1998), 58–60; Davis, *Bombing the European Axis Powers*, 571–574.

15 Davis, *Bombing the European Axis Powers*, 571.

16 Portal papers, Letter from Harris to Portal, January 18, 1945.

17 Miller, *Masters of the Air*, 438.

18 Davis, *Bombing the European Axis Powers*, 571.

19 Schaffer, *Wings of Judgment*, 65.

20 Quotation and details in the last paragraph from Shaffer, *Wings of Judgment*, 50.

21 See Davis, *Bombing the European Axis Powers*, 418–435.

22 See, for instance, Würzburg Stadtarchiv, Karl Zimmermann, Am Main, auf der Feste, August 18, 1949. In a similar vein, Dean Schadewitz of the St. Stephans-Notkirche made no reference to the Jews in his sermon for the victims of the bombing on its first anniversary. See Würzburg Stadtarchiv, Brüder und Schwestern unter dem Kreuz. Gadächtnisgottesdienste in den evangelischen Kirchen, March 18, 1949, and Würzburg Stadtarchiv, Ich sah einen neuen Himmel und eine neue Erde, March 15, 1949.

23 Susanne Eckelmann and Cord Pagenstecher, *Zwangsarbeit in Berlin 1940–1945* (Erfurt: Sutton Verlag, 2000), 64.

24 Gunnar Heinson, *Lexikon der Völkermorde* (Hamburg: Rowohlt Tb, 1998), 115.

25 Overy, *The Air War*, 122.

26 A. Harris, *Despatch on War Operations 23rd February, 1942 to 8th May, 1945* (London: Frank Cass, 1995), 33–38; Biddle, *Rhetoric and Reality in Air Warfare*, 282.

27 Gerd-Ulrich Herrmann, *Von der Schulbank in den Krieg* (Seelow: Gedenkstätte Seelower Hoehen, 2006).

28 Carl Spaatz papers, B 135: U.S. Strategic Bombing Survey, APO 413, Interview with Dr. Tank, President, Focke-Wulf Aircraft Co., May 19, 1945.

29 Overy, *The Air War*, 123.

30 The Economic Effects of the Air Offensive against German Cities, 8–12.

31 The point is even stronger if one accepts a recent line of argument that holds that the Allies' great material advantages vis-à-vis Germany made defeat far more likely than not. See Tooze, *The Wages of Destruction*.

32 Ira Eaker papers, Box I: 17, The American Bombing Report: The United States Air Force Strikes Hard in Europe, September 4, 1943. Also see Memo from Alfred R. Maxwell, Director of Operations, February 18, 1945.

33 Carl Spaatz papers, Box I: 135, Combined Intelligence Objectives Sub-Committee: Interrogation of Albert Speer—Former Minister for Armaments and War Production, 7–8.

34 Carl Spaatz papers, Box I: 136, Interview of Robert A. Lovett by Dr. Bruce C. Hopper, June 7, 1945.

35 Carl Spaatz papers, Box I: 135, Combined Intelligence Objectives Sub-Committee: Interrogation of Albert Speer—Former Minister for Armaments and War Production, 10.

36 PRO AIR 20/4299, Note on the Role and Work of Bomber Command, June 28, 1942.

37 Davis, *Bombing the European Axis Powers*, 567–569.

38 Biddle, *Rhetoric and Reality in Air Warfare*, 251.

39 Carl Spaatz papers, Box I: 135, United States Strategic Bombing Survey, APO 143, Minutes of a Meeting with Reichsminister Albert Speer, May 19, 1945, 3.

40 PRO AIR 41, The RAF in the Bombing Offensive against Germany (official narrative), Vol. VI, 209.

41 Though there might have been more cloud cover by day than by night. A more detailed study of historical weather reports would be needed to establish or refute this point.

42 Carl Spaatz papers, Box I: 135, Combined Intelligence Objectives Sub-Committee: Interrogation of Albert Speer—Former Minister for Armaments and War Production, 3. Emphasis in original.

43 For a critical discussion of the production miracle, see Tooze, *The Wages of Destruction*, chapter 17.

44 Carl Spaatz papers, Box I: 135, Combined Intelligence Objectives Sub-Committee: Interrogation of Albert Speer—Former Minister for Armaments and War Production, 2.

45 *The Strategic Air War against Germany 1939–1945*, 58–60.

46 Harris's view was neither unique nor new. As Tedder put it in the late 1920s: "As the bombers used for the offensive are not readily interchangeable with the fighters used for the defence, and in fact cannot be efficiently used for defensive purposes, the demand for a stronger defence cannot be immediately met unless there are fighters available to be drawn from other theatres of war. Ultimately to strengthen the defences one must weaken the offence, and in such a way that it cannot quickly and easily be strengthened again. We can only increase the number of fighters by devoting a greater part of our available resources to the construction and manning of fighters in place of bombers." *Royal Air Force Museum*, Tedder Papers, B 270, Lecture on "Air Power," 6th lecture, February 2, 1928.

47 Interview with RAF pilot Sidney "Tom" Wingham, Bury-St.-Edmunds, May 5, 2003.

48 As suggested by Taylor, *Dresden*, 403.

49 Quoted in Taylor, *Dresden*, 362.

50 Thus, in October 1943, the Air Ministry urged the destruction of Augsburg, Brunswick, Gotha, Kassel, and Leipzig as centers of the German aircraft industry. PRO AIR 20/4832, Memorandum on Extent to which the Eight USAAF and Bomber Command have been able to implement the GAF Plan and on further measures for its execution, October 7, 1943. Even here, however, Air Staff complained that Hamburg and Berlin, which Harris was bombing, had little to do with the German Air Force and suggested that precision bombing again be attempted. See PRO AIR 20/4832, Note: the Bomber Offensive, September 30, 1943.

51 See D. Richards, Introduction. In A. Harris, *Bomber Offensive* (London: Greenhill Books, 1998).

52 Cox, Introduction. In Harris, *Despatch on War Operations 23rd February, 1942 to 8th May, 1945*, xii.

53 Quoted in Cox, Introduction. In Harris, *Despatch on War Operations 23rd February, 1942 to 8th May, 1945*, xii. Emphasis added. See also Sir Charles Webster and Noble Frankland, *The Strategic War Offensive against Germany 1939–1945*, Vol. 4 (London: HMSO, 1961), Appendix 8, Document xxii, 144.

54 PRO Directive, Air Vice-Marshal Bottomley to Air Marshal JEA Baldwin, London, February 23, 1942. Emphasis added.

55 Cox, Introduction. In Harris, *Despatch on War Operations 23rd February, 1942 to 8th May, 1945*, xii.

56 PRO AIR 19/189, Letter from A.W. Street to Churchill, October 28, 1943.

57 *Royal Air Force Museum*, Tedder Papers, B 270, Lecture on "RAF Staff Organization," RAF Staff College, 9th lecture, June 15, 1931.

58 *Royal Air Force Museum*, Tedder Papers, B 270, Lecture on "RAF Staff Organization," RAF Staff College, 9th lecture, June 15, 1931.

59 Carl Spaatz papers, Box I: 136, Letter from Arnold to Doolittle, August 2, 1944, and Letter from Arnold to Spaatz, August 14, 1944.

60 PRO AIR 20/438, German Cities Closely Related to GAF Fighter Assembly Plants, September 14, 1943.

61 See PRO AIR 19/189, Letter from Bottomley to Harris, December 23, 1943 (quoted above). Also see Davis, *Bombing the European Axis Powers*, 275.

62 PRO AIR 19/189, Letter from the Air Staff to the Secretary of State, January 19, 1944.

63 Harris, *Bomber Offensive*, 220.

SELECTED BIBLIOGRAPHY

PRIMARY SOURCES

1 Interviews and eyewitness reports
Alfred Abels, DFC (RAF 102 Squadron)
Günther Ackerhans (Berlin)
Karl-Heinz Alfeis (Hamburg)
Ruth Arloth (Lübeck)
Egon Asmus (Lübeck)
Wolfgang Bardorf (Berlin)
Günther Becker (Lübeck)
Else Birth (Essen)
Irmgard Blomberg (Wuppertal)
Gerhard Böhmer (Flak Helper, Berlin)
Auguste Brandt (Mülheim an der Ruhr)
Elke Brandt (Mülheim an der Ruhr)
Renate Brockmüller (Lübeck)
Udo Bungert (Mülheim an der Ruhr)
Anneliese Burger (Essen)
Detlev Burghardt (Dresden)
Sybille Cappius (Essen)
Oktavia Christ (Hamburg)
John B. Daniels (450th Bomb Group, Fifteenth Air Force)
Robert A. Davis (450th Bomb Group, Fifteenth Air Force)
Rita Deichmann (Lübeck)
Gottfried Elfes (Krefeld)
Johann Engels (Essen)
Kurt-Rolf Enters (Wuppertal)
Gertrud Everding (Hamburg)
Erich Felgenhauer (Würzburg)

Franz Ferring (Würzburg)
Roland Flade (Würzburg)
Helmut Försch (Würzburg)
Karl Heinz Gersch (Essen)
Heinrich Giesecke (Würzburg)
Walter F. Gilbert (450th Bomb Group, Fifteenth Air Force)
Walter Grave (Essen/Dresden)
Ernst-Günther Haberland (Hamburg)
Edith Hahn (Hamburg)
Christel Hansen (Mönkhagen)
Hans Heer (Würzburg)
Mrs. Heissing (Essen)
Rolf Hering (Lübeck)
Gertraud Herrmann (Lübeck)
Emmie Heuser (Sprockhövel)
Gerhard Hickmann (Mülheim an der Ruhr)
Horst Hirche (Flak Helper, Berlin)
Hildegard Högner (Essen)
Volker Holtmann (Lübeck)
Martin Honecker (Würzburg)
Paul Huben (Mühlheim an der Ruhr)
Ursula Huben (Mühlheim an der Ruhr)
Harry Hughes, DFC, DFM (RAF 102 Squadron)
Hedi Irle (Essen)
Hermann Josef-Baum (Düsseldorf)
Marlies Jung (Krefeld)
Ernst Kahlbaü (Berlin)
Wolfgang Kämmerling (Krefeld)
Elly Kammermeier (Würzburg)
Christal Kausen (Lübeck)
Ruth Klaus (Essen)
Hans-Georg Kleine-Limberg (Essen)
Hildegard Klemm (Dresden)
Wilbur Klint (303rd Bomb Group, Eighth Air Force)
Peter Koch (Würzburg)
Mrs. Koglin (Berlin/Potsdam)
Heinz Kretzer (Würzburg)
Gisela Kretzschmar (Mülheim an der Ruhr)
Volker Kuhlwein (Hamburg)
Gisela Kundt (Essen)
Manfed Kunze (Bad Oeynhausen)
Friedhelm van Laak (Dinslaken)
Gehard Lange (Hamburg)
Friedhelm Ludwig (Essen)
Carmen Lyken (Krefeld)

Stefan Mehren (Berlin)
Julia Meseck (Essen)
Theo Michell (forced laborer, Würzburg)
Hans-Werner Mihan (Potsdam)
Alwine Mismahl (Essen)
Ursula Mohnke (Berlin)
Ursula Müller (Essen)
Karl-Heinz Nissen (Lübeck)
Herbert Osner (formerly Oechsner, Würzburg)
Hans Pauels (Aachen)
Hermann Paus (Essen)
Mr. Pfeil (Wuppertal)
Helga Pfromm (Lübeck)
Stefan Pick (Cologne)
Hildegard Plum (Düsseldorf)
Jack Pragnell (RAF 102 Squadron)
Wilfried Reichert (Essen)
Robert Reichlin (son of Matthew A. Reichlin, U.S. Fifteenth Air Force)
Ellen Reinhart (Essen)
Christa Renken (Hamburg)
Marianne Richter (Würzburg)
Horst Riewer (Mülheim an der Ruhr)
Maria Rotermund (Wülfrath)
Margarete Röttinger (Würzburg)
Horst Rübenkamp (Mülheim an der Ruhr)
Eleonore Rudolph (Hamburg)
Werner Schenk (Berlin)
Fritz Schleede (Hamburg)
Gusti Schmitt (Würzburg)
Ruth Schomaker (Essen)
Lisa Schomberg (Hamburg)
Gerda Schroeder (Wuppertal)
Otti Schultz (Cologne)
Anita Schwarte (Essen)
Kurt Segering (Essen)
Elfriede Sindel (Hamburg)
Hans Smits (Krefeld)
Anne-Gerd Smola (Mülheim an der Ruhr)
Edith Stampe (Hamburg)
Sigrid Strauss (Lübeck)
Hilde Stringer (Essen)
Gertrud Türk (Cologne)
Rudolf Vetter (Flak Helper, Berlin)
Beke Wagner (Hamburg)
Heino Weiss (Lübeck)

Helmut Wender (Essen)
Werner Wendland (Würzburg)
Heinrich Weppert (Würzburg)
Paul Werner (Essen)
Hannelore Will (Essen)
Richard Wilson (RAF 102 Squadron)
Sidney "Tom" Wingham (RAF 102 Squadron)
Karl-Heinz Wirsing (Würzburg)
Gerd Woldeit (Essen)
Horst Zimmermann (Berlin)
Gertrud Zimner (Essen)
Paul Zsigmond (Mülheim an der Ruhr)

2   *Archives (cited documents)*
GREAT BRITAIN
Christ Church, Oxford
The Private Papers of Sir Charles Portal

Churchill College, Cambridge
Sydney Bufton papers
Winston Churchill papers
Sir Arthur Harris papers

Nuffield College, Oxford
Lord Cherwell papers

Public Record Office (National Archives), London
AIR 2
AIR 8
AIR 14
AIR 19
AIR 20
AIR 25
AIR 40
AIR 41
CAB 121
PREM 3

The Royal Air Force Museum, London
Sir Arthur Tedder papers

GERMANY
Cologne city archive
Police reports, 1939–1945

Federal Archives of Germany (Bundesarchiv), Koblenz
Photo collection

Hamburg city archive
Police reports, 1943
Fire Brigade reports, 1943

Lübeck city archive
Materialsammlung zum Luftangriff 1942
HS 1192, *Aufnahmen über Zerstörungen durch den Luftangriff auf Lübeck in der Nacht zum 29. März 1942.*
Collected newspaper clippings, March 1942 raid

Würzburg city archive
Berichte über die Angriffe im Raum Würzburg
Newspaper collections on the March 16, 1945, raid

UNITED STATES
Library of Congress manuscripts collection, Washington, DC
Henry H. Arnold papers
James Doolittle papers
Ira Eaker papers
Curtis LeMay papers
Carl Spaatz papers

SECONDARY SOURCES

Ayres, Travis L. *The Bomber Boys: True Stories of B-17 Airmen.* Bloomington, IN: Author House, 2005.

Bartov, O., Atina Grossmann, & Mary Noland. *Crimes of War: Guilt and Denial in the Twentieth Century.* New York: The New Press, 2002.

A Battle for Truth: Canadian Aircrews Sue the CBC over Death by Moonlight: Bomber Command. Agincourt, ON: Ramsay Business Systems Limited, 1994.

Bauer, K. Fritz. *Würzburg im Feuerofen.* Würzburg: Echter Verlag, 1985.

Beck, E.R. *Under the Bombs: The German Home Front, 1942–1945.* Lexington, KY: University Press of Kentucky, 1986.

Biddle, Tami Davis. *Rhetoric and Reality in Air Warfare.* Princeton, NJ: Princeton University Press, 2002.

Big-Scale Air Offensive Fortresses Bomb Germany Record RAF Raid on Hamburg. Hamburg Smoke at 24,000 Feet, Fires Seen 200 Miles Away. *Times,* July 29, 1943.

Bläsi, Herbert, & Christhard Schrenk. *Leben und Sterben einer Stadt.* Heilbronn: Stadtarchiv Heilbronn, 1995.

Bohl, Hans Werner, Bodo Keipke, & Karsten Schröder (eds.). *Bomben auf Rostock.* Rostock: Konrad Reich Verlag, 1995.

Bomb Damage at Essen. *Times,* March 21, 1942.

Brecht, B. Hamburg geht Unter. *Hamburg 1943. Literarische Zeugnisse zum Feuersturm.* V. Hage (ed.) Frankfurt, Fischer: 2003.

Breuilly, J. Hamburg: The German City of Laissez-Faire. *The Historical Journal* 35 (1992): 701–712.

Briol, John J. *Dead Engine Kids: World War Two Diary of John J. Briol, B-17 Ball Turret Gunner.* Rapid City, SD: Silver Wings Aviation, 1993.

Brown, Louis. *A Radar History of World War II.* London: CRC Press, 1999.

Brüggemeier, Franz-Josef. *Leben vor Ort—Ruhrbergleute und Ruhrbergbau 1889–1919.* Munich: C.H. Beck, 1984.

Churchill, Winston. *Memoirs of the Second World II: An abridgement of the six volumes of the Second World War, with an epilogue by the author on the postwar years written for this volume.* Boston: Houghton Mifflin, 1959.

Coffey, Thomas S. *Hap: Military Aviator.* New York: Viking Press, 1982.

Colville, John R. *The Fringes of Power.* New York: W.W. Norton and Company, 1985.

Connolly, Kate. Germans call Churchill a war criminal. *Daily Telegraph,* November 19, 2002.

Cowling, Maurice. *The Impact of Hitler: British Politics and British Policies, 1933–1940.* Chicago: Chicago University Press, 1977.

Craven, Wesley Frank, & James Lea Cate. *The Army Forces in World War II. Volume III: Argument to V-E Day.* Chicago: University of Chicago Press, 1951.

Crosby, Harry H. *A Wing and a Prayer: The "Bloody 100th" Bomb Group of the U.S. Eighth Air Force in Action over Europe in World War II.* New York: HarperCollins, 1992.

Davidson, Eugene. *The Making of Hitler.* New York: Macmillan, 1977.

Davis, Richard G. *Bombing the European Axis Powers: A Historical Digest of the Combined Bomber Offensive, 1939–1945*. Maxwell, AL: Air University Press, 2006.

Davis, Richard G. *Carl A. Spaatz and the Air War in Europe*. Washington, DC: The Smithsonian Institute, 1992.

Davis, Richard G. *Henry (Hap) Arnold, Military Aviator*. Washington, DC: Air Force History and Museum Program, 1997.

De Groot, Gerard J. *Liberal Crusader: The Life of Sir Archibald Sinclair*. London: C. Hurst; New York: New York University Press, 1993.

Die Nacht als Essen unterging. *NRZ: Zeitung für Essen*, March 6, 1993.

Eckelmann, Susanne, & Cord Pagenstecher. *Zwangsarbeit in Berlin 1940–1945*. Erfurt: Sutton Verlag, 2000.

Ecker, Ulrich P. *Freiburg 1944–1994: Zerstörung under Wiederaufbau*. Freiburg: Stadtarchiv, 1994.

Edkins, Major Craig R. *Anonymous Warrior: The Contributions of Harold L. George to Strategic Air Power*. Montgomery, AL: Air Force University, 1997.

Effects on Bombing Inside Germany: New Propaganda Note. *Times*, June 21, 1943.

Fest, Joachim. *Speer: The Final Verdict*. London: Weidenfeld & Nicolson, 2001.

Fischer, Klaus P. *Nazi Germany*. New York: Continuum, 1995.

Fletcher, G.P. Liberals and Romantics at War: The Problem of Collective Guilt. *The Yale Law Journal* 111 (2002): 1499–1573.

Förschler, Andreas. *Unser Stuttgart geht unter: Die Bombenangriffe im Juli und September 1944*. Wiesenthal: Wartberg Verlag, 2004.

Fort, Adrian. *Prof: The Life of Frederick Lindemann*. London: Jonathan Cape, 2003.

Fortresses Bomb Germany, Gelsenkirchen and Bonn, Over 20 Fighters Down. *Times*, August 13, 1943.

Freeman, Roger A. *The Mighty Eighth*. New York: Orion Books, 1970.

Freeman, Roger A. *Mighty Eighth War Manual*. London: Jane's, 1984.

Friedrich, Jörg. *Der Brand: Deutschland im Bombenkrieg 1940–1945*. Munich: Ullstein Heyne, 2002.

Friedrich, Jörg. *The Fire: The Bombing of Germany 1940–1945*. New York: Columbia University Press, 2006.

Furse, Anthony. *Wilfred Freeman: The Genius behind Allied Survival and Air Supremacy*. Kent: Staplehurst, 1999.

Galland, Adolf. *The First and the Last: The Rise and Fall of the German Fighter Forces, 1938–1945*. New York: Buccaneer Books, 1954.

Gretzschel, M. Hamburg im Feuersturm. *Hamburger Abendblatt* (2003): 1–2.

Hansell, Haywood S. *The Strategic Air War against Germany and Japan: A Memoir*. Washington, DC: Office of Air Force History, United States Air Force, 1986.

Harriman, William A., & Elie Abel. *Special Envoy to Churchill and Stalin, 1941–1946*. New York: Random House, 1975.

Harris, Arthur. *Bomber Offensive*. London: Collins, 1947.

Harris, Arthur. *Despatch on War Operations 23 February, 1942 to 8th May, 1945*, Preface and Introduction by Sebastian Cox and a German View by Horst Boog. Portland, OR: Frank Cass, 1995.

Harrod, Roy. *The Prof: A Personal Memoir of Lord Cherwell*. London: Macmillan, 1959.

Hastings, Max. *Armageddon: The Battle for Germany 1944–45.* London: Macmillan, 2004.

Hastings, Max. *Bomber Command.* London: Pan Books, 1999.

Hawkins, Ian L. *The Munster Raid: Before and After.* Trumbull, CT: FNP Military Division, 1999.

Heinson, Gunnar. *Lexikon der Völkermorde.* Hamburg: Rowohlt Taschenbuch Verlag, 1998.

Heute vor 60 Jahren in Hamburgs Zeitungen. *Hamburger Abendblatt,* July 22, 2003. Hamburg: 12.

Hough, Richard A. *Winston and Clementine: The Triumph of the Churchills.* New York: Bantam Books, 1991.

Jenkins, Roy. *Churchill: A Biography.* London: Macmillan, 2001.

Keegan, John. We Wanted Beady-Eyed Guys Just Absolutely Holding the Course. *Smithsonian Magazine* 14 (August 1983): 34–43.

Kerr, E. Bartlett. *Flames over Tokyo: The U.S. Army Air Forces Incendiary Campaign against Japan 1944–1945.* New York: Donald Fine Inc., 1991.

Kershaw, Ian. *Hitler, 1889–1936: Hubris.* London: W.W. Norton & Company, 1998.

Kershaw, Ian. *Hitler, 1936–1945: Nemesis.* London: Penguin, 2000.

Kimball, Warren F. *Forged in War: Roosevelt, Churchill, and the Second World War.* New York: W. Morrow, 1996.

Kirby, Maurice W. *Operational Research in War and Peace: The British Experience from the 1930s to 1970.* London: Imperial College Press, 2003.

Kucklick, Christoph. *Feuersturm: Der Bombenkrieg gegen Deutschland.* Ellert & Richter: GEO, 2003.

Lacker, Erich. *Zielort Karlsruhe: Die Luftangriffe im Zweiten Weltkrieg.* Karlsruhe: Badenia Verlag, 1996.

Lieber, Francis. *Instructions for the Government of Armies of the United States in the Field.* New York: D. Van Nostrand, 1863.

Longmate, Norman. *The Bombers: The RAF Offensive against Germany.* London: Hutchinson, 1983.

Lowe, Keith. *Inferno: The Devastation of Hamburg, 1943.* London: Viking, 2007.

MacKay, Kenneth. *Kesselring: The Making of the Luftwaffe.* London: B.T. Batsford Ltd., 1978.

Manson, Paul. A Poor Display of Canada's Military History. *Globe and Mail,* January 9, 2007.

Manvell, Roger. *Der Reichsmarschall: Aufstieg und Fall des Hermann Göring.* Rastatt: Pabel-Moewig Verlag, 1987.

Martens, Stefan. *Herman Goering: Erster Paladin des Führers und Zweiter Mann im Reich.* Paderborn: Ferdinand Schöningh, 1985.

Maser, Werner. *Hermann Göring: Hitlers janusköpfiger Paladin.* Berlin: Quintessenz Verlag, 2000.

Messenger, Charles. *Cologne: The First 1000-Bomber Raid.* London: Ian Allan Ltd., 1982.

Middlebrook, Martin. *The Battle of Hamburg.* London: Cassell & Co, 2002.

Middlebrook, Martin. *The Berlin Raids.* London: Cassell Military Paperbacks, 2002.

Middlebrook, Martin. *The Schweinfurt-Regensburg Mission*. London: Allen Lane, 1983.

Middlebrook, Martin, & C. Everitt. *The Bomber Command War Diaries: An Operational Reference Book, 1939–1945*. Harmondsworth, UK: Viking, 1985.

Mierzejewski, Alfred C. *The Collapse of the German War Economy, 1944–1945: Allied Air Power and the German National Railway*. Chapel Hill, NC: University of North Carolina Press, 1988.

Mierzejewski, Alfred C. When Did Albert Speer Give Up? *Historical Journal* 31, 2 (1988): 391–97.

Miller, Donald L. *Masters of the Air: America's Bomber Boys Who Fought against Nazi Germany*. New York: Simon and Schuster, 2006.

Mosley, Leonard. *The Reich Marshall: A Biography of Hermann Goering*. Garden City, NY: Doubleday, 1974.

Murphy, Robert D. *Diplomat among Warriors*. Garden City, NY: Doubleday, 1964.

Neillands, Robin. *The Bomber War: Arthur Harris and the Allied Bomber Offensive 1939–1945*. London: John Murray, 2001.

New York Times, March 30, 1942.

Nicholl, John, & Tony Rennel. *Tail-End Charlies: The Last Great Battles of the Bomber War*. London: Thomas Dunne, 2006.

Nissen, Margret. *Sind Sie die Tochter Speer?* Munich: Deutsche Verlags-Anstalt, 2005.

Oppelt, Hans. *Würzburger Chronik des denkwürdigen Jahres 1945*. Würzburg: Verlag Ferdinand Schöningh Würzburg, 1947.

Overy, Richard. *The Air War, 1939–1945*. New York: Stein and Day, 1980.

Overy, Richard. *Goering: The "Iron Man."* London: Routledge, 1984.

Parton, James. *"Air Force Spoken Here": General Ira Eaker and the Command of the Air*. Bethesda, MD: Adler & Adler, 1986.

Paul, Wolfgang. *Wer war Hermann Goering*. Esslingen: Bechtle Verlag, 1983.

Phillips, J. Alwyn, DFM. *The Valley of the Shadow of Death*. Chippenham, Wiltshire: Antony Rowe Ltd., 1992.

Pogt, Herbert (ed.). *Bomben auf Wuppertal*. Wuppertal: Born Verlag, 1993.

Probert, Henry. *Bomber Harris: His Life and Times*. London: Greenhill Books, 2001.

Proctor, Robert N. *Racial Hygiene: Medicine under the Nazis*. Cambridge, MA: Harvard University Press, 1988.

R.A.F. Targets in Germany: Comparison of Bombing Damage. *Times*, January 1, 1943.

Read, Simon. *The Killing Skies: RAF Bomber Command at War*. Stroud: Spellmount, 2006.

Richards, Denis. *Portal of Hungerford*. London: Heinemann, 1977.

Rockenmaier, D.W. *Als vom Himmel Feuer fiel: so starb das alte Würzburg*. Echter Würzburg: Fränkische Gesellschaftsdruckerei, 1995.

Saward, Dudley. *Bomber Harris: The Story of Marshal of the Royal Air Force, Sir Arthur Harris*. Garden City, NY: Doubleday, 1985.

Saward, Dudley. *The Bomber's Eye*. London: Cassell, 1959.

Schaffer, Ronald. *Wings of Judgment: American Bombing in World War II*. New York: Oxford University Press, 1985.

Schmidt, Matthias. *Albert Speer: Das Ende eines Mythos.* Bern: Scherz Verlag, 1982.

Schönherr, Hans. *Lübeck: Aufbau aus dem Chaos.* Lübeck: GmbH Buchverlag Lübeck, 1962.

Sereny, Gitta. *Albert Speer: His Battle with the Truth.* London: Picador, 1996.

Speer, Albert. *Inside the Third Reich: The Classic Account of Nazi Germany by Hitler's Armaments Minister.* London: Phoenix, 2003.

Speer, Albert. *Inside the Third Reich: Memoirs.* New York: Macmillan, 1970.

Sweetman, John. *Bomber Crew.* London: Little Brown, 2004.

Taylor, Eric. *Operation Millennium: "Bomber" Harris' Raid on Cologne, May 1942.* London: Robert Hale, 1987.

Taylor, Frederick. *Dresden: Tuesday, February 13, 1945.* New York: HarperCollins, 2005.

U-Boat Yard Blazes Night and Day. *Daily Sketch*, March 30, 1942.

Vaccaro, Tony. *Entering Germany 1944–1949.* Cologne: Taschen, 2001.

Van Der Vat, Dan. *Der Gute Nazi.* Berlin: Henschel, 1997.

Webster, Sir Charles, & Noble Frankland. *The Strategic Offensive against Germany 1939–1945*, Vol. 3. London: HMSO, 1961.

Webster, Sir Charles, & Noble Frankland. *The Strategic Offensive against Germany 1939–1945*, Vol. 4. London: HMSO, 1961.

Weinberg, G.L. *A World at Arms: A Global History of World War II.* Cambridge: Cambridge University Press, 2005.

Wilde, Lutz. *Bomber gegen Lübeck: Eine Dokumentation der Zerstörungen in Lübecks Altstadt beim Luftangriff im März 1942.* Lübeck: Verlag Schmidt-Römhild, 1999. [Consulted in Lübeck city archives, L II 2995.]

Willems, Susanne. *Der entsiedelte Jude: Albert Speers Wohnungsmarktpolitik für den Berliner Hauptstadtbau.* Berlin: Edition Hentrich, 2000.

Wilson, Kevin. *Bomber Boys: The RAF Offensive of 1943.* London: Weidenfeld & Nicolson, 2005.

INDEX

VIII Corps, 231

7th Army, 231

10 Squadron, 69–70

XII Fliegerkorp, 112

100th Squadron, 176–77

4445th Bomb Group, 207

Aachen (Germany), 154, 175, 207–8, 230

Aalborg (Denmark), 21

absenteeism, 23, 202, 287–88

Academic Assistance Council, 56

Adam, Ronald, 29

Air Corps Tactical School, 38–40

Air Ministry, 20

    characterization of area bombing,
161,   157–67

    denies civilians are bomber targets, 163

    frustration with Harris, 141–42

    inconsistency of position on area
        bombing, 164, 166–67

    kept in dark about Harris's plans, 294

    opposes bombing of transportation, 180

    pressurizes USAAF to join in area
        bombing, 202–3

    reaction to Hamburg raid, 142

air raids. *See also* air-raid shelters; area
    bombing; precision bombing

    civilian casualties, 8, 11, 18, 19, 52–54,
        93, 101, 119, 139, 149, 201, 210,

        220–22, 225–27, 236, 241, 248, 254,
        260, 263, 279, 283, 325n8

    imprecision of, 12, 18, 20–21, 22, 138,
        280

Air Service Command, 45

Air Staff

    dissatisfaction with Harris, 327n50

    support for precision bombing, 294,
        327n50

aircraft industry

    affected by German bombing, 44

    bombed in Operation Argument, 174–75

    primary target of RAF, 22

    seen by Mitchell as a target, 38

air-raid shelters, 3–6, 92–93, 264

    as death traps, 6–7

    Jews barred from, 286

    underground stations used as, 10, 17–18

Alfeis, Karl-Heinz, 119

Allied Air Forces Bombing Committee,
    180

Allied Expeditionary Force, 172

Anderson, Fred, 126, 127, 169, 170, 173,
    174, 184

    advocates bombing of oil, 181

    cautions against bombing of Auschwitz,
        196

Anti-Aircraft Command, 107

anti-aircraft defense, 12, 71, 115, 144–45, 176
  elements, 112
  German focus on, 286–87
Antwerp (Belgium), 229, 230
Ardennes, Battle of the, 229–39
area bombing
  adopted by RAF, 22–26, 31
  characterization by Air Ministry, 157–67
  effect on morale doubted, 29
  effect on postwar Germany, 277–78
  effectiveness of, 85, 124, 202, 280–81
  Harris's view of, 102–3
  justifiability, 279–80, 296–97
  and Nuremberg principles, 296
  public backlash against, 155–56, 157, 269–70, 273, 292–93
  purpose of, 65–66, 162–66
  questioned in House of Commons, 164, 259–60
  self-fulfilling logic, 255, 256, 292
  study commissioned by Lord Cherwell, 57–59
  by USAAF, 247–48, 251–52, 254–55, 282
Arnold, Henry Harley "Hap," 33–35, 72, 203
  appointment as Deputy Chief of Staff for Air, 42
  assigns Eaker to head Eighth Air Force Bomber Command, 45–46
  belief in independent U.S. air force, 45
  at Casablanca Conference, 85, 87
  confidence in precision bombing, 131–32, 134
  directive makes oil primary bombing target, 208
  impatience with progress of U.S. bombing campaign, 126, 127, 251, 294
  mandate to expand air force, 41
  orders bombing of smaller towns, 255
  orders destruction of Luftwaffe, 169
  perception of air forces' role, 53
  personality, 33–34

  support for Mitchell, 37, 38
  visits Britain, 43–44
Atlantic Conference, 44
Attlee, Clement, 274
Augsburg (Germany), 150, 175
Auschwitz extermination camp, 80, 191–93
Auschwitz Protocols, 191–93
aviation, predicted effect on warfare, 28–29, 37

B-17 bomber, 43, 46, 134, 137
ball bearings plants, 88, 102, 125–31, 138, 141, 176, 183, 237, 242–43, 281, 282
Battle of Berlin, 141–51
Battle of Britain, 17–19, 21
Battle of Hamburg, 3–13, 103, 109–16, 118–20
Battle of the Barges, 70
Battle of the Bulge. See Ardennes, Battle of the
Battle of the Ruhr, 91–94, 95–103
Beaverbrook, Lord, 43, 44
Becker, Günther, 55
Belfast (Northern Ireland), 19
Bennett, John, 177
Berlin (Germany), 282, 327n50
  Battle of, 141–51, 224, 225
  Bloody Monday, 176–77
  as bombing target, 89, 90, 175
  daylight raid proposed, 197
  Operation THUNDERCLAP, 201–2
  Spaatz's regret over bombing, 275
  Speer commissioned to redesign, 77–78
  strategic value of bombing, 149–50
  U.S. bombing of, 247–48, 251–52
Bernal, Desmond, 57
Beur (Germany), 210
Bielefeld (Germany), 198
"Big Week," 173–75
Billancourt, (France), 51–52
Birkenau extermination camp, 193, 195
Birmingham (England), 18, 276
Blechhammer (Germany), 191, 196
Blenheim bomber, 20
blind bombing, 138, 204, 282, 283

Blitz, 17–19, 75
Bloemetz, Günther, 234
Bloody Monday, 176–77
Bochum (Germany), 219, 225
Bock, Elfriede, 4–5, 9–11, 276
Bohlen (Germany), 185
Bomber Command
    ability to carry out precision bombing,
        283
    Battle of the Ruhr losses, 94
    conservatism of early strategy, 19–20, 31,
        44
    demand for U.S. bombers, 44–45
    denied a campaign medal, 274
    improvement under Harris, 99
    inability to bomb Auschwitz, 195
    independence from Fighter Command,
        292
    morale, 31–32
    opposes bombing of transportation, 180
    organization of, 45
    perception by Arnold as defeatist, 43–44
    precision bombing raids, 51–52, 182,
        210, 212, 221–22, 289, 290
    raid on Dresden, 253–54
    size of force, 51, 66–67
    statistics on targets, 226–27
    tasks other than area bombing, 289
"bombing on the leader," 209
bombsights, 40, 209
Bonham-Carter, Violet, 270
Bonn (Germany), 156, 198, 211, 321n31
Bormann, Martin, 123, 241
Bottomley, Norman, 189–90, 195, 212–13,
        249, 250–51, 271, 312n53
    advocates precision bombing, 130
    denies RAF intends to bomb civilians,
        162
    and Strategic Directive No. 4, 272
Bottrop (Germany), 227
bouncing bombs, 96–98
Bradley, Omar, 251
Brand, Joel, 194
Brandt, Karl, 81
Bremen (Germany), 75, 138, 154

Brereton, Lewis, 172–73, 174
Bristol (England), 18
British Intelligence Appreciation, 133–34
Brittan, Vera, 155
Brooke, Sir Alan, 132
Brown, Ken, 98
Brunner, Alois, 79
Brunswick (Germany), 174, 211, 260
Brux (Germany), 185
Bryett, Alan, 143–44
Budapest (Hungary), 194
Bufton, Sydney, 141–42, 203, 293
Burcher, Tony, 97
Butt, David, 22, 32, 57–58

Cabell, Charles, 199, 200, 202, 255
Cardiff (Wales), 19
carpet bombing. See area bombing
Carr, Roderick, 69–70
Casablanca Conference, 83–90
Cayford, Denis, 142–43
Central Department for Resettlement, 79
Chamberlain, Neville, 29
Chaney, James, 47, 48, 63
Chemnitz (Germany), 254, 259
Cherwell, Lord, 55–62, 106, 107
Christ Church (Oxford University), 56–57
Churchill, Clementine, 59
Churchill, Winston, 22, 164, 173, 174
    approves bombing of Auschwitz, 194
    approves bombing of oil, 189
    approves of The Thousand Plan, 66
    approves of Window, 107–8
    at Atlantic Conference, 44
    attention paid to Cherwell's advice, 60
    at Casablanca Conference, 83–88
    convinced of value of area bombing, 211
    convinces U.S. to delay European
        invasion, 87
    daily routine, 59–60
    desire to bomb Berlin, 89, 90, 141
    doubts effectiveness of area bombing,
        23–24
    excludes Bomber Command from VE
        speech, 273

Churchill, Winston, (*cont.*)
  lobbies Roosevelt to join night bombing, 85
  opposes bombing of transportation, 180
  opposes early invasion of France, 72
  orders bombing of Berlin, 249–50
  orders bombing of Mannheim, 21
  position on bombing campaign changes, 59
  proposes raids on smaller towns, 197–98
  qualified support of area bombing, 25
  reaction of bombing of Ruhr Valley, 94
  role in area bombing campaign, 275
  seeks to distance self from area bombing campaign, 270–71
  support for area bombing, 60, 293, 295
  support for Harris, 30
  "Winston hours," 85
cities, bombing of. *See* area bombing
civilians
  Air Ministry denies they are targets, 163
  gas attacks, 184, 199
  ground forces' efforts to minimize casualties, 296
  murdered by Peiper's Kampfgruppe, 233
  numbers killed in air raids, 8, 11, 18, 19, 52–54, 93, 101, 119, 139, 149, 201, 210, 220–22, 225–27, 236, 241, 248, 254, 260, 263, 279, 283, 325n8
  U.S. aversion to bombing, 39–40
Coastal Command, 66, 85
Cochrane, Ralph, 96
Cologne (Germany), 154, 211, 227, 254, 277, 321n31
  bombing questioned by Air Ministry, 213, 220
  chosen as target of The Thousand Plan, 69–72, 224
  Harris's defense of bombing, 214–15, 218, 222–23
  "Wild Boar" defense tested over, 142
Colyer, Douglas, 204
Committee of Operations Analysts (COA), 281–82, 295
Coryton, Alec, 150, 198

Coudenhove-Kalergi, Count Richard, 76
Coventry (England), 19, 276
Cowan, Howard, 269, 292
creepback, 8, 12
Cripps, Sir Stafford, 31–32

Daily Mirror, 293
Daily Sketch, 155–56
Daily Telegraph, 157–58
dambuster raids, 95–102, 224, 283, 289
Darmstadt (Germany), 210, 260, 277, 283
Davis, Richard, 211
day bombing
  championed by Eaker, 86–87
  imprecision of, 18, 20–21
  of London, 17–18
  by Luftwaffe, 17–18
  necessity of fighter escort, 21
  U.S. belief in, 38–39, 45–48
D-Day, 187–88, 213
de Gaulle, Charles, 84, 86, 87
Dessau (Germany), 259
Dietrich, Sepp, 231, 234
Doolittle, James, 170, 173, 197, 251–52, 255, 284
Dora forced labor camp, 131
Dornberger, Walter, 73
Dortmund (Germany), 100, 210, 211, 221, 225, 227, 259, 270
Dortmund-Ems Canal, 219
Douhet, Giulio, 37, 38–39, 283
Dresden (Germany), 253–54, 260, 272, 282
Drummer Lake, 176–77
Duisberg (Germany), 75, 211, 227
Dulles, Allen, 192
Düppel project, 108
Düren (Germany), 225
Düsseldorf (Germany), 75, 101, 154, 217

Eaker, Ira, 35–38, 137, 180, 275, 284
  appointed head of Eighth Bomber Command, 45–49
  at Casablanca Conference, 85
  makes case to Churchill for day bombing, 86–87

and Operation Argument, 171
opposition to Operation Clarion, 255
personality, 47
response to Schweinfurt raids, 169–70
support for Mitchell, 38
transferred to Mediterranean front, 170
unconvinced by Lübeck raid, 55
Eaker, Ruth, 46
Eden, Anthony, 194, 195, 197
Eder Valley dam, 98, 100
Eichmann, Adolf, 79, 192
Eighth Air Force, 235
area bombing by, 197, 209–10
attack on Luftwaffe fighters, 174, 175
bombing of Dresden, 254
bombing of railways, 291
"bombing on the leader," 209
bombs Berlin, 197
formation of, 45
given control over Ninth Air Force,
173
lack of manpower, 132, 134
losses on Bloody Monday, 177
made part of USSTAF, 170
and Operation Frantic, 193
priorities, 183
raids on oil, 190
raids on Regensburg and Schweinfurt,
125–31
response to Ardennes offensive, 232–33
statistics on targets, 226–27
Einstein, Albert, 56
Eisenhower, Dwight, 72, 88
command over strategic bombing, 200,
208
permits raids on oil, 184–85
policy of sparing buildings and
monuments, 285
publicizes raids on oil, 190
supports area bombing, 251
supports daylight raid on Berlin, 197
supports plan to bomb railways, 180–81
Emden (Germany), 75, 138, 154, 210
Emmerich (Germany), 211
Enemy Coast Ahead (Gibson), 98

energy infrastructure, 22. See also oil
infrastructure
Essen (Germany), 75, 92–93, 103, 153,
211, 227, 259, 270
Eupen (Belgium), 128
Europe, Allied invasion of, 72, 85, 87–88,
131–32, 172, 187–88. See also
Normandy (France), invasion of
Evill, Sir Douglass, 198

Fairchild, Muir, 38
Fellowship, 155
Ferson, Steve, 33–34
Fifteenth Air Force, 173, 175
ability to destroy Auschwitz-Birkenau,
193
bombing of oil, 204
made part of USSTAF, 170
priorities, 183
raid on Ploesti, 184
statistics on targets, 226–27
Fighter Command, 45
independence from Bomber Command,
291–92
judged by Luftwaffe to be spent force,
18
opposes use of Window, 107
First Army, 207–8
Five Group, 260
Flying Training Command, 67
Frankfurt (Germany), 75, 150, 210, 277
Franklin, Noble, 94
Fraser, John, 97
Freeman, Wilfred, 65
Freiburg (Germany), 198, 226
Freisler, Roland, 252–53
Fritsche, Hans, 155
Funk, Walter, 123

Galland, Adolf, 135–36, 177, 185, 187,
206, 234, 272
Gebhardt, Dr. Karl, 175
Gee, 51–52, 293
Gelsenkirchen (Germany), 219–21, 225
George, Harold, 38–39

Gerhart, John, 138–39

Germany
  aircraft production, 287
  anti-aircraft defenses, 12, 71, 112, 115,
    144–45, 176, 286–87
  armament production, 124–25, 138
  Battle of the Ardennes, 229–39
  damage to British aircraft industry, 44
  declares war on U.S., 80
  defense of oil supply, 205–6
  effect of precision raids on war
    production, 185–86, 280–81,
    287–88
  fear of daylight raids, 130, 131, 134,
    135
  fuel shortages, 190, 210, 233, 236,
    243–44, 289
  housing shortage, 91
  invasion of Low Countries, 20
  morale undamaged by air raids, 39,
    54–55
  oil production depleted, 212
  oil production recovers, 223
  overproduction of consumer goods,
    93–94
  postwar reconstruction, 277
  resistance along western front, 207–8

Gibson, Guy, 96, 97, 98

Giesecke, Heinrich, 259–60, 263, 276

Giessen (Germany), 320n31

Gilbert, Walter, 205

Giraud, Henri, 84, 86

Glasgow (Scotland), 19

Goebbels, Joseph, 77, 248
  advocates mass conscription, 241–42
  and expulsion of Berlin Jews, 79
  orders synagogues destroyed, 78

Göring, Hermann, 18, 73–75, 112, 123,
  129, 186–87
  denial of Allied air strength, 135–36
  scraps Düppel project, 108
  sentenced to hanging, 274

Granberg, Herie, 247

Grierson, C. M., 269

Ground-Air Support Command, 45

Haberland, Ernst-Günther, 3–4, 9, 10, 276

Hagen (Germany), 103, 227

Halifax, Lord, 30, 74

Hallendorf (Germany), 227

Hamburg (Germany), 75, 277, 280–81,
  284, 310–11n4, 327n50
  Battle of, 3–13, 103, 109–16, 118–20,
    156
  considered as target of "The Thousand
    Plan," 67
  evacuation, 10, 12

Hamm (Germany), 227

Hanau (Germany), 242

Hanke, Karl, 76–77

Hansell, Haywood, 38, 39–40, 42–43

Harburg (Germany), 221

Harriman, Averell, 63, 85

Harris, Sir Arthur "Bomber," 27–32, 180
  appointed head of Bomber Command,
    30–32
  autonomy over bombing plans, 293–94
  belief that bombing would win war, 149,
    150, 161
  bombs cities in defiance of Portal,
    217–23
  as commander, 292
  complains about U.S. aversion to area
    bombing, 284
  convinces Churchill of value of area
    bombing, 210–11
  defends area bombing, 212–16, 292
  defends bombing of Dresden, 271
  denied peerage, 274
  disregard for POINTBLANK directive,
    294
  encourages Americans to join in area
    bombing, 46, 64
  excluded from VE Day ceremonies, 273
  focuses on Ruhr Valley, 91–92, 100
  improvement of Bomber Command
    under, 99
  inaccuracy of arguments against
    precision bombing, 295
  interest in bombing Berlin, 141
  opposes bombing of railways, 181–82

ordered to bomb Berlin, 250–51
personality, 34, 47
proposes daylight raid on Berlin, 197
provides USAAF with bases, 48
on purpose of area bombing, 65–66, 161–62, 163–65
reaction to POINTBLANK directive, 88–90
reaction to Williams's article, 159–61
refusal to bomb Schweinfurt, 130, 138
reluctantly bombs oil plants, 220–22, 290
resumes control over strategic bombing, 208
skepticism toward bouncing bombs, 96
skepticism toward precision bombing, 189–90, 215, 225–27, 235–39, 244–45
support of Window, 107
The Thousand Plan, 66–67, 68, 224
threatens to resign, 246
views on area bombing, 102–3
willingness to risk high losses, 225
Harris, Craig, 209
Harris, Jill, 47
Harrod, Roy, 57
Hasting, Max, 208
Heer, Hans, 260, 264, 267, 276
Heilbronn (Germany), 227, 260
Heinicke, Herbert, 120
Heinsberg (Germany), 225
Henrietta, James, 248
Herrmann, Hajo, 147
high explosives, 7, 65
Himmler, Heinrich, 175
Hitler, Adolf, 91, 241
   abandons UK for Russian front, 19
   and Battle of the Ardennes, 229–30, 234
   commissions Speer to renovate Chancellery, 77
   declares war on U.S., 80
   denial of Allied air strength, 135
   and extermination of Jews, 81
   meets with oil industry, 186–87
   at Nuremberg rallies, 41

and Operation Northwind, 234–35
   orders bombing of British cities, 18
   orders fighter production halted, 206
   perception of Göring, 73
   reaction to Schweinfurt raid, 129
   refuses to visit Hamburg, 124
   remains in Berlin, 149
Hitler Youth, 119
Hodges, Courtney, 207
Holocaust, 80–81, 191–93, 196, 285
Homburg (Germany), 217, 221
Hopgood, John "Hoppy," 97
Hopkins, Harry, 41, 63, 86
Hornibrook, Kevin, 143–44, 148
Horowitz, Jules, 275
Hughes, Richard, 199–200
Hull (England), 58, 62

incendiary bombs, 7, 64–65, 282
   dropped on London, 30
"industrial web," 39
Ismay, Sir Hastings, 197, 198
Italy, 285

Japan
   attack on Pearl Harbor, 45
   bombing of, 285
Jeschonnek, Hans, 112, 129–30
Jewish Agency for Palestine, 194
Jewish Agency Rescue Committee, 192
Jews
   barred from air-raid shelters, 286
   expelled from Berlin, 79
   extermination of, 80–81, 191–93, 196, 285
Jodl, Alfred, 230
Jones, R. V., 107
Josef-Baum, Hermann, 101
Journal of the United Services Institute, 274
Jülich (Germany), 225

Kaiserslautern (Germany), 198
Kammhuber, Joseph, 111–12
Kammhuber Line, 111–13, 144, 147
Karlsruhe (Germany), 154, 227

Kassel (Germany), 148, 160, 209, 260
Kastner, Rudolf, 192
Katzenberger, Dr. Helmut, 275
Kaufmann, Karl, 12, 124
Kehrl, Hans, 186–87
Keitel, Wilhelm, 186–87, 241
Kepner, William, 170, 173
Kiel (Germany), 75, 175, 210
King, Cecil, 293
Kirk, Irving, 173
Klemperer, Victor, 286
Kleve (Germany), 211
Klint, Wilbur, 128–29, 137
Knerr, Hugh, 232
Koblenz (Germany), 198, 221, 222
Königsberg (Germany), 260
Kopecky, Dr. Jaromir, 192
Krefeld, (Germany), 101
Kristallnacht, 78, 79, 260
Kuter, Laurence, 38, 42–43, 202

Lange, Gerhard, 117–19, 275–76
Leigh-Mallory, Sir Trafford, 107–8, 172,
    180, 182
Leipzig (Germany), 174, 175
LeMay, Curtis, 126–28, 131, 135, 209
Leuna, (Germany), 186
Ley, Robert, 123
Lindemann, Frederick. *See* Cherwell, Lord
Lindenbaum, Shalom, 196–97
Lippert, Julius, 78
Liverpool (England), 18, 19
Lloyd George, David, 28
Lofthouse, Charles, 142–43
London (England)
    daylight raids, 17–18, 19
    night raids, 30
    postwar reconstruction, 276
Lovett, Robert, 42
Lowry, G. C., 106
Lübeck, (Germany), 52–55, 154, 155–56
Ludlow-Hewitt, Sir Edgar, 19–20
Luftwaffe
    Allied campaign to destroy, 63–64,
        169–74, 180–81, 211–12

bombing of London, 17–19, 30
concentrates fighters on oil defense, 186
destruction, 234, 291
fighter strength, 128–29, 133, 137,
    145–47, 158–59, 171
fuel shortages, 190, 288–89
losses on Bloody Monday, 176–77
nuisance raids on Casablanca
    Conference, 84
regains fighter strength, 217
"Wild Boar" defense, 147
Luftwaffenhelfer, 145
Lützendorf (Germany), 185, 187

Macmillan, Harold, 86
Magdeburg (Germany), 187
Mahncke, Otto, 119–20
Mainz (Germany), 154, 198
Maltby, David, 98
Manchester (England), 19
Mannheim (Germany), 21, 148, 175, 210,
    254
Manser, Leslie, 71
Manteuffel, Hasso von, 231–32
Marshall, George, 42, 63, 87, 251
Martin, Micky, 70–71, 97–98
Maudslay, Henry, 98
Maxwell Field, 38–40
McAuliffe, Anthony, 232
McClelland, Roswell, 192–93
McCloy, John, 193, 195, 196, 284
McDonald, George, 256, 284
Mediterranean campaign, 88
Merseburg-Leuna (Germany), 185, 187,
    191
Mihan, Hans-Werner, 145
Mikkelson, Vernon, 205
Milch, Erhard, 75, 112, 123, 135, 175–76,
    186–87, 274
Miller, Henry J. F., 184
Ministry of Economic Warfare (MEW),
    181, 200, 215, 221, 237–38, 242, 295
Mitchell, Billy, 35, 37–38
Model, Walter, 233
Möhne dam, 95–100

Mönchengladbach (Germany), 210
Monowitz concentration camp, 191
morale
    as general target of bombing campaigns,
        38
    of military leaders undermined, 188
    seen as invulnerable to bombing raids,
        19, 39, 62, 75, 88, 249, 255, 256
    as target of British bombing campaign,
        22–26, 58, 65–66
    as target of U.S. bombing campaign, 199
Mordowicz-Rosin Report, 192
Morrison, Herbert, 107
Moseley, Sgt. P., 110–11
Mülheim an der Ruhr (Germany), 101
Munich (Germany), 75, 148, 175, 204, 242,
    251, 260
Münster (Germany), 138, 139, 154, 210,
    227, 282
Murphy, Robert, 86

Netherlands, invasion of, 20
Neuss (Germany), 210, 227
newspapers, coverage of war, 153–59
night bombing
    adopted by RAF, 21
    goal of, 163–65
    imprecision of, 8, 12–13, 22–23
    by Luftwaffe, 19
Ninth Air Force, 172, 174
Norden, Carl L., 40
Normandy (France), invasion of, 187–88,
    213
North Africa campaign, 85, 87
Nuremberg (Germany), 150, 209, 241,
    260, 277
Nuremberg Principles, 296
Nuremberg rallies, 41, 77
Nuremberg war trials, 274

Oancia, Steven, 98
Oberhausen (Germany), 217, 227
Oechsner, Herbert, 259, 262–63
oil infrastructure, 20–22, 88, 89, 179–86,
    200, 204–5, 207, 243–44

made primary target, 208, 244
Oldenburg (Germany), 198
Olds, Archie, 127
Operation Argument, 171–77
Operation Chastise, 95–102
Operation Clarion, 255–56, 284
Operation Crossbow, 184, 197
Operation Frantic, 193
Operation Gomorrah, 3–13
Operation Market Garden, 207
Operation Northwind, 234–35
Operation OVERLORD, 172, 181
Operation THUNDERCLAP, 201–2, 248,
    250, 252
Order of the White Feather, 248
Osnabrück (Germany), 75, 198
Osner, Herbert, 324n5
Osterfeld (Germany), 227
Overy, Richard, 287

P-38 fighter, 173
Parton, James, 86
Passchendaele, Flanders, 27
Patton, George, 86, 233
Pauels, Hans, 119
Peck, Sir Richard, 162, 273
Peenemünde (Germany), 131, 147–48
Pehle, John, 192–93, 196
Peiper, Joachim, 233
Peirse, Sir Richard, 21, 22, 30, 43, 44
Perry, Colin, 17
Pforzheim (Germany), 254
Phillips, Tom, 29
Phipps, Sir Eric, 73–74
Pirmasens (Germany), 198
Ploesti (Romania), 183–86, 187, 204,
    321n31
Plymouth (England), 19
POINTBLANK directive, 88–90, 132,
    294
    superseded by Operation Crossbow, 184
Politz (Poland), 242
Portal, Sir Charles, 46, 294
    accuracy of arguments for precision
        bombing, 295

Portal, Sir Charles, (*cont.*)
  admits necessity of European invasion, 85
  and adoption of area bombing, 31, 293
  appointed head of Bomber Command, 20, 29
  approves The Thousand Plan, 66
  at Casablanca Conference, 83
  confidence in area bombing, 23–26, 45
  defied by Spaatz, 183–84
  directive makes oil primary bombing target, 208
  endorses raids on oil, 189
  loses patience with Harris, 242–44
  opposes bombing of smaller towns, 198–99
  opposes integration of air forces, 180
  orders Harris to bomb railways, 182
  perceived by Arnold as defeatist, 44
  sides with Spaatz on role of fighters, 172
  and Strategic Directive No. 2, 212
  and Strategic Directive No. 3, 244
  support for precision bombing, 22, 132–34
  supports daylight raid on Berlin, 197
  tolerance of Harris's insubordination, 90, 141–42, 216, 218–25, 227–28
  urges Harris to bomb oil plants, 236–37
  views on value of bombing cities, 225
Portsmouth (England), 19
Posen (Poland), 174
Potsdam (Germany), 272
Pound, Sir Dudley, 63
Pragnell, Jack, 67, 105, 111, 113
precision bombing
  abandoned by RAF, 31
  aided by development of bombsights, 40, 209
  aided by Gee, 51–52, 293
  aided by radar, 51–52, 282
  casualty rate, 227, 283
  dambuster raids, 95–100
  dependence on weather, 216
  effect on morale of military leadership, 188
  inaccuracy of, 22, 138, 280
  increasing accuracy, 96–98, 99
  not always distinct from area bombing, 282
  seen as helpful on Russian front, 250
  U.S. belief in, 38–39
prisoners of war, murdered by Germans, 233
Probst, Christopher, 252
public opinion, of bombing campaign, 155–57, 269–70, 273, 292–93

QUADRANT Conference, 131–34, 141

radar, 282
  development of Gee, 51–52
  H2X, 138, 284
  interference with, 105–8, 109–15, 144
railways, 20, 39, 180–82, 188, 209, 212, 235, 291
Regensburg (Germany), 126, 127, 131
Reichstag, 74
Remscheid (Germany), 101
resource transfers, 287–88
Reston, James, 176
retaliatory bombing, 197–99
Riegner, Gerhart, 192
Rockwell Field, 35, 36
Röhm, Ernst, 74
Roosevelt, Franklin
  at Atlantic Conference, 44
  at Casablanca Conference, 84–85, 88
  confidence in air power, 41
  policy of sparing buildings and monuments from bombing, 284–85
  support for area bombing, 251, 279–80
  transfers planes to Britain, 45
  urged to bomb Auschwitz, 194
Rostock (Germany), 64–65, 154
Rothenberg ob der Tauber, 284
Rotterdam (Netherlands), 20

Royal Air Force (RAF). *See also* Bomber
    Command; Coastal Command;
    Fighter Command
  bombing of Hamburg, 3–13
  commitment to precision bombing, 43
  creation of, 28
  expansion, 20
  focus on precision bombing, 21
  losses during Battle of Berlin, 150
  organization of, 19
  preference for area bombing, 283–84
  pressurizes USAAF to join area
      bombing, 46–47, 55
  Strategic Directive No. 2, 212
  Strategic Directive No. 3, 244
  Strategic Directive No. 4, 272
  support of Warsaw uprising, 195
  switches to area bombing, 22–26
  switches to night bombing, 21
  various commands not integrated, 292
Royal Flying Corps, 28
Royal Naval Air Service, 28
Royal Navy, supported by RAF bombers,
    43
Rübenkamp, Horst, 92–93
Ruhland (Germany), 187
Ruhr, Battle of the, 91–94, 95–103
Ruhr Valley, 75, 91–94, 95–103, 224–25,
    259, 290
  evacuation of, 155
  Speer reports on destruction, 230
Russian front, 80

Saarbrücken (Germany), 175, 198
Saundby, Robert, 66–67
Schaefer, Georg, 275
Schaub, Julius, 136
Schenk, Werner, 145
Schmidt, Anna Lies, 11–12
Schmitt, Gusti, 266
Scholl, Hans, 252
Scholl, Sophie, 252
Schwabedissen, Walter, 111, 113
Schweinfurt (Germany), 126–31, 137, 138,
    169, 175, 275, 312n53

scientists, smuggled out of Germany, 56
Scripture, Ellis, 138–39
searchlights, 112–13, 145
Second Schweinfurt Memorial Association
    (SSMA), 275
Shannon, David, 98
Sheffield (England), 19
Shertok, Moshe, 194
shipping, as bombing target, 21, 43, 70,
    289
Shipway, A. C., 114
Simmons, Bruce, 33
Sinclair, Sir Archibald, 99–100, 153–54,
    156, 158, 164, 194–95, 249–50, 313n2
Slessor, John C., 43
Smuts, Jan, 59, 158
Solingen (Germany), 198, 220
Sorpe dam, 96, 98, 100
Spaatz, Carl "Tooey," 35–36, 174, 275,
    284
  advocates bombing of oil, 179–85
  appointed as head of USSTAF, 170
  aversion to bombing civilians, 283
  campaign to destroy Luftwaffe, 169,
      171–73, 181, 216, 217
  at Casablanca summit, 86
  confidence in daylight precision
      bombing, 45, 282
  defies Portal, 183–86
  dispatched to Britain, 43
  oil bombing campaign, 204–5, 207,
      208–9
  opposition to area bombing, 202, 203
  orders area bombing, 251–52
  orders end to area bombing, 256–57
  perception of air forces' role, 55
  raids on Budapest, 194
  resumes command over strategic
      bombing, 208
  sets priorities for air forces, 183
  and Strategic Directive No. 2, 212
  and Strategic Directive No. 3, 244
  and Strategic Directive No. 4, 272
  support for Mitchell, 38
Spaatz, Ruth, 36

Speer, Albert, 75–80
  assessment of dambuster raids, 100,
    101–2
  assumes control of armament
    production, 123
  and Battle of the Ardennes, 230–31,
    233–35
  on effectiveness of precision bombing,
    290–91
  given control over war production, 82
  hospitalized, 175
  ignores order to halt fighter production,
    206
  informs Hitler of damage to oil plants,
    190–91
  opposes mass conscription, 241–42
  reaction to bombing of oil, 185–86
  reaction to Hamburg raids, 123–24
  reaction to Schweinfurt raid, 131,
    137–38
  sentenced at Nuremberg, 274
  views on area bombing, 281, 288
Speer, Albert Sr., 775–76
Speyer (Germany), 198
spin recovery, 56
Spoden, Peter, 145–47
Springfield (home of Bomber Harris), 47
Stade (Germany), 111
Stimson, Harry, 41–42, 284
Stokes, Sir Richard Rapier, 164–65, 269–70
Street, Sir Arthur, 161–63
Stumpf, Hans-Jürgen, 112
Stuttgart (Germany), 75, 150, 175, 201,
    210
Swansea (Wales), 19, 153

Taylor, Frederick, 254
Tedder, Sir Arthur, 170, 294, 316n5,
    327n46
  convinced of value of oil raids, 186
  endorses oil raids, 190
  makes V-1 rocket sites priority target,
    184
  opposes raids on smaller towns, 198
  and Strategic Directive No. 4, 272

support for precision bombing, 190, 272
  supports bombing of transportation,
    180, 181
Temple, William (Archbishop of
    Canterbury), 156
terror bombing. See area bombing
Tessenow, Heinrich, 76, 78
Third Army, 233
The Thousand Plan, 66–67, 69–72, 224,
    292
The Times, 153–55, 156
Tizard, Sir Henry, 105–6
  opposition to bombing cities, 60–62
Todt, Fritz, 80–82
total war
  as envisioned by Douhet, 37, 38, 283
  Second World War as, 296
transportation infrastructure, 20, 39,
    180–82, 209, 212, 291
  gains top priority as bombing target,
    212
Treblinka extermination camp, 81
Trenchard, Hugh, 28
Tresfon, Adeline, 29
Tresfon, Jean, 29
Trident conference, 171
Trzebina (Poland), 196
Türk, Gertrud, 71–72
Turner, Geoff, 116
Tutow (Germany), 174
Twining, Nathan, 170

U-boats, as bombing targets, 22, 85, 89
Udet, Ernst, 74–75
Ulm (Germany), 236
underground stations, as air-raid shelters,
    10, 17–18
Union of Soviet Socialist Republics
    (USSR)
  as beneficiaries of precision bombing,
    250
  as beneficiaries of UK bombing
    campaigns, 158–59
  calls for opening of second front, 63
  Operation Frantic, 193

United Kingdom
  aircraft production, 287
  aircraft production hindered by German
    bombing, 44
  declares war on Germany, 29
  delays invasion of Europe, 87–88,
    131–32
  focus on North Africa, 85, 87
  lobbies U.S. to join night bombing, 85
  morale unaffected by Blitz, 19
  production of bombers, 61
  recovery from Second World War,
    276–77
United States
  agrees to delay European invasion,
    87–88
  aircraft production, 287
  area bombing by, 138–39
  aversion to area bombing, 39–40, 45, 46,
    47–48, 85, 202–3
  Congress agrees to fund Army Air
    Corps, 41
  considers retaliatory bombing of smaller
    towns, 200, 202
  desire to invade France, 72, 85, 131–32
  enters Second World War, 45
  German declaration of war on, 80
  goal of destroying German economy, 88
  goal of invading Europe, 61
  losses at Battle of the Ardennes, 235
  philosophy of precision bombing, 38–39
  production of warplanes, 58
United States Army Air Corps, 41, 42
United States Army Air Forces (USAAF).
    See also Eighth Air Force; Fifteenth
    Air Force; Ninth Air Force
  area bombing by, 247–48, 251–52,
    254–55, 282
  aversion to area bombing, 85, 282
  campaign to destroy Luftwaffe, 61, 169,
    171–73, 181, 211–12, 216–17
  destruction of Luftwaffe, 291
  expansion, 134
  frequency of oil raids, 290
  independence from RAF, 46–47, 55

  losses in "Big Week," 175
  losses on Bloody Monday, 176, 177
  plan for air war (AWPD-1), 42–43
  precursors, 34, 35–36, 38–40, 41
  response to Ardennes offensive, 232–33
  role of fighters, 171–72
  status relative to Army and Navy, 55
  Strategic Directive No.2, 212
  Strategic Directive No.3, 244
  Strategic Directive No.4, 272
United States Army Signal Corps Aviation,
    35–36
United States Aviation Service, 34
United States Strategic Air Forces in
    Europe (USSTAF), 170, 180

V-1 rockets, 148, 184, 198
V-2 rockets, 131, 148, 251
Vaccaro, Tony, 273
Vandenberg, Hoyt, 232
Vienna (Austria), 284
Vögler, Albert, 230–31
Vrba, Rudolf, 191–93
Vrba-Wetzler Report, 191–93

Walker, Kenneth, 38, 42–43
Wallis, Barnes, 95–96
Wanne-Eickel (Germany), 210
War Refugee Board, 192
Warsaw uprising, 195
Wattson-Watt, Robert, 106–7
weather, and effectiveness of air raids,
    12–13, 67, 127, 138, 204, 209, 213,
    214, 216, 232
Webster, Sir Charles, 94
Weicker, Lowell, 199–200
Weizmann, Chaim, 194
Welch, John, 247
Wendland, Werner, 5–9, 13, 276
Weppert, Heinrich, 260, 265–66, 276
Werner, Paul, 92–93
Wesel (Germany), 273
Wetzler, Alfred, 191–93
Wiesbaden (Germany), 198
Wilckens, Vomar, 275

Williams, Howard, 157–58
Williams, Robert, 126, 127
Wilson, Donald, 38
Wimperis, Harry Egerton, 106
Winant, John Gilbert, 72
Window, 105–8, 109–15, 142
    defeated by "Wild Boar" defense,
        144–48
Wingham, Sidney Thomas "Tom," 291–92
Wirsing, Karl-Heinz, 266
Wiskemann, Elizabeth, 192
Wismar (Germany), 75
Witzigmann, Alexander, 176
Wolters, Rudolf, 79
World Jewish Congress, 192, 196

Worms (Germany), 198
Wuppertal (Germany), 100, 101
Würzburg (Germany), 259–67,
    270, 277
Wycombe Abbey School, 48

Young, Dinghy, 98

Zeitz (Germany), 185
Zionist Rescue Committee, 194
Zuckerman, Solly, 57
    advocates bombing transportation,
        179–80
    opposition to area bombing, 61–62
Zwickau (Germany), 185